FROMMER'S

COMPREHENSIVE TRAVEL GUIDE

ST. LOUIS &
KANSAS CITY
2ND EDITION

by Beth Reiber

D1557076

PRENTICE HALL TRAVEL

NEW YORK • LONDON • TORONTO • SYDNEY • TOKYO • SINGAPORE

FROMMER BOOKS

Published by Prentice Hall General Reference
A division of Simon & Schuster Inc.
15 Columbus Circle
New York, NY 10023

ISBN 0-671-84763-5
ISSN 1051-6840

Design by Robert Bull Design
Maps by Geografix Inc.

FROMMER'S ST. LOUIS & KANSAS CITY 2nd Edition

Editor-in-Chief: Marilyn Wood
Senior Editors: Judith de Rubini, Alice Fellows, Lisa Renaud
Editors: Thomas F. Hirsch, Peter Katucki, Sara Hinsey Raveret, Theodore
    Stavrou
Assistant Editors: Margaret Bowen, Ian Wilker
Managing Editor: Leanne Coupe

Special Sales

Bulk purchases of Frommer's Travel Guides are available at special discounts. The publishers are happy to custom-make publications for corporate clients who wish to use them as premiums or sales promotions. We
can excerpt the contents, provide covers with corporate imprints, or create
books to meet specific needs. For more information write to Special Sales,
Prentice Hall Travel, Paramount Communications Building, 15 Columbus
Circle, New York, NY 10023

CONTENTS

PART TWO—KANSAS CITY

LIST OF MAPS

ST. LOUIS

KANSAS CITY

INVITATION TO THE READERS

In researching this book, I have come across many wonderful establishments, the best of which I have included here. I am sure that many of you will also come across special hotels, inns, restaurants, guesthouses, shops, and attractions. Please don't keep them to yourself. Share your experiences, especially if you want to comment on places that have been included in this edition that have changed for the worse. You can address your letters to:

Beth Reiber
St. Louis & Kansas City 2nd Edition
c/o Prentice Hall Travel
15 Columbus Circle
New York, NY 10023

A DISCLAIMER

Readers are advised that prices fluctuate in the course of time and travel information changes under the impact of the varied and volatile factors that affect the travel industry. Neither the author nor the publisher can be held responsible for the experiences of readers while traveling. Readers are invited to write to the publisher with ideas, comments, and suggestions for future editions.

SAFETY ADVISORY

Whenever you're traveling in an unfamiliar city or country, stay alert. Be aware of your immediate surroundings. Wear a moneybelt and keep a close eye on your possessions. Be particularly careful with cameras, purses, and wallets—all favorite targets of thieves and pickpockets.

CHAPTER 1

INTRODUCING ST. LOUIS & KANSAS CITY

In 1803, Thomas Jefferson made one of the best real estate deals in history: the Louisiana Purchase, for which the United States paid France $15 million (about 3¢ an acre), doubling the nation's size. This heralded the start of the great westward expansion, and throughout the 1800s Americans and newly arrived immigrants streamed through the middle of the continent in search of a better life.

Some settlers recognized Missouri as that better life and settled in places with such names as St. Louis and the Town of Kansas—later changed to Kansas City. Most, however, used St. Louis and the Town of Kansas as springboards for their journeys to someplace else, traveling westward on the California and Oregon trails and later on the railroads.

Kansas City and St. Louis have had a complex about this situation ever since. The automobile has replaced the Conestoga wagon, but travelers still race through the Midwest on their way to someplace else, giving Kansas City and St. Louis nothing more than a passing glance from their cars on I-70. Although the natives have always been convinced that their hometowns were especially pleasant, the two cities have not been tourist meccas. That situation is slowly changing, especially in these times as economically minded Americans search for affordable vacation destinations close to home.

1. BACKGROUND

CULTURAL LIFE

In the past decade, both St. Louis and Kansas City have undergone a renaissance. They have shaken off the dust of their frontier and backwater image, renovated their downtowns, capitalized on their rich historic legacies, assumed once again their roles as leaders in blues and jazz, and regained the pride that they once had when both cities served as bustling gateways to the West. Vacationers may still go

✔

WHAT'S SPECIAL ABOUT THE ST. LOUIS AREA

Monument
☐ Gateway Arch, America's tallest monument; honors westward expansion in the 1800s.

Parks/Gardens
☐ Forest Park, now the home of the St. Louis zoo, Science Center, St. Louis Art Museum, St. Louis History Museum, and recreational facilities.
☐ Missouri Botanical Garden, the oldest botanical garden in the country.
☐ Laumeier Sculpture Park, a 96-acre park with sculpture from more than 30 artists.

Shopping
☐ Union Station, the world's largest rail terminal when built in 1894, now a shopping center with more than 80 specialty shops.
☐ St. Louis Centre, one of the largest downtown enclosed malls in the country.
☐ Antique Row, with more than 50 antiques shops on one street.
☐ Soulard Market, St. Louis's city market.

Food
☐ Great Italian restaurants, particularly in the Hill district.

☐ New American cuisine, innovative dishes combining regional specialties with international spices and ingredients.

Free Attractions/Clubs
☐ Free admission to many top attractions, including the St. Louis Art Museum, St. Louis zoo, Anheuser-Busch Brewery, and Grant's Farm.
☐ Many nightclubs with free or inexpensive entertainment, in Laclede's Landing and Soulard.

A Paradise for the Kids
☐ Six Flags Over Mid-America, a theme park loaded with rides, amusements, and entertainment.
☐ St. Louis Zoological Park.
☐ Grant's Farm, a 281-acre estate with a zoo, a game preserve, and the Ulysses S. Grant cabin.
☐ St. Louis Science Center and the Magic House, where children learn through hands-on displays.

racing by, but they also stop over in numbers greater than ever before and are astonished at all the things to do. If it's been ten years since you've seen either Kansas City or St. Louis, you're in for a huge surprise.

Tourism now rates as one of Missouri's top-three revenue-producing industries and is one of the fastest-growing factors in the state's economy. St. Louis, after all, is within a day's drive of almost one third of the nation's population, and Kansas City is less than a four-hour drive farther west. According to a recent survey conducted by the St. Louis Convention and Visitors Commission, 88% of the visitors polled said that St. Louis was their destination, 35% said that it was their summer vacation spot, and 46% said that it was a weekend getaway.

It's easy to see why. For one thing, Kansas City and St. Louis offer a staggering variety of things to see and do. Both towns have first-rate professional baseball teams; a score of unusual museums, including renowned art museums; historic homes and buildings; theme parks that do a roaring business; nearby horseracing tracks; and riverboat rides.

In St. Louis alone there are the 630-foot Gateway Arch, symbolizing the nation's westward expansion; the renovated Union Station, with its shops and restaurants; the St. Louis Zoological Park; the Missouri Botanical Garden; the Anheuser-Busch Brewery; and museums as diverse as the National Bowling Hall of Fame and the Dog Museum. Laclede's Landing, a riverfront warehouse district where the city's history began, is now the most popular nightlife district. St. Louis is one of the best places to hear rhythm and blues, much of it absolutely free, and the city dishes out some of the best Italian food in the country.

Kansas City adds to the list of attractions with Country Club Plaza, the nation's oldest shopping center, modeled after Seville, Spain; the Harry S Truman Library and Museum and the President's boyhood home in adjacent Independence; the nation's only museum devoted to World War I; the NCAA Visitors Center; and a steamboat museum based around a century-old cargo boat. History lives on in three restored forts near Kansas City—Fort Osage, Fort Scott, and Fort Leavenworth. But most surprising to visitors is the architectural wealth of Kansas City, where more than 1,000 structures have been entered into the National Register of Historic Places. Whereas the old buildings in many cities were torn down in the zeal for urban renewal, Kansas City's buildings have survived, thanks in large part to decades of abandonment and neglect. In fact, some of the nation's best examples of art deco can be seen in the heart of Kansas City. And, of course, Kansas City is famous the world over for its barbecue, steaks, and jazz.

Not only are Kansas City and St. Louis good destinations for what they have to offer, but also they are very affordable. Prices for accommodations, meals, and entertainment run as much as 30% less than those on either coast, making these cities great places for family vacations. Many St. Louis attractions are absolutely free, and both cities have scores of things for youngsters to do, ranging from educational yet also fun learning centers to theme parks.

GEOGRAPHY

Both Kansas City and St. Louis owe their existence to rivers—St. Louis mostly to the Mississippi, Kansas City mostly to the Missouri. Also, both are located on the Missouri border—St. Louis in the east next to Illinois, Kansas City in the west adjacent to Kansas. (Actually, Kansas City is part of a metropolitan area including Kansas.) They are separated by approximately 250 miles of rolling Missouri countryside, with I-70 serving as the main highway between the two. In the central and southern parts of the state are the Missouri Ozarks, a recreational getaway for both metropolitan areas.

St. Louis, with a population of about 397,000, is some 295 miles from Chicago, 345 from Cincinnati, 545 from Cleveland, and 545

WHAT'S SPECIAL ABOUT THE KANSAS CITY AREA

Food
- [ ] Some of the best barbecue in the country, with more varieties of barbecue sauce than anywhere else in the world.
- [ ] Kansas City steaks, including huge cuts at low prices.
- [ ] Ethnic foods, including Mexican, Italian, and Greek.

Jazz
- [ ] Many jazz clubs, including piano bars, classic jazz clubs, and the Mutual Musicians Foundation's after-midnight jam sessions.
- [ ] A Jazz Hotline, with tips on what's going on in Kansas City's jazz scene.

Buildings
- [ ] The Garment District downtown, with buildings dating from the 1800s.
- [ ] Some of the best examples of art deco architecture in the country.

Shopping
- [ ] Country Club Plaza, the nation's oldest shopping center (modeled after Seville, Spain), with a notable collection of art.
- [ ] Crown Center, financed by Hallmark Cards Inc., with more than 50 boutiques, shops, and restaurants.
- [ ] City Market, especially on Saturday.

Historic Forts
- [ ] Fort Leavenworth, established in 1827 to protect travelers on the Santa Fe Trail, now a U.S. Army education center.
- [ ] Fort Osage, a reconstruction of the first U.S. outpost following the Louisiana Purchase.
- [ ] Fort Scott, established in 1842 and now restored.

from Detroit. Kansas City, MO, with a population of about 435,000, is about 605 miles from Denver, 500 from Dallas, and 460 from Minneapolis. Metropolitan St. Louis has some 2.5 million inhabitants. Metropolitan Kansas City, including Kansas City, KS, has some 1.5 million inhabitants.

2. THE PEOPLE

The most compelling reason to visit the Midwest is the Midwesterners themselves. They're friendly, open, honest, neighborly, and down-to-earth with few pretensions. It's little wonder that the region has produced three of the nation's presidents: Harry S Truman from Independence, MO; Dwight D. Eisenhower from Abilene, KS; and Abraham Lincoln from Springfield, IL. The people of the Midwest are hard workers, products of the people who came before them—waves of immigrants from first France and then Germany, Italy, Sweden, and other European countries, lured to these rich lands to hunt, trap, farm, set up shop, and make better lives for themselves. Their rich ethnic heritage lives on to this day and is most visible in small towns such as the French settlement of Ste. Genevieve, the German Rhine–like town of Hermann, and the Swedish community of Lindsborg, all of which make good overnight excursions from Kansas City or St. Louis.

However, Kansas City and St. Louis are markedly different from each other, despite the fact that they're both Midwestern towns and have intertwined histories. Although St. Louis has always looked eastward, identifying itself with Chicago and even New York City, Kansas City has always been distinctly western, perhaps because it was here that the trails for Santa Fe, Oregon, and California began.

With all the diversity the Midwest has to offer, vacationers are stopping by these days to take in the sights, delight in the food, and revel in the music and people of the heartland of America.

3. HISTORY

Before white people came, the Mississippian, Osage, Kansa, and other Native Americans lived and hunted the hills and plains that are now known as Kansas, Missouri, and Illinois. The first white people to venture into this vast interior were Spanish, seeking gold and fortune, and they were followed by French explorers, trappers, and traders. In the mid-1730s the French established the region's first permanent white settlement, Ste Genevieve. For the next 30 years this tiny outpost on the west bank of the Mississippi River survived alone in this vast Upper Louisiana Territory. But then in 1764 French fur traders Auguste Chouteau and Pierre Laclede founded St. Louis as a trading post 65 miles farther north. Naming their post after King Louis IX of France, they soon had a lucrative business trading with the Osage, Missouri, Sauk, and Fox tribes. Because game was plentiful and the post's excellent location near the confluence of the Mississippi and Missouri rivers gave it quick and easy transport on to New Orleans, St. Louis was destined to become the largest settlement in the state and one of the nation's larger cities. By the 1770s St. Louis was a town of 339 white settlers, 33 free blacks, and 274 Native American and black enslaved persons. By 1800 the number of inhabitants had grown to 2,447. Ste Genevieve, on the other hand, remained a small settlement, and it is still in existence today,

DATELINE

- **700–1500** Mississippian Indians settle along the Mississippi River.
- **1735** Ste Genevieve founded, first permanent white settlement west of the Mississippi.
- **1764** St. Louis founded as a fur-trading post.
- **1803** Louisiana Purchase.
- **1804** Lewis and Clark depart St. Louis for their 7,689-mile expedition west.
- **1817** The first steamboat arrives in St. Louis.
- **1820** Missouri Compromise allows slavery in Missouri but forbids it in all future western and northern states.
- **1821** Missouri admitted to the Union as a slave state. A fur-trading post established on the Missouri River

(continues)

DATELINE

later becomes
Kansas City.

1827 Wagon
trains depart Independence on the
Santa Fe Trail. Fort
Leavenworth established.

1833 John C.
McCoy establishes
outfitters' post in
Westport on the
Santa Fe Trail, rivaling Independence.

1841 First organized wagon train
leaves Westport for
Oregon. St. Louis
ranks second in the
nation in river traffic,
behind New Orleans.

1849 Cholera epidemic in St. Louis
kills 7,000; fire also
destroys 400 buildings.

1854 Kansas-
Nebraska Act allows
people of Kansas
and Nebraska to decide whether they
want slavery.

1857 Supreme
Court's Dred Scott
decision.

1860 St. Louis
(pop. 160,000) is
eighth-largest U.S.
city.

1861 Civil War.
Missouri, a slave
state, stays in the
Union.

1863 The anti-
slavery town of Lawrence is ransacked,
and 150 men are
killed by a posse led
by William Quantrill.

1864 Battle of
Westport, the last
major Civil War bat-
(continues)

boasting 50 buildings from its French colonial times.

In 1803 Napoleon Bonaparte, anxious to rid himself of the vast and troublesome frontier so that he could wage more effective war against England, sold the Louisiana Territory to the United States for a mere $15 million. To find out what he had acquired, President Thomas Jefferson sent two trusted explorers, Lewis and Clark, to explore the region. They left St. Louis in 1804 and covered 7,689 miles during the next two years.

The Louisiana Purchase opened the West to a flood of eager newcomers. Anglo-Americans flocked to St. Louis. Although it wasn't long before the English language became dominant, St. Louis's early French influence is still reflected in such street and district names as Laclede's Landing, Chouteau, LaSalle, and Soulard.

In 1820 the Missouri Compromise was struck, allowing slavery to continue in Missouri but forbidding it in all future states north of an imaginary line extending west and north. As a result, when Missouri was admitted to the Union in 1821, it entered as a slave state. During that same year, a fur-trading post was established on the western end of the state, on land that is now Kansas City. For years, however, it remained nothing more than a trading post for a few French families, while nearby Independence grew as the starting point for wagon trains departing on the Santa Fe Trail as early as 1827.

Then in 1833 an entrepreneur named John C. McCoy saw that there was money to be made from the Santa Fe Trail, so he set up an outfitters store in a place called Westport. His scheme worked, and it wasn't long before Westport rivaled Independence as an equipment center. Its dusty streets—if you could call them that—were filled with Native Americans, Mexicans, mountain men, buffalo hunters, and mule skinners, all hoping to cash in on the riches of the trade. Westport, an outpost of whisky and guns, was crude, rowdy, and undisciplined. To protect the interests of the Santa Fe Trail, which was primarily a commercial trail for merchants traveling the 900 miles back and forth between Santa Fe and Westport, forts such as Fort Leavenworth and Fort Scott were established in Kansas. In 1838 McCoy founded the Town of Kansas four miles north of Westport on the banks of the Missouri River, on land that is now downtown Kansas City.

While the western edge of Missouri remained a rough frontier, St. Louis became gentrified. After it was proved in 1815 that sternwheelers could travel upriver on the Mississippi, St. Louis found new prosperity as a port town, as steamboats brought new products from Europe via New Orleans. By 1841 St. Louis was outranked only by New Orleans in terms of the nation's river traffic, with 186 steamboats landing in St. Louis that year.

But goods weren't the only things the steamboats transported. They also brought people by the thousands, many of whom stayed in St. Louis but most of whom traveled onward via the Missouri River to Independence and Westport, where they then joined others on the Oregon Trail. By 1860, as many as 100,000 emigrants had dared the five-month, 2,000-mile journey to Oregon. As for St. Louis, between 1830 and 1860 it grew from a town of only 5,825 to a city of 160,000, making it the eighth-largest city in the nation. As many as 50% of the newcomers were European immigrants, most of them Germans fleeing religious persecution back home and Irish escaping the Potato Famine.

CIVIL WAR St. Louis seemed destined for greatness, but then in 1861 came an event that thwarted its ambitions—the Civil War. As a slave state, Missouri had already attracted national attention with the Dred Scott case, which had opened in 1846 in the new St. Louis Courthouse. Dred Scott, a slave, had sued for freedom after his owner had taken him to free territory, but after years of court battles the U.S. Supreme Court finally ruled that Scott was not a citizen and therefore couldn't sue.

The Supreme Court also ruled that Congress couldn't exclude slavery in the territories. With the passage of the Kansas-Nebraska Act, the people in Kansas and Nebraska were given the option of deciding whether to permit slavery. To help swing the vote, the New England Emigrant Aid Company sent both men and weapons to keep Kansas a free state, while armed "border ruffians" rode over from Missouri to fight for slavery. Civil war broke out with the first shots fired in "bleeding Kansas." In 1863 the

DATELINE

tle west of the Mississippi River.
- **1865** Missouri-Pacific Railroad reaches Kansas City.
- **1869** Hannibal Bridge, the first to span the Missouri River, allows Kansas City to establish railroad links east and west.
- **1874** Eads Bridge completed over the Mississippi River, linking St. Louis with the east.
- **1880** St. Louis becomes the nation's fourth-largest city.
- **1894** St. Louis's Union Station built, the largest rail terminal in the world.
- **1900** Kansas City hosts the Democratic National Convention, which selects William Jennings Bryan.
- **1904** St. Louis World's Fair attracts 19 million visitors.
- **1926** Charles Lindbergh makes the first nonstop flight from New York to Paris in the "Spirit of St. Louis," backed by St. Louis businessmen. The St. Louis Cardinals win the World Series against the New York Yankees led by Babe Ruth.
- **1928** Republican National Convention held in Kansas City.
- **1945** Harry S Truman of Indepen-
(continues)

DATELINE

dence becomes president of the United States.

● **1965** Gateway Arch, the nation's tallest monument, completed in St. Louis.

● **1976** Kansas City hosts the Republican National Convention.

● **1985** St. Louis's Union Station re-opens as a luxury hotel and a shop-ping-and-dining complex.

antislavery town of Lawrence was attacked by a posse of proslavery men led by William Quantrill, killing 150 Lawrence men and setting fire to the town.

The Civil War tore Missouri in half. Although Missouri was a slave state, its governor was driven from office after trying to align the state with the Confederacy. And even while Missouri remained with the Union throughout the Civil War, it sent men to both sides in the conflict. But the biggest blow to Missouri occurred when the Confederates blocked the Mississippi River and the Union placed trade restrictions on the state, depriving St. Louis of its livelihood. By default, Chicago emerged as the Midwestern giant in trade, attracting the railroads and the support of New York merchants. It would be years before St. Louis would recover.

The Civil War also crippled Kansas City because warfare cut off trade along the Santa Fe Trail. In 1860 Kansas City had boasted 9 boarding houses, 16 hotels, and 26 saloons, with as many as 700 steamboats landing each year. As the Civil War raged, half the city's population simply packed their bags and left, while Confederate sympathizers were ordered to leave by official decree. Throughout the state, as many as 20,000 Missourians sympathetic to the South were driven from their homes. Kansas City, once a booming, bawdy, and raucous frontier city, was transformed into a virtual ghost town. In 1864 the last major Civil War battle west of the Mississippi took place in Westport.

BOOMTOWNS   Once the war was over, Kansas City jumped to its feet in its bid to attract the railroad. Competition was fierce because every town around knew that the railroads were the key to success in any city's future. But Kansas City ultimately won, beating out Leavenworth and Lawrence, and in 1865 the Missouri-Pacific reached the town. That was followed in 1869 with the completion of the Hannibal Bridge over the Missouri River, which meant that Kansas City could now ship goods both east and west. Kansas City turned its back on the river and before long emerged as one of the largest rail centers in the country and the marketing hub of the Great Plains.

Between 1865 and 1870 Kansas City's population surged from a mere 6,000 to 32,000. It was also the beginning of Kansas City's cowtown era and the cattle boom, as Texas longhorns were driven north along the Chisholm Trail to Abilene and then shipped to the stockyards of Kansas City. Wild Bill Hickok, Wyatt Earp, Jesse James, Bat Masterson, and Doc Holliday all strolled the streets of Kansas City, rubbing elbows with cowboys, merchants, more immi-grants, and a newly emerging wealthy class. Before long, the bustling cowtown boasted a public library, an opera house, a board of trade, a stock exchange, a medical college, and uniformed police and firemen. By 1900 Kansas City had come so far that it was chosen as the site for the Democratic National Convention, which nominated William Jennings Bryan. Later, in 1928 and again in 1976, it would serve as headquarters for Republican conventions.

St. Louis, too, slowly recovered from setbacks suffered during the Civil War, growing as a commercial and manufacturing center for meat-packing, brewing, refining, and mining. By 1870 the city boasted 31 flour mills, 85 brickyards, and 40 breweries. In 1874 the Eads Bridge was completed, spanning the Mississippi River and finally linking the city with the east. Like Kansas City, St. Louis turned its back on the river and concentrated its energies on the growth of the city, installing city parks and public facilities.

By 1880 St. Louis was the nation's fourth-largest city, a position that it would retain for the next four decades. To accommodate the waves of people pouring in off the railroads, the city constructed Union Station. Completed in 1894, it was the world's largest rail terminal, twice as big as its nearest competitor in Boston. In 1894 St. Louis also established a convention bureau, the purpose of which was to advertise St. Louis to the rest of the world.

20TH CENTURY The convention bureau's efforts bore fruit in 1904 with the St. Louis World's Fair. A celebration of the 100-year anniversary of the Louisiana Purchase, the fair was held in Forest Park in the western end of the city and began with an address by William Howard Taft and music conducted by John Philip Sousa. Approximately 50 nations participated, erecting a total of 1,576 buildings and drawing more than 19 million visitors. Among the many exhibits was Thomas Edison's display of his newfangled phonograph and the light bulb. The seven-month fair is also credited with serving the first hot dog, iced tea, and ice-cream cone.

Throughout the 20th century, both Kansas City and St. Louis have continued to enjoy steady growth and prosperity. St. Louis led the way with the revitalization of its riverfront when its Gateway Arch was erected in 1965, followed through the next decades with the renovations of Laclede's Landing and Union Station. Today Kansas City and St. Louis are Missouri's two largest cities, with a combined metropolitan-area population of about 4 million.

4. NOTED CITIZENS

FAMOUS ST. LOUISANS

Thomas Hart Benton (1782–1858) Missouri's first senator, serving in that capacity for 30 years, Benton was a noted Congressional orator and historian. He was responsible for the eastern portion of the Missouri Pacific Railroad starting at St. Louis, thus making the city a 19th-century railroad center.

Chuck Berry (b. 1926) This rock-and-roll legend grew up in St. Louis listening to recordings of Charlie Christian, T. Bone Walker, and Carl Hogan, first imitating and then expanding on his guitar techniques. By 1954 he was packing them in at the Cosmo Club in East St. Louis, performing his own compositions and covering the blues, country, and pop demanded by his audiences. Blueberry Hill, a bar in University City in St. Louis, claims to have more Chuck Berry memorabilia than anywhere else in the country, including the guitar on which he composed "Roll over Beethoven."

William S. Burroughs (b. 1914) A beat generation novelist,

Burroughs was born in St. Louis and lived here until he was 10, later returning to work as a cub reporter for the *St. Louis Post-Dispatch* in 1935. His 1960 novel *The Naked Lunch* had wide influence. He now resides in Lawrence, near Kansas City.

Adolphus Busch (1838–1913) A German-born American brewer, businessman, and philanthropist, Busch (with his father-in-law) founded the Anheuser-Busch Brewery, today the world's largest.

Kate Chopin (1851–1904) Kate Chopin grew up in St. Louis, moved to Louisiana when she married, and returned to St. Louis with her children after she was widowed. In St. Louis she wrote her most well known book, *The Awakening,* about a woman who seeks love outside a stuffy, middle-class marriage.

Gen. William Clark (1770–1838) An explorer, a military officer, and a public official, Clark is best known for the expedition he led with Meriwether Lewis to explore the Louisiana Purchase, departing St. Louis in 1804 and returning two years later. Clark remained in St. Louis, becoming the Indian Agent for Missouri Territory.

T. S. Eliot (1888–1965) Critic, author, and winner of the Nobel Prize for Literature in 1948, Eliot is considered St. Louis's most famous poet, even though he left the city for Harvard as a student and eventually moved to London, where he lived most of his adult life.

Eugene Field (1850–95) A writer and journalist, Field is best known as the "children's poet" for such works as *Wynken, Blynken and Nod* and *Little Boy Blue*. His boyhood home in St. Louis is now a museum containing a large collection of antique toys and dolls.

Scott Joplin (1868–1917) The legendary "King of Ragtime," Joplin spent some of his most formulative and productive years in St. Louis, where he composed "The Cascades" and "The Entertainer." His St. Louis home is now open to the public, after years of careful restoration.

Stan Musial (b. 1920) Inducted into the Baseball Hall of Fame in 1969, "Stan the Man" is known as a gentleman both on and off the field. Playing his entire 22-year professional career with the St. Louis Cardinals, he had a lifetime .331 batting average, with 3,630 base hits and 475 home runs. In addition to winning seven National League batting titles and three NL Most Valuable Player awards, he helped the Cardinals win three world championships.

Charles M. Russell (1864–1926) Born in St. Louis, he moved to Montana at the age of 15 to become a cowboy. Russell was an artist who captured the essence of the American West in more than 3,000 paintings, drawings, and sculptures.

Mark Twain (1835–1910) Born in Hannibal, a small river town north of St. Louis, Mark Twain lived for several years in St. Louis, where he wrote and set type on the *St. Louis Evening News and Intelligencer* and began his career as a river pilot.

Tennessee Williams (1911–83) Playwright Thomas Lanier "Tennessee" Williams grew up in St. Louis, living in several locations with his family before he headed for the East Coast. The view from the apartment described in *The Glass Menagerie* fits the view from an apartment that he lived in during his youth in St. Louis. Williams won Pulitzer Prizes for the plays *A Streetcar Named Desire* and *Cat on a Hot Tin Roof.*

FAMOUS KANSAS CITIANS

Count Basie   (1904–84) A composer and band leader, Basie was largely responsible for bringing Kansas City to the fore of jazz. He performed with the Benny Moten Band in local clubs from 1929 to 1936 before moving on to greener pastures on the East Coast.

Thomas Hart Benton   (1889–1975) One of Kansas City's best-known artists, Benton has many works in the Nelson-Atkins Museum of Art as well as a mural at the Harry S Truman Library in Independence. The Kansas City home where Benton lived and painted from 1937 until his death is now a state historic site.

Walt Disney   (1901–66) Although born in Chicago, Disney came to Kansas City as a young man in 1919 and found employment first as a commercial artist and then as an animator for Kansas City *Film Advertising.* He then formed his first—and soon bankrupt—production company. After this, he moved to Hollywood in 1923, where he went on to produce *Pinocchio, Fantasia,* and other Disney greats.

Charlie Parker   (1920–55) Born in Kansas City, Charlie "Yard-bird" Parker was a great jazz alto saxophonist and great improviser. He first gained recognition playing in jam sessions around Kansas City, including stints with Count Basie's musicians and Jay McShann's band. After moving to New York, he developed—along with Dizzy Gillespie—a new style of jazz known as bop or bebop.

Harry S Truman   (1884–1972) Thirty-third president of the United States, Truman is one of Missouri's most famous native sons. He served as a Jackson County judge, U.S. senator, and vice president before taking office as president in 1945 upon Franklin D. Roosevelt's death. He was elected to a full term in 1948. The home where he lived with his wife, Bess, and the Truman Library and Museum, where the Trumans are buried, are open to the public in Independence.

5. RECOMMENDED BOOKS & FILMS

ST. LOUIS
BOOKS

Ebenhoh, Tom, *Arch Celebration* (Spiritgraphics, 1990). This book celebrates the 25th anniversary of the Gateway Arch with color photographs, interviews, and reflections on the meaning of St. Louis's role as the gateway to the West.

Fifield, Barringer, *Seeing St. Louis* (WA University Campus, 1987). This is a guidebook divided into specific tours and written from an architect's point of view. It is not pedantic, and can be enjoyed by a wide audience.

Kirschten, Ernest, *Catfish and Crystal* (Patrice Press, 1989). Less scholarly in tone than the book below, this is an older history book that has just been rereleased.

Primm, James N., *Lion in the Valley* (Pruett, 1990). This is the most exhaustive history of St. Louis and the area.

FILMS

Meet Me in St. Louis, a 1944 musical set in St. Louis. Starring Judy Garland, it depicts a typical St. Louis family in the year 1903.

The Pride of St. Louis, a 1952 film starring Dan Daily, who plays Dizzy Dean, the Arkansas mountain boy who became a great St. Louis Cardinal pitcher. Popular for his homespun sense of humor and pitching prowess, Dean is injured and forced to turn to a career as sportscaster, where he is no less popular.

White Palace, a 1989 film based on a novel by St. Louis writer Glenn Savan. Filmed in South St. Louis, it stars James Spader who falls for an older woman played by Susan Sarandon.

KANSAS CITY
BOOKS

Grant, William D., *The Romantic Past of the Kansas City Region* (Lowell Press, 1987). This is a portrait of Kansas City from 1540 to 1880.

Reddig, William, *Tom's Town: Kansas City and the Pendergast Legend* (University of Missouri Press, 1986). Tom Pendergast was the undisputed "Boss" of Kansas City politics in the 1920s and through the Great Depression; although the years of his regime were undoubtedly corrupt, it was also under him that many of the city's art deco buildings were constructed. Interesting reading.

FILM

Mr. and Mrs. Bridge, a 1991 film based on a novel by Evan S. Connell. It stars Paul Newman and Joanne Woodward as a well-to-do couple whose personal lives are influenced by the changing world of the mid-20th century.

PLANNING YOUR TRIP

This chapter will help you prepare for your trip to St. Louis and Kansas City. Reading through this guide's other chapters before leaving home will also help you plan your travels.

1. INFORMATION

One of the best and easiest ways to prepare for your trip is to send for the wealth of brochures and pamphlets just waiting for you. For general information on Missouri, send for the free 140-page annual booklet called *Missouri Travel Guide,* which has information on everything from attractions and campgrounds to wineries and caves. Contact the **Missouri Division of Tourism,** Truman State Office Building, Department MT-90, P.O. Box 1055, Jefferson City, MO 65102 (tel. 314/751-4133).

A similar booklet on Kansas, called *A Guide to Kansas,* which lists attractions city by city, is available from the **Kansas Department of Commerce,** Travel & Tourism Division, 400 W. 8th St., 5th floor, Topeka, KS 66603-3957 (tel. 913/296-7091, or toll free in Kansas 800/2-KANSAS). Maps and a calendar of events also are available.

For information specifically on St. Louis, including a map of the city and brochures, contact the **St. Louis Convention and Visitors Commission,** 10 S. Broadway, Suite 1000, St. Louis, MO 63102 (tel. 314/421-1023, or toll free 800/247-9791 or 800/325-7962).

Similarly, for information and a map on Kansas City, contact the **Convention & Visitors Bureau of Greater Kansas City,** City Center Square, 1100 Main St., Suite 2550, Kansas City, MO 64105 (tel. 816/221-5242, or toll free 800/767-7700).

If you plan to visit Hannibal or Springfield, you may also wish to contact that city's local tourist office before you depart. Refer to Chapter 11 for the addresses and telephone numbers of the local tourist offices for each town.

Both Kansas and Missouri maintain a number of state information centers to assist travelers arriving by car. For a list of these centers and their locations, refer to the "Getting There" section later in this chapter.

2. WHEN TO GO

The most pleasant time to visit the Midwest as far as weather is concerned is in late spring or early autumn, except then you miss out on all those festivals and events that make the rest of the year so much fun. If you're willing to brave the elements, Kansas City and St. Louis make good destinations at any time of the year.

CLIMATE   There's a saying around these parts that the weather is so fickle, it can change in the amount of time it takes you to visit the outhouse. About the only thing you can rely on is that the weather is reliably unpredictable—which means that it can be cold and chilly or warm and sunny in both July and November and sometimes even both of those extremes in the same day. But one of the great things about the weather is that the sky is often a deep blue, with more than 200 sunny days per year.

One can say with certainty, however, that Missouri has four distinct seasons. Winters are usually brisk and stimulating but seldom severe, with snowfalls up to a depth of 10 inches or more very rare. More likely are snowfalls of only an inch or two, with the average yearly snowfall ranging from about 17 to 20 inches per year. Winter temperatures usually remain around 30°F, although December 1989 brought the coldest reading of the century, when an Arctic cold front sent the mercury to a freezing 23 degrees below zero in Kansas City. Usually, however, temperatures of zero or below occur only two or three days a year, usually in January.

Early spring brings a period of frequent and rapid fluctuations in weather, including those great thunderstorms that roll in from the west off the prairies. Of course, each thunderstorm can bring the thing that got Dorothy out of Kansas—a tornado. Tornado season is April through June, but even though I've lived in Kansas most of my life, I've never seen one. In St. Louis in the past 116 years there have been only four tornadoes that have produced extensive damage and/or loss of life. Both television and radio stations carry weather alerts, and almost every town around has warning sirens.

Summer can be very hot and humid, with temperatures of 90° or more occurring 35 days a year and a humidity of 70 to 80 percent. Autumn is glorious as the leaves change color and the sky turns that incredibly deep shade of blue. Indian summers are frequent, and the first frost usually occurs in late October.

For a tape-recorded message of the temperature and forecast, call St. Louis at 314/321-2222 or Kansas City at 816/471-4840.

Missouri's Average Daytime Temperature & Days of Rainfall

	Jan	Feb	Mar	Apr	May	June	July	Aug	Sept	Oct	Nov	Dec
Temp. (°F)	29	33	43	55	65	75	80	79	71	59	44	34
Rainy days	8	8	11	11	11	9	8.6	7.6	8	8.3	9	9.5

ST. LOUIS & KANSAS CITY AREA CALENDAR OF EVENTS

If you're lucky, your trip may coincide with one of the area's many annual festivities, most of which are linked to the Midwest's rich ethnic heritage or historical events. All those listed here are easily accessible, with either free admission or tickets sold at the gates as you enter.

MARCH

☐ **St. Patrick's Day Parade, Kansas City** More than 300,000 people flock to downtown Kansas City to take part in this annual event, the country's third-largest St. Patrick's Day parade. The parade route runs from Crown Center via Grand Avenue to 6th Street, followed by a street party in Westport. March 17, from noon. For more information, call 816/931-7373.

✪ *ST. PATRICK'S DAY PARADE, ST. LOUIS This parade has been an annual event for more than 25 years.*
   ***Where:** Downtown, starting at 12th and Washington and ending at the Old Courthouse. **When:** Saturday before St. Patrick's Day. **How:** Just show up. For more information, call 314/421-1800.*

MAY

☐ **Storytelling Festival, St. Louis** This annual festival features both nationally recognized and local storytellers, with a special performance for the hearing impaired. At the Gateway Arch in early May (dates vary). For more information, call 314/553-5911.

JUNE

☐ **Good Old Days, Fort Scott, KS** Free entertainment, a parade, eight blocks of arts and crafts, and an antiques show are just some of the events of this re-creation of an 1890 street fair. At Fort Scott on the first weekend after Memorial Day. For more information, call 316/223-2334.
☐ **Kansas State Barbecue Championship, Lenexa, KS** Lenexa, a suburb of Kansas City, is host to a statewide competition with free samples. At Sar-Ko-Par Park, 87th and Lackman on the fourth Saturday in June. For more information, call 913/541-8592 or 888-6570.

JULY

✪ *VEILED PROPHET FAIR, ST. LOUIS This is one of the nation's largest July 4 celebrations, featuring three or four days of events, including air shows, water shows, craft booths, live entertainment, a parade, and a fireworks display.*
   ***Where:** Gateway Arch, Mississippi riverfront, Laclede's*

Landing. **When:** *Three or four days around July 4.* **How:**
For more information, call 314/535-FAIR.

☐ **Soulard Bastille Day, St. Louis** A weekend of French-themed celebrations, including a kickoff ball, jazz performances, an arts festival, a bicycle race, and abundant French cuisine. In the Soulard district on the weekend after July 4. A $10 ticket entitles bearer to five samples of French cuisine from participating Soulard restaurants. For more information, call 314/436-0828.

☐ **Kansas City Indian Club Pow Wow, Kansas City** Midwest Indians compete in dance and skill during a three-day event. At the Wyandotte County Fairgrounds, 98th and State, in Mid-July, usually third weekend. For more information, call 816/421-0039.

✪ **KANSAS CITY BLUES AND JAZZ FESTIVAL, KANSAS CITY** *This two-day event is Kansas City's largest annual free concert, drawing more than 100,000 spectators and top local and national musicians.*

Where: Penn Valley Park and the Liberty Memorial, 100 W. 26th St. **When:** *Last weekend in July.* **How:** *Free admission. For more information, call 816/272-2700.*

AUGUST

☐ **Jazz and Heritage Month, Kansas City** August heralds a month-long celebration of Kansas City's jazz heritage with more than 50 events around town. These include free concerts at Barney Allis Plaza downtown, Crown Center, and Country Club Plaza. The highlight of the month is the 18th and Vine Heritage Festival, a weekend of free concerts on the sidewalk saluting the cross streets that constitute Kansas City's birthplace of jazz. For more information, contact the Kansas City Jazz Commission at 816/272-2700.

☐ **Festival of Festivals, St. Louis** St. Louis celebrates a different culture each August weekend amid the beauty of the Missouri Botanical Garden. Included are music and dance, ethnic food, crafts, and activities. For more information, call 314/577-5100.

☐ **Illinois State Fair, Springfield, IL** Illinois's biggest, this fair features livestock shows, tractor pulls, milking contests, horse racing, music, and more. At the Illinois State Fair Grounds for 11 days, beginning the second Thursday in August. For more information, call 217/789-2360, or toll free 800/545-7300.

SEPTEMBER

☐ **Renaissance Festival, Bonner Springs, KS** This is a great medieval getaway, complete with bards, musicians, beggars, damsels, knights, royalty, jousts, and sorcerers. A benefit of the Kansas City Art Institute, this re-creation of a 16th-century village features crafts, food booths, and old-fashioned games as well as continual entertainment on a number of stages the entire day. At the Agricultural Hall of Fame, off I-70. Weekends only, from Labor Day weekend to mid-October. Tickets are available at the gate or in advance by writing 207 Westport Rd., Kansas City, MO 64111. For more information, call 816/561-8005, or toll free 800/373-0357.

✪ *SPIRIT FESTIVAL, KANSAS CITY* *Entertainment from gospel to jazz and blues, cultural activities, food booths, and fireworks are featured in this annual festival celebrating things unique to Kansas City.*
Where: *Liberty Memorial, Penn Valley Park.* *When:* *Labor Day weekend.* *How:* *Admission is $3 for adults, free for children under 12 and senior citizens. Tickets are available at the gate. For more information, call 816/221-4444.*

☐ **Santa-Cali-Gon Days, Independence, MO** This celebration of pioneer heritage—when the Santa Fe, California, and Oregon trails led westward from Independence—features an arts-and-crafts fair, entertainment, an interpretive area with demonstrations, and food and crafts booths. At Independence Square, downtown on Labor Day weekend, Friday to Monday. For more information, call 816/252-4745 or 836-8300.

☐ **Plaza Fine Arts Fair, Kansas City** This arts fair on Country Club Plaza has been a tradition for more than 60 years. Artists from around the country display and sell their work, including oils, watercolors, drawings, prints, photography, and sculpture. Dates vary. For more information, call 816/753-0100.

OCTOBER

☐ **Historic Folklife Festival, Hannibal, MO** Street musicians, artisans demonstrating crafts of the mid-1800s, storytellers, and abundant food make Mark Twain's river town come alive. Third weekend in October. For more information, call 314/221-6545.

NOVEMBER

✪ *AMERICAN ROYAL LIVESTOCK, HORSE SHOW AND RODEO, KANSAS CITY* *Since 1899 the American Royal has attracted competitors from across the nation to one of Kansas City's most famous traditions, a 15-day event that includes a livestock show, a rodeo, livestock auctions, and a barbecue contest.*
Where: *1701 American Royal Court and Kemper Arena.* *When:* *First Saturday in November to mid-November.* *How:* *Ticket prices vary for each event. For more information, call 816/221-9800.*

☐ **Plaza Christmas Lighting Ceremony, Kansas City** Every Thanksgiving evening, Kansas Citians crowd the streets of Country Club Plaza to see the turning on of more than 155,000 colored bulbs that outline the 14-block district. The lights remain on throughout the Christmas season. For more information, call 816/221-5242 or 753-0100.

3. TIPS FOR THE DISABLED

For a list of hotels, restaurants, and tourist attractions in St. Louis that provide handicapped parking and wheelchair accessibility, contact the **Office on the Disabled,** City Hall, Room 30, St. Louis, MO 63103 (tel. 314/622-3686 for voice, 622-3692 for TTY). This office's brochure listing these facilities is called "Access St. Louis." As for public transportation, many buses in St. Louis are equipped with lifts for wheelchairs. For more information on these buses, call the **Bi-State Transit System** at 314/231-2345 (outside Missouri, toll free 800/2233-BUS).

For information in Kansas City about access to city buildings, programs and activities, and so forth, contact the **Mayor's Office on the Disabled,** City Hall, 414 E. 12th St., 29th floor, Kansas City, MO 64105. (tel. 816/274-1235).

4. GETTING THERE

St. Louis and Kansas City are located in the heart of America, making them easy to reach by plane, train, car, and bus. St. Louis, for example, is within a four-hour flight of every major city in the country and within a day's drive of almost one-third of the nation's population.

BY AIR

PLANE ECONOMICS

Ever since the Airline Deregulation Act of 1978, the airfare market has been a free-for-all, allowing such special fares as APEX (advanced-purchase excursion fare), discount travel agents, and other options. In 1992 airlines were trying to simplify the fare structure, so be alert for the latest developments.

Your best strategy for securing the lowest airfare is to shop around. Use the toll-free lines to call all the airlines that go to your destination and then call several travel agents to see whether they can find a better deal. Always ask for the lowest-priced fare available. Sometimes you can purchase a low-priced ticket at the very last minute, because airlines will discount tickets if the flight is not fully booked. Another good strategy is to consult the travel sections of major newspapers, since they often carry advertisements for cheap fares and special promotions.

Most airlines offer an assortment of fares, ranging from first class, the most expensive, to business class to economy. First and business class offer large seats with more leg room, more personal service, and better meals. Economy is the lowest-priced regular fare, of which there are usually two types: one that carries no special restrictions or requirements and one that is cheaper and carries some restrictions, such as tickets that are only 50% refundable. Of course, you can also assume that seats in economy class will be small and cramped and that you'll be served typical airline food. All these classes can be booked at the last minute, if there's space on the flight.

If you're trying to save money, the cheapest way to travel is by a promotional fare, the most common of which is usually called APEX but can also be referred to as Excursion, Super Saver, and other names. Offering savings as much as 35% off the regular fare, they carry stringent restrictions, which vary but usually include a 7- or 14-day advance-purchase requirement, may require a Saturday night stay, usually allow no changes, and are nonrefundable and nontransferable.

Airlines that serve both Kansas City and St. Louis include **American** (tel. toll free 800/433-7300), **Continental** (tel. toll free 800/525-0280), **Delta** (tel. toll free 800/221-1212), **Northwest** (tel. toll free 800/225-2525), **Southwest** (tel. 816/474-1221 in Kansas City, 314/421-1221 in St. Louis), **TWA** (tel. toll free 800/221-2000; 816/842-4000 in Kansas City, 314/291-7500 in St. Louis), **United** (tel. toll free 800/241-6522; 816/471-6060 in Kansas City, 314/241-6522 in St. Louis), and **USAir** (tel. toll free 800/428-4322).

FARES Fares can vary widely among the airlines, which frequently offer a variety of tariffs between the same cities. The fares listed here should be used only as a guideline. From New York, round-trip fares on TWA to St. Louis at the time this book went to press were $790 for first class, $730 for business class, $670 for economy class with no restrictions, $330 for economy class with some restrictions, and $290 for APEX fare. To Kansas City, round-trip fares on United from New York were $870 for first class (there is no business class), $660 for economy class with no restrictions, $400 for economy with some restrictions, and $340 for APEX fare.

From Los Angeles, TWA round-trip flights to St. Louis cost $1,180 for first class, $790 for business class, $670 for economy class with no restrictions, $320 for economy class with some restrictions, and $290 for APEX fare. Round-trip fares from Los Angeles to Kansas City on United were $960 for first class (there is no business class), $500 for economy class with no restrictions, $280 for economy class with some restrictions, and $250 for APEX fare.

If you wish to fly between Kansas City and St. Louis, the round-trip fare on TWA is $440 for first class, $400 for business class, $360 for economy class with no restrictions, and $116 for APEX fare.

 FROMMER'S SMART TRAVELER: AIRFARES

1. Shop all the airlines that fly to Kansas City or St. Louis.
2. Keep calling the airlines, since the availability of cheap seats changes daily. As the departure date nears, you might be able to obtain a seat at a great discount, since an airline would rather sell a discounted seat than fly with it empty.
3. Read the advertisements in newspaper travel sections, since they often offer special deals and packages.
4. You can save money by buying your ticket as early as possible, since the cheapest fares, such as APEX (advance-purchase excursion), require that you purchase your ticket usually 7 or 14 days in advance.

Also, watch for other inexpensive fares, as low as $39 for a one-way ticket that carries no restrictions and does not require advance purchase. Be sure to shop around.

OTHER OPTIONS Besides contacting airlines and travel agencies and consulting newspapers, you may also contact a discount travel agent. Each agent has his or her own set of rules and usually charges small fees for such services as delivering tickets and changing reservations. Discount travel agencies that serve customers nationwide are **Travel Avenue** in Chicago (tel. 312/876-1116, or toll free 800/333-3335), **Travelbrokers** in New York City (tel. toll free 800/999-8748), and **Smart Traveller** in Miami (tel. 305/448-3338, or toll free 800/226-3338).

BY CAR

According to a survey conducted by the St. Louis Convention and Visitors Commission, approximately 86% of that city's visitors arrive by car. St. Louis is easily reached by I-70, as well as from I-55 from Chicago and New Orleans, I-44 from Oklahoma City, and I-64 from Norfolk, Virginia. Driving time to St. Louis is approximately 10 hours from Atlanta, 5 hours from Chicago, 12 hours from Dallas, 16 hours from Denver, 34 hours from Los Angeles, 13 hours from New Orleans, and 18 hours from New York.

Kansas City is served by two major highways: I-70 from Denver and St. Louis and I-35 from Minneapolis and Dallas. Kansas City is about a four-hour drive west of St. Louis on I-70.

Missouri law requires that all front-seat passengers wear seat belts. In addition, a child under four must be in a child safety seat in the front or wear a seat belt in the back. If you need emergency assistance on a Missouri highway or wish to report an accident, intoxicated drivers, or vehicle problems, call toll free 800/525-5555.

If you arrive in Missouri by car, you'll find state information centers on I-44, near the Oklahoma border; on I-270 in north St. Louis, just west of the Missouri-Illinois state line at the Riverview exit; in southeast Missouri on the north-bound lane of I-55, near Marston; on I-29 in northwest Missouri; in Hannibal on U.S. 61; and in east Kansas City, near the Truman Sports Complex on I-70.

Kansas Visitor Information Centers are located west of Kansas City on I-70 (for westbound traffic only), on I-70 in Abilene, on I-70 in Goodland in western Kansas, and on U.S. 55 near Fort Scott.

BY TRAIN

One of the most interesting ways to travel between Kansas City and St. Louis and enjoy the Missouri countryside is by Amtrak. Two trains depart daily from each direction, and the trip takes slightly more than five hours. Tickets cost $38 one way and $39 round trip.

You can also reach both Kansas City and St. Louis by Amtrak from Los Angeles, Chicago, New Orleans, and points in between. The round-trip fare from Chicago is $39 to St. Louis and $77 to Kansas City. From Los Angeles, the round-trip fare is $212 to both Kansas City and St. Louis.

For information on **Amtrak,** call toll free 800/872-7245 or 800/USA-RAIL.

BY BUS

The cheapest way to get to St. Louis or Kansas City via public transportation is probably by bus, with **Greyhound/Trailways.** The cost of a round-trip bus ticket with no restrictions from New York to Kansas City, for example, is $228.30. Promotional and seven-day advance-purchase tickets also are available. For more information, contact your nearest bus carrier.

CHAPTER 3

FOR FOREIGN VISITORS

f you're traveling to St. Louis or Kansas City, you'll have most likely visited the United States at least once before—it is rare to find a visitor in the Midwest who has not already seen New York and California. However, should you have questions about your stay, this chapter will hopefully answer them. Be sure, too, to read Chapters 1, 2, 4, and 12.

1. PREPARING FOR YOUR TRIP

ENTRY REQUIREMENTS

Except for Canadian nationals (who need only proof of residence) and British and Japanese nationals (who no longer need visas but only passports), each foreigner entering the United States must have two documents: (1) a valid **passport,** with an expiration date at least six months longer than the scheduled end of the visit to the United States, and (2) a tourist **visa,** available without charge from the nearest U.S. consulate (you must fill out a special form and provide a passport photograph).

In most instances, you will be given your visa immediately or at least within 24 hours. Try to avoid the summer rush in June, July, and August, when Consulates may be packed. If applying by mail, enclose a large, stamped, self-addressed envelope and expect to wait at least two weeks for the visa. You can obtain visa application forms from U.S. consulates as well as from airline offices and leading travel agents. The U.S. tourist visa (visa B) is theoretically valid for a year and good for any number of entries, but in reality the U.S. consulate issuing your visa will determine the length of stay for a multiple- or single-entry visa. Keep in mind that there is some latitude here, so dress neatly and responsibly if applying in person; it helps if you can give the address of a relative, friend, or business connection living in the United States.

MEDICAL REQUIREMENTS No inoculations are required for entry into the United States unless you come from, or have stopped over in, an area known to be infectious, especially for cholera or yellow fever. Only applicants for immigration visas are required to undergo a screening test for AIDS.

If you have an ailment requiring treatment with syringes or

medications containing narcotics or drugs, be certain to carry a valid, signed prescription from your physician to avoid any suspicions from Customs officials that you are carrying illegal drugs.

TRAVEL INSURANCE [BAGGAGE, HEALTH & LOSS]

Insurance—even health insurance—is voluntary in the United States. However, because of the very high cost of medical care, you'd be wise to arrange for appropriate coverage before setting out. There are specialized insurance companies that will, for a relatively low premium, cover the following: loss or theft of your baggage; trip-cancellation costs; guarantee of bail in case you are jailed; sickness or injury costs (medical, surgical, and hospital); and costs of an accident, repatriation, or death.

Such packages may be sold by insurance companies, travel agencies, banks, some airports, and even automobile clubs. If you carry a lot of camera equipment, it's worth getting the equipment insured as well. I can't stress enough the importance of having medical insurance.

2. GETTING TO THE UNITED STATES

Travelers from overseas can take advantage of APEX (advance-purchase excursion) fares, which are offered by all major U.S. and European airlines. In addition, Icelandair from Luxembourg offers inexpensive fares to New York or Orlando, and Virgin Atlantic is an inexpensive way to get from London to New York via Newark Airport or Miami.

Some airlines (such as TWA, Northwest, United, and Delta) offer discount tickets on their transatlantic or transpacific flights under the name Visit USA, allowing travel between a set number of U.S. destinations at minimum rates. Such tickets are not for sale in the United States and must therefore be purchased before you leave your foreign point of departure. This system is the best way to cover much of the country at a low cost.

FAST FACTS **THE FOREIGN TRAVELER**

Accommodations Hotel and motel chains are big business in the United States, accounting for the majority of accommodations nationwide. Chain hotels offer uniformity in the quality of their rooms, as well as their prices, but they lack the charm of privately owned, smaller hotels. Generally speaking, motels, which are one- or two-story accommodations often located near highways, are cheaper than hotels, particularly those on the outskirts of town. Another choice in inexpensive accommodations are bed-and-breakfasts, which are similar to pensions in Europe. Bed-and-breakfasts are often historic homes offering half a dozen or so guest rooms with or without private bathrooms.

Refer to the accommodations chapters for St. Louis and Kansas City for more information on the various types of hotels, motels, and bed-and-breakfasts.

Auto Organizations If you plan to travel by automobile, you may wish to join an auto club, which entitles you to maps, recommendations on routes, guidebooks, accident insurance, and emergency road service. One of the largest automobile clubs is the **American Automobile Association** (AAA), which maintains an office in St. Louis at 3917 Lindell Blvd. (tel. 314/531-0700) and in Kansas City at 3245 Broadway (tel. 816/931-5252). A one-year membership for both Americans and foreigners is $45.

Business Hours Most **government offices and businesses** are open Monday through Friday from 9am to 5pm. **Banks** usually are open Monday through Friday from about 9am to 3 or 4pm, with slightly longer hours sometimes offered on Friday and morning hours offered on Saturday. **Post offices** generally are open Monday through Friday from 8am to 5:30 or 6pm and Saturday from 8am to noon.

Stores in downtown areas usually are open only during regular business hours—that is, Monday through Saturday from 9 or 10am to about 5:30 or 6pm. **Shopping malls** have longer hours, usually Monday through Saturday until 9pm and Sunday until 5 or 7pm. **Drugstores and supermarkets** are open even later—and in some cities they never close. Some Americans, to avoid crowds, do all their grocery shopping in the middle of the night.

Museum hours vary widely. The average hours for large museums are Tuesday through Saturday from 10am to 5pm, opening perhaps at noon on Sunday and closed on Monday. Some of the major museums are open on national holidays, with the exception of Thanksgiving, Christmas, and New Year's Day.

Climate See "When to Go" in Chapter 2.

Currency/Exchange The U.S. monetary system has a decimal base: one **dollar** ($1) = 100 **cents** (100¢). The most common denominations are $1 (a "buck"), $5, $10, $20, $50, and $100 notes—all mostly green in color. There's also a $2 bill, but it's rarely used. Most store clerks do not like taking a $50 or $100 bill for a small purchase.

There are six denominations of coins: 1¢ (one cent, or penny); 5¢ (five cents, or nickel); 10¢ (ten cents, or dime); 25¢ (twenty-five cents, or quarter); 50¢ (fifty cents, or half dollar); and the $1 piece (both the older, large silver dollar and the newer, small Susan B. Anthony coin).

The foreign-exchange bureaus so common in Europe are rare even at airports in the United States and nonexistent outside major cities. Try to avoid having to change foreign money or traveler's checks denominated in foreign currency—it may prove to be more of a nuisance than it's worth. The best policy is to put the bulk of your money into U.S. dollar traveler's checks and then bring a credit card. If you must change money, there are major banks in Kansas City and St. Louis that will do so for you. In St. Louis, try the **Mercantile Bank,** 8th and Locust (tel. 314/425-2525), open weekdays from 8:30am to 4:30pm; or the **Commerce Bank of St. Louis Coun-**

ty, 8000 Forsyth on the corner of Merimac (tel. 314/854-7463), open Monday to Thursday from 9am to 4pm and Friday from 9am to 6pm. In Kansas City, a convenient place to exchange foreign currency is downtown at the **United Missouri Bank,** 1010 Grand (tel. 816/860-7000), open Monday to Thursday from 8am to 4:30pm and Friday from 8am to 5pm.

Customs/Immigration Every adult visitor to the United States may bring in the following free of duty: one liter of wine or hard liquor (which isn't much, regrettably); 1,000 cigarettes or 100 cigars (but *no* cigars from Cuba) or three pounds of smoking tobacco; and $400 worth of gifts. These exemptions are offered to travelers who spend at least 72 hours in the United States and who have not claimed the exemptions in the preceding 6 months. It is absolutely forbidden to bring into the country foodstuffs (particularly cheese, fruit, cooked meats, and canned goods) and plants (vegetables, seeds, tropical plants, and so on). Foreign tourists may bring in or take out up to $5,000 in U.S. or foreign currency with no formalities. Larger sums must be declared to Customs on entering or leaving.

No matter what your point of entry into the United States, you should anticipate a long wait. U.S. Customs and Immigration officials are among the slowest and most suspicious on earth. At some of the busiest international airports, such as New York's John F. Kennedy Airport, you may have to wait two hours just to get your passport stamped. When you add to that the time it takes to clear Customs and get your luggage, it'll become clear that you should allow at least three hours if you're changing planes.

It's a different story altogether if you're arriving by car or rail from Canada because border-crossing formalities between the two neighbors are little more than that. And for some flights by air from Canada, Bermuda, and some points in the Caribbean, Customs and Immigration are handled at the point of *departure,* which is much quicker and less painful.

Drinking Laws Americans can't drink until they reach 21 years of age in Missouri and Kansas. That applies to visitors as well. For hours of operation of liquor stores and bars, check the individual city listings.

Electricity Although in Europe the current is 220 volts and 50 cycles, in the United States it's 110 to 115 volts and 60 cycles.

Embassies/Consulates All embassies are located in Washington, D.C.; consulates in the Midwest are usually located in Chicago. For the telephone number of your nation's embassy in Washington, D.C., call information at 202/555-1212.

Emergencies Throughout the United States, dial 911 to get the police or an ambulance or to report a fire. U.S. hospitals usually have emergency rooms, with a special entrance for quick attention. See the Fast Facts section for each city for more information under "Dentists/Doctors," "Drugstores," and "Hospitals."

Gasoline [Petrol] One U.S. gallon equals 3.75 liters, while 1.2 U.S. gallons equals one Imperial gallon. Almost all gasoline sold is unleaded.

Holidays Banks, government offices, and post offices are closed on the following national holidays: New Year's Day (January 1); Martin Luther King, Jr., Day (third Monday in January); Presidents Day/Washington's Birthday, (third Monday in February); Memorial Day (last Monday in May); Independence Day (July 4); Labor Day (first Monday in September); Columbus Day (second

Monday in October); Veterans Day/Armistice Day (November 11); Thanksgiving (fourth Thursday in November); and Christmas Day (December 25).

If Christmas or New Year's Day falls on a Sunday, the following Monday is a holiday. The Tuesday following the first Monday in November is Election Day and is a legal holiday every four years during the presidential election (1992, 1996).

Information For local tourist information, refer to the "Getting to Know St. Louis" and "Getting to Know Kansas City" chapters. If you wish to obtain information before your trip, see Chapter 2, "Information," for telephone numbers and addresses of local and state tourist offices.

Legal Aid The foreign tourist will probably never come up against the U.S. legal system. The most that's likely to happen is that you'll be pulled over for speeding (65 miles per hour is achingly slow if you're used to German autobahns), in which case you should never attempt to pay the fine directly to the police officer. It could be interpreted as a bribe and land you in serious trouble. Pay fines by mail or directly into the hands of the clerk of the court. If you're accused of a more serious offense, it is wise to say and do nothing before consulting a lawyer. Under U.S. law, an arrested person is allowed one telephone call to a party of his or her choice. Call your embassy or consulate.

Mail Mailboxes in the United States are painted blue with a red-and-white stripe and carry the inscription "U.S. Mail." Don't forget to add the five-figure postal code (Zip code) to all letters addressed to a U.S. destination. If you're unsure of the postal code, inquire at any post office.

You can receive your mail on your vacation, even if you aren't sure of your address, by having your mail sent to you in care of **General Delivery** at the main post office of the city where you expect to be. You must pick it up in person and produce proof of identity (driver's license, credit card, or passport). If you want your mail forwarded, you need only to fill out a change-of-address card at any post office. The post office will also hold your mail for you up to one month.

Medical Emergencies See "Emergencies," above. Also refer to the "Getting to Know St. Louis" and "Getting to Know Kansas City" chapters for information on local hospitals and doctors.

Newspapers/Magazines Most newspapers in the United States are local, not national. In St. Louis it's the *St. Louis Post-Dispatch;* in Kansas City it's the *Kansas City Star.* National newspapers available in both cities are *USA Today, The New York Times, The Wall Street Journal,* and the *Christian Science Monitor.* As for magazines, weekly news magazines include *Newsweek, Time,* and *U.S. News & World Report.* It is difficult to obtain airmail editions of foreign newspapers and magazines in the Midwest—and they're often out of date by the time they get here.

Radio/Television Most hotels have televisions in their rooms, so you'll have a chance to see that most American of institutions—commercials. There are five coast-to-coast broadcast networks—ABC, CBS, NBC, Fox, and the Public Broadcasting System (PBS), as well as many national cablecasters, such as Cable News Network (CNN), MTV (popular music), and ESPN (sports). Many hotels subscribe to cable, allowing viewers the choice of about a dozen channels. There are also local radio stations that each broadcast a particular kind of music—classical, country, jazz, or pop—punctuated by news broadcasts and frequent commercials. If you're hungry for international news, tune to the local National Public Radio station, which broadcasts lengthy news programs in the morning and again in the late afternoon.

Safety Whenever you're traveling in an unfamiliar city or country, stay alert. Be aware of your immediate surroundings. Wear a money belt and keep a close eye on your possessions. Never carry large amounts of cash and leave your expensive jewelry at home. Be particularly careful with cameras, purses, and wallets—all favorite targets of thieves and pickpockets.

Generally speaking, the Midwest is safe, particularly in rural areas, but there are parts of Kansas City and St. Louis where you should exercise extreme caution. Use common sense when walking at night—keep to areas where there are lots of people and the streets are well lit. Avoid such isolated areas as parks, alleys, and parking lots after dark.

Taxes There is no VAT (Value-Added Tax) in the United States. Every state, however, can set its own sales tax: in Missouri it's 4.425%; in Kansas it's 4.25%. In addition, each city can add its own general revenue tax. In St. Louis, for example, it's 1.5%. These taxes are added to almost everything you purchase, from clothing to a meal in a restaurant. Liquor taxes are even higher. Thus, if you're making a major purchase, taxes can really add up.

Telephone/Telegraph/Telex Public telephones can be found virtually everywhere—on the street and in restaurants, bars, public buildings, stores, and gas stations. Outside metropolitan areas, gas stations and stores are your best bet.

Local calls cost a quarter (25¢). For long-distance or international calls, stock up on a supply of quarters; the pay phone will instruct you when and in what quantity you should put them into the slot. For direct overseas calls, first dial 011, followed by the country code (Australia, 61; Republic of Ireland, 353; New Zealand, 64; United Kingdom, 44; and so on), and then by the city code and the number of the party you wish to call. For calls to Canada and long-distance calls in the United States, dial 1 followed by the area code and number you want. Generally speaking, it's much cheaper calling from the United States to other countries rather than the reverse. It's also cheaper if you call between 10pm and 8am or on Saturday and Sunday.

Before calling from a hotel room, always ask the hotel phone operator if there are any telephone surcharges, since these can be shockingly high. It's best to use a public phone. As a rule, telephone cards sold in England, Germany, Japan, and many other countries are not usable here.

For reversed-charge or collect calls and for person-to-person calls dial 0 (zero, not the letter O) followed by the area code and the number you want. The operator will then come on the line, and you should specify that you are calling collect, or person-to-person (the most expensive way to call), or both. If your operator-assisted call is international, ask for the overseas operator.

If you need local directory assistance, dial 411. If you need a long-distance number, dial 1, followed by the appropriate area code and 555-1212. Thus, if you're in Kansas City and need a number in St. Louis, dial 1-314-555-1212.

Telegraph and telex services are provided by private corporations (as is the telephone system), such as ITT, RCA, and above all, Western Union. You can bring your telegram in to the nearest Western Union office or even dictate it over the phone (tel. toll free 800/325-6000). You can also telegraph money or have it telegraphed to you very quickly over the Western Union system. Some hotels also provide these services.

Telephone Directories There are two kinds of telephone directories available, both of which should be in your hotel room. The general directory is the so-called **White Pages,** which contains private residential numbers and business subscribers, listed in alphabetical order. The inside front cover contains the emergency number for police and other vital numbers, such as a poison control center and a crime hotline. It also contains a guide to long-distance and international calling, complete with country codes and area codes.

The second directory is printed on yellow paper—and therefore called the **Yellow Pages**—and lists all local services, businesses, and industries by type of activity, with an index in the back. The listings cover everything from restaurants to specialized shops and services. The book also includes a city map. In small cities, the *Yellow Pages* and *White Pages* often are combined into one directory.

Time The United States is divided into four time zones (with the exception of Alaska and Hawaii), and both St. Louis and Kansas City follow Central Standard Time (CST). When it's noon in Kansas City, it's 1pm in New York and 10am in Los Angeles. Kansas City is seven hours behind Central European Time, which means that when it's noon in Kansas City, it's already 7pm in much of Europe. Daylight Saving Time is in effect from the last Sunday in April (when clocks are set one hour ahead) through the last Saturday in October (when clocks are set one hour back).

Tipping Tipping is very much a part of the American way of life. Indeed, waiters and waitresses depend on it for the majority of their income. Here are some rules of thumb:

Bartenders: 10%–15%
Bellhops: at least 50¢ per piece; $2–$3 for a lot of baggage
Cab drivers: 15% of the fare
Cafeterias, fast-food restaurants: no tip
Chambermaids: $1 a day; more in upper-class hotels
Cinemas, movies: no tip
Checkroom attendants: 50¢ per garment
Doormen (hotels or restaurants): not obligatory, but $1 at top hotels
Hairdressers: 10%–15%
Parking-lot attendants: $1 or $2
Porters (airport and railroad stations): at least 50¢ per piece; $2–$3 for a lot of baggage
Restaurants, nightclubs: 15%–20% of the check to your service person

Toilets The United States does not have as many public toilets as you'll find in many other countries. Rather, Americans use those in bars, fast-food restaurants, hotels, museums, department stores, or gasoline stations. Often the toilets are clean, but sometimes they are not, with those at gasoline stations the worst offenders. I usually carry some pocket tissues with me in case toilet paper is nonexistent.

Some gas stations and restaurants have signs saying that restrooms (as public toilets are often called) are for the use of patrons only. Buy a cup of coffee if you must. And although it is now rare, some public toilets require you to insert a dime (10¢) or quarter (25¢) into a slot on the door before the door will open.

Traveler's Checks/Credit Cards   In some categories, the United States is moving toward becoming a cashless society. Going about with only cash, it seems, is just too risky, since there may not be enough to pay for unforseen accidents or expenses. In fact, many hotels and most car-rental agencies will not deal with customers who cannot produce a credit card.

Paying with credit cards (and personal checks), therefore, is a widely used method in the United States. Most common are VISA (BarclayCard in Britain), MasterCard (EuroCard in Europe, Access in Britain, Diamond in Japan, and so on), American Express, Diners Club, Carte Blanche, and Discover Card. Of these, VISA and MasterCard seem to be preferred by the greatest number of establishments. Credit cards can be used in almost all hotels and motels and in most restaurants and shops (except for liquor stores). A credit card can serve as a deposit when you rent a car or allow you to draw cash from banks that accept them. It is also accepted as proof of identity, sometimes carrying more weight than a passport.

As for traveler's checks, buy them in U.S. dollars. They're accepted as cash almost everywhere. It's best to have both $20 and $100 denominations. There's no fee charged for cashing them.

See Also   "Fast Facts: St. Louis" in Chapter 4 and "Fast Facts: Kansas City" in Chapter 12.

AMERICAN SYSTEM OF MEASUREMENT

LENGTH

1 inch (in.)	=	2.54cm
1 foot (ft.)	=	12 in. = 30.48cm = 0.305m
1 yard (yd.)	=	3 ft. = 0.915m
1 mile	=	5,280 ft. = 1.609km

To convert miles to kilometers, multiply the number of miles by 1.61. Also use to convert speeds from miles per hour (mph) to kilometers per hour.

To convert kilometers to miles, multiply the number of kilometers by .62. Also use to convert to mph.

CAPACITY

1 fluid ounce (fl. oz).	=	0.03 liters
1 pint	=	16 fl. oz. = 0.47 liters
1 quart	=	2 pints = 0.94 liters
1 gallon (gal.)	=	4 quarts = 3.79 liters = 0.83 Imperial gal.

To convert U.S. gallons to liters, multiply the number of gallons by 3.79.

To convert liters to U.S. gallons, multiply the number of liters by 0.26.

To convert U.S. gallons to Imperial gallons, multiply the number of U.S. gallons by 0.83.

To convert Imperial gallons to U.S. gallons, multiply the number of Imperial gallons by 1.2.

WEIGHT

1 ounce (oz.)	=	28.35g
1 pound (lb.)	=	16 oz. = 453.6g = 0.45kg
1 ton	=	2,000 lb. = 907kg = 0.91 metric tons

To convert pounds to kilograms, multiply the number of pounds by 0.45.

To convert kilograms to pounds, multiply the number of kilograms by 2.2.

AREA

1 acre	=	0.41ha
1 square mile	=	640 acres = 259ha = 2.6km²

To convert acres to hectares, multiply the number of acres by 0.41.

To convert hectares to acres, multiply the number of hectares by 2.47.

To convert square miles to square kilometers, multiply the number of square miles by 2.6.

To convert square kilometers to square miles, multiply the number of square kilometers by 0.39.

TEMPERATURE

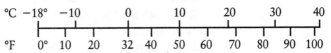

To convert degrees Fahrenheit to degrees Celsius, subtract 32 from the number of degrees Fahrenheit, multiply by 5, then divide by 9 (example: 85°F − 32 × 5/9 = 29.4°C).

To convert degrees Celsius to degrees Fahrenheit, multiply the number of degrees Celsius by 9, divide by 5, and add 32 (example: 20°C × 9/5 + 32 = 68°F).

PART ONE

ST. LOUIS

CHAPTER 4

GETTING TO KNOW ST. LOUIS

1. ORIENTATION
- **WHAT THINGS COST IN THE ST. LOUIS AREA**
- **NEIGHBORHOODS IN BRIEF**

2. GETTING AROUND
- **FAST FACTS: ST. LOUIS**

This chapter will answer any questions that you might have upon your arrival in St. Louis and during your stay—from how to get to your hotel from the airport and around the city to numbers to call during an emergency.

1. ORIENTATION

Located on the western shore of the Mississippi River, which divides the state of Missouri from the state of Illinois, St. Louis prides itself on having been the gateway to the West.

ARRIVING

BY PLANE

Lambert–St. Louis International Airport (tel. 314/426-8000) is conveniently located 10 miles northwest of the city, just north of I-70. Facilities include the usual restaurants, car-rental companies, lockers for storage of luggage, shoe-shine stands, and a hair salon, but of most interest to arriving visitors is the **St. Louis Visitor Information** booth located on the lower level near the luggage carousels. Be sure to pick up a copy of *St. Louis Quick Guide,* with information on the city's top attractions, as well as brochures and a map of the city.

GETTING INTO TOWN The easiest way to get to your hotel is by **taxi,** which costs about $18 for the ride downtown and takes approximately 40 to 60 minutes, depending on traffic. Fares from Lambert Airport to the suburb of Clayton or the communities in Mid-County run about $15. Up to five passengers can ride and share the meter fare, making a taxi ride very reasonable if there are several of you.

By summer 1993, Lambert–St. Louis airport is scheduled to be connected to downtown St. Louis by a light rail service called **Metro Link**. Station stops will include Central West End, Union Station, Busch Stadium, 8th and Pine (in the heart of downtown), St. Louis Centre, and Laclede's Landing. The one-way fare has been set at $1.80.

An alternative is to take the **Airport Express** (tel. 314/429-4940), which is a six- or eight-passenger van depositing passengers directly at hotels. The fare is $8 one way or $14 round trip. The hours of operation from the airport are daily from 6:30am to 10:30pm.

Among the many hotels served by Airport Express in the downtown area are the Adam's Mark, the Clarion, the Holiday Inn Downtown/ Riverfront, the Hotel Majestic, the Marriott Pavilion Downtown, the Embassy Suites, the Hyatt Regency St. Louis at Union Station, the Doubletree Mayfair Suites, the Drury Inn Gateway Arch, and the Drury Inn Union Station. Other accommodations served by Airport Express include the Cheshire Inn and Lodge and the Radisson and Ritz-Carlton hotels in Clayton. Even if you aren't staying at one of these hotels, you may find it cheaper to take the limousine to the hotel nearest your destination and then continue your trip by taxi.

WHAT THINGS COST IN THE ST. LOUIS AREA	U.S. $
Taxi from airport to downtown St. Louis	$18.00
Bus from downtown to Clayton	1.00
Local telephone call	0.25
Double at Adam's Mark Hotel (expensive)	175.00
Double at Drury Inn Union Station (moderate)	90.00
Double at Coral Court Motel (inexpensive)	40.00
Lunch for one at Grappa (moderate)	10.00
Lunch for one at Miss Hullings (budget)	5.00
Dinner for one, without wine, at Tony's (expensive)	49.00
Dinner for one, without wine, at Gian-Peppe's (moderate)	24.00
Dinner for one, without wine, at Rigazzi's (budget)	8.00
Pint of beer	2.25
Coca-Cola	1.00
Cup of coffee	0.75
Roll of SAS 100 Kodacolor film, 36 exposures	5.50
Admission to Gateway Arch and Tram	3.50
Movie ticket	5.50
Ticket to The Muny	5.00 to 30.00

The cheapest way to travel from the airport to downtown is via **public bus no. 4,** known as the Natural Bridge bus and operated by the **Bi-State Transit System** (tel. 314/231-2345). The fare is $1, and the final destination is Broadway and Olive streets in the heart of downtown.

BY TRAIN

If you're arriving in St. Louis via train, you'll most likely arrive at the main **Amtrak** terminal at 550 S. 16th St. (tel. toll free 800/872-7245) in downtown St. Louis. Taxis are easily available here.

BY CAR

If you're driving to St. Louis, the main thing to keep in mind is to time your arrival so that you miss rush hour. Particularly bad is the bottleneck that develops on the Poplar St. Bridge crossing the Mississippi from Illinois, which is also the route served by highways 70, 55, and 64. As in most big cities, traffic here is worst heading into St. Louis in the morning and again after 5pm as commuters head back for the suburbs.

Since parking can be expensive in St. Louis, you'll probably save a lot by staying in a hotel that offers free parking. (Check Chapter 5 for parking information for individual hotels.) Generally speaking, hotels on the outskirts are more apt to provide free parking than those in the downtown area. As for public parking facilities, St. Louis has parking garages everywhere to accommodate the crowds that flock to Busch Stadium, Union Station, the Arch, and other top attractions.

BY BUS

The new **St. Louis Bus Terminal** (tel. 314/231-7800), served by Greyhound, is set for construction at 13th and Cass streets, just north of downtown St. Louis.

TOURIST INFORMATION

The main information office is the downtown **St. Louis Convention and Visitors Commission,** 10 S. Broadway (tenth floor of the Equitable Building) Suite 1000, St. Louis, MO 63102 (tel. 314/421-1023)—open daily from 8:30am to 5pm. Stop here to arm yourself with brochures, guides, and maps of St. Louis and vicinity.

There's another visitor center located in the **Mansion House Center,** 445 N. Memorial Drive (tel. 314/241-1764)—open daily from 9:30am to 4:30pm—and also one on the airport's lower level that is open daily from 10am to 8pm.

For a quick rundown of what's happening in St. Louis, call the "Fun Phone" at 421-2100 for a recorded message outlining special exhibits and music and theater events and even giving a schedule of Cardinal home baseball games.

CITY LAYOUT

St. Louis was founded on the western bank of the Mississippi, and here its heart remains. Downtown St. Louis, watched over by the shining Gateway Arch, includes Busch Stadium, Union Station, and a restored warehouse district now containing restaurants and bars, called Laclede's Landing. Less than a 10-minute drive due west from downtown is Forest Park, site of St. Louis Zoological Park, a fantastic art museum, two golf courses, and a number of other fine attractions. St. Louis city is a separate administrative unit, apart from any county in Missouri. Spreading like a fan to the north, west, and south is St.

IMPRESSIONS

The first time I saw St. Louis I would have bought it for $6 million. It is bitter now to look abroad over this domed and steepled metropolis, this solid expanse of brick and mortar, and remember that I allowed this opportunity to go by. . . .
—MARK TWAIN (1874)

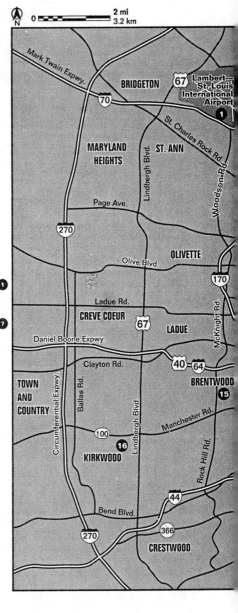

Louis County, which contains a number of well-known communities. Locals often refer to locations in St. Louis County as North County, West County, South County, and Mid-County. The last identifier includes Brentwood, Clayton, Kirkwood, Richmond Heights, and University City. Incidentally, the city of East St. Louis is across the Mississippi in Illinois. Many residents of East St. Louis commute across the river to work in the St. Louis area.

270 Circumferential Expwy.

MISSOURI

ILLINOIS

Frost Ave.

170 BERKELEY FERGUSON

Airport Rd.

West

DELLWOOD

BELLEFONTAINE
NEIGHBORS

Chambers Rd.

Halls Ferry Rd.

Florissant Ave.

Elizabeth Ave.

Broadway

Riverview Dr.

Hanley Rd.

JENNINGS

NORTHWOODS

ST. JOHN

Mississippi River

GRANITE
CITY

NORMANDY

Riverview Blvd.

Union Blvd.

MADISON COUNTY

Hall St.

Natural Bridge Rd.

UNIVERSITY
CITY ②

PAGEDALE

St. Louis Ave.

70

Hodiamont Ave.

Newstead Ave.

Grand Blvd.

③

Hanley Rd.

④

Kings highway Blvd.

Page Ave.

CLAYTON

Forest Park

⑤

⑨

⑪

RICHMOND
HEIGHTS

40

100

64

⑥ ⑫

MAPLEWOOD

McCausland Ave.

44

ST. LOUIS

⑧ ⑦ ⑩

100

⑭

EAST
ST. LOUIS

WEBSTER
GROVES

Hampton Ave.

Morganford Rd.

Daniel Boone Expwy.

366

Jefferson Ave.

⑬

Broadway

55

366

Grand Blvd.

Mississippi River

ST. CLAIR COUNTY

Watson Rd.

Gravois Rd. 30

55

ST. LOUIS COUNTY

MISSOURI

Mississippi River

ILLINOIS

MAIN ARTERIES & STREETS For orientation downtown, let
the Gateway Arch be your guide. Located on an expanse of green
called Jefferson National Expansion Memorial National Historic Site
beside the Mississippi River, the Arch serves as the gateway to the
West both in symbol and in fact. From about the middle of the Arch
stretching west is Market Street, which passes the Old Courthouse
and continues on to Union Station. It's one of the most important

streets in the city, serving as a dividing line for the north and south street addresses. Some of the streets running westward and parallel to Market Street were named in the 1800s after trees. Walnut, Chestnut, Pine, Olive, and Locust are all downtown streets lined with office buildings, restaurants, and shops.

Crossing Market Street are numbered streets that run north and south. At 18th and Market streets is Union Station, 18 blocks west of the Mississippi River. Because Market Street is the dividing line between north and south addresses, North 4th Street is north of Market Street, while South 4th Street is south of Market.

Downtown St. Louis is connected to the rest of the county via a number of major thoroughfares and highways. Most important for east-west traffic are I-70 (which leads past Lambert-St. Louis International Airport and continues through Missouri to Kansas City); U.S. Highway 40/I-64 (also called Daniel Boone Expressway), which skirts Forest Park; and I-44, which continues on to Six Flags and Meramec Caverns. Also passing through downtown is I-55 in its run from Chicago on to the Ozarks. If you picture greater St. Louis as a fan spreading out from the Mississippi, its outer perimeter is marked by I-270, a circumferential expressway. Another important thoroughfare that loops the area is Lindbergh Boulevard.

FINDING AN ADDRESS   As previously mentioned, downtown St. Louis is composed of a grid, with numbered streets paralleling the Mississippi River and running north and south and named streets running east to west. Remember that Market Street divides the north and south street designations. Thus, the Holiday Inn at 200 N. 4th Street is located two blocks north of Market; and the Campbell House Museum at 1508 Locust is located near the intersection of Locust Street and 15th Street.

MAPS   The St. Louis Visitor Information Center offers a free map that includes both an outline of the city and its vicinity and a detailed map of the downtown area. It's adequate for most purposes, but if you wish to explore the backroads of St. Louis, you might wish to purchase one of many city maps available. H. M. Gousha, for example, offers a handy *FastMap*™ covering St. Louis and vicinity.

NEIGHBORHOODS IN BRIEF

Laclede's Landing   A neighborhood of restored 19th-century warehouses just north of the Gateway Arch and beside the river, Laclede's Landing is where the city of St. Louis was born. It was here that Pierre Laclede, a French fur trapper, set up a trading post on the banks of the Mississippi in 1764, and it was from here that the city grew and prospered. Today Laclede's Landing is a nine-block area of brick buildings and cobblestone streets, filled with restaurants, clubs, shops, and offices. This is one of St. Louis's most famous nightlife districts, noted for its many establishments offering live music from blues and jazz to rock and roll.

Central West End   In the late 1880s, with the increase in smog and noise, many well-to-do St. Louisans moved farther west to greener pastures, and this is where many of them settled. By the time the World's Fair opened in nearby Forest Park in 1904, the Central

West End was a booming residential area of imposing mansions and neighborhood stores. Stretching along Euclid Avenue between Delmar and Forest Park boulevards and branching off onto side streets such as Maryland Avenue and McPherson, today the Central West End is one of the city's most interesting neighborhoods, a lively mix of trendy clothing boutiques, sidewalk cafés, art galleries, antiques shops, and restaurants.

The Hill   No trip to St. Louis would be complete without a visit to the Hill, perhaps to sample some great Italian cuisine. This is the city's Italian district, where even the fire hydrants are painted red, white, and green, the colors of the Italian flag. Practically every block has its own Italian eatery, some of which are very expensive and hushed within, others of which are riots of families and noise. There are also Italian bakeries; mom-and-pop specialty grocery stores; and neatly maintained small brick homes, many of which take pride in their lawn ornaments. The heart of the Hill is the St. Ambrose Church, located at the corner of Wilson and Marconi streets, where there's a bronze statue memoralizing the Italian immigrants who came to America to begin new lives. The Hill, which is not much of a hill at all, is located south of Forest Park and west of the Botanical Gardens.

Soulard   Located south of downtown on and around Russell Boulevard, Soulard (pronounced "sue-*lard*") is another neighborhood of brick homes, these built primarily by 19th-century German immigrants, many of whom worked in the city's breweries. In fact, Soulard is where you'll find Anheuser-Busch, the area's only surviving brewery, where tours are offered most days of the week. Soulard Market, the city's main produce market, at Seventh and Lafayette, has been selling fruit, vegetables, meats, and spices since 1845. Near Soulard is Cherokee Street, lined with dozens of antiques shops. But the main draws of Soulard are its small music clubs and restaurants, where jazz, blues, and Irish music reign supreme.

NEARBY NEIGHBORHOODS

The Loop   Named after an old streetcar turnaround, the Loop is a five-block area between 6200 and 6700 Delmar Boulevard in University City, a community adjacent to St. Louis. It is the closest thing the St. Louis area has to a SoHo. The Loop is home to a number of art galleries, an alternative movie theater, ethnic restaurants serving everything from Mexican to Ethiopian food, bookstores, and bars. Blueberry Hill, a bar that pays tribute to rock and roll, is said to have the world's best jukebox, and out on the sidewalk is a Walk of Fame, with markers highlighting the lives of such famous St. Louisans as Tennessee Williams, Chuck Berry, and baseball great Stan Musial.

Clayton   Located in Mid-County west of Forest Park, the separate city of Clayton is an important corporate and financial center. The home of many of the area's most notable hotels and restaurants, it has the subdued and relaxed pace of suburbia but also the flair of metropolitan smartness. Clayton is a convenient spot from which to explore greater St. Louis.

2. GETTING AROUND

St. Louis cannot compete with European or East Coast cities when it comes to public transportation—in the Midwest, most people get around in their own cars. Even most visitors arrive by car.

BY PUBLIC TRANSPORTATION

LIGHT RAIL   Metro Link is a new 18-mile light rail line, with an expected opening in summer 1993. It will run from Lambert–St. Louis International Airport through downtown to East St. Louis in Illinois. Metro Link will have 20 stations, including stops at Delmar Boulevard, Forest Park, Central West End, Union Station, Busch Stadium, 8th and Pine (in the heart of downtown), St. Louis Centre, and Laclede's Landing. The fare will be $1.80. For more information, contact the St. Louis Visitor Information Center.

BUS   St. Louis's bus network is operated by the Bi-State Transit System. Most bus routes start downtown and then fan out to outlying districts, which means that buses are convenient if you're traveling to or from the downtown area. Bus stops do not identify the destination or route of buses that stop there, so you'll need to know beforehand the route of the bus you want to take. Bus no. 93, for example, begins at 3rd and Washington downtown and passes through St. Louis University and the Central West End on its way past Forest Park to Clayton. Bus no. 40 is convenient for travel from Washington Avenue downtown to Anheuser-Busch and Soulard Market. For more information on specific bus routes, call the **Bi-State Transit System** at 231-2345 (outside Missouri, you can call Bi-State by dialing toll free 800/2233-BUS). Simply say where you are and where you want to go and you'll be told which bus to board. Bus maps are available at the Bi-State office at 707 N. 1st Street and at public libraries and city hall.

Most buses are equipped with lifts for wheelchairs and operate from approximately 5am to 11pm or midnight, with slightly shorter hours on Sunday and holidays. Fares for local buses are $1 for adults and 50¢ for children 5 through 12. Express buses (identified with an X added to their number, as in 140X) cost $1.30 for adults and 65¢ for children. Transfers between buses cost 20¢.

For visitors, the great news is that you can ride throughout the downtown area for free. Downtown is known as the Free Ride Zone, in which passengers can ride from one point to any other point without paying, all year round. In addition, from May to December there's the **Levee Line,** special buses that transport passengers between Union Station and the Gateway Arch, with stops along the way such as at Laclede's Landing and the St. Louis Centre. The Levee Line is also free, and the buses are easily identifiable because they are painted like paddlewheel steamboats. Hours of operation for the Levee Line are daily from about 10:50am to 9:40pm (to 5:55pm on Sunday). Pick up a map of the Levee Line's route at the St. Louis Visitor Information Center.

BY TAXI

There are approximately 20 taxicab companies listed in the St. Louis *Yellow Pages,* each with its own fare schedule. **County Cab**

Co. (tel. 991-5300), in business since 1937, serves the entire St. Louis County and charges $2.45 for the first mile and $1 for each additional mile. **Allen Cab** (tel. 241-7722) charges 85¢ when you get into the cab, then $1 per mile. Most companies also charge an extra $1 for an additional passenger, and some also add a 50¢ gasoline surcharge. It costs approximately $18 to take a taxi from Lambert–St. Louis Airport to the downtown area.

BY CAR

That St. Louis is a driving town is evident during rush hour. A plus is that drivers in the Midwest tend to be courteous, civil, and forgiving, qualities to be grateful for if you're navigating unfamiliar territory.

Arm yourself with a good map and keep in mind that during rush hour the freeways tend to be congested. In the downtown area, it seems that every street is one-way, so you'll probably want to park and then walk around. Unless otherwise posted, you can turn right at red lights after coming to a full stop.

Have plenty of coins handy if you plan to park at meters along the street. Since meters must be fed approximately every hour-and-a-half in the downtown area, you'll probably want to park at a lot or garage. Parking can run more than $5 for a couple hours near the Gateway Arch. You'll find public parking at various locations downtown, at the Arch, Laclede's Landing, and Union Station. Some downtown parking lots offer early-bird specials for less than $4 for the entire day if you park before 9am. Check the parking lots east and west of Busch Stadium for such specials.

In St. Louis you'll also come across valet parking, very much the mode at the city's better hotels and restaurants. Hotels charge extra for valet parking, so you can save money by parking yourself. At some restaurants, valet parking is offered as a courtesy to diners, though you're expected to tip $1 or $2. At some downtown locations where parking is a problem, valet parking is a real godsend. Otherwise, it seems a bit superfluous to have a car attendant drive your car 20 feet to the nearest available stall.

If you need to rent a car, **Avis** has an office both downtown (tel. 241-5780) and at the airport (tel. 426-7766), as do **Hertz** (tel. 421-3131 downtown; 426-7555 airport) and **National** (tel. 621-0060 downtown; 426-6272 airport). The base price for rentals begins at about $40 per weekday, which includes unlimited mileage but excludes gas. Cheaper rates are offered on weekends.

ON FOOT

There are many parts of the St. Louis area that you'll want to explore on foot, including the downtown area, the Hill, Forest Park and its many museums, the Loop in University City, and the Central West End. It's approximately 16 blocks from the Arch to Union Station (about a mile), which you can walk in less than half an hour.

 ST. LOUIS

This section is designed to make your stay in St. Louis as problem-free as possible. Keep in mind, too, that the concierge at your hotel is an invaluable source of information, as is the **St. Louis Convention and Visitors Commission** (tel. 314/421-1023).

Airport   Lambert–St. Louis International Airport (tel. 314/426-8000) is conveniently located 10 miles northwest of the city. Refer to "Orientation," above, for more information.

American Express   American Express Travel Services is located downtown at 1 Mercantile Center, 7th and Washington (tel. 314/241-6400). It's open Monday to Friday from 9am to 5pm.

Area Code   The telephone area code for St. Louis is **314.** On the Illinois side of the Mississippi River, in East St. Louis, it's **618.**

Auto Rentals   See "Getting Around," above, for information on car-rental agencies and prices.

Babysitters   Most of St. Louis's major hotels provide babysitting services or can contact a babysitter should the need arise.

Buses   Many bus routes start in the downtown area and then fan out to the outskirts, but of most interest to visitors is the fact that passengers can travel within the downtown area absolutely free. Refer to "Getting Around," above, for more information.

Business Hours   As a rule, **office hours** are weekdays from 9am to 5pm, and most **banks** are open weekdays from about 8:30 or 9am to about 4pm. **Shops** are open longer, especially those at such shopping centers as Union Station and the city's many enclosed shopping malls. Although hours vary, most **shopping centers** are open Monday through Saturday from about 10am to 9 or 10pm, until 5pm on Sunday.

Car Rentals   See "Auto Rentals," above.

Climate   See "When to Go" in Chapter 2.

Dentists/Doctors   Some of the expensive hotels offer the services of an in-house doctor or a doctor on call. Otherwise, check the *Yellow Pages* for a list of area doctors. An alternative is to call the **Doctor Referral Service of the St. Louis Metropolitan Medical Society** (tel. 314/371-5225) or the **Dentist Referral Service of the Dental Society of Greater St. Louis** (tel. 314/965-5960).

Driving Rules   See "Getting Around," above.

Drugstores   Many drugstores have normal business hours. If you need a prescription in the middle of the night, **Walgreens,** 4 Hampton Village Plaza on the corner of Chippewa and Hampton (tel. 314/351-2100), fills prescriptions 24 hours a day.

Emergencies   As throughout the United States, the number to call in an emergency is **911** for police, fire, and ambulance. Also see "Dentists/Doctors" and "Hospitals" in this section.

Eyeglasses   If you need to replace eyeglasses in a hurry, a convenient location is **Lenscrafters,** 176 Crestwood Plaza in Southwest County (tel. 314/968-9090). It can supply you with a new pair within a few hours.

Gay Hotline   The local gay and lesbian hotline is 314/367-0084, available only in the evening from 6 to 9pm.

Hairdressers/Barbers   If your hotel does not have a barber shop or beauty salon, the concierge may be able to direct you to one to suit your style. Otherwise, refer to the *Yellow Pages*.

Holidays   For a list of U.S. national holidays, see "Fast Facts: The Foreign Traveler" in Chapter 3. For information on St. Louis' special annual events, see "When to Go" in Chapter 2.

Hospitals   There are approximately 30 hospitals in the St.

Louis area. Some of the most centrally located include **Barnes Hospital,** Barnes Hospital Plaza (tel. 362-5000), which specializes in surgery and transplants; **Deaconess Hospital,** 6150 Oakland (tel. 768-3000); **St. Mary's Health Center,** 6420 Clayton Rd. (tel. 768-8000), which also has a doctor-referral service; **St. John's Mercy Medical Center,** 615 S. New Ballas Rd. (tel. 569-6000); **St. Louis Children's Hospital,** 400 S. Kingshighway (tel. 454-6000); **St. Louis Regional Medical Center,** 5535 Delmar Blvd. (tel. 361-1212); and **St. Louis University Hospital,** 3635 Vista at Grand Blvd. (tel. 577-8777).

Information Locations of the St. Louis visitor centers are given in "Orientation," above.

Laundry/Dry Cleaning All of the expensive and most of the medium-priced hotels offer laundry and/or dry-cleaning service. Some of the budget-priced ones offer coin-operated laundry machines. If yours does not, ask the staff where the most convenient laundry facility is.

Liquor Laws The minimum drinking age is 21. Otherwise, liquor laws vary somewhat according to municipality. Bars close by 1:30am throughout much of the city, except in selected nightlife areas, such as Laclede's Landing, where they often stay open until 3am. Liquor stores stay open until 1:30am, but nowhere can you buy liquor at a store on Sunday, even though it is served in restaurants and bars.

Lost Property There is no central lost-property office. If you lose something, call the nearest police station to report the loss.

Luggage Storage Lambert–St. Louis Airport has lockers for storing luggage in all its concourses.

Mail The main **post office** of St. Louis is located at 1720 Market St. (tel. 436-4458), next to Union Station. It's open Monday through Friday from 7am to 8pm and Saturday from 8am to 3pm. Vending machines selling stamps are accessible 24 hours a day. In addition, a full 24-hour retail postal center is located at the **Lambert–St. Louis Airport Mail Facility,** 9855 Air Cargo Rd., just east of the airport's East Terminal.

Maps The St. Louis visitor centers distribute a free map of the downtown area and city vicinity. In addition, hotels often carry maps of their surrounding region.

Newspapers/Magazines The local newspaper is the *St. Louis Post-Dispatch.* Other newspapers readily available include *The Wall Street Journal, USA Today,* and *The New York Times.* It's difficult to find international newspapers in St. Louis. Foreign magazines are a bit easier to locate, and your best bet for doing so is at **World News,** which has three locations: 314 N. Broadway in downtown (tel. 621-8686)—open Monday through Friday from 7am to 6pm; 4 S. Central Ave. in Clayton (tel. 726-6010)—open Monday through Friday from 7am to 11pm, Saturday from 7am to midnight, and Sunday from 7am to 10pm; and 308 West Port Plaza in West Port (tel. 434-9449)—open Monday through Friday from 8am to 10pm, Saturday from 10am to 11pm, and Sunday from 10am to 6pm. **The Daily Planet,** 243 N. Euclid in the Central West End (tel. 367-1333), is also a good source for newspapers and magazines. It's open Monday through Saturday from 8am to 8:30pm and Sunday from 8am to 7:30pm.

Photographic Needs Both Union Station and the St. Louis Centre downtown have photo shops that specialize in quick film processing and also sell film. Otherwise, ask the concierge at your hotel for the nearest photo shop.

Police The emergency number for police is **911**.

Post Office See "Mail."

Radio/Television You'll find CBS on channel 4, NBC on channel 5, and ABC on channel 2. The local PBS station is on channel 9. Among the many radio stations in St. Louis, KMOX (AM 1120) is your best bet for international news, with newscasts, talk shows, and sports broadcasts throughout the day.

Religious Services The Saturday edition of the *St. Louis Post-Dispatch* carries a religious section with a list of area churches and times of their services.

Restrooms If you need to use a public restroom, your best bet is a hotel or fast-food outlet.

Safety Whenever you're traveling in an unfamiliar city or country, stay alert. Be aware of your immediate surroundings. Wear a money belt and keep a close eye on your possessions. Never carry large amounts of cash and leave your expensive jewelry at home. Be particularly careful with cameras, purses, and wallets—all favorite targets of thieves and pickpockets.

St. Louis's crime rate is as high as that in any major U.S. city, so exercise caution, especially at night. Keep your car locked at all times and do not wander from nightlife districts at night. You are perfectly safe walking around Laclede's Landing, Soulard, or the Central West End at night, especially if there are two or more of you. The downtown area, however, tends to empty out after the shops and businesses close, so keep to lighted areas if you're walking from Laclede's Landing to a downtown hotel.

Shoe Repair You can have your shoes repaired while you wait at the **Cobblestone Shoe Care,** located in the second level of the St. Louis Centre, 6th and Washington streets (tel. 231-4014). It's open Monday through Saturday from 10am to 6pm. Another shop downtown is **Broadway Shoe Repair,** 308 N. Broadway (tel. 342-9983), open Monday through Friday from 8am to 5:30pm.

Taxes A 5.925% tax is added to the price of all goods, food, and services bought in St. Louis; it's composed of a 4.425% Missouri sales tax and a 1.5% General Revenue tax. If you're staying in a downtown hotel, both the 5.925% tax and a 3.75% hotel tax will be added to your bill (for a total of 9.675%), as well as a $2 occupancy fee per room per night; if you're staying in a hotel outside the downtown area, the total tax added to your bill will be 13.175%, but there is no occupancy fee.

Taxis Refer to "Getting Around," above, for information on taxis and fares.

Telephone A local telephone call from a pay phone costs 25¢. Be sure to ask at your hotel whether a surcharge is added to calls made from your hotel room, since these surcharges can be stiff, even if you're making a credit-card call. If you need directory assistance, dial 1-411. For local numbers when calling from a pay phone, dial 411.

Time Zone St. Louis follows Central Standard Time. If it's noon in St. Louis, it's 1pm in New York and 10am in Los Angeles.

Tipping As elsewhere in the United States, serving people should be tipped 15% to 20%, and bartenders should get at least 10%. Bellhops should receive 50¢ for each piece of luggage, cab drivers expect a tip of 15% of the fare, and chambermaids should be left $1 per night of stay. Valet parking is in vogue in a big way at St. Louis' hotels and better restaurants, where attendants expect $1 or $2 in tips, even if they just drive your car across the parking lot.

Transit Information   For information on St. Louis's Bi-State Transit System, call 314/231-2345. Outside Missouri, you can call Bi-State toll-free by dialing 800/2233-BUS.

Weather   For a recorded message of the time and temperature, call 321-2522. Weather information and the forecast can be obtained by dialing 321-2222 or 421-5555.

CHAPTER 5

ST. LOUIS AREA ACCOMMODATIONS

As in any city, your biggest expense in St. Louis will be for a place to sleep at night. Luckily, there's a wide choice in accommodations, from deluxe hotels near the Gateway Arch to inexpensive motels on the outskirts of town and even quaint bed-and-breakfasts and a youth hostel. No matter where you stay, you won't be very far from the city's main attractions.

The rates given below are the standard rack rates, but remember there are often discounts available but only if you ask. In fact, most hotels offer so many discounts and packages that virtually no one ever ends up paying the full rack rate. Many hotels, for example, offer weekend discounts that amount to 50% off the rack rate and corporate rates for business travelers; others offer cheaper rates in winter. In any case, keep in mind that in addition to the rates given, a hotel tax will be added to your bill. If you're staying at a downtown hotel, a 9.675% tax will be added to your bill, as well as a $2 occupancy fee per room per night. If you opt for a hotel outside the downtown area, a tax of 13.175% will be added to your bill, but there is no occupancy fee.

Keep in mind, too, that although every effort was made to be accurate, rates may go up—or down—during the lifetime of this book. It's always a good idea to reserve a room in advance to avoid disappointment or wasting time searching for accommodations. In addition, rooms downtown become scarce if there's a big convention at the convention center or if the Cardinals are enjoying a good season.

Many hotels now include in their rates a continental breakfast of rolls, coffee, and perhaps juice and fruit. Some even offer complimentary cocktails during afternoon happy hours. Some offer free parking as well, while others may charge as much as $8 to $12 per night for a space. (Note: In the listings below quoted parking rates are per day.) Some offer free local phone calls from your room, while others add a stiff surcharge. It pays to shop around, asking for the absolutely best rate and keeping in mind what services and extras are included. Toll-free reservation numbers have been included below. Sometimes the best rates can be procured by calling the hotel directly, however, since central offices of hotel chains don't always provide special rates offered by member hotels. The best strategy is to call both the hotel and the toll-free number, and compare prices.

IMPRESSIONS

The inhabitants of St. Louis believed in enjoying life. There was a
fiddle in every house, and dance somewhere every night. They
were honest, hospitable, inviting and generous. . . .
—JOHN DARBY (1818)

Hotels are divided according to their location and are further
subdivided according to price. (Unless otherwise noted, all provide
private baths.) The **expensive** hotels charge more than $120 per
night for two persons but provide first-rate accommodations and a
wide range of services, which may include health clubs and swimming pools guests can use for free, concierges to help you with any
problems, cocktail lounges with live music, and fine restaurants.
Hotels in the **moderate** category charge $60 to $120 for two
persons and offer comfortable rooms with all the usual amenities—
TVs, with cable programs or in-house movies at an extra charge;
radios; and telephones. Some have swimming pools as well. **Budget**
lodgings, offering rooms for under $60, are simple but adequate, with
all the basics. If you'd like to spend less, consider staying in the **youth
hostel** in Soulard or at one of the outlying **campgrounds.**

The big dollar symbol at some listings denotes an especially good
value for the money, and the star symbol indicates one of my
particular favorites, usually assigned for a combination of outstanding service, ambience, and comfort.

1. DOWNTOWN

These hotels are within easy walking distance of the Gateway Arch,
newly enlarged Cervantes Convention Center, Laclede's Landing,
and other downtown attractions. Downtown is an especially convenient place to stay if you do not have a car, because buses provide
service from here to much of the rest of the St. Louis area.

EXPENSIVE

**ADAM'S MARK HOTEL, 4th and Chestnut Sts., St. Louis,
MO 63102. Tel. 314/241-7400,** or toll free 800/444-
ADAM. Fax 314/241-9839. 814 rms, 96 suites. A/C TV TEL
$ Rates: $160–$170 single; $175–$185 double; $210 double
Concorde Executive Level. Extra person $15. Children under 17
stay free in parents' room. Weekend, family, senior-citizen, and
corporate discounts available. AE, CB, DC, DISC, MC, V. **Parking:** $9.

Located in the shadow of the Gateway Arch, the Adam's Mark
is one of St. Louis's premier hotels, the flagship of the Adam's
Mark group. Its lobby is a three-story atrium, impressive
though a bit glitzy, with such features as half a dozen Regency
chandeliers in the foyer and a pair of nine-feet-tall cast-bronze horses

Adam's Mark Hotel 8

Clarion (Regal Riverfront) Hotel 9

Courtyard By Marriott 11

Days Inn at the Arch 4

Doubletree Mayfair Suites 5

Drury Inn Gateway Arch 3

Drury Inn Union Station 13

Embassy Suites 1

Hampton Inn 11

Holiday Inn Downtown/ Riverfront 7

Hotel Majestic 6

Hyatt Regency St. Louis 12

Marriott Pavillion Downtown 10

Super Inn 2

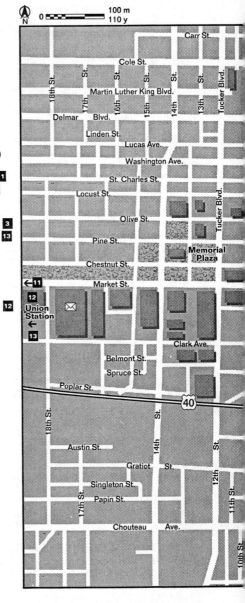

galloping across the marble floor. Many visitors to St. Louis include a stroll through the hotel, stopping off for a meal at one of its fine restaurants, an afternoon tea at Tiffany Rose, or a beer at AJ's, one of downtown's most popular night spots—which means that the hotel can also be noisy and busy. The Adam's Mark indoor and outdoor pools are on the roof, offering breathtaking views of the city.

Each room provides all amenities and comforts you'd expect from a first-class hotel, including cable TV with in-house movies, an extra

Carr St.

2

Cole St.

Collins St.

2nd St.

Waddingham

Commercial St.

1st St.

1

**M.L. King Jr.
Memorial Bridge**

10th St.

9th St.

7th St.

6th St.

Broadway

**Cervantes
Convention
Center**

Delmar Blvd.

3

11th St.

70

Lucas Ave.

4

**Eads
Bridge**

Washington Ave.

St. Charles St.

Jefferson

5

8th St.

Locust St.

National

Lenore K. Sullivan Blvd.

✉

Olive St.

Expansion

6

7

Memorial

4th St.

N.H.S.

Mississippi River

Pine St.

8

Chestnut St.

**Kiener
Plaza**

Memorial

Drive

Market St.

10

Walnut St.

10th St.

**Busch
Memorial
Stadium**

Spruce St.

9

**Stadium
Plaza**

Broadway

4th St.

Cerre St.

2nd St.

1st St.

55 70

**Poplar St.
Bridge**

Gratiot St.

Cerre St.

Gratiot St.

Papin St.

Lombard St.

**MacArthur
Municipal Bridge
(closed)**

Chouteau Ave.

Chouteau Ave.

9th St.

8th St.

7th St.

55

Post Office

✉

phone in the bathroom, and full-length mirrors. There's a no-smoking floor. As in many downtown hotels, rooms facing the Arch and the mighty Mississippi are more expensive (and worth it), but if you really want to splurge, consider staying on the hotel's Concorde Executive Level, which includes its own concierge services, a lounge, and a full-service complimentary breakfast in its rates.

Dining/Entertainment: Faust's is the place to go for fine dining in an atmosphere of old-world charm, where continental and

American cuisine are complemented by an extensive wine list. Chestnut's is the hotel's more casual restaurant, where an international buffet is offered every Friday and Saturday evening. Tiffany Rose features afternoon tea and live piano or jazz music on Monday through Saturday, while Players caters to sports fans with screens depicting the latest in ESPN sports. AJ's draws in a nightly crowd with its live music, dance floor, and special events.

Services: 24-hour room service, babysitting referral, airport shuttle, laundry/shoe shine, concierge desk.

Facilities: Indoor and outdoor pools, racquetball courts, whirlpool, sauna, exercise room, aerobic classes, gift shop, florist, barber/beauty shop, airline/car-rental services, business center.

CLARION [REGAL RIVERFRONT] HOTEL, 200 S. 4th St., St. Louis, MO 63102. Tel. 314/241-9500, or toll free 800/325-7353. Fax 314/241-6171. 799 rms, 29 suites. A/C TV TEL

$ Rates: $130 single or double; from $275 suite. Extra person $10. Children under 17 stay free in parents' room. AE, DC, DISC, MC, V. **Parking:** $9.

Popular as a convention hotel, the Clarion can be crowded and noisy at times, but maybe that's the excitement you're looking for. The hotel features two towers of rooms; the North Tower is taller, with 27 floors topped by a revolving restaurant. Each room features a TV with pay video, an alarm clock, and a sink and counter space separate from the bathroom. Rooms with refrigerators also are available, as well as no-smoking rooms. Unfortunately, rooms are not soundproofed against traffic noise; pets are allowed.

Dining: Top of the Riverfront, the city's only revolving restaurant, offers a bird's-eye view of the Arch and the city. The Lobby Bar also has a view of St. Louis's famous landmark. The Dugout Bar is a popular pregame watering hole, while Café in the Park offers casual dining.

Services: Room service until 11pm, laundry, concierge.

Facilities: Indoor and outdoor pools, exercise room, game room, gift shop, barber shop, beauty salon, coin-operated laundry.

NOTE: After undergoing major renovation, the Clarion is expected to be renamed the **Regal Riverfront Hotel** in early 1993. The rate structure may be altered at that time.

EMBASSY SUITES, 901 N. 1st St., St. Louis, MO 63102. Tel. 314/241-4200, or toll free 800/362-2779. Fax 314/241-6513. 297 suites. A/C MINIBAR TV TEL

$ Rates (including American breakfast): $145 single or double. Extra person $15. Children under 18 stay free in parents' room. Weekend rates and senior-citizen discounts available. AE, CB, DC, DISC, MC, V. **Parking:** $5.75.

Located in the historic district of Laclede's Landing, just north of the Arch, Embassy Suites is part of a nationwide chain of hotels that does its best to provide guests with extra touches and services that make staying here a pleasure. Its eight-story inner atrium is a comfortable oasis complete with a courtyard, a bubbling fountain, and well-tended plants. Breakfast, which is cooked to order and includes eggs and pancakes, is served beside the fountain; in the early evening, from 5 to 7pm, there also are complimentary cocktails.

Every room at the Embassy Suites, as its name implies, is a two-room suite, all of which ring the atrium and have windows on the outside overlooking the city. Rooms on the lowest floor have balconies, but those higher up facing the Arch have better views, all at the same price. The living room of each suite contains a sofa-bed, a refrigerator, and a coffee machine and coffee, and in each suite are two remote-control TVs with pay movies, two telephones, and two sinks. Handicapped-equipped and no-smoking suites are available.

Dining: The hotel's bar is the Landing's Lounge. Joe B's Restaurant offers everything from chili dogs to prime rib, including a bargain lunch buffet on Monday through Friday.

Services: Room service until 11pm (until 1am weekends), valet, same-day laundry, 24-hour fax.

Facilities: Indoor pool, exercise room, sauna, whirlpool, pool tables, video games, coin-operated laundry, gift shop.

THE HOTEL MAJESTIC, 1019 Pine St., St. Louis, MO 63101. Tel. 314/436-2355, or toll free 800/451-2355. Fax 314/436-2355. 91 rms. A/C MINIBAR TV TEL

$ Rates (including continental breakfast): $170 single or double. Extra person $15. Children under 12 stay free in parents' room. Weekend, corporate, and other packages available. AE, CB, DC, DISC, MC, V. **Parking:** $8 (free on weekends).

 FROMMER'S SMART TRAVELER: HOTELS

VALUE-CONSCIOUS TRAVELERS SHOULD TAKE ADVANTAGE OF THE FOLLOWING:

1. Weekend discounts of up to 50% available at most expensive and moderate hotels in the St. Louis area.
2. Corporate rates available to business travelers. Even if you're on vacation, it doesn't hurt showing a business card and asking for corporate rates.
3. Winter discounts offered at some inexpensive hotels.
4. Hotels on the outskirts of the city, which are often cheaper than those downtown.
5. Accommodations that include breakfast in their price.
6. A youth hostel and campgrounds at rock-bottom prices.
7. In St. Louis, rooms without a view of the Arch, which are usually cheaper than rooms with a view.

QUESTIONS TO ASK IF YOU'RE ON A BUDGET

1. Is breakfast included in the price? Is it buffet-style, allowing you to eat as much as you want?
2. Is there a parking charge? (In many downtown St. Louis hotels, as much as $8 to $12 may be charged for each overnight stay. Valet parking costs more. Parking is free at hotels outside the downtown area.)
3. Is there a surcharge on local and long-distance telephone calls? (Some hotels offer free local phone calls.)
4. Are discounts available? (Weekend rates are sometimes half the rack weekday rates.)

⭐ If your idea of a fine hotel is a smaller, older establishment with old-world European charm, this hotel is for you. First opened in 1913 and built in the Renaissance revival style, the Hotel Majestic is a National Historic Landmark that has long been a guarded St. Louis secret. Both businesspeople and visiting stars stay here for the privacy it affords (Billy Joel was checking in during one of my visits) as well as for all the extra amenities and facilities, including one of the city's liveliest jazz restaurants. There is no front desk—check in is at a concierge desk that provides the individualized treatment repeat customers appreciate.

All guest rooms are slightly different, but each is outfitted with either a king-size or two double beds, a hairdryer, two-line phones, a remote-control TV with pay movies, terrycloth robes, a minibar, and a coffee machine. There's maid service twice a day, including turndown service with chocolates. Although the hotel itself does not have a health club, guests can use free of charge a nearby YMCA, which includes a pool, racquetball courts, and a gym. No-smoking rooms are available.

Dining/Entertainment: Just Jazz is the hotel restaurant, serving continental cuisine to the accompaniment of live jazz every night.

Services: Complimentary fruit plate on arrival, complimentary shoe shine, free morning newspaper, free shuttle downtown, 24-hour room service, babysitting, same-day laundry, 24-hour concierge.

MARRIOTT PAVILION DOWNTOWN, 1 Broadway, St. Louis, MO 63102. Tel. 314/421-1776, or toll free 800/228-9290. Fax 314/331-9029. 670 rms, 11 suites. A/C TV TEL

$ **Rates:** $120 single; $135 double; Concierge Floor $15 extra. Extra person $10. Children under 18 stay free in parents' room. Weekend and other packages available. AE, DC, DISC, MC, V.
Parking: $9.

Located beside Busch Stadium and just two blocks from the Gateway Arch, this is a large hotel with a lot of facilities, attracting both baseball fans and convention groups. It consists of an east tower and a newer, taller west tower, and some rooms even provide a view of the stadium or the Arch at no extra charge. All rooms are comfortable, each containing two phones and remote-control cable TV with pay movies; some rooms also have small refrigerators. There are also no-smoking rooms and rooms for the handicapped. If you really feel like being pampered, stay on the 22nd, 23rd, or 24th Concierge floors of the west tower, where you'll have a king-size bed, an automatic shoe polisher, and a communal lounge in which you'll receive a complimentary continental breakfast and afternoon hors d'oeuvres.

Dining: The Pavilion Restaurant offers everything from a buffet breakfast or light snack to a quick lunch and hearty dinner. J. W. Carver's is more elegant and formal. One Broadway, a sports bar, is the place to meet for pregame cocktails.

Services: Room service until 1am, same-day laundry, concierge desk, free newspaper available weekdays.

Facilities: Indoor pool, whirlpool, sauna, health club with weight room, gift shop, business center, travel agency, game room.

MODERATE

DAYS INN AT THE ARCH, 333 Washington Ave., St. Louis, MO 63102. Tel. 314/621-7900, or toll free 800/325-2525. Fax 314/421-6468. 179 rms. A/C TV TEL

Ⓕ FROMMER'S COOL FOR KIDS: HOTELS

Cheshire Inn and Lodge *(p. 59)* The child in everyone will be enchanted by the nine Fantasy Suites here, which include the Tree House and the Safari Country.

Henry VIII Hotel *(p. 64)* Kids will love the game room, pool, and tennis courts here, plus the space outside to run around in.

Holiday Inn Airport West *(p. 64)* Kids love the facilities of the Holidome, including its indoor pool, whirlpool, video-game room, indoor putting green, billiards table, and Ping-Pong tables.

Hyatt Regency St. Louis *(p. 55)* The Hyatt Regency is a great place for a family vacation. Not only is it located in Union Station—with its many shops, restaurants, and diversions—but also the hotel itself offers children's menus from room service and in its restaurants, plus a welcome check-in packet for kids.

The Ritz-Carlton *(p. 58)* The Ritz Kids Package is a special weekend offer that includes a special gift; children's menus and complimentary hot-fudge sundaes at two of the hotel's restaurants; toys, games, and children's movies available on request; a free comic book; and an indoor pool. Babysitting services are available, too.

$ Rates: $65 single; $85 double. Extra person $10. Children under 18 stay free in parents' room. AE, DC, DISC, MC, V. Winter discounts available. **Parking:** $4.50.

With a great location just a stone's throw from Laclede's Landing and the Arch, this 25-year-old property has recently been renovated. Simple but comfortable, each of its rooms features double-paned windows to shut out traffic noise, full-length mirrors, an alarm clock with radio, and a large bathroom with counter space. Rooms facing the Arch have the best view, and there are also no-smoking rooms.

This Days Inn contains a restaurant and a lounge. Its facilities include an indoor pool and a coin-operated laundry, and fax service and free morning coffee and newspaper (available in the lounge) are offered.

DOUBLETREE MAYFAIR SUITES, 806 St. Charles St., St. Louis, MO 63101. Tel. 314/421-2500, or toll free 800/ 444-3313 or 800/528-0444. Fax 314/421-0770. 165 rms and suites. A/C MINIBAR TV TEL

$ Rates: $80–$100 single; $95–$115 double; suites from $120 single, $135 double. Extra person $15. Children under 17 stay free in parents' room. Weekend packages available. AE, DC, DISC, MC, V. **Parking:** $7 weekdays, $4 weekends.

Built in 1925 and completely renovated in 1990, the Doubletree Mayfair is located in the heart of downtown and is on the National Historic Register. Its lobby, restored to the original style, is small and comfortable, and the original hand-operated elevators still take guests to their floors. Guest rooms have been modernized and remain spacious with features like old-fashioned double-paned windows. There are only 12 rooms and suites per floor, and every other floor is designated as no-smoking. Each room is decorated with floral-print bedspreads and curtains and features a remote-control TV with pay movies, a clock-radio, two-line telephones. There's even a small TV in the bathroom. Most rooms are Grand Suites, each with French doors separating the bedroom from the parlor and TVs in both rooms. The Mayfair's most expensive suites on the 18th floor each boast a fireplace and Jacuzzi. All guests receive free freshly baked chocolate-chip cookies on arrival.

Besides a restaurant, the Mayfair features a rooftop outdoor pool and sundeck and a fitness and exercise room. Also offered are 24-hour room service, free morning newspapers, and same-day laundry service.

DRURY INN GATEWAY ARCH, 711 N. Broadway, St. Louis, MO 63101. Tel. 314/231-8100, or toll free 800/325-8300. Fax 314/231-3817. 142 rms, 36 suites. A/C TV TEL

$ Rates (including continental breakfast): $79–$90 single; $90–$100 double; suites from $100 single, $112 double. Extra person $10. Children under 18 stay free in parents' room. Free cribs available. Corporate rates available. AE, DC, MC, V. **Parking:** Free.

This new hotel near the Convention Center and Laclede's Landing makes it easy to understand why the Drury Inn chain is taking the Midwest by storm. Offering a variety of services but without a correspondingly high price tag, it's a great choice for both the business traveler and families. Guests start their day with a complimentary QUIKSTART breakfast consisting of cereals, fruit, doughnuts, muffins, coffee, and juice, served buffet-style in the airy atrium near the indoor pool. The building itself, built in 1925, once served as the city market; the hotel's cool and spacious lobby is on the ground floor, and the two top floors contain the guest rooms. In between is a parking garage. Rooms face either the inner atrium or the outside, with soundproof windows to cut down on noise. Particularly good deals are the suites, each of which comes with a microwave, a refrigerator, and two satellite TVs with remote control. A couple of suites even feature lofts. There are also no-smoking and handicapped-accessible rooms.

Although there are no restaurants in the hotel, there are many in the immediate area. Free local phone calls and evening cocktails are offered to guests, who can also use the indoor pool and the whirlpool. All in all, you can't go wrong staying here.

HOLIDAY INN DOWNTOWN/RIVERFRONT, 200 N. 4th St., St. Louis, MO 63102. Tel. 314/621-8200, or toll free 800/325-1395. Fax 314/621-8073. 371 rms, 87 suites. A/C TV TEL

$ Rates: $98 single; $109 double; suites $140–$330. Extra person

$10. Children under 12 stay free in parents' room. Free cribs available. Package discounts available. AE, DC, DISC, MC, V. **Parking:** $6.

This downtown property was built in 1974 as an apartment complex, and that is reflected in the enormity of most of the hotel's rooms. Some even have balconies, while others have kitchenettes complete with stoves and refrigerators (but without pots and pans). There are also no-smoking rooms. Close to the Gateway Arch and all downtown sights, the Holiday Inn boasts a rooftop pool with an observation deck offering a great view of the city. Although there's no health club in the hotel, guests can use a nearby YMCA for free.

For dining, there are a restaurant and a deli. Facilities include a coin-operated laundry, a gift shop, and a beauty shop. Also offered are a concierge desk, room service until 10pm, and same-day laundry service.

BUDGET

SUPER INN, 1100 N. 3rd St., St. Louis, MO 63102. Tel. 314/421-6556. 48 rms. A/C TV TEL

$ Rates: $38–$49 single or double. Winter discounts available. AE, MC, V. **Parking:** Free.

Located off I-70 near the 6th Street exit, this older hotel doesn't look like much from the outside since it's a bit seedy, but it offers inexpensive lodging in the heart of the city. Rooms were recently refurbished, each with a double- or king-size bed, a desk, a TV with pay movies, and a sink and counter space separate from the bathroom. Complimentary coffee is served mornings in the lobby, where there are vending machines selling sodas. The hotel is a bit isolated from the rest of downtown by an undeveloped strip of land, but you can't beat the price. Recommended for young people who are interested only in a bed for the night.

2. UNION STATION AREA

Only a mile or so from the Gateway Arch, the Union Station area is practically a city in itself, with a myriad of diversions. It's a great place to stay for the entire family.

EXPENSIVE

HYATT REGENCY ST. LOUIS, Union Station, St. Louis, MO 63103. Tel. 314/231-1234, or toll free 800/233-1234. Fax 314/436-4238. 522 rms, 20 suites. A/C TV TEL

$ Rates: $140 single; $165 double; Regency Club $180 single, $200 double. Extra person $20. Children under 18 stay free in parents' room, half price in separate room. Weekend packages available. AE, CB, DC, DISC, MC, V. **Parking:** $11 (valet).

The Hyatt Regency is one of the most talked about hotels in St. Louis. Occupying part of Union Station, which was built in 1894, it boasts one of the most magnificent lobbies I've ever seen—six stories high with a barrel-vaulted ceiling, Romanesque arches, elaborate plasterwork highlighted in gold leaf, and stained glass. Once serving as the waiting room for train passengers, it's a feast for the eyes, and there's a lobby lounge where you can slowly take it all in.

Rooms are simple yet comfortable, with standard units occupying a new free-standing structure right in the middle of the station. Each room features an extra cordless phone, a hairdryer, a small TV and clothesline in the bathroom, full-length mirrors, a TV with pay movies, and all the luxuries you'd expect from a first-class hotel. Regency Club rooms, which occupy the original rooms of the historic Terminal Hotel and are reached by private elevator, offer turn-of-the-century charm along with their own concierge, a free continental breakfast, complimentary evening cocktails, daily newspapers, and personalized matchbooks with each guest's name. Children love this hotel not only for its many facilities but also because of the welcome packet they receive at check-in. A great place for a family vacation.

Dining: The Station Grille is housed in Union Station's original oak-paneled dining hall and offers steaks and seafood. Italian cuisine, including California-style pizza cooked in a wood-burning stove, is featured in Aldo's. The Grand Hall in the lobby is open daily for an executive lunch as well as for evening cocktails.

Services: 24-hour room service, babysitting, concierge desk, laundry and dry cleaning.

Facilities: Outdoor pool, health club, sauna, business center.

MODERATE

COURTYARD BY MARRIOTT, 2340 Market St., St. Louis, MO 63101. Tel. 314/241-9111, or toll free 800/321-2211. Fax 314/241-8113. 139 rms, 12 suites. A/C TV TEL

$ Rates: $85 single; $95 double; suites from $100 single, $115 double. Extra person free. Weekend rates and discounts for longer stays available. AE, DC, DISC, MC, V. **Parking:** Free.

This chain hotel is conveniently located about two blocks west of Union Station and about a mile and a half from the Gateway Arch (and it's within the free bus zone). As in all hotels in the Courtyard group, rooms are built around an inner courtyard that contains an expanse of green and a terrace. Rooms on the third and fourth floors even have miniature balconies with views of downtown and the Arch. All units feature TVs complete with VCRs (approximately 90 rental videos are available from a vending machine in the hotel), clock-radios, telephones with 18-foot cords, sinks separated from the bathrooms, large working desks, and in-room coffee service. Half the rooms are no-smoking, and most have king-size beds and sofas. Complimentary coffee (tea or decaffeinated coffee on request) is offered.

The Courtyard has a restaurant and a lounge with outdoor seating. Its facilities include an indoor pool, a sunning terrace, a whirlpool, an exercise room, and a coin-operated laundry.

DRURY INN UNION STATION, 201 S. 20th St., St. Louis, MO 63103. Tel. 314/231-3900, or toll free 800/325-8300. 174 rms, 2 suites. A/C TV TEL

$ Rates (including continental breakfast): $79–$90 single; $90–$100 double; suites from $100 single, $112 double. Extra person $10. Children under 18 stay free in parents' room. Free cribs available. Corporate rates available. AE, CB, DC, DISC, MC, V. **Parking:** Free.

Drury Inn does it again with this imaginative use of what was once a YMCA, built in 1907 to serve transient railroad workers. Located beside Union Station, it has been lovingly restored utilizing many of the building's original features, including its large fireplaces, leaded-glass windows, oak paneling, and interior columns with marble bases. Rooms are clean and comfortable, with everything you might need. Some face inside with views over the pool; others face outside. Some of the suites are stocked with refrigerators and microwaves. The complimentary breakfast includes everything from doughnuts and muffins to fruit, juice, and coffee. This hotel is one of St. Louis's best-kept secrets.

For dining, the Drury Inn boasts an Italian restaurant. It offers free local phone calls and evening cocktails and features an indoor pool and a whirlpool.

HAMPTON INN, 2211 Market St., St. Louis, MO 63101. **Tel. 314/241-3200,** or toll free 800/HAMPTON. 239 rms. A/C TV TEL
$ Rates (including continental breakfast): $65–$80 single; $75–$92 double. Extra person free. AE, CB, DC, DISC, MC, V. **Parking:** Free.

Located a couple of blocks west of Union Station, this simple hotel offers clean, comfortable, and cheerful rooms decorated in pastels and tiled bathrooms. Unfortunately, even though it's a tall building, the Hampton is built at an angle providing no room with a view of downtown. Approximately half are no-smoking rooms.

The Hampton Inn's restaurant specializes in seafood. The hotel offers free local phone calls and same-day laundry service. Its facilities include an indoor pool, a whirlpool, an exercise room, and a coin-operated laundry.

3. CENTRAL WEST END

Located near Forest Park and only a 10-minute drive from downtown, the Central West End is a fun part of town to be in, with many restaurants, shops, and bars along Euclid Avenue. But it's also a quiet residential area, with large stately homes on tree-lined streets.

BED-&-BREAKFAST

COACHLIGHT, 4612 McPherson Ave., St. Louis, MO 63108. Tel. 314/367-5870. 3 rms (all with bath). A/C TV TEL
$ Rates (including continental breakfast): $65–$80 for two persons. Extra person $15. AE, MC, V. **Parking:** On the street.

Dating back to 1904 when the St. Louis World's Fair was held in nearby Forest Park, this brick home has been lovingly restored by a personable couple in their 30s, Susan and Chuck Sundermeyer. Susan, who used to work as director of sales for the Hotel Majestic and thus is very familiar with the hotel business, has decorated her home and guest rooms with antiques, soft down comforters, and Laura Ashley prints but also has installed such modern conveniences as private bathrooms, telephones, ceiling fans, and color TVs. Breakfast is a generous array of home-baked breads, muffins, fruit, coffee, and tea. Children three and older are welcome. Because there's a dog in residence, however, no pets are allowed.

4. CLAYTON

Located just west of the city of St. Louis, Clayton is a nucleus for business offices, and most hotels here cater to the business traveler. Only 15 to 20 minutes from downtown and 10 minutes from the airport, it's also a convenient spot from which to explore the rest of the city. Richmond Heights borders Clayton on the south, Ladue is just west, and University City is just north.

EXPENSIVE

THE RITZ-CARLTON, 100 Carondelet Plaza, Clayton, MO 63105. Tel. 314/863-6300, or toll free 800/241-3333. Fax 314/863-7486. 268 rms, 33 suites. A/C MINIBAR TV TEL
$ Rates: $155–$200 single to triple occupancy; Ritz-Carlton Club executive floors $235; from $380 suite. Children under 18 stay free in parents' room. Weekend and other packages available. AE, CB, DC, DISC, MC, V. **Parking:** $8.

The fine tradition of the Ritz-Carlton was brought to the St. Louis area with the 1990 opening of this spectacular property, featuring $5-million worth of original 18th- and 19th-century fine art and antiques. Filling the hotel are 52 chandeliers as well as fantastic bouquets of Hawaiian imports. The lobby is elegant with its marbled floor and chandeliers yet is comfortable and intimate with its overstuffed chairs and Persian rugs. Because of its quiet location on the edge of Clayton's business district, the Ritz-Carlton is spared the foot traffic that sometimes plagues downtown hotels. And, of course, the service here is excellent in every detail. Many consider this the area's top hotel.

Each guest room, handsomely decorated with mahogany furniture and plush chairs, features a remote-control TV, a two-line phone, an in-room safe, a vanity table with lighted makeup mirror and hairdryer, a marble bathroom, and all the amenities that you'd expect from a first-rate hotel. All rooms open up onto small balconies—those facing west have views of an outdoor fountain and Clayton; those facing east have views of the downtown skyline. If you feel like splurging, the Ritz-Carlton Club on the 17th and 18th floors provides guests with an exclusive lounge, private concierge service, a complimentary continental breakfast, afternoon tea, cocktails, and hors d'oeuvres.

Dining/Entertainment: Besides cocktails, the Lobby Lounge serves afternoon tea daily from 2:30 to 5pm, featuring delicate sandwiches, scones, chocolates, and strawberries with Devonshire cream served on Rosenthal china to the accompaniment of classical music. The Grill serves grilled specialties for dinner. The signature restaurant, called simply The Restaurant, features continental and American cuisine.

Services: 24-hour room service, free morning newspaper, twice-daily maid service, babysitting, same-day laundry and dry cleaning, complimentary shoe shine.

Facilities: Indoor pool, Jacuzzi, fitness and exercise center, business center, gift shop.

MODERATE

CHESHIRE INN AND LODGE, 6300 Clayton Rd., Richmond Heights, MO 63117. Tel. 314/647-7300, or toll free 800/325-7378. 107 rooms and suites. A/C TV TEL

$ Rates (including continental breakfast Mon–Fri only): $102–$130 single; $115–$140 double; Fantasy Suites $150–$270 double. Extra person $10. Children under 18 stay free in parents' room. AE, CB, DC, DISC, MC, V. **Parking:** Free.

This lodging, located in Richmond Heights between Forest Park and the Clayton business district, will appeal to the child in all of you. Walk into its mock English Tudor–style building, and you leave St. Louis far behind. The decor is heavy English, almost medieval, with a lot of dark woods, reds, and kitsch. But the real treasures here are the so-called 13 Fantasy Suites, each designed on a different theme—all weird, whimsical, corny, and wonderful. The Tree House suite, for example, the hotel's most popular room, features a waterfall in the room, along with a Jacuzzi, a king-size waterbed, and numerous mirrors and plants. The Safari Country suite boasts a king-size four-poster bed and decor that looks like an attraction at Disneyland. The decorator must have had fun here. The hotel's regular rooms carry on the theme with dark reds and more kitsch, and some of those on the first floor have doors leading out directly to the pool. However, if you can afford it and appreciate corniness, opt for one of the Fantasy Suites. They're in a class by themselves, certainly not your usual hotel experience.

Cheshire Inn has a restaurant and two pubs. Among the services it offers are a free shuttle to downtown and Clayton, free newspapers, room service until 9:30pm (until 1am on weekends), free local phone calls, and same-day laundry service. Its facilities include a covered year-round pool with a sunning patio, a sauna, a whirlpool, a health club, and a gift shop.

DANIELE HOTEL, 216 N. Meramec, Clayton, MO 63105. Tel. 314/721-0101, or toll free 800/325-8302. Fax 314/721-0609. 82 rms, 6 suites. A/C TV TEL

$ Rates: $119 for up to 4 in a room. Corporate and weekend rates available. AE, CB, DC, MC, V. **Parking:** Free.

It's easy to see why business travelers keep coming back to this small hotel with its friendly and outgoing staff. Although the Daniele has recently been renovated and is modern in every sense of the word, it still manages to create a European-style atmosphere, in part because of its intimate size and in part because of its subdued and tasteful decor. The lobby is cozy, while the guest rooms are very pleasant, done in soothing mint green and cool pink. Each room has a separate vanity area, and each bathroom has a large counter with lots of room to spread out. There are also no-smoking rooms. In short, this is a good choice for those who shun large hotels but demand quality in service and accommodations.

MISSOURI

St. Louis

Jefferson City

Caverly Farm
  and Orchard **1**
Cheshire Inn
  and Lodge **14**
Coachlight **7**
Coral Court Motel **2**
Daniele Hotel **3**
Henry VIII Hotel **4**
Holiday Inn—Airport/
  Oakland Park **11**
Holiday Inn Airport
  West **5**
Huckleberry Finn
  Youth Hostel **6**
Lafayette House **9**
Motel 6 **9 10**
Oak Grove Inn **8**
Old Convent
  Guesthouse **12**
Radisson Hotel Clayton **3**
Seven Gables Inn **3**
Sheraton Plaza Hotel **13**
Sheraton West Port Inn **13**
The Ritz-Carlton **3**

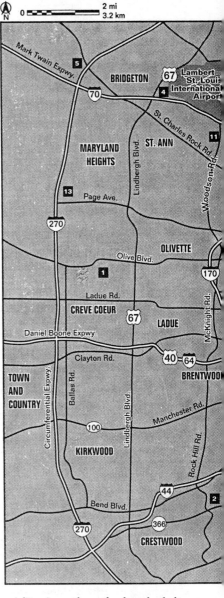

Dining: A restaurant specializes in steak, seafood, and salads.
  Services: Free limousine to airport and Clayton vicinity, same-
day laundry, room service until 10pm.
  Facilities: Outdoor pool, free access to nearby health club.

**RADISSON HOTEL CLAYTON, 7750 Carondelet Ave.,
Clayton, MO 63105. Tel. 314/726-5400,** toll free
800/333-3333. Fax 314/726-6105. 204 rms, 8 suites. A/C TV
TEL

IMPRESSIONS

St. Louis, as you approach it, shows like all the other French towns in this region, to much the greatest advantage at a distance. The French mode of building, the white coat of lime applied to the mud or rough stone walls, gives them a beauty at a distance. . . .
—TIMOTHY FLINT (1826)

$ Rates: $94 single; $104 double. Extra person $10. Children under 18 stay free in parents' room. Corporate rates and other packages available. AE, CB, DC, DISC, MC, V. **Parking:** Free.
Formerly called Clayton Inn, the Radisson Hotel Clayton recently underwent a complete renovation, from the reception area and lobby to the guest rooms. It provides a wide range of facilities. Guest rooms, including those on no-smoking floors, are comfortable—each with a refrigerator, a remote-control TV, an alarm clock, and a full-length mirror.

Dining: The popular Joe Hanon's restaurant specializes in steaks and seafood. The hotel also has a bar.

Services: One free continental breakfast, free shuttle to airport, one-day laundry and valet, room service until 11pm, free happy-hour hors d'oeuvres and cocktails.

Facilities: Indoor and outdoor pools, health club, Jacuzzi, sauna, steam room, exercise room.

SEVEN GABLES INN, 26 N. Meramec, Clayton, MO 63105. Tel. 314/863-8400, toll free outside Missouri 800/433-6590. Fax 314/863-8846. 26 rms, 6 suites. A/C TV TEL

$ Rates: $105–$140 single or double; from $175 suite. Extra person free. Weekend rates available. AE, CB, DC, DISC, MC, V. **Parking:** $4 (valet).

This may well be the smallest hotel in the St. Louis area, and it achieves even more distinction by virtue of its two well-known restaurants. With only 32 rooms and suites, this inn was built in the 1920s as an apartment complex and was designed to resemble Nathaniel Hawthorne's *The House of Seven Gables,* from which the hotel takes its name. It has since become a landmark with its white-washed timbered facade and is listed on the National Register of Historic Monuments. Catering largely to business travelers who come back regularly for its homey and peaceful atmosphere, the Seven Gables offers rooms on three floors (there is no elevator), each room unique but outfitted with a remote-control TV and a two-line phone.

Dining: Some St. Louisans consider Chez Louis the best restaurant around for traditional and innovative French and continental cuisine. Bernard's, decorated like a turn-of-the-century French bistro, offers more casual dining, and in summer there's even outdoor seating in an inner courtyard.

Services: Room service until 11pm, same-day laundry.

Facilities: Free access to nearby health club with pool and tennis courts.

5. IN & AROUND SOULARD DISTRICT

Only minutes from downtown St. Louis, Soulard and vicinity are known for Soulard Market, the Anheuser-Busch Brewery, Antique Row on Cherokee Street, and a number of live music houses.

BED-&-BREAKFASTS

LAFAYETTE HOUSE, 2156 Lafayette Ave., St. Louis, MO

63104. Tel. 314/772-4429. 4 rms (with and without bath), 1 apt. A/C

$ Rates (including breakfast): $50 double without bath, $60 double with bath; $75 apt. double with bath. Extra adult $15, extra child $10. No credit cards. **Parking:** Street parking only.

Overlooking Lafayette Park, this bed-and-breakfast is an 1876 Queen Anne brick mansion built by James Eads (of Eads Bridge fame) for his daughter, Martha. Now owned by Sarah and Jack Milligan, who have run it since 1983, Lafayette House is a bit cluttered with mementos of a lifetime and is home to four cats. Sarah is friendly and helpful with advice on what to see and do, and, for a small fee, you'll be fetched from the airport or bus or train depot. Families will find the third-floor apartment with its own kitchen, living area with TV, and private bathroom especially appealing. A refrigerator on the second floor is stocked with soda, wine, and beer free to guests, and there's a communal lounge with a VCR. Sarah serves a full breakfast, including her famous cinnamon-raisin French toast.

THE OLD CONVENT GUESTHOUSE, 2049 Sidney St., St. Louis, MO 63104. Tel. 314/772-3531. 5 rms (with and without bath). A/C

$ Rates (including breakfast): $45 double without bath, $55 double with bath, $95 double with bath and Jacuzzi. No credit cards. **Parking:** Street parking only.

This bed-and-breakfast takes its name from the fact that it served as quarters of the Sisters of St. Joseph from the early 1900s until 1971. Built in 1881 by a cooper who made beer barrels, it contains an incredible 64 windows, 6 coal-burning fireplaces (no longer used), walnut and maple floors, and high ceilings. Light, open, and airy, it has been tastefully redecorated in a modern style that utilizes the best of the past. Each guest room is different from the others, ranging from the French room to the art nouveau room to the Oriental room. A couple of rooms even have their own Jacuzzi. The hosts are Paul and Mary LaFlam; breakfasts here are especially good, a reflection of the fact that Paul worked as a professional chef for 20 years. Almost half the people who stay here are local St. Louisans getting away for a weekend.

YOUTH HOSTEL

HUCKLEBERRY FINN YOUTH HOSTEL, 1904–6 S. 12th St., St. Louis, MO 63104. Tel. 314/241-0076. 30 beds. **Bus:** 73, 21 or 5 to 12th & Russell.

$ Rates: $11 per night members, $14 nonmembers. Sheets $2. Discounts for stays of a week or longer. No credit cards.

If all you're looking for is an inexpensive place to lay down your head at night, this youth hostel should suit your needs. The dormitory-style rooms, accommodating men and women separately, are lined with bunk beds. Facilities include lockers; a kitchen stocked with pots and pans; and a communal room with cable TV, public phone, and piano. Air-conditioning may have been installed by the time you read this. Walk-ins are welcome. If you wish to make a reservation, only written reservations with a check or money order are accepted. Check-in is after 6pm. The Huckleberry Finn is located in three brick buildings built in the 1870s, about a mile south of the Arch.

6. NEAR THE AIRPORT

These hotels are convenient if you wish to be close to Lambert–St. Louis International Airport or if you're arriving in St. Louis on I-70 from Kansas City and don't wish to drive all the way downtown.

MODERATE

HENRY VIII HOTEL, 4690 N. Lindbergh, Bridgeton, MO 63044. Tel. 314/731-3040, toll free 800/325-1588; in Missouri toll free 800/392-1660. Fax 314/731-4210. 195 rms, 190 suites. A/C TV TEL

$ Rates: $105 single; $115 double; from $125 suite. Extra person $10. Children under 18 stay free in parents' room. Weekend and corporate rates available. AE, CB, DC, DISC, MC, V. **Parking:** Free.

Situated on 50 acres in Bridgeton, just minutes from the airport near I-70 and I-270, this large hotel is built in mock Tudor style. In keeping with its Henry VIII theme, it has a timber-frame facade, stained-glass windows, a suit of armor in the lobby, chandeliers, and gleaming polished wood. Striving to appeal to business travelers, tourists, and convention groups, this hotel offers a wide range of facilities, from a game room for the kids to a quarter-mile jogging and nature trail. Each room has a refrigerator and a remote-control TV, while each suite offers an additional phone and a TV in both the bedroom and the living room. No-smoking rooms are available.

The Henry VIII contains a restaurant and an Irish pub. Besides offering a free shuttle to and from the airport, room service until 11pm, and same-day laundry service, the hotel features a game room, indoor and outdoor pools, fitness equipment, a sauna, a whirlpool, tennis courts, and a jogging trail.

HOLIDAY INN AIRPORT WEST, I-270 at St. Charles Rock Rd., Bridgeton, MO 63044. Tel. 314/291-5100, or toll free 800/HOLIDAY. Fax 314/291-3546. 250 rms. A/C TV TEL

$ Rates: $75 single; $85 double. Extra person $8. Children under 18 stay free in parents' room. Weekend and special packages available. AE, CB, DC, DISC, MC, V. **Parking:** Free.

This Holiday Inn in Bridgeton is similar to other hotels in this chain across the country, including its inner, spacious Holidome recreation center. Kids love the facilities here, which means that the hotel is packed with families. Rooms are clean and comfortable and face toward either the indoor pool or the outside of the building.

For dining, the Holiday Inn has a restaurant and a lounge. The hotel's services include a free shuttle to and from the airport, room service until 10pm, and same-day laundry service. Facilities include an indoor pool, a sauna and whirlpool, workout equipment, a video-game room, an indoor putting green, a billiards table, Ping-Pong tables, a business center, a gift shop, and a coin-operated laundry.

HOLIDAY INN—AIRPORT/OAKLAND PARK, 4505 Woodson Rd., Woodson Terrace, MO 63134. Tel. 314/

427-4700, or toll free 800/426-4700 or 800/HOLIDAY. Fax 314/427-6086. 154 rms, 9 suites. A/C TV TEL

$ Rates: $77 single; $82 double; $120–$170 suite. Extra person $5. Children under 19 stay free in parents' room. Weekend and corporate rates available. AE, CB, DC, DISC, ER, MC, V. **Parking:** Free.

If you shun generic chain hotels, you'll love this family-owned hotel (operated under license from Holiday Inns) in Woodson Terrace, just south of the airport. Its walls serve as a gallery for 300 paintings, most done by the owner. The Oakland Park strives for a European flavor and style, providing its mostly business clientele with a cozy home away from home. Rooms, 20% of which are reserved for nonsmokers, each feature a cable remote-control TV, full-length mirrors, bedtime mints, and such amenities as shampoo and sewing kits.

The hotel—with a restaurant and a pub—offers a free shuttle to the airport and the immediate vicinity, free coffee and newspapers, same-day laundry service, and room service until 10pm. Its facilities include an outdoor pool, a whirlpool and sauna, an exercise room, a video-game room, and a library.

BUDGET

MOTEL 6, 4576 Woodson Rd., Woodson Terrace, MO 63134. Tel. 314/427-1313. 106 rms. A/C TV TEL

$ Rates: $32.95 single; $38.95 double. Extra person $7. Children under 18 stay free in parents' room. AE, CB, DC, DISC, MC, V. **Parking:** Free.

Located across the street from the Oakland Park Holiday Inn (south of I-70, half a mile east of the 236 exit), Motel 6 provides modest accommodations at low prices. Rooms are simple but comfortable and provide individual air-conditioning and heating controls and showers. In addition, local phone calls and in-house movies are free. There are also an outdoor pool and soda-vending machines.

7. WEST COUNTY

The following accommodations are located just off I-270 in the western part of St. Louis County. They're somewhat distant from downtown St. Louis but fairly close to Clayton and University City.

EXPENSIVE

SHERATON PLAZA HOTEL, 900 West Port Plaza, Maryland Heights, MO 63146. Tel. 314/434-5010, or toll free 800/822-3535. Fax 314/434-0140. 204 rms, 5 suites. A/C TV TEL

$ Rates: $112–$130 single; $123–$140 double; from $150 suite. Extra person $10. Children under 18 stay free in parents' room. Weekend and other packages available. AE, CB, DC, DISC, MC, V. **Parking:** Free.

The Sheraton Plaza Hotel and the Sheraton West Port Inn (below) are located on opposite ends of a shopping-and-entertainment complex called West Port Plaza, just off I-270 and Page Avenue. Each of the hotels has an individual character: The West Port Inn is in the style of a country chalet and overlooks a lake; the Plaza is a modern high-rise that caters to corporate businesspeople. The view at the Inn may be better, but I prefer the rooms at the Plaza, which are large, bright, and cheerful, with breezy rattan furniture and Asian-influenced artwork. Some even have small balconies. Be sure to walk through West Port Plaza, an open-air complex designed like an Alpine village and boasting 16 restaurants and numerous shops and boutiques. Guests of both Sheratons can use a nearby health club free of charge.

There are a restaurant and a bar on the premises. The Plaza's services include a free shuttle to and from the airport, complimentary morning coffee and newspaper, a concierge desk, laundry service, room service until 1am, and free local phone calls. Its facilities include an indoor pool, a whirlpool, sunning deck, and a sauna.

SHERATON WEST PORT INN, 191 West Port Plaza, Maryland Heights, MO 63146. Tel. 314/878-1500, or toll free 800/822-3535. Fax 314/878-2837. 291 rms, 9 suites. A/C TV TEL
$ Rates: $112–$130 single; $123–$140 double; from $175 suite. Extra person $10. Children under 18 stay free in parents' room. Weekend and other packages available. AE, CB, DC, DISC, MC, V. **Parking:** Free.

Built in the style of a country lodge, the West Port Inn feels like a resort hotel. Its lobby, casual and intimate, emphasizes the Alpine theme with stone walls and wooden beams, while the outdoor pool overlooks an artificial lake complete with ducks. Rooms, all with balconies, are in two buildings—the main building and an adjoining tower with newer and slightly more expensive units. Regardless of where you stay, it's worth paying more for a lakeside room. The suites are particularly roomy, each with a large living area, a bar area and sink, two TVs, two phones, two bathroom sinks, and a clothesline and hairdryer in the bathroom. Hotel guests have free use of a nearby health club.

The hotel features a restaurant and a bar. Among its services are a free shuttle to and from the airport, complimentary coffee and morning newspaper, a concierge desk, same-day laundry service, room service until 1am, and free local phone calls. There also are an outdoor pool and a jogging track.

BED-&-BREAKFAST

CAVERLY FARM AND ORCHARD, 389 N. Mosley Rd., Creve Coeur, MO 63141. Tel. 314/432-5074. 3 rms (1 with bath). A/C
$ Rates (including breakfast): $45 single without bath, $50 single with bath; $50 double without bath, $55 double with bath. Extra person $5. Children stay free in parents' room. No credit cards. **Parking:** Free.

Originally built as a farmhouse in the 1880s but added on to through the years, this red-clapboard house is located in a very quiet and wooded residential town called Creve Coeur. Owned by David and Nancy Caverly, the Caverly is decorated in a casual country style, with rooms that are cheerful and comfortable. Breakfast includes berries from the back yard as well as homemade breads, eggs, and jam and jelly made from fruit of the small orchard out back. This is a good choice for families because there's a lot of room for children to run free and play. Note that no smoking is allowed in the house.

8. SOUTH COUNTY

The following accommodations, located in the southern part of St. Louis County, offer inexpensive lodging.

BUDGET

CORAL COURT MOTEL, 7755 Watson Rd., Marlborough, MO 63119. Tel. 314/962-3000. 74 rms. A/C TV TEL

$ Rates: $35 one bed; $40 two beds; $46 three beds. AE, MC, V. **Parking:** Free.

Nostalgic for the days of Route 66 and highway motels? This is a classic—located near the St. Louis city line on the original Route 66—a motel of yellow tile and glass brick, very art deco, spread like a village underneath a canopy of oak trees. Construction on the motel began around 1940, was halted because of World War II, and then began again in the 1950s. The Coral Court has changed little since then. Most units have attached garages complete with garage doors. The rooms themselves are a bit worn around the edges, are a bit too dark, and have furniture that looks like its been there since the 1950s (including Murphy beds in some units). Even though the motel looks better on the outside than it does on the inside, for a bit of novel Americana straight from the past, you can't beat this place. Rates are based on the unit and the number of beds it contains, not on the number of people.

MOTEL 6, 6500 S. Lindbergh Blvd., Mehlville, MO 63123. Tel. 314/892-3664. 118 rms. A/C TV TEL

$ Rates: $29.95 single; $37.95 double. Extra person $7. Children under 19 stay free in parents' room. AE, CB, DC, DISC, MC, V. **Parking:** Free.

Located near the intersection of I-55 and I-270, this hotel is convenient if you're coming into town from the south. Not too far from downtown St. Louis, it offers large rooms containing just the basics. No-smoking rooms are available, and local telephone calls are free. Small pets are allowed. All rooms are on the ground floor, so you can park right in front of your room. There are also an outdoor pool and a family-style restaurant next to the hotel.

OAK GROVE INN, 6602 S. Lindbergh Blvd., Mehlville, MO 63123. Tel. 314/894-9449, or toll free 800/435-7144. 98 rms. A/C TV TEL

$ Rates: $28.50 single; $34–$37 double. Extra person $2. Crib or rollaway $3.50. AE, CB, DC, DISC, MC, V. **Parking:** Free.

Just down the street from Motel 6, Oak Grove Inn offers slightly better rooms, although they're still pretty basic. Local calls here also are free. Complimentary coffee and juice are served in the lobby, and there's a coin-operated laundry. The TV offers cable and HBO as well as pay movies. If you feel like splurging, the most expensive room offers a king-size bed and a whirlpool bathtub. There's a family-style restaurant next door.

9. CAMPING

ARCHWAY MANOR, 7474 St. Charles Rock Rd., St. Louis County, MO 63133. Tel. 314/726-6992. 40 trailer sites, 5 tent sites.
$ Rates: $20 for complete hookup; $15 for tent site. MC, V. **Season:** Year round.

Located in the northern part of the county just off the I-170 Inner Belt Expressway in the Bridgeton area, this small 4.5-acre campground offers mainly RV hookups, including electricity, water, and sewage disposal.

KOA OF ST. LOUIS SOUTH, 8000 Metropolitan Blvd., Barnhart, MO 63012. Tel. 314/479-4449. 94 trailer sites, 20 tent sites.
$ Rates (based on double occupancy): $16 for full hookup; $13 for tent site. Extra person $1.50. DISC, MC, V. **Season:** Mar 1–Nov 1.

This KOA campground is located south of St. Louis near Barnhart, Missouri, off I-55 at the 185 exit. About a 40-minute drive from downtown St. Louis, it offers such facilities as a store, flush toilets, hot showers, fireplaces and firewood, a pool, and a game room.

PINEWOODS CAMP AND FISHING PARK, 1500 Pinewoods Dr., Wentzville, MO 63385. Tel. 314/327-8248. 305 trailer sites, 86 tent sites.
$ Rates (based on double occupancy): $13.50 for full hookup; $10 for tent site. Extra person $1. MC, V. **Season:** Mar 1–Nov 30.

Located off I-70 in Wentzville about 40 minutes from downtown St. Louis, this 100-acre campground has such recreational facilities as a pool, a game room, a playground, and fishing.

RV PARKING, 2nd and Poplar Sts., St. Louis, MO 63101. Tel. 314/241-7777. 50 trailer sites.
$ Rates: $4 without hookup; $8 with hookup. No credit cards. **Season:** Year round.

Conveniently located just south of the Gateway Arch underneath the Poplar Street Bridge, this RV park offers only electric hookup—nothing else. The well-lit park is enclosed by a fence.

ST. LOUIS RV PARK, 900 N. Jefferson, St. Louis, MO 63106. Tel. 314/241-3330. 100 trailer sites.
$ Rates: $23.50 for full hookup. MC, V. **Season:** Mid-March to mid-Nov.

Located in the heart of St. Louis near the crossroads of Jefferson and Martin Luther King Jr. Boulevard, this RV park with full hookups offers such facilities as a convenience store, a laundry room, a pool, and a game room.

CHAPTER 6

ST. LOUIS AREA DINING

Nowhere does St. Louis's ethnic diversity express itself more joyously and thoroughly than in its cuisine. Italian food reigns supreme, and hardly a visitor passes through the city without consuming at least one pizza or pasta or veal dish. The Hill is the old Italian enclave, filled with family-owned restaurants that range from neighborhood mom-and-pop diners to plush establishments with valet parking. All St. Louis natives have their favorite Italian restaurant, and exactly which is the very best is a hotly debated topic. Be sure to try the appetizer unique to St. Louis— toasted ravioli, consisting of ravioli filled with ground beef and vegetables and then deep-fried to a crispy golden brown.

In addition to Italian food, St. Louis boasts a great variety of other cuisines— from French, German, and Mexican to seafood and steaks. The past decade or so has ushered in a whole new generation of young chefs who aren't afraid to experiment with regional and ethnic foods, resulting in innovative and surprising combinations. No longer is St. Louis a backwater when it comes to dining; and even best is the fact that eating out here costs a fraction of what it costs in other parts of the country.

When choosing a restaurant, keep in mind that many establishments offer different lunch and dinner menus, and you can save money by eating your big meal at noon. You should make reservations for the more expensive and moderately priced restaurants, especially on weekend nights. Note that many close from about 3 to 5pm and that a 5.9% sales tax will be added to your bill. Tips are generally 15% to 20% of the total bill. Very much in fashion at St. Louis's expensive restaurants is valet parking, for which attendants expect a $1 or $2 tip, even if they drive your vehicle only 20 feet.

The following restaurants have been divided according to location and then further subdivided according to price. Note that restaurants located in hotels have been grouped under a separate heading in the "Specialty Dining" section at the end of the chapter. Expect to pay about $30 or more per person (not including drinks) for dinner in the **expensive** restaurants, while the **moderate** establishments should run you about $20 to $30. Recommendations listed in the **inexpensive** category should average about $9 to $20, depending on choice of main course, while **budget** establishments are those that offer meals for less than $9. A circled dollar sign by a listing denotes good value for money spent; a circled star signifies one of my particular favorites.

In addition to the restaurants listed here, be sure to check Chapter 10 for bars and entertainment establishments that also serve food.

1. DOWNTOWN

All the restaurants listed in this section are within walking distance of the Gateway Arch. Because many cater to office workers in the area, they tend to be closed on Sunday.

EXPENSIVE

AL'S STEAK HOUSE, 1200 N. 1st St. Tel. 421-6399.
Cuisine: STEAK/SEAFOOD. **Reservations:** Recommended.
$ Prices: Main courses $22–$37. AE, MC, V. **Parking:** Valet.
Open: Mon–Sat 5–11pm. **Closed:** Sun and hols.
Located north of Laclede's Landing in a riverfront industrial area, Al's has been a longtime favorite ever since it opened its doors in 1926. There is no printed menu; rather, a tray of what's available is brought to each table—laden with steak, veal, rack of lamb, and fresh seafood—and the waiter elaborates on how each dish is prepared. This restaurant is a favorite destination for St. Louisans celebrating special occasions. Jackets and ties are required for men.

CAFE DE FRANCE, 410 Olive St. Tel. 231-2204.
Cuisine: TRADITIONAL FRENCH. **Reservations:** Imperative.
$ Prices: Appetizers $7.50; main courses $19–$24. AE, CB, DC, DISC, MC, V. **Parking:** Valet.
Open: Mon–Thurs 5:30–10pm, Fri–Sat 5:30–11pm.
Many consider this their favorite French restaurant in St. Louis. From the minute you walk into this intimate and elegant establishment, with its chandeliers and fresh flowers on the tables, you're whisked away to the adventures of another continent, a different cuisine, and a whole new way of looking at food. Owner/chef Marcel Keraval, born in France, is well known for the artful presentation of his dishes, which are so beautiful to look at that you almost hate to eat them.

But who could resist hot smoked salmon with dill sauce, veal scaloppine stuffed with crab and glazed with lobster and hollandaise, lamb with honey-ginger sauce, or duckling with red currants? There are always daily specials not listed on the menu, as well as fixed-price three- to five-course meals ranging from $22.50 to $29.50. Although Keraval describes his cuisine as being traditional French, some of his creations border on nouvelle. Start your meal with gooseliver pâté, but be sure to leave room for the fantastic homemade French pastries. Jackets and ties are required for men.

KEMOLL'S, 1 Metropolitan Square, 211 N. Broadway. Tel. 421-0555.
Cuisine: ITALIAN. **Reservations:** Recommended, especially on weekends.
$ Prices: Lunch main courses $10.95–$14.95; dinner main courses $19–$27; pasta $10.95–$16. AE, DC, MC, V.
Open: Lunch Mon–Fri 11am–2pm; dinner Sun–Thurs 5–9pm, Fri–Sat 5–10pm.
Kemoll's, a well-known name in the St. Louis Italian dining scene,

was established in 1927 and moved in 1990 to its new downtown location just a block from the Old Courthouse. To make its longtime customers feel at home, the new location is a faithful reproduction of its former self, including the same artwork, decor, and other fixtures. Although the restaurant can accommodate 250, the interior is divided into themed dining rooms, allowing for greater intimacy.

Popular for business lunches, it offers various pasta dishes, served with a salad and a vegetable, as well as individual-size pizzas served with a salad and garlic bread, including a vegetarian pizza with onions, four cheeses, zucchini, sundried tomatoes, grilled eggplant, mushrooms, peppers, and sweet basil. The dinner menu is much more extensive. You might wish to start with toasted ravioli, fried fresh artichokes, oysters, or mussels, then follow with veal scalloppine, veal saltimbocca, filet mignon, or shrimp and artichokes in cream-mustard sauce. Recommended pasta dishes include fettucine al Toscano (fettucine with smoked salmon, capers, cream, and parmesan cheese) and linguine tossed with shrimp, mussels, clams, and lobster-tail meat in wine-flavored cream sauce. Men should wear jackets and ties.

TONY'S, Equitable Building, 10 S. Broadway. Tel. 231-7007.

  Cuisine: ITALIAN. **Reservations:** Necessary.

$ Prices: Appetizers $8; pasta $8–$9; main courses $20–$29, fixed-price dinners $49. AE, CB, DC, DISC, MC, V. **Parking:** Valet.

  Open: Mon–Sat 5–11:30pm. **Closed:** Sun and hols.

I could write an entire article on Tony's alone, as indeed many have. Although there may be a few dissenters, most St. Louisans agree that this is the city's finest restaurant, as reflected in the fact that it's one of only two restaurants in the entire United States to hold both a five-star *Mobil Travel Guide* Award and an AAA Five Diamond Award. One reason is that diners are never disappointed—the food is always fantastic. What's more, diners are treated with deference whether they're famous or just folks from out of town. The restaurant has had since 1949 to perfect its style.

Part of that calculated style is reflected in the staff's attentive yet unobtrusive service. However, oldtimers lament the demise of one of the restaurant's most endearing acts of showmanship when it moved to its present site in 1992—the maître d' used to show the way walking backward up the stairs, so that he never turned his back on his customers. The new location, alas, has no stairs. Still, coat- and car-claim tickets aren't given because the staff members remember which item belongs to whom; and doggie bags are waiting in the car when the customer leaves.

As for the food, it's sublime. I've never been quite the same since trying the cappellini primavera. Equally good are the smoked salmon filled with imported Italian cheese, the lobster Albanello (perhaps the star dish), various veal dishes, and steaks. All pasta dishes are cooked to order, the veal chops are four inches thick and are the best you'll find anywhere, the beef is dry-aged by the restaurant, and the seafood is flown in fresh daily. Even basil grows fresh in the kitchen. In fact, the kitchen is so spotlessly clean, orderly, and amazing that it should be on a tour. The kitchen floors are swept every hour and mopped every two hours, the silver is polished twice a week, and even the ceilings are washed down according to a strict schedule. I've never

ST. LOUIS
Downtown

Al's Steak House ❶
Boston's ⑭
Café de France ❾
Caleco's ❽
Charlie Gitto's ❼
Dierdorf & Hart's ⑭
Faust's ⑮
Food Court ⑭
Kemoll's ❸
Key West ⑭
La Sala ❻
Lettuce Leaf ⑰
Lt. Robert E. Lee ⑬
Miss Hullings ❺
Old Spaghetti Factory ❷
Premio ⑪
Ruth's Chris Steak
    House ⑩
Station Grille ⑭
A Taste of St. Louis ❹
Tony's ⑫
Top of the Riverfront ⑯

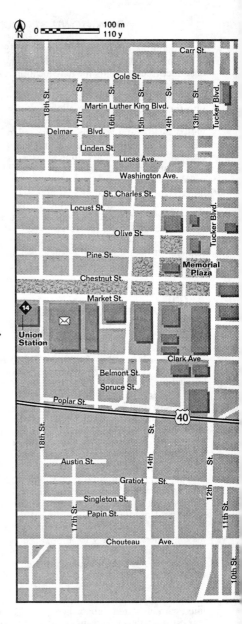

seen anything like it. All things considered, Tony's gets my vote as the best restaurant in town. Jackets are required for men.

MODERATE

LT. ROBERT E. LEE, 100 S. Lenore K. Sullivan Blvd. Tel. 241-1282.
    Cuisine: AMERICAN. **Reservations:** Recommended.

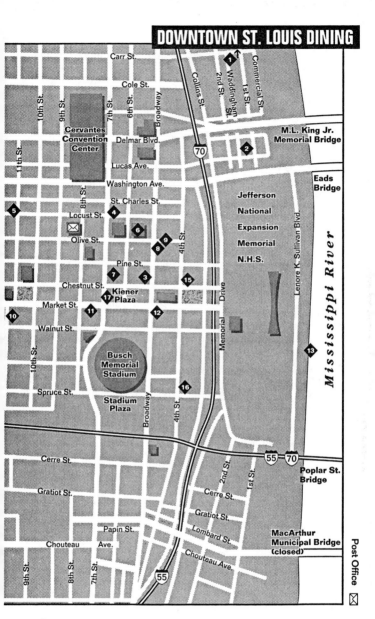

DOWNTOWN ST. LOUIS DINING

Carr St.

Cole St.

Delmar Blvd.

Lucas Ave.

Washington Ave.

St. Charles St.

Locust St.

Olive St.

Pine St.

Chestnut St.

Kiener Plaza

Market St.

Walnut St.

Busch Memorial Stadium

Spruce St.

Stadium Plaza

Cerre St.

Gratiot St.

Papin St.

Chouteau Ave.

Carr St.

Commercial St.

Waddingham St.

2nd St.

1st St.

Collins St.

M.L. King Jr. Memorial Bridge

Eads Bridge

Jefferson National Expansion Memorial N.H.S.

Lenore K. Sullivan Blvd.

Mississippi River

Memorial Drive

Cerre St.

Gratiot St.

Lombard St.

Chouteau Ave.

Poplar St. Bridge

MacArthur Municipal Bridge (closed)

Post Office

Cervantes Convention Center

9th St.

10th St.

11th St.

8th St.

7th St.

6th St.

Broadway

4th St.

9th St.

8th St.

7th St.

10th St.

$ **Prices:** Lunch main courses $6–$10; dinner main courses $12.25–$20. AE, DC, DISC, MC, V.

Open: Lunch daily 11:30am–3pm; dinner Mon–Thurs 5–10pm, Fri–Sat 5–11pm; Sun brunch 10am–2pm.

Dine right on the Mississippi on this boat moored near the Gateway Arch, built to resemble the sternwheelers that once ruled the river. It offers various options in dining, including a main dining room specializing in steaks, prime rib, and seafood. On Sunday, there's a brunch featuring live Dixieland jazz. If you want to be entertained while you dine, you might consider spending an evening in the Natchez Room with the Showboat Jubilee variety show (see Chapter 10 for more information).

PREMIO, Gateway One Building, 701 Market St. Tel. 231-0911.

  Cuisine: ITALIAN. **Reservations:** Recommended for lunch.

$ Prices: Lunch pasta $6–$10.50, main courses $7–$13; dinner appetizers $5.50–$8, pasta $8–$13, main courses $15–$23. AE, DC, MC, V.

  Open: Lunch Mon–Fri 11am–2pm; dinner Mon–Thurs 5–10pm, Fri–Sat 5–11pm.

Brought to you by the same folks who own four-star Dominic's on the Hill (see the "In or Near the Hill District" section below), Premio caters to the downtown business crowd with its light contemporary Italian cuisine and its prime location on Market Street behind the Old Courthouse. A modern restaurant that relies on plants as its main decoration, it offers outdoor seating (with a great view of the Arch) as well as a separate bar. Its main business is at lunch, when it offers 11 different pasta dishes, including cannelloni, fettuccine with veal sauce, linguine with fresh seafood, and ravioli filled with ricotta cheese in tomato-and-basil sauce. Risotto dishes of Northern Italy also are on the menu, as are fresh seafood, chicken, and veal. The dinner menu offers the same pasta and appetizers but with additional entrées.

RUTH'S CHRIS STEAK HOUSE, 101 S. 11th St. Tel. 241-7711.

  Cuisine: STEAK. **Reservations:** Recommended on weekends.

$ Prices: Salads and Appetizers $3–$7; main courses $15.50–$23.50. AE, DC, DISC, MC, V.

  Open: Daily 5–11pm.

Part of a chain of steak houses that originated in New Orleans, Ruth's Chris Steak House has achieved a devoted following by serving only the best U.S. prime, corn-fed Midwestern beef, cut by hand, broiled to perfection, and then served sizzling hot. An upmarket restaurant with white tablecloths and modern decor, this steak house is located in the basement of a striking brick building that once served as a warehouse. In addition to its steaks, it serves lamb chops, veal chops, chicken, and lobster. There are nine different selections of potato dishes, from cottage fries to potatoes au gratin served in cream sauce and topped with sharp Cheddar.

INEXPENSIVE

CALECO'S, 420 Olive. Tel. 421-0708.

  Cuisine: ITALIAN/AMERICAN.

$ Prices: Appetizers $3.50–$5.50; main courses $5.25–$14. AE, DC, DISC, MC, V.

  Open: Mon–Fri 11am–3am, Sat–Sun noon–3am.

This is a local success story, beginning in 1974 with the opening of a college establishment that has now expanded to more than half a dozen locations across the city. The downtown Caleco's, on the corner of Olive and Broadway, is a casual bar and grill that caters to local businesspeople, families, and tourists. Its menu includes a bit of everything—such as pizza, fajitas, chicken pasta salad, burgers, sandwiches, prime rib, veal, and stir-fried vegetables—but it's best known for its offerings of more than a dozen different kinds of pasta. There are daily lunch specials as well as a children's menu. On Friday and Saturday there's live rock-and-roll music after 10pm, for which there is no cover charge.

Other Caleco's locations include 14 Marilyn Plaza in the Central West End (tel. 361-8505); 10567 Old Olive St. (tel. 567-6047) in Creve Coeur; and 3815 Laclede St. (tel. 534-7878) in Midtown.

LA SALA, 513 Olive. Tel. 231-5620.
  Cuisine: MEXICAN.
$ Prices: Appetizers $2.70–$5.50; main courses $5.75–$7.95. AE, MC, V.
  Open: Mon–Sat 11am–11pm.
La Sala means "living room" in Spanish—and that's the atmosphere this cozy restaurant tries to evoke. Dimly lit and comfortable, it's been a longtime favorite with the locals, especially during happy hour "attitude adjustment" offered on Monday through Friday from 4:30 to 6pm, when large margaritas go for only $2.25. The menu includes nachos, enchiladas, tamales, tacos, mole verde, burritos, tostadas,

---

 FROMMER'S SMART TRAVELER: RESTAURANTS

VALUE-CONSCIOUS DINERS SHOULD TAKE ADVANTAGE OF THE FOLLOWING:

1. Lunch menus offering main courses at cheaper prices than those on dinner menus; save money by eating a big meal at noon.
2. Daily specials offered by many restaurants, which are not on the regular menus and may offer a main course and side dish at a good price.
3. Fixed-price meals, each of which includes an appetizer or soup, a main course, and a dessert, at prices much cheaper than when ordering à la carte.
4. Inexpensive main courses, such as chicken or pasta, offered by some of the more expensive restaurants, where even budget travelers can dine in style by choosing carefully.
5. St. Louis's many Italian restaurants in all price categories.
6. A view of the Gateway Arch from a few of St. Louis's downtown restaurants—request a table by the window when making your reservation.
7. Food offered by many pubs, bars, and taverns, usually hearty portions at bargain prices.

QUESTIONS TO ASK IF YOU'RE ON A BUDGET

1. Does the main course come with a side dish such as a vegetable or potato? (If so, it may be all you want to order, unless you have a voracious appetite.)
2. Is there a special of the day or a fixed-price meal not listed on the regular menu?

quesadillas, chimichangas, chile rellenos, and taco salads. There's a variety of alcoholic concoctions made with tequila and Kahlúa.

BUDGET

CHARLIE GITTO'S, 207 N. 6th St. Tel. 436-2828.
Cuisine: ITALIAN. **Reservations:** Not accepted.
$ Prices: $4.50–$9.50. AE, DC, DISC, MC, V.
Open: Mon–Thurs 11am–10:30pm, Fri–Sat 11am–11:30pm, Sun 3–9:30pm (Cardinal game days only). **Closed:** Sun when there are no games.

There's no better place to go on baseball-game days than this St. Louis institution, even though it may be packed and accepts no reservations, except for large groups. It's been *the* sports place ever since it opened more than 15 years ago in a small brick building that today looks out of place amidst the surrounding high-rises. It's filled with photos and sports memorabilia and is popular with athletes. Tommy LaSorda has his own table here, and he makes it a point to drop in whenever he's in town. The specialty is pasta, for which there are more than 20 different offerings, most available in small or large servings. There are also sandwiches; lunch and dinner specials; and a few choices of low-calorie, low-fat dishes.

LETTUCE LEAF, 107 N. 6th St. Tel. 241-7773.
Cuisine: SALADS/SANDWICHES.
$ Prices: $3.50–$7.25. AE, DISC, MC, V.
Open: Mon–Fri 11am–7:30pm (in winter until 4pm).

This casual restaurant, decorated with cane and rattan furniture and hanging plants, specializes in more than a dozen salads and a variety of sandwiches that change with the seasons. The summertime fare features light food, including fruit plates, while the winter menu includes heartier dishes. Baked-potato soup is a year-round favorite, and the huge salads are meals in themselves.

Two other Lettuce Leafs are at 7823 Forsyth (tel. 727-5439) in Clayton and 620 Westport Plaza (tel. 576-7677) in West County.

MISS HULLINGS, 1103 Locust St. Tel. 436-0840.
Cuisine: AMERICAN.
$ Prices: $3.70–$7. AE, DC, DISC, MC, V.
Open: Summer, Mon–Sat 6am–8pm; winter Mon–Thurs 10:30am–7pm, Fri–Sat 10:30am–8pm.

A St. Louis tradition since 1928, Miss Hullings is an old-fashioned cafeteria offering home-style cooking. Pink is its trademark—hence the pink walls, pink aprons worn by the staff, and pink napkins. It offers 4 different soups each day, 14 types of vegetables, 26 salads, sandwiches, and a variety of entrées that changes daily. Selections may include such main dishes as fried chicken, prime rib, and ham, along with such side dishes as hot creamed spinach, broccoli, and corn. There's also a wide selection of cakes, pies, and other desserts.

THE OLD SPAGHETTI FACTORY, 727 N. 1st St., Laclede's Landing. Tel. 621-0276.
Cuisine: PASTA.
$ Prices: $4.50–$7.50. MC, V.
Open: Summer Mon–Thurs 4:30–10pm, Fri 4–11pm, Sat 3–11:30pm, Sun 3–10pm; winter Mon–Thurs 5–10pm, Fri 5–11pm, Sat 4–11:30pm, Sun 3:30–10pm.

Its name leaves little doubt about the specialty served in this casual family restaurant located in the heart of Laclede's Landing. The Spaghetti Factory is in the basement of a beautiful six-story cast-iron–and–brick building that once housed a tobacco company. There are antiques throughout the restaurant, including a 1920 streetcar that now contains some dining tables and a nine-foot Tiffany window commissioned by a Chicago cattle baron. Approximately a dozen selections of spaghetti and pasta are offered, all of which come with a salad, French bread, a drink, and ice cream. There's also a children's dinner.

A TASTE OF ST. LOUIS, 4th floor, St. Louis Centre, between 6th and 7th and Washington and Locust Sts. Tel. 231-5522.
   Cuisine: VARIED FAST FOOD.
$ Prices: $2–$5. No credit cards.
   Open: Mon–Sat 10am–7pm, Sun noon–7pm.
If you're looking for a fast meal at a cheap price, your best bet downtown is the fourth floor of the St. Louis Centre shopping mall. Popular at lunch with local office workers and shoppers, this food court consists of counters specializing in various foods—from tacos and quiche to barbecued food, stir-fried vegetables, gyros, pizza, and salads. O'Connell's, an Irish pub famous for its hamburgers, also has a concession here.

2. UNION STATION

In addition to the Union Station restaurants described below, Houlihan's (listed in Chapter 10) serves a wide variety of American food.

MODERATE

BOSTON'S, Union Station, 18th & Market. Tel. 621-3474.
   Cuisine: SEAFOOD. **Reservations:** Recommended on weekends.
$ Prices: Lunch main courses $5.50–$12; dinner appetizers $5.50–$7.50, main courses $15–$18. AE, CB, DC, MC, V.
   Open: Sun–Thurs 11am–10pm, Fri–Sat 11am–11pm.
Decorated like a Victorian saloon, Boston's is known for its affordable seafood, especially its lobster tail served with potatoes and fresh vegetables for less than $12. It's located on the second level of Union Station, with an outdoor patio overlooking a small lake. The dinner menu includes a raw bar sampler with shrimp, oysters, and clams, as well as such seafood fare as shrimp, scallops, Alaskan king crab legs, and fish ranging from Norwegian salmon to swordfish and mahimahi. For landlubbers, there are also beef and chicken selections. The lunch menu offers salads, sandwiches, a few main courses (including lobster), and more than half a dozen specials.

DIERDORF & HART'S, Union Station, 18th and Market. Tel. 421-1772.

Cuisine: STEAK/SEAFOOD. **Reservations:** Recommended.
$ Prices: Lunch main courses $6–$12; dinner main courses $14–$33. AE, CB, DC, DISC, MC, V.
Open: Mon–Thurs 11am–11pm, Fri–Sat 11am–midnight, Sun 11am–10pm.

Established by former Cardinal star football players Dan Dierdorf and Jim Hart, this posh establishment claims to offer the best steak in St. Louis (don't they all?). Its walls lined with sketches of sports celebrities, Dierdorf & Hart's boasts an extensive bar and wine list. It offers for lunch egg dishes, burgers, sandwiches, seafood, and steaks and for dinner New York strip (how about a 26-ounce cut?), filet mignon, T-bone, fresh fish, and lobster. **Another D & H** is in Westport Plaza in West County (tel. 878-1801).

BUDGET

FOOD COURT, Union Station, Upper Level, 18th and Market. Tel. 421-4314.
Cuisine: VARIED FAST FOOD.
$ Prices: $1–$5. No credit cards.
Open: Mon–Thurs 10am–9pm, Fri–Sat 10am–10pm, Sun 11am–7pm.

Perched along the walkway of Union Station's upper level, this food court offers a variety of inexpensive dishes from many vendors, including burgers, sandwiches, barbecued food, pizza, and hot dogs, as well as a few ethnic choices ranging from Mexican and Greek to Chinese. You'll find good people-watching here.

KEY WEST, Union Station, 18th and Market. Tel. 241-2566.
Cuisine: SEAFOOD/AMERICAN.
$ Prices: $5.25–$10. AE, DC, MC, V.
Open: Daily 11am–1:30am.

Key West favorites—including conch fritters, Key lime pie, fish sandwiches, shark, Florida rock shrimp, and even alligator marinated

 FROMMER'S COOL FOR KIDS: RESTAURANTS

Blueberry Hill *(p. 86)* Teenagers and adults alike will enjoy a burger at this St. Louis area attraction (in University City), dedicated to rock and roll, with memorabilia relating to Chuck Berry, Elvis, the Beatles, and other music greats.

Busch's Grove *(p. 89)* There's no better setting for a family outing than this long-standing institution with private cabanas offering outdoor dining.

Rigazzi's *(p. 82)* This family-style Italian restaurant on the Hill is inexpensive, fun, and lively—just the kind of atmosphere kids love.

in a spicy Cajun mixture and then grilled in garlic-lemon butter—are served at this combination bar/restaurant. There are also a dozen different versions of hamburgers with toppings and hot dogs. Happy hour is Monday through Friday from 4 to 7pm, when oysters are offered at half price and drink specials are available. There's a wide selection of domestic and imported beer.

3. IN OR NEAR THE HILL DISTRICT

The Hill, located just west of the Missouri Botanical (Shaw's) Gardens, is St. Louis's Italian district, famous for its many restaurants.

EXPENSIVE

DOMINIC'S, 5101 Wilson. Tel. 771-1632.
   Cuisine: ITALIAN. **Reservations:** Recommended; necessary on weekends.
   $ Prices: Appetizers $4.50–$10; main courses $17–$25. AE, CB, DC, DISC, MC, V. **Parking:** Valet.
   Open: Mon–Sat 5pm–midnight. **Closed:** Sun and hols.

Any discussion of the Hill's best Italian restaurants will include Dominic's, a formal affair where the waiters wear bow ties and black suits and the decor includes statues reminiscent of those in old Rome, chandeliers, and enough paintings on the walls to make the restaurant look like a museum. It's borderline pretentious—but all is forgiven due to the careful and exact service, subdued lighting, and, most important, great Italian food (it has a four-star *Mobil Travel Guide* listing). After your meal, you'll think you've dined and gone to heaven. The menu includes both Italian and American selections, including fresh seafood, chicken, beef tenderloin, steaks, rack of lamb, and veal. The veal saltimbocca and the chateaubriand are especially recommended. The wine list is extensive, and there's also a bar where you can come for only a drink if you wish. Jackets and ties are required for men.

GIOVANNI'S, 5201 Shaw. Tel. 772-5958.
   Cuisine: ITALIAN. **Reservations:** Strongly recommended, especially on weekends.
   $ Prices: Appetizers $6.50–$7.50; pasta $14–$18; main courses $17–$30. AE, DC, MC, V. **Parking:** Valet.
   Open: Mon–Sat 5pm–11pm. **Closed:** Sun and hols.

Giovanni's has a slight edge over Dominic's (above), by virtue of the fact that it was asked to prepare a pasta dish for former President Reagan's inaugurations in 1981 and 1985. In fact, Giovanni's may well have the best pasta in town, which is no mean feat considering the competition. Winner of four stars in the *Mobil Travel Guide* for the past decade, it is certainly a top contender for the best Italian restaurant in town. Elegant and romantic in the style of the Italian Renaissance, it's a great place for a splurge.

You'll probably want to include pasta with your meal. If you want what Reagan had, order the Presidential Farfalline Al Salmone, pasta in a rich cream sauce with fresh salmon. For a main course, you might choose veal saltimbocca or picante veal cooked with wine and lemon. There are also chicken breast cooked with champagne, fresh seafood, filet mignon, and rack of lamb. Jackets and ties are required for men.

MODERATE

GIAN-PEPPE'S, 2126 Marconi. Tel. 772-3303.
   Cuisine: ITALIAN. **Reservations:** Advised on weekends.
$ Prices: Lunch main courses $6.80–$14; dinner main courses $14–$24; pasta $12. AE, CB, DC, MC, V. **Parking:** Valet.
   Open: Lunch Tues–Fri 11am–2pm; dinner Tues–Sat 5–11pm.

Quickly closing in on the two restaurants listed above in the fierce battle of best Italian eatery, this relative newcomer is more youthful in clientele and decor. Its dining room is small, intimate, and comfortable, with crisp white tablecloths and fresh flowers on every table. The staff is friendly and efficient, and the customers tend to be regulars. You might wish to come for lunch, when you can choose half an order of pasta or have it as an entrée or opt for one of the many veal dishes. For dinner, too, the pasta is not to be missed, and you can order it as a main dish or a side dish. Fresh fish, veal piccata, an intriguing selection of chicken dishes, rack of lamb, and steaks round out the menu. Jackets are required for men.

GIAN-TONY'S, 5356 Daggett at Macklind. Tel. 772-4893.
   Cuisine: ITALIAN.
$ Prices: Lunch main courses $4.50–$12; dinner pasta $7.50–$11, main courses $12–$15. AE, MC, V.
   Open: Lunch Tues–Fri 11am–2pm; dinner Tues–Fri 5–10pm, Sat 5–11pm, Sun 4:30–9pm.

Although Gian-Tony's is a newcomer on the Hill, proprietor Tony Catarinicchia is not. He served as a chef for 16 years at nearby Giovanni's before deciding to open a restaurant of his own and has quickly won over a faithful and discerning clientele. A simple restaurant where the emphasis is on the cuisine rather than the decor, it offers the usual pasta and veal dishes, including such favorites as chicken cacciatore, veal saltimbocca, and veal Fiorentina (veal scaloppine with artichoke hearts and mushrooms in a sauce of white wine and cream). This restaurant is on the road to becoming an established winner.

INEXPENSIVE

CUNETTO HOUSE OF PASTA, 5453 Magnolia. Tel. 781-1135.
   Cuisine: ITALIAN. **Reservations:** Not accepted.
$ Prices: Lunch $5–$9; dinner $7–$12. AE, DC, MC, V.
   Open: Lunch Mon–Fri 11am–2pm; dinner Mon–Thurs 5–10:30pm, Fri–Sat 5–11:30pm.

This family-style restaurant has been immensely popular for more than 15 years, in part because of its low prices but mostly because of its great Italian food. In fact, this place is so popular that you're guaranteed a wait—no reservations are accepted for dinner. No matter, head for the bar. The food is worth the wait, with more than two dozen selections of pasta alone. The dinner menu is more extensive and includes no-cholesterol, low-salt pasta, sirloin steaks, fish, veal, and chicken selections.

LOU BOCCARDI'S, 5424 Magnolia. Tel. 647-1151.

Cuisine: ITALIAN.

$ Prices: Lunch $5–$8.50; dinner pasta and pizza $5.50–$8, main courses $8–$13.

Open: Mon–Thurs 11am–12:30am, Fri–Sat 11am–1:30am, Sun 3–11pm.

This is a very unpretentious neighborhood restaurant that has changed little since opening in 1972. Occupying three levels of an old house, with hand-painted murals on some of the walls, Boccardi's is best known for its thin-crust pizza, great if you prefer to fill up on topping rather than crust. In fact, people get so hooked on the pizza that some have ordered it delivered by Federal Express after they've left town. In addition to pizza, it serves pasta, sandwiches, fish, steaks, veal, and chicken. From Monday to Friday, it offers for $4.50 lunch specials that include an entrée, salad, and side dish of pasta.

ZIA'S, 5256 Wilson. Tel. 776-0020.

Cuisine: ITALIAN.

$ Prices: Lunch main courses $6–$7.25; dinner pastas $6.50–$7.50, main courses $6.50–$14.50. AE, MC, V.

Open: Mon–Thurs 11am–10pm, Fri–Sat 11am–11pm.

This plainly decorated family-style restaurant is a popular choice for casual dining on the Hill, with dinner main courses ranging from veal scaloppine and chicken parmigiana to filet mignon, all served with a salad and a side order of pasta or a fresh vegetable. Pasta dishes include various linguine, fettuccine, and ravioli choices, including seafood ravioli and linguine prepared in a spicy cream sauce with shrimp, crabmeat, clams, mushrooms, and marinara.

BUDGET

AMIGHETTI BAKERY, 5141 Wilson. Tel. 776-2855.

Cuisine: ITALIAN.

$ Prices: $4–$6. No credit cards.

Open: Tues–Thurs 9am–8pm, Fri 9am–8:30pm, Sat 7:30am–5:30pm. **Closed:** Sun, Mon, and hols.

Located in the heart of the Hill district, on the corner of Wilson and Marconi avenues across from the St. Ambrose Catholic Church, this establishment first opened as a bakery in 1921 and still uses traditional ovens to bake its great breads. A St. Louis tradition, Amighetti's is presided over by Mrs. Amighetti herself, called Mrs. A by people who know her. She specializes in mouthwatering sandwiches, the best known of which is the Amighetti Special, made with ham, beef, salami, Swiss cheese, lettuce, tomato, pickle, onion, pepperoncini pepper, and Mrs. A's special dressing. There are also pizza, pasta, salads, and homemade gelato.

Mrs. A has other branches at 101 N. Broadway (tel. 241-3700) and at 1010 Market (tel. 241-8555), both downtown, 8696 Telegraph Rd. (tel. 846-6636), and 8000 Carondelet in Clayton (tel. 725-8081).

O'CONNELL'S PUB, Kingshighway and Shaw. Tel. 773-6600.

Cuisine: BURGERS/SANDWICHES.

$ Prices: $3.50–$5. AE, MC, V.
  Open: Mon–Sat 11am–midnight.

Popular and unanimous consensus names O'Connell's as having the best burgers in town. A simple pub with a wooden floor, pressed-tin ceiling, and wooden tables, it also serves sandwiches filled with roast beef, Italian sausage, ham, salami, and other fillings, and on tap are Guinness and Watney's. If this place is too far to go for a burger, there's an O'Connell's concession on the fourth floor of the St. Louis Centre downtown.

RIGAZZI'S, 4945 Daggett Ave. Tel. 772-4900.
  Cuisine: ITALIAN.
$ Prices: Lunch buffet $4.25; pasta dinners $8; pizzas $6–$8. AE, MC, V.
  Open: Mon–Thurs 7am–11:30pm, Fri–Sat 7am–12:30am.

Another neighborhood tradition for more than 30 years, Rigazzi's is an informal family-style restaurant located in a simple brick building. Its red-and-white vinyl tablecloths are often lined elbow-to-elbow with an enthusiastic dining public who come for the lunch buffet or the dinner pasta specials, which include a salad and garlic bread. There are also sandwiches, burgers, meat dishes, pizza, and seafood. You won't want to pass up the specialty, the so-called "fishbowls" of beer, a full 32 ounces of the brew. No wonder everyone here looks so enthusiastic.

4. CENTRAL WEST END & FOREST PARK

These restaurants, many of them inexpensive and catering to a young, upwardly mobile crowd, are convenient if you're window-shopping in the Central West End or visiting the attractions in Forest Park.

MODERATE

BALABAN'S, 405 N. Euclid Ave. Tel. 361-8085.
  Cuisine: FRENCH/CONTINENTAL. **Reservations:** Accepted until 7pm.
$ Prices: Café main courses $6–$12; restaurant main courses $17–$22. AE, DISC, MC, V.
  Open: Café: Lunch Mon–Fri 11am–3pm, Sat 8am–11am, Sun 10:30am–3pm; café dinner Mon–Thurs 6–11:30pm, Fri–Sat 5:30–11:30pm, Sun 5–10:30pm. Restaurant: Mon–Thurs 6–10:40pm, Fri–Sat 5:30–11:15pm.

Open since the early 1970s, this café/restaurant sets the pace for the Central West End, serving gourmet food to a discerning and hip clientele. It's actually two restaurants in one, each with its own menu and atmosphere. The café, with a bistrolike feel, extends along the front of the building, with windows overlooking the sidewalk, and serves inexpensive food in a casual setting. Lunch includes sandwiches, pasta, roasted-pepper–and–pesto pizza, hamburgers, chicken curry, and fresh Missouri trout, while dinner adds a few more items, such as pork chops and seafood.

The main restaurant, on the other hand, is open only for dinner and is a lot more artsy, with brick walls, a wooden floor, and a more innovative menu. Fresh seafood is the restaurant's forté—from seared yellowfin tuna with citrus beurre blanc and kumquats to mussels from Maine. Beef Wellington with a golden-raisin sauce has been popular for years, and there are also sweetbreads with fennel-and-chervil sauce, half roast duckling with wild rice and blackberry sauce, and grilled tournedos of beef. All in all, Balaban's is a fun, laid-back, and eclectic place. A separate bar is open throughout the day and evening.

GRAPPA, 512 N. Euclid Ave. Tel. 361-2021.

Cuisine: AMERICAN. **Reservations:** Recommended for dinner.

$ Prices: Lunch main courses $5.50–$9; dinner appetizers $7–$9, main courses $14–$20. AE, DC, DISC, MC, V.

Open: Lunch Mon–Sat 11am–3pm; dinner Mon–Thurs 5–11pm, Fri–Sat 5pm–midnight.

A newcomer to the Central West End dining scene, Grappa has been quick to gain a faithful following with its contemporary and eclectic American cuisine and bright and cheerful decor. Located in the historic Pierce Arrow building on the corner of Washington and North Euclid avenues, it boasts a gracefully curved facade of glass that lets in lots of sunshine, while the tiled floor, palm trees, starched white tablecloths, and flowers on each table create an atmosphere that's both comfortable and trendy. Its menu changes every four months but always features organically raised meats; fresh fish; free-range veal and chicken; flatbreads; salads; and a selection of grappas, ports, Madeiras, and other wines. Past lunch selections have included yellowfin tuna salad with Southwestern influences on jalapeño cornbread, while dinner has offered roast leg of lamb and grilled lamb sausage with a fennel, grilled eggplant, and marjoram salad, plus saffron polenta; roasted farm-raised rabbit with a mushroom sauce and a turnover of wild mushrooms and goat cheese; and grilled beef tenderloin with a roasted garlic-thyme potato cake and black pepper, shallot, and herb butter. A full-service bar remains open throughout the day.

NANTUCKET COVE, 40 N. Kingshighway Blvd. (enter on West Pine). Tel. 361-0625.

Cuisine: SEAFOOD. **Reservations:** Recommended.

$ Prices: Appetizers $5–$7; main courses $12–$30. AE, CB, DC, MC, V. **Parking:** Valet.

Open: Mon–Thurs 5:30–10pm, Fri–Sat 5:30–10:30pm. **Closed:** Sun and hols.

Yes, you can have fresh seafood even in the Midwest, thanks to air travel. Nantucket Cove has been serving what many St. Louisans consider to be the best seafood in the city for more than 30 years, so it must be doing something right. It's decorated to resemble what you might find on the New England coast—with rustic wooden walls and ceiling, galley lamps, boat fixtures, and antiques collected from the days when Nantucket Island was the whaling center of the world. Fresh lobsters, flown in daily from Maine and kept alive in a tank until you choose the one you want, are a specialty, but there are also blackened redfish, charcoal-broiled fresh fish, fried catfish, shrimp stuffed with crab legs, scallops, and Alaskan king crab legs. For landlubbers there are steak and chicken breast. There are also an extensive white wine list and a bar where you can wait for your table or enjoy happy-hour specials on oysters. Nantucket Cove is located just off Kingshighway Boulevard on West Pine, northeast of Forest Park.

INEXPENSIVE

DUFF'S, 392 N. Euclid Ave. Tel. 361-0522.
   Cuisine: INTERNATIONAL.
$ **Prices:** Lunch $5.50–$7.50; appetizers, pizzas, and pastas $5–$8.50; dinner main courses $13–$17. AE, CB, DC, DISC, MC, V.
   Open: Lunch Tues–Thurs 11am–4pm, Fri 11am–4pm, Sat 10am–4pm; dinner Tues–Thurs 5:30–10pm, Fri–Sat 5:30pm–midnight; Sun 10am–10:30pm.

Opened in 1972 in a building dating back to 1907, this is a casual, friendly, and earthy place, with an exposed-brick wall, wooden floors, and ceiling fans. A venue for once-a-month poetry readings and occasional story readings, Duff's offers an interesting menu that changes with the seasons. A summertime lunch menu, for example, is likely to include such light fare as quiche, pizza, salads, and sandwiches ranging from the BLT to an avocado-sprout sandwich, and a dinner menu may feature Thai peanut chicken, orange-mustard shrimp, pecan catfish, and chicken marsala.

MUSEUM CAFE, in the St. Louis Art Museum, Forest Park. Tel. 721-5325.
   Cuisine: CONTINENTAL.
$ **Prices:** Lunch $5.50–$8; dinner main courses $7–$13; Sun brunch $11.50. AE, MC, V.
   Open: Lunch Tues–Sat 11am–3:30pm; dinner Tues 5–8:30pm; Sun brunch 10am–2pm.

If you're in Forest Park visiting the wonderful attractions, you can't find a more cheerful place to eat than this restaurant located inside the St. Louis Art Museum. It certainly looks like a museum café, bright and cheery, with a view of the courtyard's artificial waterfall and sculpture. Its eclectic and changing menu shows influences from around the world and ranges from a grilled chicken sandwich with Thai-curry mayonnaise to Italian frittata. Dinner is available one night a week; the great Sunday brunch features a spread varied enough to please the adventuresome and the traditionalist.

REDEL'S, 310 DeBaliviere Ave. Tel. 367-7005.
   Cuisine: AMERICAN. **Reservations:** Accepted only for parties of five or more.
$ **Prices:** $3.80–$16. AE, MC, V.
   Open: Lunch Mon–Fri 11:30am–2:30pm; dinner Mon–Wed 5:30–11pm, Thurs–Sat 5:30–11:30pm, Sun 5–10pm.

This avant-garde restaurant, located north of Forest Park, met with instant success when it opened a few years ago. Its decor is a zany mix of the American Southwest and the classical, with a cactus placed beside a Greek pillar, a display of antique cameras and radios, a changing exhibition of artwork on the walls, and glass bricks. The effect is breezy and very upmarket, and the clientele is young and well-heeled. The menu includes such sandwich standbys as the BLT, club sandwich, and Reuben, but there are also fresh seafood, baby-back ribs, pasta, chicken teriyaki, and very popular pizzas with toppings you can choose yourself. There's a bar where you can wait for your table, and at each table are crayons that you can use to draw the evening away.

BUDGET

CULPEPPERS, 300 N. Euclid Ave. Tel. 361-2828.
   Cuisine: BAR FOOD.
$ **Prices:** $4.75–$6.50. AE, MC, V.
   Open: Mon–Sat 11am–midnight (last order), Sun noon–11pm.
This is a simple neighborhood watering hole that may have looked pretty hip at one time but now seems outdated with its brown walls and decor. But it's still a place to be seen—and almost everyone who comes here can't resist the dish Culpeppers is famous for: spicy chicken wings (less than $5 for a pound). Other bar food includes cold shrimp, melts, hamburgers, tuna salad, and sandwiches. No children under 12 are allowed.

THE PASTA HOUSE COMPANY, 309 N. Euclid Ave. Tel. 361-7811.
   Cuisine: PASTA.
$ **Prices:** Pasta, pizza, and sandwiches $4–$9.50; main courses $8–$16. AE, DISC, MC, V.
   Open: Sun–Thurs 11am–11pm, Fri–Sat 11am–1am.
This is an enormously successful pasta chain begun in 1974 that now has 25 locations throughout the St. Louis metro area, each offering more than two dozen inexpensive pasta dishes. The Central West End location occupies the lobby of a former hotel, with high stucco ceilings, pillars, and green-checked tablecloths. One of the rooms is huge, with windows that overlook Euclid Avenue, and there are also a long full-service bar and even outdoor seating in summer. Everything from toasted ravioli and rigatoni to flat noodles with asparagus is offered, as well as several selections of pizza and sandwiches; there are also a children's menu and carry-out. The Special Salad with unlimited refills, can't be beat.
   Other locations include 6214 S. Lindbergh (tel. 894-9161) in South County and 295 Plaza Frontenac (tel. 569-3040) in Mid-County.

SAINT LOUIS BREAD COMPANY, 4651 Maryland Ave. Tel. 367-7636.
   Cuisine: SANDWICHES.
$ **Prices:** $3.50–$4.50. No credit cards.
   Open: Mon–Thurs 6:30am–8pm, Fri–Sat 6:30am–10pm, Sun 7am–8pm.
The Saint Louis Bread Company is famous for its freshly baked breads, including approximately a dozen different kinds, ranging from sourdough and French to nine grain, cracked wheat, and cinnamon raisin. The choice of sandwich fillings includes everything from tuna salad, to breast of turkey, to avocado with lettuce and tomato. About a dozen varieties of muffins, croissants, espresso, and cappuccino are also available. Dining here is simple, with additional tables placed outside in warm weather. You can also pick up the fixings for a picnic in one of the area's parks.
   Other locations include 6309 Delmar Blvd. (tel. 726-6644) and 6655 Delmar (tel. 721-8007), both in University City, and also the St. Louis Galleria shopping center (tel. 727-5300).

Cuisine: BAR FOOD.

$ Prices: $4–$6. AE, CB, DC, DISC, MC, V.

Open: Mon–Sat 11am–midnight (last order), Sun 11am–11pm.

Blueberry Hill rates as a St. Louis area attraction and is worth a visit even if you don't eat here. Dedicated to rock-and-roll, it's packed with memorabilia relating to Chuck Berry and Elvis Presley, the Beatles, and much more; also, there are seven dart boards. Its CD juke box, which a selection of more than 2,000 songs at any one time, has been rated the best in the country. So gaze and listen as you munch on a burger, a sandwich, or soup.

BURRITO BROTHERS, 6600 Delmar, University City. Tel. 726-2767.

Cuisine: MEXICAN.

$ Prices: $2–$4.40. No credit cards.

Open: Summer Sun–Thurs 11am–10pm, Fri and Sat 11am–midnight; winter Mon–Thurs 11am–8pm, Fri–Sat 11am–10pm, Sun noon–8pm.

This self-serve fast-food joint is about as casual as you can get. Eat at one of the booths indoors or sit outside and watch the action along The Loop. Burrito Brothers offers tacos, fajitas, quesadillas, enchiladas, tostadas, burritos, and chimichangas—all available with red or green sauce and with bean, pork, roast beef, chicken, or steak, fillings.

6. CLAYTON & MID-COUNTY

EXPENSIVE

AL BAKER'S, 8101 Clayton Rd., Richmond Heights. Tel. 863-8878.

Cuisine: ITALIAN/CONTINENTAL. **Reservations:** Recommended.

$ Prices: Appetizers $4.50–$7.50; pasta dishes $12–$15; main courses $14–$27. AE, CB, DC, DISC, MC, V. **Parking:** Valet.

Open: Mon–Sat 5pm–midnight.

In a world of increasing trendiness where sparse decor is all the rage, Al Baker's remains steadfastly comfortable. Its corridor is lined with photographs of people who have dined here, and its dining room is richly decorated in deep red, with flickering sconces along the walls. An institution since 1965, it's still the place to go for a special occasion, with attentive service, many dishes prepared tableside, and live music nightly.

Al Baker's is well known for its pasta dishes, so you may wish to start with one of its dozen offerings. Among its main courses, the Veal Oskar (breaded veal and whole lobster tail garnished with asparagus and topped with cream sauce), Greek-style rack of lamb, and stuffed tenderloin are outstanding. There are also fresh fish and a low-cholesterol menu kind to your heart (and approved by the Cardiovascular Risk Reduction Center at St. Louis University). Its wine cellar is probably the best in the city, with approximately 20,000 bottles. Jackets are required for men.

CARDWELL'S, 8100 Maryland, Clayton. Tel. 726-5055.

Cuisine: NEW AMERICAN. **Reservations:** Recommended.

$ Prices: Lunch $8–$13; dinner main courses $15–$23; fixed-price dinners about $16. AE, MC, V.
Open: Mon–Thurs 11:30am–10pm, Fri–Sat 11:30am–11pm.

★ This upstart restaurant hit it off big in the St. Louis area and is already considered one of the great establishments around. The dining area is cooly comfortable and elegant, with a tiled floor, polished wood ceiling beams, palm trees, and artwork ⑤ on the walls. French doors open onto an outdoor patio in summer. Because of its prime location in the business district of Clayton, it's a favorite place for a business lunch.

The menu changes often, reflecting what's available and fresh. Thus, homegrown tomatoes offered by a local farmer or perhaps fish from a special delivery from Boston may suddenly appear on the night's menu. Past selections have included chilled gazpacho with pepper vodka and crispy corn tortilla chips; pan-roasted breast of pheasant prepared with muscat wine, green peppercorn, and fresh peach sauce; and grilled herb-marinated naturally raised chicken with summer-squash salsa, basil butter, and crispy potato straws. On Monday through Saturday there's a fixed-price dinner that includes a salad or soup, an entrée, and a dessert. Don't pass up the souffle for dessert.

FIO'S LA FOURCHETTE, 1153 St. Louis Galleria, Richmond Heights. Tel. 863-6866.
Cuisine: NOUVELLE FRENCH. **Reservations:** Recommended.
$ Prices: Appetizers $8–$9; main courses $20–$22; fixed-price dinners $45. AE, DC, MC, V.
Open: Tues–Sat 6–10pm.

★ Don't let its location in a mall deter you because the food here is fun, avant-garde, and imaginative. Owner/chef Fio Antognini isn't afraid to experiment by blending traditional French haute cuisine with international and nouvelle cuisine and adding his own personal touches.

Main courses may include Norwegian salmon stuffed with shiitake mushrooms and fresh herbs, served with grilled peppers and lemon sauce; and grilled medallions of beef tenderloin with roast-garlic sauce. There's also a selection of entrées with reduced fat for those watching calories. But the restaurant is most famous for its six-course fixed-price menu that might include a free-range veal-and-pistachio pâté on decorated herb sauce, followed by chilled smoked Missouri trout and Louisiana crayfish Napoleon, grilled Hawaiian swordfish, salad, dessert, and coffee or espresso with petits fours.

L'AUBERGE BRETONNE, 200 S. Brentwood Blvd., Clayton. Tel. 721-0100.
Cuisine: TRADITIONAL FRENCH. **Reservations:** Recommended, especially on weekends.
$ Prices: Lunch main courses $6.50–$15; dinner appetizers and soups $3.25–$9, main courses $15–$26. AE, CB, DC, MC, V.
Open: Lunch Mon–Fri 11:30am–3pm; dinner Mon–Sat 5:30–10:30pm.

Formerly located in Frontenac until its move to Clayton, L'Auberge Bretonne was the St. Louis area's pioneer French restaurant and is still highly recommended for its traditional classic cuisine. The service is impeccable, and the comfortable dining room is a great place for lunch or dinner because the dark windows screen out harsh sunlight, providing a romantic atmosphere even at high noon. The lunch menu is basic, consisting of sandwiches, salads, pasta, burgers, steaks, seafood, and omelets; at dinner traditional French food might include appetizers like snails in garlic butter or angel-hair pasta with scallops and basil, followed by baked boneless breast of duckling with port-wine sauce, tenderloin, rack of lamb, chateaubriand béarnaise, veal with lobster and asparagus, or lobster Wellington.

MODERATE

BUSCH'S GROVE, 9160 Clayton Rd., Ladue. Tel. 992-0011.
Cuisine: AMERICAN. **Reservations:** Imperative outdoors, recommended indoors.
$ **Prices:** Lunch $6.50–$11; dinner main courses $12.50–$20; fixed-price dinners $16–$19. AE, CB, DC, MC, V. **Parking:** Valet.
Open: Tues–Thurs 11am–11pm, Fri–Sat 11am–midnight.

A great place for outdoor dining with its 20 screened cabanas, individual shelters with ceiling fans and table service (the smallest ones seat 2 to 8 persons). It's so popular that reservations sometimes must be made two weeks in advance. The indoor dining hall is not nearly as interesting, but it's often full as well. Located in the community of Ladue at the crossroads of Clayton and Price roads, this white-frame restaurant has been a local institution for a hundred years.

The food is simple American cooking, if a bit predictable, and the younger generation will enjoy the children's menu. Lunch offers everything from burgers to lemon-pepper catfish filet, including sandwiches, chicken, seafood, and steak. For dinner there are chicken, veal, beef, and seafood selections. Whatever you choose, include a bowl of the homemade soup and some cottage fries. There's a nightly fixed-price dinner, the most popular being Wednesday's barbecue ribs and Saturday's prime rib.

INEXPENSIVE

CAFE NAPOLI, 21 S. Bemiston St., Clayton. Tel. 863-5731.
Cuisine: ITALIAN.
$ **Prices:** Lunch $4.50–$7; dinner pasta $8.25–$10, main courses $11–$15. MC, V.
Open: Lunch Mon–Fri 11am–2pm; dinner Mon–Thurs 5–10pm, Fri–Sat 5–11pm, Sun 5–9pm.

IMPRESSIONS

I have spent many years out of America, but the Missouri and Mississippi rivers have made a deeper impression on me than any other part of the world.
—T. S. ELIOT (1948)

This relatively new Italian restaurant has already gained a loyal following due to its dependably good food at very reasonable prices and its friendly service. Casual and usually crowded, Café Napoli is a small place with tables so close together that diners receive little privacy, especially during lunch, when the room is packed with business people. At dinner the establishment is transformed by candles and lots of small white lights on the ceiling that twinkle like distant stars. The menu offers various pasta, chicken, veal, beef, and fish selections; the wines are affordable. You can't go wrong here.

GIRARROSTO, 101 S. Hanley, Clayton. Tel. 726-4900.

Cuisine: ITALIAN/AMERICAN.
$ Prices: Lunch fixed-price menu $5.95–$7.95; dinner appetizers $3.95–$5, pasta $8, main courses $8.50–$13. AE, CB, DC, MC, V.
Open: Lunch Mon–Fri 11:30am–2:30pm; dinner Mon–Thurs 5:30–10pm, Fri–Sat 5:30–11pm.

A cheerful place for both lunch or dinner, Girarrosto bills itself as an American rotisserie (it has an open rotisserie) specializing in Tuscan-style classic cooking with an emphasis on light sauces, fresh herbs, and olive oil. Appropriate for both businesspeople (its bar is open throughout the day) and families, it offers three or four pastas every evening and, for real pasta fans, a pasta sampler special every Monday evening. Wednesday evenings feature a five-course Tuscan fixed-price meal for $14.95. Free appetizers are offered on Monday to Friday from 4 to 7pm, along with reduced-price drinks. Main courses on the regular dinner menu include rotisserie chicken stuffed with Tuscan bread, pancetta and herbs, double loin pork chops, leg of lamb with garlic and thyme, and baby-back ribs. Incidentally, all the waiters here go by the name of "Pepino," while all waitresses answer to "Lucia."

SCHNEITHORST'S HOFAMBERG INN, Lindbergh and Clayton Rds., Ladue. Tel. 993-5600.

Cuisine: GERMAN.
$ Prices: Lunch $6.50–$17; dinner main courses $9.50–$18. AE, CB, DC, DISC, MC, V.
Open: Lunch Mon–Sat 11am–4pm; dinner Mon–Thurs 5–10pm, Fri–Sat 5–11pm, Sun 2–8pm; Sun brunch 10am–1:30pm.

Schneithorst's first opened in 1917 and has been in this location since 1957, under the same family management. A huge establishment with four dining rooms and eight private banquet rooms, all decorated to resemble those in a Bavarian lodge, it boasts the largest beer stein in the world. The "Pig-skin Room," featuring genuine pigskin wallpaper and wood carvings, is the most popular room, while the main dining room containing a beer stein collection and booths along one wall is romantic. Most customers, however, are family groups and senior citizens.

Although the menu contains some German specialties, it offers much more than sauerbraten (marinated beef) and Wienerschnitzel, notably steaks, country fried chicken, pork tenderloin médallions, and catfish. There are also nightly specials; if it's available, I'd suggest you order the German Sampler—sauerbraten, bratwurst, and beef roulade—along with a side order of crisp potato pancakes. The wine list is extensive. Schneithorst's 60-item Sunday brunch is enormously popular ($9.95 for adults and $3.95 for children).

BUDGET

YEN CHING, 1012 S. Brentwood Blvd., Richmond Heights. Tel. 721-7507.
  Cuisine: CHINESE.
$ **Prices:** Lunch $4.50–$5.50; dinner main courses $6.50–$9. AE, DC, MC, V.
  Open: Lunch Mon–Fri 11:30am–2pm; dinner Mon–Thurs 5–9:30pm, Fri–Sat 5–10:30pm, Sun 4:30–9pm.

Located across from the St. Louis Galleria and in operation since the early 1970s, this Chinese restaurant specializes in Peking and Szechuan food. Considered by some to be the best Chinese restaurant in the area, it has a decor that is restrained, with only its red tablecloths, Chinese lanterns, and a bit of Chinese artwork to give it away. At lunch a dozen selections include spicy-hot chicken wings, broccoli beef, and a vegetable combo, all of which come with hot-and-sour soup, an egg roll, fried rice, and tea. Dinner is much more extensive, with more than 60 entrées of pork, poultry, beef, seafood, and vegetables. Recommended dishes include the twice-cooked pork braised with vegetables and hot peppers, snow-white breasts of chicken cooked with mushrooms and peas, Peking duck ($20.75—order in advance), sliced beef marinated in garlic sauce, and deep-fried prawns.

7. IN & AROUND SOULARD

The following restaurants are convenient if you're visiting the Soulard Market, the Anheuser-Busch Brewery, Antique Row, and other sights in the Soulard district south of downtown St. Louis.

MODERATE

PARK AVENUE CAFE, 1923 Park Ave. Tel. 241-9122.
  Cuisine: CONTINENTAL/NEW AMERICAN.
$ **Prices:** Lunch $7–$9.50; dinner main courses $14–$19. AE, MC, V.
  Open: Lunch Mon–Sat 11am–2:30pm; dinner Fri–Sat 6–11pm.

Located across the street from Lafayette Park, this is a very fashionable and chic café, with a polished wooden floor, white tablecloths, fresh flowers, modern lighting, and white walls serving as an art gallery. Lunch features cashew chicken salad, an American crab sandwich on English muffins with tomato sauce, and a broiled chicken sandwich on French bread with brie. For dinner there are approximately 10 entrée choices, which may include chicken breast with spinach, wild rice, lingonberries, brie, and mustard; sea scallops grilled with pineapple and papaya in ginger sauce; and lamb chops with rosemary in brandy-mint sauce.

PATTY LONG CAFE, 1931 Park Ave. Tel. 621-9598.
  Cuisine: AMERICAN/CONTINENTAL.
$ **Prices:** Lunch $7–$8.30; dinner $13.20–$19. AE, DC, MC, V.
  Open: Lunch Mon–Fri 11am–2pm; dinner Fri–Sat 6–10pm; Sun brunch 10am–3pm.

This establishment is more earth-bound than neighboring Park Avenue, with exposed-brick walls and daily specials written on a chalkboard—but it's still classier than the usual café due to the changing exhibitions of artwork on the walls and the white table-cloths and flowers. There is no smoking anywhere in the restaurant. The lunch menu may include curry-chicken salad, quiche, Thai-style pork tenderloin, croque monsieur (puff pastry with turkey and Swiss cheese filling), and grilled chicken. Dinner main courses, most served with a salad, seasonal vegetables, and rice or potato, change often and range from fresh seafood to vegetable cannelloni.

BUDGET

DE MENIL MANSION RESTAURANT, 3352 De Menil Place. Tel. 771-5829.
   Cuisine: AMERICAN.
$ **Prices:** $6–$9. AE, MC, V.
   Open: Tues–Sat 11:30am–2pm.
Located in the former carriage house of a stately mansion that's now restored and open to the public, this is a very pleasant place for lunch. If the weather's fine, you'll want to dine in the garden. The lunch fare, primarily salads and sandwiches, is light and healthy. There are the California Sunshine whole-wheat sandwich with avocado, bacon (well, maybe not so healthy, but bacon is that food you hate to love), American cheese, tomato, and alfalfa sprouts; a smoked turkey sandwich; and a vegetable garden salad. Also offered are a wide selection of desserts, including cheesecakes and such alcoholic concoctions as strawberry-mint lemonade and chocolate-almond cream, the latter made with Amaretto, Irish Cream, and hot chocolate (perfect for winter).

NORTON'S CAFE, 808 Geyer. Tel. 436-0828.
   Cuisine: AMERICAN.
$ **Prices:** $4–$10. AE, MC, V.
   Open: Mon–Thurs 11am–11pm, Fri–Sat 11am–midnight, Sun 11am–10pm.
A casual café in the heart of Soulard's nightlife district, housed in an ivy-covered brick building dating from the mid-1800s, it's popular for its hearty portions of Irish- and Cajun-inspired food. Norton's has sandwiches served with Irish potatoes and also a changing menu that may include blackened shark, raspberry chicken, steak, and pasta. The desserts are a must, especially the cheesecakes.

8. SOUTH ST. LOUIS

INEXPENSIVE

BEVO MILL, 4749 Gravois Ave., near Morganford Rd. Tel. 481-2626.
   Cuisine: GERMAN.
$ **Prices:** Lunch main courses $4.95–$8; fixed-price lunch $5.95;

dinner main courses $11.95–$15.95; Sunday brunch $8.95 adults, $2.50 children. AE, CB, DC, MC, V.
Open: Lunch Mon–Sat 11am–4pm; dinner Sun–Thurs 4–9pm, Fri–Sat 4–10pm; Sun brunch 10am–2pm.

A longtime St. Louis institution, Bevo Mill is the reigning king of kitsch, from the imitation windmill that towers above the restaurant and the fake storks on the chimney to its interior of Gothic vaulted ceilings, wooden ceiling beams, stained-glass windows, wainscoting, and antlers lining the walls. Popular with families and senior citizens, it specializes in traditional German food, including sauerbraten (marinated beef), Schnitzel (breaded veal cutlet), and beef Rouladen (round steak with bacon, onion, and pickle)—all served with such typical German side dishes as potato dumplings, sauerkraut, spaetzel (noodles), or potato pancakes. Seafood, steaks, veal, and chicken dishes are also available. On Thursday, Friday, and Sunday evenings, diners are serenaded by strolling musicians. Especially popular is the Sunday brunch. Bevo Mill is located about a 15-minute drive southwest of downtown.

9. SPECIALTY DINING

HOTEL DINING

The restaurants listed here represent the best of St. Louis's hotel dining. Jackets usually are required for men.

DOWNTOWN

Expensive

FAUST'S, in the Adam's Mark Hotel, 4th and Chestnut Sts. Tel. 241-7400.
Cuisine: NOUVELLE AMERICAN. **Reservations:** Recommended for lunch, imperative for dinner.
$ Prices: Lunch $7.50–$15; dinner main courses $18–$30. AE, CB, DC, DISC, MC, V. **Parking:** Valet (free).
Open: Lunch Mon–Fri 11:30am–2pm; dinner Sun–Thurs 5:30–10pm, Fri–Sat 5:30–10:30pm.

The signature restaurant of this premier hotel, it's decorated like a European baron's castle, with stone walls, wooden beams, and chandeliers. Rustic and elegant at the same time, it adjoins Pierre's Lounge, where you can relax with a cocktail before or after dinner and listen to a jazz trio and even dance. A few tables have a view of the Gateway Arch, but you should request one when making your reservation.

The creative menu changes often to reflect what's in season. For lunch you might start with bow-tie pasta au gratin with three cheeses and vodka sauce, followed by Norwegian salmon grilled with fresh thyme and ground lemon pepper. For dinner you might opt for an appetizer of smoked Missouri ham with an assortment of fruit or râgout of wild hare; for the main course you may choose pheasant and venison seared with a rosemary, juniper, and game glaze or jumbo shrimp and abalone. Save room for the Oreo-crusted white-chocolate cheesecake with raspberry sauce. Suits and ties are required for men.

UNION STATION

Expensive

STATION GRILLE, in the Hyatt Regency St. Louis, Union Station at 18th and Market Sts. Tel. 231-1234.
   Cuisine: STEAKS/SEAFOOD. **Reservations:** Recommended.
$ Prices: Appetizers $7.50–$9; main courses $16–$25. AE, CB, DC, DISC, MC, V.
   Open: Mon–Thurs 5:30–10:30pm, Fri–Sat 5:30–11pm.
Housed in Union Station's original oak-paneled dining hall, once occupied by the famous Fred Harvey restaurant, this is the Hyatt Regency's signature restaurant. It's an elegant place to dine and still reminiscent of the railroad era with art deco motifs, brass, lots of warm woods, an open copper grill, plants, and white tablecloths. The waiters and waitresses wear crisp black-and-white uniforms, much like they did back in the 1890s when the station first opened.

Dinner at the Station Grille could begin with a selection from its raw bar, including cherrystone clams, Chesapeake Bay oysters, mussels, shrimp, and Alaskan king crab—all flown in daily. Other appetizers include blackened carpaccio and turkey-and-roasted-pepper sausage. Entrées are mainly seafood and steaks, as well as such dishes as roasted rack of lamb, Long Island duck, and spit-roasted chicken.

CLAYTON

Expensive

CHEZ LOUIS, in the Seven Gables Inn, 26 N. Meramec, Clayton. Tel. 863-8400.
   Cuisine: FRENCH/CONTINENTAL. **Reservations:** Recommended.
$ Prices: Lunch $6.50–$11; dinner main courses $16–$20. AE, CB, DC, DISC, MC, V.
   Open: Lunch Mon–Fri 11am–2pm; dinner Mon–Sat 5–10pm.
This place looks so French that you almost expect a "Bonjour" when you walk through the door—there are white curtains that cover only the bottom half of the window, crisp linen tablecloths, artwork on the walls, and fresh flowers. But even better is the fact that the food lives up to the restaurant's image. *The New York Times* once named Chez Louis one of the best hotel restaurants in the country.

The food is classic French and continental, beautifully presented, with an eye on current trends emphasizing health without sacrificing taste. The lunch menu changes daily but always includes a large selection of salads, a crêpe du jour, egg dishes, and fish. Listed alongside the main courses are recommended wines that best complement the food. For dinner, you might start with frog's legs cooked with butter, garlic, and lemon or perhaps escargots in rich garlic cream sauce with puff pastry. For the main course, choose from medallions of veal with sweetbreads; grilled loin of lamb with Montrachet, pine nuts, and lamb essence; or pan-seared shrimp or duck breasts in hoisin sauce with raspberries.

THE RESTAURANT, in The Ritz-Carlton, 100 Carondelet Plaza, Clayton. Tel. 863-6300.
   Cuisine: AMERICAN/CONTINENTAL. **Reservations:** Recommended.
$ Prices: Lunch $8–$18; dinner main courses $22–$35. AE, CB, DC, DISC, MC, V.
   Open: Lunch Mon–Sat 11:30am–2:30pm; dinner daily 6–11pm; Sun brunch 11am–2:30pm.

The Restaurant is everything you'd expect from the Ritz-Carlton's best dining hall: richly enameled walls adorned with 18th- and 19th-century art, a crystal chandelier, fantastic flower arrangements, and food served under silver domes on scalloped Hutschenreuther china. Even lunch is an experience in luxury: Although the menu changes often, perhaps you'll begin with the sautéed soft-shell crab appetizer or the Missouri corn chowder and proceed to such entrées as grilled swordfish, veal rib-eye steak, or chicken breast filled with leek, prosciutto, spinach, and grain-mustard sauce. Dinner is even more elaborate, with appetizers in the past including Beluga caviar; smoked lamb loin, artichoke, and feta cheese in peppered garlic vinaigrette; and baked rabbit loin with spinach and a mushroom-mustard glaze and cardamom sauce. The dinner main courses also change with the seasons, but examples of past dishes include sautéed Dover sole with crabmeat; Maine lobster with black-pepper–and-basil fettucine in rosemary sauce; broiled prime New York strip with red wine and truffles; and roasted milk-fed lamb loin with caraway ratatouille and pinot noir sauce. For the health-conscious, both lunch and dinner offer dishes that are low in fat, cholesterol, sodium, and calories—in accordance with guidelines set by the American Heart Association.

DINING WITH A VIEW

MODERATE

TOP OF THE RIVERFRONT, in the Clarion [Regal Riverfront] Hotel, 200 S. 4th St. Tel. 241-9500.
   Cuisine: AMERICAN. **Reservations:** Recommended.
$ Prices: Lunch main courses $6–$12; dinner main courses $14–$23; Sun brunch $12.95. AE, DC, DISC, MC, V.
   Open: Lunch Mon–Fri 11am–2pm; dinner daily 5–11pm; Sun brunch 9am–2pm.

Although this hotel restaurant doesn't measure up to the quality of those listed above, it does have something the others don't—a bird's-eye view of the Gateway Arch. St. Louis's only revolving restaurant, it's located downtown and makes a complete turn every hour. There's piano music on Monday through Saturday evening. Besides salads and sandwiches, lunch offers such entrées as fresh fish and St. Louis Bake, which is smoked breast of turkey with broccoli and mushrooms served on a croissant with sharp Cheddar-cheese sauce. Dinner is a lot fancier, with a menu that offers such main courses as St. Louis pepper steak, roast duck, scampi and linguine, and grilled swordfish. **Note:** The Clarion Hotel is expected to be renamed the Regal Riverfront in early 1993.

LIGHT, CASUAL & FAST FOOD

MCDONALD'S, 322 South Leonor K. Sullivan Blvd. Tel. 231-8895.
 Cuisine: HAMBURGERS.
$ **Prices:** 60¢–$2.25. No credit cards.
 Open: Sun–Thurs 7am–midnight; Fri–Sat 7am–1am.
Fast-food chains are not what guidebooks are all about, but you won't find a McDonald's more unusual than this one—a riverboat on the Mississippi under the shadow of the Gateway Arch. There are even tables outside so you can enjoy the view. Nearby is another riverboat for Burger King.

TED DREWES, 6726 Chippewa St. Tel. 481-2652.
 Cuisine: FROZEN CUSTARD.
$ **Prices:** $1.25–$3.25. No credit cards.
 Open: Daily 11am–midnight.

A St. Louis tradition! When evening comes, the crowds start lining up at the windows of this roadside parlor specializing in frozen custard. Begun by the present owner's father over 60 years ago with a small cart on Chippewa, Ted Drewes now packs them in with its dips (called Concretes), shakes, malts, sundaes, and sodas in flavors ranging from chocolate chip and strawberry to Heath Bar and Oreo. For many fans, it's the perfect way to complete a night on the town.

There's a second stand set up during summer only at 4224 S. Grand (tel. 352-7376), but most people patronize the crowded Chippewa location just for the experience in camaraderie.

SUNDAY BRUNCH

All the hotels in the expensive and moderate ranges have restaurants that serve breakfast. A great bird's-eye view of the Arch is afforded by **Top of the Riverfront,** a revolving restaurant atop the Clarion Hotel downtown. Sunday brunch here, served from 9am to 2pm, costs $12.95 for adults and $6.95 for children. And if money is no object, dine in sinful luxury at the Ritz-Carlton's **The Restaurant** on Sunday between 11am and 2:30pm—$28 for adults and $14 for children.

The Museum Café, located in the St. Louis Art Museum, is a bright and airy venue for Sunday brunch served from 10am to 2pm, where $11.50 for adults and $5.50 for children gives you breakfast and lunch items and a view of an artificial waterfall. **Schneithorst's,** a German restaurant in Ladue, was the first in the area to offer Sunday brunch and still does so from 10am to 1:30pm, when approximately 60 items are offered—$9.95 for adults and $3.95 for children. **Balaban's,** located in the Central West End, is a great place to rub elbows with the natives and dine on anything from smoked trout with dill sauce or cheese blintzes to eggs Benedict. Prices for individual dishes here range from about $5.50 to $9. Hours are Sunday from 10:30am to 3pm.

And finally, another great place for breakfast on Saturday and Sunday—from 10am to 2:30pm—is the **Sunshine Inn,** also in the Central West End, known for its vegetarian and natural foods.

Dishes, from about $4.50 to $8, include scrambled tofu, a Mexican omelet, and potato or multigrain pancakes, but sandwiches, salads, quiche, a vegetarian burrito, and a steamed vegetable platter also are available.

For more information on the locations and addresses of these establishments, refer to the individual listings earlier in this chapter.

AFTERNOON TEA

This English tradition is carried on in St. Louis at two of its most impressive hotels, the Adam's Mark and the Ritz-Carlton. At the **Adam's Mark,** located downtown across from the Gateway Arch, tea is served in the lobby lounge's Tiffany Rose on Monday through Saturday from 2 to 5pm; this tea features pastries and desserts for $5.25 to $9.95, along with music provided by a jazz trio and a pianist.

It would be difficult to find a fancier setting than the **Ritz-Carlton's** Lobby Lounge for afternoon tea, served daily from 2:30 to 5pm and costing $11.50 for the works. Included in the price are delicate sandwiches, tea cakes, scones with Devonshire cream, and fruit tarts served on Rosenthal china—all to the strains of classical music.

PICNIC FARE & WHERE TO EAT IT

For a great selection of breads, muffins, sandwiches, and so forth, try one of the four locations of the **Saint Louis Bread Company,** discussed in Section 4 of this chapter. Also try one of the places listed below.

KOPPERMAN'S, 386 N. Euclid Ave., Central West End. Tel. 361-0100.

Open: Sun–Thurs 7:30am–9pm, Fri–Sat 7:30am–10pm.

This grocer's and Kosher-style deli has been serving the surrounding Central West End neighborhood since 1897 and is well stocked with breads, rolls, cheeses, salads, vegetables, fruit, wines, and spirits (it's one of the few places to sell liquor on Sundays). Half the store serves as a casual cafeteria, where such items as homemade chili, hickory-smoked chicken wings, baby-back ribs, sandwiches, seafood, and desserts are offered for takeout or for immediate consumption at the indoor or sidewalk tables. Box lunches also are available.

SOULARD MARKET, bounded by 9th, 7th, Carroll, and Lafayette Sts.

Open: Tues–Sat 6am–4pm.

Saturday is the big day for St. Louis's city market, with stalls selling fruit, vegetables, meat, eggs, fish, deli meats, and T-shirts. Pick up your basics here or wander through for the atmosphere.

Note: The best place to picnic is the biggest park in town: Forest Park, less than a 10-minute drive west of downtown. There are acres here to spread a blanket and relax, and after eating you can visit such cultural attractions as the St. Louis Art Museum and the Zoological Park. Other parks worth a picnic are Lafayette Park near Soulard and Laumeier Sculpture Park on Geyer and Rott roads, which features a sculpture garden. Of course, you can simply sit down beside the Mississippi at Jefferson National Expansion Memorial National Historic Site and watch the river drift by.

CHAPTER 7

WHAT TO SEE & DO IN THE ST. LOUIS AREA

One of the great things about the St. Louis area is that it offers such a wide range of things to see and do. You can go up the Gateway Arch, shop at Union Station, stroll through one of the nation's best botanical gardens, visit the zoo, sample beer at a brewery, watch the Cardinals play baseball at Busch Memorial Stadium, and much more. Many attractions are absolutely free, making the St. Louis area a perfect destination for a family vacation.

SUGGESTED ITINERARIES

To help you get the most out of your visit, here are some suggested itineraries to guide you to the most important attractions in the city and its environs.

IF YOU HAVE ONE DAY

Get up early and head straight for the Gateway Arch, perhaps the Midwest's best-known landmark, which symbolizes the westward expansion of the United States. Since the tram to the top of the Arch is sometimes so packed that there's a two- or three-hour wait in summer and on the weekend, buying your tram ticket should be your first priority. Then you can stroll through the Museum of Westward Expansion and watch the 35-minute *Monument to the Dream*, a film about the construction of the Arch. If time permits, visit the nearby Old Courthouse, with a museum tracing the history of St. Louis.

For lunch, you might wish to dine at Top of the Riverfront, a revolving restaurant with a bird's-eye view of the Arch, or on the *Lt. Robert E. Lee,* a riverboat moored on the Mississippi. Spend the afternoon at the Missouri Botanical Garden, the oldest botanical garden in the United States, or at the St. Louis Art Museum, ranked as one of the top art museums in the country. If you have children in tow, you may wish instead to go to the St. Louis Zoological Park or to Grant's Farm, which includes a small-game preserve, a zoo, and a ride on a trackless train in its tour.

By late afternoon, you should make your way to Union Station.

Built in the 1890s and once the largest and busiest passenger terminal in the world, it now houses a wonderland of shops, restaurants, bars, and other diversions. Eat dinner at Union Station or go to the Hill, St. Louis's Italian district, for some of the best Italian food in the country. For evening entertainment, take a stroll through Laclede's Landing, a 19th-century warehouse district just north of the Arch that now serves as one of the city's top nightlife spots.

IF YOU HAVE TWO DAYS

Day 1 Spend the morning at the Gateway Arch as outlined above, adding Busch Memorial Stadium with its St. Louis Cardinals Hall of Fame, the Old Courthouse, the Eugene Field House and Toy Museum, or perhaps the St. Louis Centre shopping mall to your itinerary. After lunch, head south to the Anheuser-Busch Brewery, where you can tour one of the world's largest breweries and sample its products. Afterward, visit the historic De Menil Mansion (you may wish to come here first to eat lunch in its carriage house) and then stroll down nearby Cherokee Street with its many antiques shops.

By late afternoon, head for Union Station as described above. Stay for dinner or head straight for Laclede's Landing for dining and entertainment.

Day 2 You may wish to start the morning at Missouri Botanical Garden, especially if it's summer and the weather is hot. Afterward, head directly north for the Central West End, a fashionable neighborhood of shops, galleries, restaurants, and cafés. Stop here for lunch. After you feel replenished, go to the St. Louis Art Museum for a look at one of the country's great collections. In the evening, attend the theater or a musical production at one of the many venues outlined in Chapter 10.

IF YOU HAVE THREE DAYS

Days 1–2 Follow the itinerary outlined above.

Day 3 Pursue your own special interests: a trip to the St. Louis Zoological Park; the Laumeier Sculpture Park; one of the city's historic homes now open to the public; or an offbeat museum, such as the Dog Museum or the National Bowling Hall of Fame. If you have children, there are many other options also available—including the Magic House, with its hands-on approach in explaining wonders of the world; the newly expanded St. Louis Science Center, with its workshops for kids; and Grants Farm, with its animals and a cabin built by Ulysses S. Grant. In addition, Six Flags Over Mid-America, located about 30 miles southwest of St. Louis, is an enormous theme park with roller coasters and other amusement rides. Enjoy the evening at one of the popular live-music spots in historic Soulard.

IF YOU HAVE FIVE DAYS OR MORE

Days 1–3 Follow the itinerary outlined above.
Days 4–5 Head farther afield. If you feel like taking an overnight excursion, good destinations outside St. Louis include Hannibal, Missouri, hometown of Mark Twain, and Springfield, Illinois, former home of Abraham Lincoln with a number of historical attractions. For more information on excursions outside St. Louis, refer to Chapter 11.

1. THE TOP ATTRACTIONS

GATEWAY ARCH, Jefferson National Expansion Memorial National Historic Site, between Memorial Drive and Lenore K. Sullivan Blvd. Tel. 425-4465.

Perhaps no monument is as well known in the Midwest as the Gateway Arch, America's tallest monument, a graceful rainbow of shining steel soaring 630 feet into the air. Located beside the Mississippi River in the heart of the city, it was erected to honor the westward expansion of America through the 1800s. St. Louis is an appropriate site for such a monument, because it was from here that Lewis and Clark set out to explore the riches of Thomas Jefferson's Louisiana Purchase. In addition, throughout the 19th century St. Louis served as a gateway to the West for explorers, pioneers, immigrants, cowboys, and entrepreneurs setting out to seek their fortune. In 1990 the Arch celebrated its 25th birthday and now welcomes 2.5 million visitors a year.

For most visitors, the most thrilling experience is riding the small tram to the top, where an observation room provides a panoramic view east and west. The tram—not for the claustrophobic—consists of eight tiny capsules, each of which holds only five passengers and is designed to stay vertical throughout the four-minute ride to the top. Be sure to purchase your tram ticket immediately upon your arrival at the Arch, since tickets are for a specific time and often booked solid for two or three hours in advance in the summer and on the weekend.

While waiting for your trip up the Arch, be sure to go underneath to visit the **Museum of Westward Expansion,** which traces the westward journey of Lewis and Clark, who were followed by pioneers, immigrants, and others traveling West. Displays spread in a semicircle from the entrance, cleverly giving the illusion of expansion. Be sure, too, to watch the 35-minute film *Monument to the Dream,* which depicts the construction of the Arch from its conception to the placement of its last section. Movies are shown every 45 minutes.

Admission: $1 National Park entrance fee for adults; senior citizens 62 and older and children under 17 free. Tram ride $2.50

adults, 50¢ children 3–12. Movie tickets $1 for all visitors 3 and older.

Open: Tram rides daily Memorial Day to Labor Day 8:30am–9:10pm (last ride); winter 9:30am–5:10pm (last ride). **Closed:** Thanksgiving, Christmas, New Year's Day.

UNION STATION, 18th and Market Sts. Tel. 421-4314.

First opened in 1894, Union Station soon became the largest and busiest passenger-rail terminal in the United States. More than twice the size of its nearest competitor, it served more than 100,000 passengers per day before finally closing in 1978 because people were using other forms of transportation.

Since it's reopening as a shopping, dining, and entertainment center in 1985, Union Station has become as popular a destination for visitors as the Gateway Arch. In fact, I know one family who came to Union Station's Hyatt Regency for a vacation and ended up staying there the entire time. While that seems a bit demented considering everything else that St. Louis has to offer, it does illustrate the fact that Union Station is practically a city in itself. In addition to a hotel, it contains more than 80 specialty shops, more than two-dozen food outlets and restaurants in all price categories, a 10-screen cinema, and even a small lake. Throughout the station are 22 plaques describing its architecture and what life was like when the rails were king and also display cases containing memorabilia relating to the station donated by former employees and travelers.

For real rail buffs, Memories Theater presents films relating to the history of Union Station and the building of the railroads in America, with shows running daily from 11am to 5:15pm in summer and on Friday, Saturday, and Sunday from 11am to 5:15pm in winter.

For more information on Union Station and a brochure of its shops and services, stop by the Information Booth in Union Station, located near the 18th St. entry.

Admission: Free to Union Station; Memories Theater admission 75¢.

Open: Shops open Mon–Thurs 10am–9pm, Fri–Sat 10am–10pm, Sun 11am–7pm. Restaurants open later, usually weekdays until 11pm and weekends until midnight.

MISSOURI BOTANICAL GARDEN, 4344 Shaw. Tel. 577-5100.

The Missouri Botanical Garden is the oldest botanical garden in the nation, opened to the public in 1859 and located less than a 10-minute drive from downtown. Locals refer to it as Shaw's Garden, after the wealthy businessman Henry Shaw, who conceived, designed, and directed the garden until his death in 1889 at the age of 89.

Covering 79 acres, the Botanical Garden is divided into various individual areas, including two rose gardens with more than 6,000 roses, an iris garden, a daylily garden, and an azalea/rhododendron garden. The 14-acre Japanese Garden is the largest one in North America and contains a lake with huge carp (just like in Japan, where there isn't a pond without carp), a teahouse, stone lanterns, and traditional bridges. In the Scented Garden are plants chosen for their strong fragrance or textured leaves, and visitors are encouraged to touch and smell, with signs also in Braille.

There are also greenhouses, the most interesting of which is the

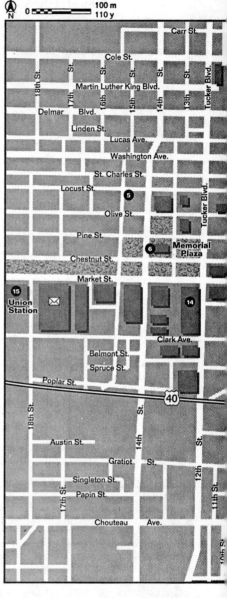

Climatron, the world's first geodesic-domed greenhouse, containing beautifully landscaped tropical vegetation that includes orchids. Interested visitors will want to stop by the Home Gardening Center, dedicated to providing the public with practical information. In addition to the thematic garden plots and displays, staff members are on hand to answer gardening questions on everything from rose-bushes to vegetables.

Throughout the Botanical Garden are sculptures, including works

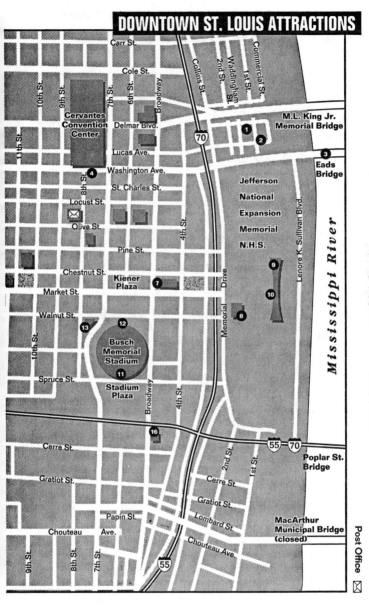

DOWNTOWN ST. LOUIS ATTRACTIONS

Carr St.

Cole St.

Delmar Blvd.

Lucas Ave.

Cervantes Convention Center

Washington Ave.

St. Charles St.

Locust St.

Olive St.

Pine St.

Chestnut St.

Kiener Plaza

Market St.

Walnut St.

Busch Memorial Stadium

Spruce St.

Stadium Plaza

Cerre St.

Gratiot St.

Papin St.

Chouteau Ave.

10th St.

9th St.

7th St.

6th St.

Broadway

Collins St.

Waddingham St.

2nd St.

1st St.

Commercial St.

M.L. King Jr. Memorial Bridge

Eads Bridge

Jefferson National Expansion Memorial N.H.S.

Lenore K. Sullivan Blvd.

Mississippi River

Memorial Drive

4th St.

Poplar St. Bridge

Cerre St.

Gratiot St.

Lombard St.

Chouteau Ave.

MacArthur Municipal Bridge (closed)

Post Office

11th St.

8th St.

9th St.

by Henry Moore and Carl Milles. A 25-minute tram ride winds through the park and stops at the Japanese Garden. There's also a restaurant open for breakfast and lunch with indoor and outdoor seating.

Admission: $2 adults, $1 senior citizens 65 and older; children under 12 free. Tram ride $2; children under 6 free.

Open: Memorial Day to Labor Day daily 9am–8pm; winter daily 9am–5pm. **Closed:** Christmas.

ST. LOUIS ART MUSEUM, Forest Park. Tel. 721-0067.

Occupying the crest of a hill in Forest Park, a 10-minute drive from downtown, the St. Louis Art Museum is housed in the only permanent building constructed for the 1904 World's Fair, built in the American Renaissance style. It was the first art museum in the world created by a citizens' vote to finance it through taxation. Now ranked as one of the top museums in the country, it contains collections from every significant period of art history—from ancient Egypt and Asia through the Middle Ages, the Renaissance, and 19th-century Europe, up to modern America. Its pre-Columbian and German Expressionist collections are considered among the top in the world. Other galleries show Islamic and ancient art; the museum's exceptional Asian collection; and art from Africa, Oceania, and the Americas. The Egyptian collection's newest acquisition is a mummy. There also are displays of Chinese, European, and American decorative arts, including furniture, vases, ceramics, silver, and armor. Finally, there's a museum shop, as well as the Museum Café serving meals and Sunday brunch.

Admission: Free to the permanent collection. Temporary exhibitions charge varying admission Wed–Sun, free on Tues.

Open: Tues 1:30–8:30pm; Wed–Sun 10am–5pm. **Closed:** Thanksgiving, Christmas, New Year's Day.

BUSCH MEMORIAL STADIUM AND ST. LOUIS CARDINALS HALL OF FAME, 100 Stadium Plaza. Tel. 421-FAME, or 421-3060 for ticket information.

Baseball and beer are what summers in St. Louis are all about—and of course that means watching the Cardinals at Busch Memorial Stadium. (In fact, Busch gets its name from Anheuser-Busch, and the St. Louis Cardinals, founded in 1892, are part of the Anheuser-Busch Company.) What makes this stadium special is that it's located in the heart of downtown—in fact it probably *is* the heart of downtown to Cardinal fans. If you're a true-blooded sports fanatic, you'll want to visit Busch Stadium's St. Louis Cardinals Hall of Fame, located between gates 5 and 6 on Walnut Street. It contains an overwhelming collection of St. Louis baseball memorabilia, including more than 1,000 items relating to St. Louis's immortal Stan Musial. Exhibits also include St. Louis's former American League entry, the Browns (now the Baltimore Orioles), and its two Negro League Pro teams, the Giants and the Stars. A 25-minute movie shows the Cardinals in action (they have won 9 World Championships and 15 National League pennants), and a trivia quiz game tests what you've learned in the museum. On evenings when there are games, the museum is open only to those who have tickets to the game.

Next to the Cardinals Hall of Fame is a gift shop where you can purchase everything imaginable with "Cardinals" written on it, from hats to nightlights to keychains to T-shirts. At the gift shop you can also purchase tickets for a 45-minute tour of Busch Stadium, with visits to the press box, the umpire's corridor, the dugout, and a portion of the field (only if there's no practice—otherwise you can watch some of the practice).

Admission: Free to gift shop. St. Louis Cardinals Hall of Fame $2.50 adults, $2 children 5–15. Stadium tours $3 adults, $2.50 children. Combination tickets for both Sports Hall of Fame and stadium tour $5 adults, $4 children.

Open: Sports Hall of Fame daily 10am–5pm (until 11pm on game days, open only to spectators with game tickets). Stadium tours in summer daily at 10:15 and 11am and 1, 2, and 3pm; in winter daily at 11am and 2pm (cancelled in bad weather). No tours on days when games are played in the afternoon.

ANHEUSER-BUSCH BREWERY TOUR, 13th and Lynch. Tel. 577-2153.

Anheuser-Busch claims to be the largest beer brewer in the world, with plants stretching from Tampa, Florida, to Fairfield, California. The St. Louis brewery is the company's largest facility and is also where the story of Anheuser-Busch began. Its 100 acres are an architectural delight, with old brick buildings—some very ornate, with turreted tops and detailed facades—and streets lined with shade trees. The oldest building dates from 1868; the brew house was built in 1892.

To see the brewery and sample its brew, visitors are invited to join a tour, which takes approximately 1¼ hour and covers eight blocks of walking. The tour begins with the complicated brewing process, and visitors see the huge vats, follow the fermentation process, and watch the packaging lines in action. Tour groups also see the famous Clydesdale horses in their stables (which must be one of the prettiest stables in the world). The tour culminates with complimentary samples of beer, including Busch, Budweiser, Michelob, and Bud Light.

Admission: Free, on a first-come, first-served basis.

Open: Tours leave every 10 minutes May–Oct Mon–Sat 9am–5pm; in winter every 30 minutes Mon–Sat 9am–4pm. **Closed:** Sun and hols.

2. MORE ATTRACTIONS

LAUMEIER SCULPTURE PARK, Geyer and Rott Rds., Sunset Hills, MO. Tel. 821-1209.

Located in South County near I-44 and I-270, this is one of only two contemporary outdoor sculpture parks in the United States. The park, covering 96 acres, contains the largest single collection of works by sculptor Ernest Trova, as well as pieces by more than 30 other artists, including Alexander Liberman, Carl Milles, Richard Serra, and Alice Aycock. Among the most interesting pieces are Aycock's *The Hundred Small Rooms,* a 30-foot-tall wooden sculpture painted white, and Liberman's *The Way,* a 100-foot-long piece made of storage tanks welded together and painted red. Included in the park are hiking trails, picnic sites, a museum shop, and a gallery for changing exhibitions of contemporary art.

Admission: Free.

Open: Park daily 8am–dusk; gallery Tues–Sat 10am–5pm, Sun noon–5pm.

SOULARD MARKET, bounded by 9th, 7th, Carroll, and Lafayette Sts.

I love city markets, so whenever I'm in St. Louis on a Saturday I head for Soulard. That's the market's busiest day, when vendors sell

FROMMER'S FAVORITE ST. LOUIS EXPERIENCES

Enjoying the Mississippi Riverfront Ride a tram to the top of the Gateway Arch for a view of the Mississippi and all of St. Louis. Stroll along the riverfront. Take a riverboat sightseeing cruise. In the evening, head for the restaurants, clubs, and bars of Laclede's Landing.

A St. Louis Cardinals Game Summer in St. Louis means baseball and beer at Busch Stadium with the St. Louis Cardinals.

A Drink at a Sidewalk Café The Central West End, settled at the turn of the century by St. Louis's upper class, offers a lively mix of unusual clothing stores, galleries, antiques shops, restaurants, outdoor cafés, and bars, making it a great place for window-shopping and people-watching.

A Saturday at Soulard Market The city's oldest open-air market is one of the best free shows in town on Saturday, when vendors sell everything from fruit and vegetables to live chickens.

Antique Row Even if you don't buy something, it's interesting browsing in the many antiques shops here—and who knows, you might find a treasure.

Afternoon Tea at the Ritz-Carlton For an afternoon of indulgence, feast on finger sandwiches, tea cakes, scones with Devonshire cream, and fruit tarts, served on Rosenthal china—to the accompaniment of classical music.

An Italian Meal No visit to St. Louis would be complete without at least one meal in the Italian district, the Hill, which is packed with Italian restaurants in all price categories.

A Night with the Blues St. Louis offers some of the best blues in the country, much of it for free or nearly free, so spend an evening in Soulard or Laclede's Landing at one of the many live music houses.

Frozen Custard at Ted Drewes When the late-night munchies hit, head for Ted Drewes' custard stand and join the multitude who come here to cap off a night on the town.

fruits and vegetables at bargain prices. There are also stalls selling snacks, smoked meats and sausages, flowers, T-shirts, audio cassettes, underwear, costume jewelry, bread, and more. Fun for a browse.
Admission: Free.
Open: Tues–Sat 6am–4pm.

HISTORIC BUILDINGS

OLD COURTHOUSE, 11 N. 4th St. at Market St. Tel. 425-4468.

Just two short blocks from the Gateway Arch is the Old Courthouse, one of the oldest buildings left standing in downtown St. Louis. First built in the 1820s and then reconstructed and added on to through the next few decades, the present courthouse stems from 1862. Built in Greek Revival style with a 150-foot dome, it is best known as the site of the 1847 Dred Scott trial, in which a slave sued for freedom and ultimately lost. On the ground floors of the courthouse is a museum dedicated to the history of St. Louis from its early years in the 1700s to the present. On the second floor are restored courtrooms, and on the fourth floor is an observation area around the rotunda. The building is under the administration of the National Park Service, which also maintains a gift shop selling books relating to St. Louis.

Admission: Free.

Open: Daily 8am–4:30pm. **Closed:** Thanksgiving, Christmas, New Year's Day.

CAMPBELL HOUSE MUSEUM, 1508 Locust St. Tel. 421-0325.

In the decades following the Civil War, Lucas Place was an exclusive residential street, buffered from downtown by a park. The sole survivor of Lucas Place is the Campbell House, built in 1851, residence of Robert Campbell and his family from 1854 to 1938. What makes it especially unique, however, is that, with the exception of only a few items, everything in the house is original, giving insight into the Campbell family's taste and life-style. That taste was decidedly French, financed by wealth acquired through fur trading, banking, and real estate. The Campbells had 13 children, only 3 of whom reached maturity. Visitors walk through the house on guided tours given continuously throughout the day.

Admission: $3 adults, $1 children.

Open: Tues–Sat 10am–4pm, Sun noon–5pm. **Closed:** Jan–Feb and hols.

CHATILLON–DE MENIL MANSION, 3352 De Menil Place. Tel. 771-5828.

Located three blocks south of the Anheuser-Busch Brewery, just off Cherokee Street, this historic home was first built in 1848 as a four-room farmhouse by Henri Chatillon, a fur trapper and wilderness guide. It was later acquired by Dr. Nicholas De Menil, a Frenchman who completely renovated the house in Greek Revival style and added nine rooms. Today it contains antiques dating from the latter part of the 1800s, as well as two oil portraits by famed Missouri artist George Caleb Bingham. Tours, which begin with a video presentation and last about an hour, are given continuously throughout the day. There's a gift shop in the basement, while in the carriage house is the De Menil Mansion Restaurant, open for lunch on Tuesday through Saturday from 11:30am to 2pm.

Admission: $3 adults, 50¢ children under 10.

Open: Tues–Sat 10am–3:30pm (last tour). **Closed:** Jan and hols.

SCOTT JOPLIN HOUSE, 2658A Delmar Blvd. Tel. 533-1003.

Scott Joplin, a musician and composer popularly known as the "King of Ragtime," lived in this modest four-family antebellum home from 1900 to 1903. In 1902 "The Entertainer" was published and became popular, but it was not until 1973 that it became his most famous piece when it was used as the movie theme song for *The Sting*. In 1976, the building was listed on the National Register of Historic Places as the only surviving structure associated with Scott Joplin, and after receiving the status of National Historic Landmark and undergoing years of painstaking restoration, the house was opened to the public in 1991. Twenty-minute tours include Joplin's second-floor flat with furnishings representative of the time and conclude with a player piano equipped with approximately 90 of Joplin's tunes. The most requested song is, you guessed it—"The Entertainer."

Admission: $1.25 adults, 75¢ children 6–12, 50¢ children under 6.

Open: Summer Mon–Sat 10am–4pm, Sun noon–6pm (until 5pm in winter).

ST. LOUIS CATHEDRAL, 4431 Lindell Blvd., Central West End. Tel. 533-2824.

Three blocks east of Forest Park, St. Louis Cathedral is nothing short of incredible, a magnificent piece of architecture and art. Begun in 1907 and combining Byzantine and Romanesque architecture, its claim to fame is that it contains the largest collection of mosaics in the world, some 145 million pieces of stone and glass covering 83,000 square feet of ceilings, domes, arches, and wall panels. These mosaics portray scenes from the Old and New Testaments, events in the life of St. Louis IX, and men and women prominent in the history of the Catholic Church. The cathedral's main dome is higher than a 22-story building, and the marble used in the construction of the cathedral came from almost every marble center in the world. A must see.

Admission: Free.
Open: Daily 6am–6pm.

CUPPLES HOUSE, 3673 West Pine Blvd. Tel. 658-3025.

Located on a pedestrian-only lane between Grand Boulevard and Spring Avenue on the campus of St. Louis University, the Cupples House was the home of Samuel Cupples, a self-made millionaire who made his fortune as a wood merchant. His mansion, built in 1889 at a cost of $500,000 (which would be the same as $10 to $15 million today), is in the Romanesque Revival style and is constructed of pink Missouri granite and Colorado sandstone. As many as 18 servants were employed to take care of the 42-room home, which has 20 operative fireplaces. Today Cupples House is filled with beautiful antiques and decorative objects, which visitors can view on their own. In the basement, in what was formerly a bowling alley, is the McNamee Gallery, which features changing exhibits from both the University's own collection of modern paintings and pieces lent by other institutions.

Admission: $2 adults, $1 senior citizens over 60; children under 13 free.

Open: Tues–Fri noon–4pm, Sun 2–4pm.

MORE MUSEUMS

ST. LOUIS HISTORY MUSEUM, Jefferson Memorial Building, Forest Park. Tel. 361-1424.

Built in 1913 as the nation's first national monument to Thomas Jefferson, the Jefferson Memorial Building houses both the Missouri Historical Society and the St. Louis History Museum. The museum traces important events in the history of St. Louis, the state of Missouri, and the American West and also houses memorabilia from the people who played indispensable roles in St. Louis's development, including Charles Lindbergh, Daniel Boone, and Lewis and Clark. You can learn about the 1904 St. Louis World's Fair and Lindbergh's historic flight across the Atlantic in *The Spirit of St. Louis.* You'll see early firefighting equipment, toys, and guns and sabers used in the Civil War.

Admission: Free.

Open: Tues–Sun 9:30am–4:45pm. **Closed:** Thanksgiving, Christmas, New Year's Day.

THE EUGENE FIELD HOUSE AND TOY MUSEUM, 634 S. Broadway. Tel. 421-4689.

This was the childhood home of Eugene Field, known as the "children's poet" for such works as *Wynken, Blynken and Nod* and *Little Boy Blue.* Built in 1845, the oldest residence still standing in downtown St. Louis, the Eugene Field House today contains a large collection of antique toys and dolls spanning 300 years, all donated by individuals.

Admission: $2 adults, 50¢ children under 12.

Open: Wed–Sun noon–4pm. **Closed:** Jan–Feb and hols.

NATIONAL MUSEUM OF TRANSPORT, 3015 Barrett Station Rd., near Kirkwood, MO. Tel. 965-7998.

Located just west of I-270, this 50-acre outdoor museum contains one of the largest collections of locomotives in the country, along with railway cars, automobiles, streetcars, buses, trucks, horse-drawn vehicles, and aircraft.

Admission: $3 adults, $1.50 children 5–12, $1.50 senior citizens 65 and older.

Open: Daily 9am–5pm. **Closed:** Thanksgiving, Christmas, New Year's Day.

NATIONAL BOWLING HALL OF FAME, 8th and Walnut. Tel. 231-6340.

Located across from Busch Stadium, this downtown museum salutes a sport enjoyed by millions of Americans. The history of bowling is traced from medieval Europe (even monks got into the action then), when it was pursued at country festivals, village dances, and even baptisms. Variations of the game also are presented, along with explanations of how it spread through the New World colonies and was eventually taken up also by women. A highlight is the eight-lane bowling alley in the basement, four lanes of which are automated and four of which are operated by pin setters. The museum also houses the American Bowling Congress and Women's International halls of fame.

Admission: $3 adults, $2 senior citizens, $1.50 children.

Open: Summer Mon–Sat 9am–7pm, Sun noon–7pm; winter Mon–Sat 9am–5pm, Sun noon–5pm. **Closed:** Thanksgiving; Dec 24, 25, and 31; New Year's Day.

THE DOG MUSEUM, Edgar M. Queeny Park, 1721 S. Mason Rd., Town and Country, MO. Tel. 821-3647.

Dedicated to man's best friend, the Dog Museum (located

southwest of the intersection of I-64 and I-270) contains works of art and literature depicting the dog throughout history, in an effort to promote understanding about the canine. It's housed in the Jarville House, built in 1853 in Greek Revival style, and also contains a library for research on various breeds.

Admission: $3 adults, $1.50 senior citizens, $1 children 5–14.
Open: Tues–Sat 9am–5pm, Sun noon–5pm. **Closed:** Hols.

THE NATIONAL VIDEO GAME AND COIN-OP MUSEUM, 801 N. 2nd St. Tel. 621-2900.

If you're a pinball wizard or simply wish to relive the pinball and video games of your youth, stop by this unique museum in the midst of the Laclede's Landing nightlife district. Approximately 100 classic video games, landmark pinball machines, and other coin-operated amusements are available for play—including Pong, Pac-Man, Donkey Kong, Centipede, and Humpty Dumpty (the first pinball with flippers). Admission includes four tokens for free play (all games cost one token, with the exception of the Dragon's Lair).

Admission: $3 adults, $2 children 5–12; $5 family price.
Open: Summer Mon–Sat 10am–10pm, Sun noon–8pm; winter Sun–Wed noon–8pm, Thurs–Sat noon–10pm.

3. COOL FOR KIDS

SIX FLAGS OVER MID-AMERICA, Allenton Rd., Eureka, MO. Tel. 314/938-5300 or 938-4800.

Amusement rides, arcade games, shows, food, and fun are featured in this theme park, located 30 miles southwest of St. Louis on I-44 at the Allenton exit. Among its many attractions are a dolphin show, the Screaming Eagle roller coaster (reputedly one of the longest, tallest, and fastest in the world), the NINJA roller coaster with its 360-degree loop, an old-fashioned carousel, and much more. The park is divided into six sections, each representing one of the six countries that have flown their flags over the Midwest through the centuries. Allow a whole day to tour the park.

Admission to all attractions: $20.95 adults, $15.95 children 3–11.
Open: June–Aug Sun–Thurs 10am–9pm, Fri 10am–11pm, Sat 10am–10pm; Apr, May, Sept, and Oct usually Sat and Sun only 10am–7 or 8pm. Because the park occasionally closes for private functions, telephone for verification of hours prior to leaving.

ST. LOUIS ZOOLOGICAL PARK, Forest Park. Tel. 781-0900.

Like the St. Louis Art Museum, the St. Louis Zoological Park was the first zoo in the world that was supported by a citizens' vote to tax themselves, and it remains one of the few free zoos in the world. Covering 83 acres in beautiful Forest Park, it's home to 2,800 animals—including apes, lions, tigers, jaguars, birds, penguins, and reptiles. The Herpetarium and the Primate House date from the 1920s, while the Bird Cage dates from the 1904 World's Fair as the Smithsonian Institution's walk-through bird cage.

Particularly outstanding is the newly opened Living World, an educational center designed to teach visitors about how nature works and what happens when humans upset the balance of nature, in the belief that it is no longer enough for zoos simply to display exotic animals. Approximately 150 animals are on display at Living World, chosen for their diversity, from bats and sponges to the tarantula and microscopic creatures (magnified to the size of house cats). Throughout are high-tech equipment, such as computers, videodisk presentations, and sound systems, to explain and entertain. A must see.

Admission: Free.

Open: Daily 9am–5pm. **Closed:** Christmas and New Year's Day.

GRANT'S FARM, 10501 Gravois Rd., near Crestwood, MO. Tel. 843-1700.

In 1856, several years before he became 18th president of the United States, Ulysses S. Grant built a log cabin not far southwest of St. Louis and farmed the land. Today that log cabin and farm are part of the 281-acre estate of August A. Busch, Jr. (as in Anheuser-Busch), and they are open to the public. There are also a game preserve where buffalo, longhorn sheep, deer, horses, and other animals roam free; a small zoo; a beer garden; and a stable of Clydesdale horses.

Although free, tours must be reserved in advance and are for a specific time. Lasting approximately two hours, tours start with a trackless train ride to the Tiergarten—a small zoo with deer, camels, elephants, bears, goats, and other animals—along with shows starring birds or elephants. After wandering through the zoo at your leisure, you're invited to visit the Bauernhof, built in 1913 as Busch's home and now housing his collection of horse-drawn carriages dating from the 1800s, and to sample a free glass of beer. Then it's back on the trackless train for a ride through the game preserve and past Grant's cabin. All in all, this is a great outing for the family.

Admission: Free, but advance reservations required.

Open: Jun–Aug Tues–Sun 9am–3pm (last tour); Apr 15–May 31 and Sept–Oct 31 Thurs–Sun 9am–3pm. Tours depart on the hour at 9, 10, and 11am and at 1, 2, and 3pm.

ST. LOUIS SCIENCE CENTER, Forest Park. Tel. 289-4444.

Newly expanded, the St. Louis Science Center is a great learning experience for children (and adults), with hands-on displays and equipment. Its four main galleries are devoted to Ecology and the Environment, the Human Adventure, Technology, and Aviation. Included are life-size moving dinosaurs; a laser show; an "earthquake" center where participants can feel what it's like to experience tremors; and Infomachines, where participants can learn about computer programming or haggle with a computer about the price of strawberries. In fact, there's so much to do here that you'll probably be overwhelmed, so be sure to allow at least several hours to tour the center.

In addition to the displays, there's an Omnimax Theater, as well as a Discovery Room, a hands-on activity area for children 4 to 10 that allows them to dress in Native American costumes, explore a Missouri cave, or look at items under a microscope. And, finally, there's also the Alien Research Project, a live stage show featuring an "alien xenologist" from another galaxy who has come to Earth to study our system of values and applications. He involves the audience in his research by asking them to vote on key issues. Note that these

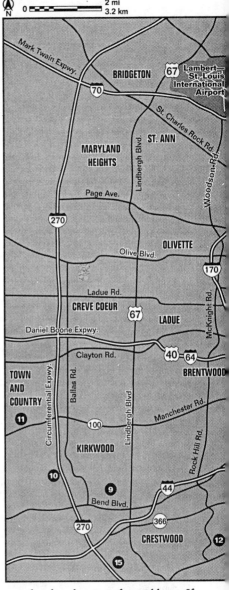

Anheuser-Busch Brewery **13**

Busch Memorial Stadium **7**

Cupples House **6**

The Dog Museum **11**

Forest Park **3**

Grant's Farm **12**

Laumeier Sculpture Park **15**

Magic House **9**

Missouri Botanical Gardens **8**

National Museum of Transport **10**

St. Louis Art Museum **2**

St. Louis Cathedral **5**

St. Louis History Museum **1**

St. Louis Science Center **14**

St. Louis Zoological Park **4**

additional programs are so popular that they are often sold out. If you're interested in visiting the Omnimax, the Discovery Room, or the Alien Research Project, it's best to arrive early in the morning.

Admission: Free to Science Center and exhibits; Omnimax Theater $4.75; Discovery Room or Alien Research Project $1.

Open: Science Center Sun–Tues 9:30am–5pm, Wed–Sat 9:30am–9pm. Omnimax Theater (shows on the hour) Mon–Fri 10am–3pm, Sat 10am–4pm, Sun 11am–4pm; evening shows Wed–Fri 7 and 8pm, Sat 6–8pm. Discovery Room Mon–Thurs 10am–

4pm, Fri–Sat 10am–7pm, Sun 11am–4pm. Alien Research Project (on the hour) Mon–Fri 10am–1pm and 4pm; Sat–Sun noon–4pm.

MAGIC HOUSE, 516 S. Kirkwood Rd., Kirkwood, MO. Tel. 822-8900.

Located one mile north of I-44 on Kirkwood Road (an extension of Lindbergh), the Magic House is filled with exhibits that encourage kids to use their senses to discover the world's wonders. There's an electrostatically charged ball that makes your hair stand on end, a human-size maze, a three-story spiraling slide, simple computers that teach letters and numbers, and room upon room packed with things to do. Children can test their reaction times, identify smells, watch the pupils in their eyes grow larger or smaller with corresponding light, or test for color blindness. There's also a special play room for children younger than 7.

Admission: $2.50; children under 2 free.

Open: Summer (Memorial Day to Labor Day) Tues–Thurs 9:30am–5:30pm, Fri 9:30am–9pm, Sat 9:30am–5:30pm, Sun 11:30am–5:30pm; winter Tues–Thurs 1–5:30pm, Fri 1–9pm, Sat 9:30am–5:30pm, Sun 11:30am–5:30pm.

ST. LOUIS CAROUSEL, Faust County Park, Olive St., Chesterfield, MO. Tel. 889-3356.

Located north of I-64 in west St. Louis County, 98-acre Faust County Park is the home of the St. Louis Carousel, built about 1920 by the Dentzel Co. of Pennsylvania and one of only 10 still in existence. It features 60 hand-carved, colorfully painted horses, 4 reindeer with real antlers, and 2 chariots.

Admission: $1 adults, 50¢ children.

Open: Wed–Sun noon–5pm.

BOB KRAMER'S MARIONETTES, 4143 Laclede Ave. Tel. 531-3313.

Bob Kramer began making puppets when he was five years old, and he has since designed and constructed more than 800 marionettes and rod puppets. You can visit his workshop (in the Central West End district) for a one-hour studio demonstration of how his puppets are made and how they work and also a brief history of puppetry. Marionette shows change with the season, ranging from a Christmas variety show to classics such as *Peter and the Wolf.* Reservations for the demonstration or the show are a must.

Admission: Studio demonstration $4.50 adults, $3.50 children. Shows $5 adults, $4 children. Combination tickets for demonstration and show $7 adults, $6 children.

Open: Studio demonstration Mon–Sat 10am and 1pm; shows Mon–Sat 11:15am and 2:15pm. **Closed:** Sun and major hols.

DENTAL HEALTH THEATRE, 727 N. 1st St. Tel. 241-7391.

This is a small theater (in the Laclede's Landing district), designed to teach kids what teeth are, why they are important, and how to take care of them. Demonstrations take place using three-foot-high fiberglass teeth that light up as an educator explains each function and how to brush and floss. Also included in the one-hour show is a film with Charlie Brown, Snoopy, and Lucy, as well as the use of puppets to further explain our teeth.

Admission: Free, but reservations required.

Open: Mon–Fri 9am–4pm. Telephone beforehand to inquire about show times.

4. ORGANIZED TOURS

BOAT CRUISES St. Louis owes its existence to the mighty Mississippi, and you can be part of its river traffic by joining a one-hour cruise with **Gateway Riverboat Cruises,** which operates three replica paddlewheelers called the *Huck Finn, Tom Sawyer,* and *Becky Thatcher.* Moored near the Gateway Arch on the riverfront, the boats are in operation daily April through December, with departures every 45 minutes between 10:15am and 5pm during summer, less frequently during the rest of the year. The cost is $7 for adults and $3.50 for children 3 to 12.

There are also longer cruises aboard the *Belle of St. Louis,* the city's newest excursion boat. Featuring a live music revue, the three-deck boat offers a two-hour day cruise on Tuesday through Sunday from noon to 2pm costing $10 for adults and $5 for children. Box lunches are available for an extra charge. The *Belle* also offers dinner-and-dancing cruises on Wednesday through Sunday from 7:30 to 10pm. These cost $28 per adult every night except Saturday, when adults pay $36. The price for children any night of the week is $18.

Finally, aboard the *Huck Finn, Tom Sawyer,* and *Becky Thatcher* are 1¼-hour Sunday-brunch cruises that cost $14.95 for adults and $5.95 for children. Another option is the Sunday brunch aboard the *Belle,* which sails from noon to 2pm at a cost of $18.50 for adults and $9.50 for children.

For more information regarding Gateway Riverboat Cruises, times of departure, and prices, call 621-4040.

BUS TOURS   Although the purpose of this book is to guide you through St. Louis and its environs on your own, for orientation purposes you may wish to join a tour upon your arrival in the city, returning later to explore sights at leisure. The **Gray Line** offers a 3½-hour Grand Tour, which includes a trip through the downtown area, Forest Park, and the Central West End, with stops at the Missouri Botanical Gardens and the New Cathedral. Departing from major hotels in St. Louis, the tour costs $15.50 for adults and half price for children 6 through 12. Tours are offered every afternoon from April 1 to October 31. For more information on exact departure times from each hotel, call 241-1224 in St. Louis, or toll free 800/542-4287.

5. SPORTS & RECREATION

For information on the Cardinals, the Blues, and other news in sports, including game times and scores, call the **Sportsline** at 321-1111. *Note:* A new stadium is planned for 1995, partly to try to lure a pro football team. (The football Cardinals departed St. Louis for Phoenix in 1988.) The stadium will be at Cervantes Convention Center in downtown.

SPECTATOR SPORTS

BASEBALL   For baseball fans, St. Louis is synonymous with the St. Louis Cardinals, who have won 9 World Championships and 15 National League pennants. Home games are played at **Busch Stadium,** located right in the heart of downtown, a ball's throw from the Gateway Arch. Baseball season runs from April through September, with approximately 80 home games. Tickets range from $4 for bleacher seats (sold two hours before the game) to $11 for box seats. General admission reserved seats are $5.50. For tickets and general information, call 421-3060. The Individual Ticket Charge Line for VISA or MasterCard is 421-2400. You can also order tickets by mail at St. Louis Cardinals Ticket Office, P.O. Box 8787, St. Louis, MO 63102, for which there's an extra $4 handling-and-postage charge. The Cardinal Ticket Lobby is open Monday to Saturday from 9am to 5:30pm.

ICE HOCKEY The St. Louis Blues ice hockey team plays at **St. Louis Arena,** 5700 Oakland, south of Forest Park. The National Hockey League season runs from October through April, with about 40 home games each season. Ticket prices range from $13 to $35. For more information, call 781-5300. Tickets can also be ordered through Dialtix at 291-7600. *Note:* The Blues plan to move to a new downtown arena, at Market and 14th streets, in fall 1994.

HORSE RACING **Fairmont Park** is a horse-racing track in Collinsville, IL, just a 15-minute drive from the Gateway Arch. Thoroughbreds race from March to November, while harness racing takes place from November to the end of December. Approximately five race cards are held each week. General admission to the grandstand costs $2, while admission to the Club House costs $3. On Tuesday, admission to the grandstand or Club House is only $1. To reach Fairmont Park from downtown St. Louis, cross the Mississippi River on the I-70 bridge, go to the Black Lane Exit, then turn left on U.S. 40. For more information on horse racing and schedules, call 436-1516 in St. Louis or 618/345-4300 in Illinois.

RECREATION

Forest Park was established in the early 1870s with nearly 1,300 acres. At one time well outside city limits, it is now completely enveloped by the city and is only a 10-minute drive from downtown. The site of the 1904 World's Fair, it contains a number of the city's most famous attractions, including the St. Louis Art Museum and the St. Louis Zoological Park. It also has a number of recreational facilities, including three golf courses, a tennis center, handball courts, a Perrier fitness parcourse, a playground, and biking and jogging trails. The **Forest Park Municipal Golf Course** (tel. 367-1337) has an 18-hole, 70-par public course, with green fees ranging from $10 to $14 on weekdays and $11 to $17 on weekends. Golf Clubs are available for rent for $14. Carts for two players are $18.

For more information on recreational facilities in St. Louis, contact the **St. Louis Convention and Visitors Commission** (tel. 421-1023 or toll free 800/247-9791).

CHAPTER 8

STROLLING AROUND ST. LOUIS

1. DOWNTOWN
2. CENTRAL WEST END

As with several major U.S. cities, particularly in the Midwest, St. Louis is best traversed by car. However, the city has a few areas that warrant exploration on foot, notably the downtown area and the Central West End. (*Note:* You'll find more details in Chapter 7 about some of the attractions mentioned below.)

WALKING TOUR 1 — Downtown

Start: Gateway Arch, between Memorial Drive and Lenore K. Sullivan Boulevard.
Finish: Union Station, 18th and Market streets.
Time: Approximately two hours, not including museum and shopping stops.
Best Times: Weekdays, when downtown is livelier.
Worst Times: Weekends, when the Gateway Arch is crowded, particularly in the afternoon.

A stroll around St. Louis's downtown brings you to the city's most famous attractions, including the Gateway Arch, Union Station, and Busch Memorial Stadium, as well as the best of St. Louis shopping. Although the total walking time of this tour is about two hours, you'll probably want to spend much longer—perhaps the entire day—exploring downtown's many offerings.

FROM THE GATEWAY ARCH TO LACLEDE'S LANDING

1. **The Gateway Arch** would be difficult to overlook—630 feet tall, it towers high above the St. Louis skyline and is the nation's tallest monument. Erected as a reminder of the westward expansion of the United States, the Arch is situated in Jefferson National Expansion Memorial National Historic Site, an expanse of green and artificial lakes. For the tram ride to the top of the Arch, try to arrive as early in the morning as possible, since lines are sometimes very long. Be sure, too, to visit the:

2. **Museum of Westward Expansion,** located underground beneath the Arch, and to see the film *Monument to the Dream,* about the construction of the Arch. (See p. 100 for details.)

   There are steps leading down from the Arch to the Mississippi riverfront, which is where St. Louis's modern history began. Among the several boats moored here, the:

3. ***Huck Finn, Tom Sawyer,*** and ***Becky Thatcher,*** operated

by Gateway Riverboat Cruises, leave every 45 minutes for an hour's cruise along the river.

REFUELING STOPS   If the ride to the top of the Arch or a riverboat cruise leave you hungry, you can refresh yourself with a meal aboard the **Lt. Robert E. Lee,** a boat moored near the Arch offering steaks and seafood in an atmosphere reminiscent of the old sternwheelers that once plied the river. If you're looking for something less formal, there are fast-food outlets occupying boats moored along the riverfront, including **McDonald's** and **Burger King.**

The northern end of Jefferson National Expansion Memorial National Historic Site is bounded by ancient-looking:

4. **Eads Bridge,** built in 1874 by James Eads. It was the first bridge to fully span the Mississippi River at the middle of its run toward the Gulf; it was also the first arched steel truss bridge in the world. Walking under the bridge, you'll find yourself at:

5. **Laclede's Landing,** a neighborhood of restored 19th-century brick warehouses and cobblestone streets. One of St. Louis's best-known entertainment centers, it also encompasses some shops, restaurants, and a couple tourist attractions. If you have children, stop by the:

6. **Dental Health Theatre,** 727 N. 1st St., a small exhibition designed to teach children the importance of teeth and how to take care of them. If you've enjoyed feeding coins into pinball machines or video games, you'll want to visit the nearby:

7. **National Video Game and Coin-Op Museum,** 801 N. 2nd St. It showcases some 100 classic video games, landmark pinball machines, and other coin-operated amusements, all available for play.

   I suggest you also wander along North 2nd Street, North 1st Street, and Lucas and Morgan streets, the heart of Laclede's Landing.

REFUELING STOP   Most establishments in Laclede's Landing don't open until late afternoon, but one open for lunch is **Kennedy's 2nd Street Co.,** 612 N. 2nd St., located in a restored warehouse with brick walls, tall ceilings, and wood-and-brick floors. It offers burgers, salads, and sandwiches for lunch and beer throughout the day. Live alternative and progressive music can be heard in the evening.

FROM LACLEDE'S LANDING TO BUSCH STADIUM   From Laclede's Landing, take Morgan Street west, underneath a highway overpass, past the Days Inn at the Arch, to 6th Street. Turn left, where you'll soon see the:

8. **St. Louis Centre,** which opened in 1985 as the largest urban enclosed shopping mall in the United States. (It's since been out-distanced.) Covering two city blocks between 6th and 7th streets and Washington and Locust, it offers four levels of shopping and dining. Its food court, by the way, is on the fourth floor. After walking through the St. Louis Centre and exiting

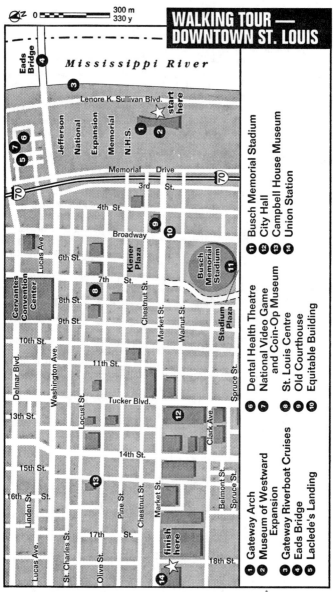

**WALKING TOUR —
DOWNTOWN ST. LOUIS**

Mississippi River

Eads Bridge

Lenore K. Sullivan Blvd.

start here

Jefferson National Expansion Memorial N.H.S.

Memorial   Drive

3rd   St.

4th St.

Broadway

Kiener Plaza

Lucas Ave.

6th St.

7th   St.

8th St.

9th St.

Cervantes Convention Center

Chestnut St.

Market St.

Walnut St.

Busch Memorial Stadium

Stadium Plaza

Delmar Blvd.

Washington Ave.

10th St.

11th St.

Tucker Blvd.

Locust St.

13th St.

Clark Ave.

14th St.

15th St.

Belmont St.

16th   St.

Linden St.

Pine St.

Chestnut St.

Market St.

Spruce St.

17th   St.

finish here

Lucas Ave.

St. Charles St.

Olive St.

18th St.

❶ Gateway Arch
❷ Museum of Westward Expansion
❸ Gateway Riverboat Cruises
❹ Eads Bridge
❺ Laclede's Landing
❻ Dental Health Theatre
❼ National Video Game and Coin-Op Museum
❽ St. Louis Centre
❾ Old Courthouse
❿ Equitable Building
⓫ Busch Memorial Stadium
⓬ City Hall
⓭ Campbell House Museum
⓮ Union Station

300 m
330 y

N

0

through the Famous-Barr department store, one of its anchors, you'll find yourself on Olive Street, where you should take a left. Olive Street is one of downtown's most important thoroughfares and is lined with office buildings. Walk two blocks to 4th Street and then take a right, and within a few minutes you'll find yourself at the:

9. Old Courthouse, 11 N. 4th St. Built in 1862 in Greek Revival style, it's managed by the National Park Service and contains a museum dedicated to the history of St. Louis, plus a gift shop with books on St. Louis.

Leaving the Old Courthouse through its back-door exit, go out onto Broadway and take a left, crossing Market Street. On your left, at 10 S. Broadway, is the:

10. Equitable Building, where on the third floor you'll find the main office of the St. Louis Convention and Visitors Commission. You can stop here for brochures, maps, and other information on St. Louis. Walking one block farther south on Broadway, you come to Walnut Street, with its unmistakable:

11. Busch Memorial Stadium, home of the St. Louis Cardinals. Baseball fans know that the Cardinals have won 15 National League pennants and 9 World Championships, all remembered in the St. Louis Cardinals Hall of Fame, located between gates 5 and 6 of the stadium on Walnut Street. There's a gift shop here, where you can purchase everything imaginable with the Cardinals logo on it. If you wish, you can also join a tour of Busch Stadium. Across the street from Busch Memorial Stadium is another hall of fame honoring another American tradition, the National Bowling Hall of Fame, at 8th and Walnut, where you can even bowl on an old-fashioned alley operated by pin setters.

REFUELING STOPS A five-minute walk away, **Top of the Riverfront** is a revolving restaurant providing a great view. Located atop the Clarion Hotel at 200 S. 4th St., it offers everything from sandwiches to fresh fish for lunch. A bit closer to the stadium is **Premio's,** 701 Market St., a modern restaurant popular with downtown businesspeople for its contemporary Italian cuisine. If the weather's fine, you may wish to dine on its outdoor patio, with an unobstructed view of the Old Courthouse and the Gateway Arch. For the budget-conscious, there's **Miss Hullings,** 1103 Locust St., a cafeteria serving home-cooked foods. It's located about halfway between Busch Memorial Stadium and the next stop on your tour, Campbell House.

FROM BUSCH MEMORIAL STADIUM TO UNION STATION From Busch Memorial Stadium, return to Market Street, where you should head west, away from the Gateway Arch. On the left corner of 12th Street (also called Tucker Memorial Boulevard) is:

12. City Hall, built as an exact copy of the Hôtel de Ville (city hall) in Paris. Take a right onto 12th Street and walk four blocks to Locust, where you should take another left. Within a few minutes you'll arrive at the:

13. Campbell House Museum, 1508 Locust St., built in 1851 as a private residence in what used to be one of St. Louis's most exclusive neighborhoods. The home is decorated almost entirely with original furnishings, providing valuable insight into life in the city in the 1800s.

Follow 15th street back to Market Street and continue walking west. After passing the main post office, you'll come upon:

14. **Union Station** on your left, at 18th and Market streets. There's no mistaking its fortresslike facade topped by a clock tower, behind which stretches what was once the largest and busiest passenger-rail terminal in the world. Today it houses a wonderland of shops, cafés, and restaurants, as well as a hotel and even an artificial lake. Since the shops stay open late here, it's a good place to end the day.

A FINAL REFUELING STOP   There are so many places to eat and drink in Union Station that the problem is not *finding* one but *deciding* on one. For elegant dining there's **Station Grille,** Union Station's former dining hall, as well as **Dierdorf & Hart's** both of which serve steaks and seafood. **Boston's** specializes in seafood, including lobster, at affordable prices. **Houlihan's Old Place** serves beer, cocktails, and food, with outdoor seating beside the lake; there's also the upper-level **Picnic Express,** a food court with vendors selling a variety of fast foods.

WALKING TOUR 2 —— Central West End

Start: North Euclid Avenue at Lindell Boulevard.
Finish: North Euclid Avenue at Washington Boulevard.
Time: Approximately one hour, not including shopping and dining stops.
Best Times: Monday through Saturday in the afternoon, when shops are open.
Worst Times: Sunday or Monday, when some galleries are closed.

Located a few miles west of downtown and bordered by Forest Park, the Central West End was settled at the turn of the century by the upper crust of St. Louis society. The elegant homes here still remain, now accompanied by a lively mix of unusual clothing shops, galleries, antiques shops, restaurants, and bars, making it a great place for strolling and people-watching. Its center is Euclid Avenue and a few side streets.

FROM NORTH EUCLID AVENUE AT LINDELL BOULEVARD STREET TO MARYLAND AVENUE   Head north on North Euclid Avenue and within a minute you'll arrive at the first of many antiques shops in the Central West End:

1. **Hirschfeld Galleries,** 234 N. Euclid Ave. Established in 1931, this family-owned shop offers rare books and antiques.
    The next intersection, Euclid and Maryland avenues, is the heart of the Central West End, with several sidewalk cafés perfect for whiling away an afternoon watching the world go by. If you turn right onto Maryland Avenue, you'll soon see:
2. **Four Seasons West,** 4657 Maryland Ave., dealing in French, English, and Chinese furniture and decorative objects from the 17th through the 19th century. Almost next door is:

3. **Saint Louis Bread Company,** 4651 Maryland Ave., considered St. Louis's best bakery, with a wide assortment of breads ranging from sourdough to rye and baguettes.

   Retrace your steps, cross back over Euclid Avenue, head in the other direction on Maryland Avenue, and you'll see Maryland Plaza, a small roundabout with a fountain. Here you'll find one of St. Louis's foremost galleries:

4. **The Greenburg Gallery,** at 44 Maryland Plaza. A contemporary art gallery focusing on post–World War II American and European paintings, sculpture, and drawings, it has carried works by Andy Warhol, Georgia O'Keeffe, Alexander Calder, Roy Lichtenstein, Helen Frankenthaler, Joel Shapiro, and many more.

   Heading back toward Euclid Avenue, you'll soon see on your right:

5. **Salamander,** 8 Maryland Plaza, a women's store specializing in ethnic clothing using natural fibers, including fashions from India, Indonesia, Guatemala, Morocco, and Nepal.

REFUELING STOPS   Saint Louis Bread Co., described above, sells sandwiches using its delicious breads, which you can eat at one of its indoor or outdoor tables. **Culpeppers,** on the corner of Euclid and Maryland avenues, is a simple neighborhood bar famous throughout St. Louis for its spicy chicken wings. The nearby ✪ **Pasta House Company,** 309 N. Euclid Ave., offers more than two dozen inexpensive pasta dishes in a pleasant setting that was once the lobby of a hotel. It, too, has outdoor seating.

FROM MARYLAND AVENUE TO MCPHERSON   Across the street from the Pasta House Company is:

6. **Boxers,** 310 N. Euclid. As the name implies, it's a shop carrying mostly boxer shorts and underwear—stop here to buy a unique present for the guy who has everything! Down the street from Boxers is another interesting shop:

7. **The Elephant Walk,** 330 N. Euclid, which specializes in African collectibles, including art, clothing, and jewelry. Continuing north on Euclid, you'll soon come to:

8. **Pershing Place** and **Hortense Place,** two residential streets lined with elegant turn-of-the-century homes. Although they are marked with a gate that says "Private Road," you can stroll down them to see how the other half lived at the time of the 1904 World's Fair, with homes built in almost every style that socialites could imagine, from Italian Renaissance to Victorian.

   Return to reality on Euclid Avenue and continue north to:

9. **Kopperman's,** 386 N. Euclid Ave., a grocer's that has been serving the needs of the neighborhood since 1897. Stock up on picnic supplies or enjoy a drink at one of its outdoor tables.

10. **Rothschild's Antiques,** 398 N. Euclid, is packed with furniture, lamps, stained-glass windows, watches, jewelry, and junk. Take a right onto McPherson, and there are more antiques shops. First, though, you may wish to satisfy a sweet tooth with a stop at:

Central
West End

ST. LOUIS

❶ Hirschfield Galleries
❷ Four Seasons West
❸ Saint Louis Bread
Company
❹ Greenburg Gallery
❺ Salamander
❻ Boxers
❼ Elephant Walk
❽ Pershing Place
❾ Hortense Place
❿ Kopperman's
⓫ Rothschild's
Antiques
⓬ Karl Bissinger
French Connections
⓭ West End Gallery
McPherson Antique
Gallery
⓮ Alice's Vintage Clothing
⓯ Fellenz Antiques
⓰ Euclid Galleries

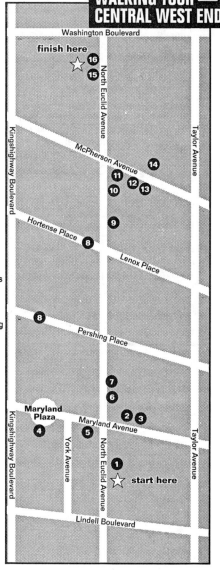

11. Karl Bissinger French Connections, a St. Louis company famous for its chocolate creations special to each season, including Valentine's Day, Easter, and Christmas. The Bissinger family, which immigrated from France, has been making chocolate for 300 years. Not far from the chocolate shop is the:

12. West End Gallery, 4732 McPherson, actually three shops in one, housing an antiques shop, a florist, and an art jeweler.

13. McPherson Antique Gallery, next door, offers four floors of antiques, collectibles, and curios, including furniture and brass hardware.

14. **Alice's Vintage Clothing,** across the street at 4703 McPherson, is crammed with men's and women's clothes from 1900 to 1960. Back on Euclid Avenue, you'll find two more shops worth checking out:

15. **Fellenz Antiques,** 439 N. Euclid, is an antiques shop specializing in architectural artifacts, including old doors, mantels, stained-glass windows, moldings, spindles, wood carvings, and old brass door hardware. Farther north is:

16. **Euclid Galleries,** 449 N. Euclid, which in one building features six different vendors selling antiques—including jewelry, furniture, cut glass, vintage clothing, and more.

FINAL REFUELING STOPS **Balaban's,** 405 N. Euclid Ave., was a forerunner of the Central West End's urban revitalization, and it still sets the pace with its French and continental cuisine. Equally well known is **Duff's,** 392 N. Euclid Ave., a casual and friendly restaurant with a menu that changes with the seasons. For a beer with a difference, head for **Dressel's Pub,** 419 N. Euclid, a true Welsh pub with imported beers from Europe and such pub fare as Welsh vegetarian pie and ploughman's lunch. This is a great place to end the day and herald the evening.

If you have a craving for Chinese food, try the bargain buffet lunches and dinners at **Silk Road,** near the corner of Euclid and Washington Boulevard. You might also enjoy **Grappa,** a trendy restaurant that features innovative American cuisine.

CHAPTER 9

ST. LOUIS AREA SHOPPING

1. ANTIQUES

2. ART & CRAFTS GALLERIES

3. MALLS & SHOPPING CENTERS

• **FROMMER'S SMART SHOPPER**

Shopping in St. Louis does not differ much from that in any other major U.S. city, with the same chains selling the same merchandise. However, in St. Louis it's *where* you shop that makes a difference: How many other cities have shopping centers that match the scale of Union Station? How many other cities have more than a dozen major shopping malls or a street devoted entirely to antiques shops? And if you're looking for something truly unique, you can find that, too—from arts and crafts produced by local artists and artisans to antiques and collectibles. In short, the best of St. Louis shopping is its shopping centers, such as Union Station; its many antiques shops; and its art galleries.

Shopping hours vary throughout the city. Downtown shops are generally open Monday through Saturday from about 9 or 10am to about 5:30 or 6pm. Shopping centers stay open longer, from about 10am to 9 or 10pm on Monday to Saturday and noon to 5 or 6pm on Sunday. A 5.925% tax will be added to the price of purchased goods.

1. ANTIQUES

ANTIQUE ROW ON CHEROKEE STREET   Located south of downtown, not far from the Anheuser-Busch Brewery, Cherokee Street is St. Louis's premier hunting ground for antiques, known to locals as Antique Row. Surrounded by an older neighborhood of two- and three-story brick homes, it boasts nearly 5 blocks (from 1900 to 2300 Cherokee Street) of more than 50 antiques shops, the oldest of which opened some 45 years ago. Most deal in 18th- to 20th-century collectibles and antiques, although some specialize in such items as furniture, art deco objects, neon, jewelry, and door handles and knobs.

Since there are so many shops, the best strategy is to cover first one side of the street and then the other. Be sure to pick up a free pamphlet on Antique Row, available at most Antique Row shops or at the St. Louis Tourist Office. It lists each shop's address, telephone number, and open hours.

Hours vary, but most shops are **open** Mon through Fri from 10 or 11am to 4 or 5pm and Sun from noon to 5pm. Some shops are open daily, but others are closed on Mon or Tues. The best shopping days are Thurs through Sat.

CENTRAL WEST END   There are approximately a dozen antiques shops in the fashionable Central West End, most clustered along North Euclid Avenue or on such side streets as Maryland Avenue and McPherson. Among these are the following:

EUCLID GALLERIES, 449 N. Euclid. Tel. 454-9330.

Located on the corner of Washington Boulevard and North Euclid, this older building houses six vendors selling everything from jewelry and antique furniture to cut glass and vintage clothing. **Open:** Tues to Sun from 10:30am to 5pm.

THE FOUR SEASONS WEST GALLERY, 4657 Maryland Ave. Tel. 361-2929.

This shop, in business since 1965, specializes in fine French, English, and Chinese furniture dating from the 17th century to the 19th century and also cut glass and such items as perfume bottles and paperweights—in all price ranges. **Open:** Mon, Wed, and Fri from 10am to 4pm, Tues from 1 to 4pm, and Sat from 10am to 5pm.

MCPHERSON ANTIQUE GALLERY, 4728 McPherson. Tel. 361-0551.

Although a bit overpriced, the antiques, collectibles, and curios here cover four floors and include a large supply of furniture, china, glassware, and crystal. **Open** Mon through Sat from 10am to 5:30pm and Sun from 11am to 5:30pm.

ROTHSCHILD'S ANTIQUES, 398 N. Euclid Ave. Tel. 361-4870.

This shop is packed with an eclectic mix of antiques and junk, with lots in between. Furniture, watches, jewelry, lamps, mounted animal heads, old radios, stained-glass windows, paintings, and more vie for the shopper's attention. Worth a browse. **Open** Mon through Thurs from 10am to 6pm, Fri and Sat from 10am to 10pm, and Sun from 11am to 6pm.

WEST END GALLERY, 4732 McPherson. Tel. 361-1059.

This is actually several stores in one, containing antiques shops and a custom-made jewelry shop. The antiques are mostly from the 18th and the 19th centuries and include furniture, silver, china, and accessories. **Open:** Mon from 11am to 5pm, Tues through Fri from 10am to 6pm, and Sat from 10am to 5pm.

ST. CHARLES   Located just northwest of St. Louis, off I-70, St. Charles was the site of Missouri's first state capitol. Today it contains the state's largest National Register Historic District, with many mid-1800s buildings authentically restored. The center of St. Charles is Main Street, where you'll find a few antiques shops as well as the St.

IMPRESSIONS

As compared with the world, St. Louis has the largest railroad station, hardware store, tobacco factories, lead works, brickyards and stove and range factories. As compared with the United States, St. Louis has the largest brewery, shoe factory, saddlery market, street-car factories, hardwood lumber market, and the finest street cars and botanical gardens. . . .
—CHARLES T. LOGAN (1897)

Charles Tourism Center, 230 S. Main, offering brochures and a map of the city.

However, the real focal point of antiques shopping in St. Charles is Frenchtown, located a few blocks north of Main Street on North 2nd Street; it offers 10 blocks of antiques shops selling American furniture, glassware, stoneware, quilts, baskets, jewelry, old toys, and collectibles. Most shops are **open** daily from 10am to 4pm. Some are closed on Mon.

2. ART & CRAFTS GALLERIES

There are more than 60 art galleries listed with the St. Louis Gallery Association, covering everything from local talent to international greats. For a copy of the Association's *Gallery Guide,* published twice a year, contact the **St. Louis Gallery Association,** P.O. Box 24226, St. Louis, MO 63130. The list that follows includes some of St. Louis's best-known galleries, plus a few of my personal favorites.

ART ST. LOUIS, St. Louis Centre, 515 N. 6th St. Tel. 241-4810.

Created in 1986 as a nonprofit organization to foster a supportive climate for the visual arts of St. Louis and regional artists, the St. Louis Artists Coalition lists more than 600 members, including professional artists, educators, designers, and art patrons. In addition to sponsoring each autumn a juried exhibition by St. Louis artists, it also stages changing exhibits by both established and emerging local artists in its first-floor gallery in the downtown St. Louis Centre shopping complex. If you want to know about the art scene in St. Louis, this place is a good start. **Open** Mon through Fri from 10am to 6pm and Sat from 10am to 4pm.

ATRIUM GALLERY, Old Post Office Building, 815 Olive St. Tel. 621-1066.

Serving both the private sector and the corporate market, this downtown commercial gallery represents contemporary artists who are active regionally and nationally. In addition to one-person shows and occasional group or theme shows, it maintains a large on-site inventory of canvases, oil and acrylic, mixed-media pieces, paper pieces, fabric works, prints, photography, and three-dimensional work. **Open** Mon through Fri from 10am to 5pm and Sat from noon to 5pm.

COMPONERE, GALLERY OF ART AND FASHION, 6509 Delmar Blvd., University City. Tel. 721-1181.

This is a fun gallery/boutique specializing in art and fashion, including wearable art, crafts, jewelry, glass, pottery, furniture, and paintings. Its collections—about 90% from local artists—are fun, funky, eclectic, and unique, making it a good place to shop for one-of-a-kind gifts. **Open** Mon through Thurs from 11am to 5pm, Fri and Sat from 11am to 9pm, and Sun from 1 to 5pm.

CRAFT ALLIANCE, 6640 Delmar Blvd., University City. Tel. 725-1151 or 725-1177.

Founded by six artisans in 1964, Craft Alliance is dedicated to exhibitions of contemporary crafts as well as to art education in the St. Louis area. Besides offering classes and workshops in everything from ceramics, weaving, painting, and metalworking, it stages nine major exhibitions per year. The work of local, national, and international artists includes contemporary and avant-garde crafts made from ceramics, wood, glass, fiber, metals, and more, used to create everything from furniture and baskets to vases and jewelry. A beautiful gallery. **Open** Tues through Fri from noon to 5pm and Sat from 10am to 5pm.

THE FORUM, 555 Washington Ave. Tel. 421-3791.

The Forum was founded in 1980 by a group of civic and arts leaders to address arts and humanities issues with a variety of exhibits and programs. Located downtown, it is a multipurpose center for the arts, with an emphasis on contemporary, historic, and civic themes. With the goal of reaching as large an audience as possible, it has dealt with a wide range of subjects—including fashion, photography, architecture, advertising art, and furniture. The Forum also sponsors musical, theatrical, and educational events. **Open** Mon through Fri from 11am to 5pm.

GALLERY AT COCA, 524 Trinity Ave., University City. Tel. 725-6555.

COCA (Center of Contemporary Arts) offers classes in dance, drama, mime, martial arts, poetry, creative writing, music, and the visual arts. Its noncommercial gallery presents local and national artists whose work is on the "cutting edge" of the art world, including mixed media, printmaking, and photography. **Open** Tues through Sat from noon to 5pm.

GREENBURG GALLERY, 44 Maryland Plaza. Tel. 361-7600.

This is one of St. Louis's premier contemporary art galleries, focusing on postwar American and European paintings as well as drawings, sculpture, and ceramics. Dealing primarily with originals rather than with prints or graphics, it is a member of the Art Dealers Association of America and represents established artists of international stature, including Georgia O'Keeffe, Andy Warhol, Alexander Calder, Frank Stella, Willem DeKooning, Henry Moore, Helen Frankenthaler, Joel Shapiro, Roy Lichtenstein, and Ken Price. It is located in the Central West End. **Open** Tues through Sat from 10am to 5pm.

LITHOS', 6301 B. Delmar Blvd., University City. Tel. 862-0674.

This gallery features the works of top black artists from all over the country as well as artists from Africa and the Caribbean. All types of media are on display, including originals, prints, silkscreens, and even posters. **Open** Mon through Fri from 10am to 7:30pm, Sat from 10am to 6:30pm, and Sun from 1 to 5pm.

PHILIP SAMUELS FINE ART, 8112 Maryland Ave., Clayton. Tel. 727-2444.

This upscale gallery carries American contemporary art, specializing in pop art. In addition to handling works by Andy Warhol, Alexander Calder, and other well-known artists, it serves as the international representative for St. Louis artists Ernest Trova and Michael Rubin. **Open** Mon through Fri from 9:30am to 4:30pm.

3. MALLS & SHOPPING CENTERS

DOWNTOWN

ST. LOUIS CENTRE, Bounded by Locust, Seventh St., Washington and Sixth Sts. Tel. 231-5522.

Upon its opening in 1985, the St. Louis Centre was hailed as the largest downtown enclosed shopping mall in the country (it no longer holds this honor). It covers four levels, the fourth containing the food court popular with downtown office workers. All together there are more than 100 shops, with Dillard's and Famous-Barr serving as anchors. Interesting shops include Abercrombie & Fitch, with upscale clothing, and St. Louis Stuff, with souvenirs of St. Louis, and there are also bookstores, boutiques, shoe stores, jewelry outlets, and much more. **Open** Mon through Sat from 10am to 6pm and Sun from noon to 5pm.

UNION STATION, 18th and Market Sts. Tel. 421-4314.

Any city would be proud of Union Station, so successfully has it been transformed from the nation's largest rail terminal into a marketplace and showplace. A National Historic Landmark, it's big, light, airy, and packed with all kinds of things to do, from shopping to dining to nighttime entertainment. Union Station has more than 100 specialty shops and restaurants, including such notable shops as the Disney Store, Eddie Bauer, Banana Republic, Crabtree and Evelyn, and the Great Train Store. The Nature Company and Brookstone always have lovely gift items on display. Missouri Peddlers has a small outlet here selling items crafted by Missouri artisans. It would be difficult to pass by the Fudgery, where employees sing, dance, and give entertaining demonstrations as they go about their work making fudge. **Open** Mon through Thurs from 10am to 9pm, Fri and Sat from 10am to 10pm, and Sun from 11am to 7pm.

ELSEWHERE

ST. LOUIS GALLERIA, Clayton Rd. and Brentwood Blvd., Clayton/Richmond Heights. Tel. 863-5500.

This is one of St. Louis's newer, smarter shopping malls, with a 100-foot-high atrium, an Italian marble interior, and three levels of shops. Dillard's, Famous-Barr and Lord & Taylor are the anchor shops, backed by more than 180 specialty shops featuring boutiques, home accessories, gifts, jewelry, books, and more—including Eddie Bauer, FAO Schwarz, The Body Shop, The Nature Company, Brooks Brothers, and Abercrombie Fitch. **Open** Mon through Sat from 10am to 9:30pm and Sun from noon to 6pm.

PLAZA FRONTENAC, Lindbergh Blvd. and Clayton Rd., Frontenac, MO. Tel. 432-0604.

Some call this the Rodeo Drive of the St. Louis area. At any rate, Plaza Frontenac, just west of Ladue, contains some 70 stores, including Neiman Marcus, Saks Fifth Avenue, Gucci, Burberrys, Ralph Lauren, Waterford Wedgwood, Bruno Magli, Williams-Sonoma, Rodier of Paris, and Leppert Roos—not to mention Banana Republic, Laura Ashley, Mondi, and Victoria's Secret. **Open** Mon through Fri from 10am to 9pm, Sat from 10am to 6pm, and Sun from noon to 5pm.

NORTHWEST PLAZA, Lindbergh Blvd. at St. Charles Rock Rd., St. Ann, MO. Tel. 298-0071.

Located only five minutes from Lambert–St. Louis Airport, this shopping center underwent complete renovation in the late 1980s and emerged as one of the largest in the city. It's the only St. Louis mall with four anchors—Dillard's, Famous-Barr, J. C. Penney, and Sears—and it also boasts more than 200 specialty shops. It also contains a family-entertainment center with video games, miniature golf, and a movie theater with nine screens. **Open** Mon through Sat from 10am to 9:30pm and Sun from noon to 6pm.

 FROMMER'S SMART SHOPPER

1. Use cash and traveler's checks when you possibly can; you will tend to overspend with a credit card.
2. Take advantage of "Sale" signs posted in windows, just as you would at home.
3. Look for discount shopping coupons in tourist booklets and newspapers.
4. Comparison shop before buying, especially in shopping centers or malls where there are many stores under one roof.

CHAPTER 10

ST. LOUIS AREA NIGHTS

1. THE PERFORMING ARTS
2. THE CLUB & MUSIC SCENE
3. THE BAR SCENE
4. MOVIES

No matter where your interests lie in evening entertainment, you're bound to find satisfaction in the St. Louis area's night scene: a Broadway production at the restored Fox Theatre, an outdoor concert underneath the stars at The Muny, or a performance of the St. Louis Symphony Orchestra. One of the most exciting developments in St. Louis's nightlife is the revitalization of North Grand Boulevard, once the heart of entertainment from the late 19th century to the mid-1950s and known as the "Broadway of the Midwest." Home of the Fox Theatre, Black Repertory Theater, and Powell Symphony Hall, the district will eventually house nine theaters by the turn of the 21st century.

If blues are your style, you have a choice of more than two dozen clubs in St. Louis and its environs that feature blues or rhythm and blues on a regular basis, ranking the area behind only Chicago and New Orleans in terms of the availability and quality of live performances. In the St. Louis area you can also listen to jazz, traditional Irish music, alternative and progressive bands, and even Top 40. But the most astounding thing about St. Louis is that many of its clubs are absolutely free.

To find out what's happening where, consult the entertainment pages of the *St. Louis Post-Dispatch* morning newspaper. Two other great sources are the weekly *Riverfront Times,* distributed free at many restaurants and establishments, and the monthly *St. Louis* magazine, available at newsstands.

1. THE PERFORMING ARTS

MAJOR PERFORMING-ARTS COMPANIES

OPERA

OPERA THEATRE OF ST. LOUIS, Loretto Hilton Center, 130 Edgar Rd., Webster University. Tel. 961-0171 for information, 961-0644 for tickets.

Opera Theatre of St. Louis has been presenting opera, both classic and new, for more than 15 years. All productions are sung in English, accompanied by the St. Louis Symphony Orchestra. There are usually four operas per season, which runs from May to June.

Prices: $9–$54.

CLASSICAL & ORCHESTRAL MUSIC

ST. LOUIS SYMPHONY ORCHESTRA, Powell Symphony Hall, 718 N. Grand Blvd. Tel. 533-2500 or 534-1700 for box office; toll free inside Missouri 800/231-1880, outside Missouri 800/232-1880.

Founded in 1880, the St. Louis Symphony Orchestra is the nation's second-oldest orchestra and is now under the dynamic direction of conductor Leonard Slatkin. A Grammy Award winner and recently named by *Time* magazine as one of the top two orchestras in the country, it plays more than 240 concerts yearly—from classical to pop, chamber, and educational.

Prices: Tickets vary; orchestral concerts $11–$40.

THEATER COMPANIES

BLACK REPERTORY COMPANY, 634 N. Grand Blvd. Tel. 534-3807.

The St. Louis Black Repertory Company was founded in 1976 to provide platforms for theater, dance, and other creative expressions from the African-American perspective, in an effort to heighten cultural awareness in its audience. Six main stage productions are offered each year in a season that runs from September through May.

Prices: $7–$25.

REPERTORY THEATRE OF ST. LOUIS, Loretto Hilton Center, 130 Edgar Rd., Webster University. Tel. 968-4925.

This professional, nonprofit live theatrical organization seeks to engage its audience in the thrill of live theater with its wide variety of classic and contemporary plays, musicals, comedies, and dramas. Each season, which runs from September through April, brings six full-length plays, of which three are new.

Prices: $9–$25.

DANCE

DANCE ST. LOUIS, 149 Edgar Rd. Tel. 534-5000 or 968-4341.

Dance St. Louis brings in national and international companies who perform traditional and contemporary ballet and modern dance. Past performances have featured the State Ballet of Missouri, the Martha Graham Dance Company, the Alvin Ailey American Dance Theater, and the American Ballet Theatre. Performances are staged at Fox Theatre, Edison Theatre, and at other university theaters, and the season runs from October through May.

Prices: $15–$35.

ST. LOUIS BALLET, Administrative office, 634 N. Grand Blvd., 10th Floor, Suite E. Tel. 652-7711 or 889-6543 for box office.

St. Louis Ballet is a professional company performing traditional and contemporary dance, under the artistic direction of Ludmila Dokoudovsky and Antoni Zalewski. Plans include the staging of many of the great but neglected ballets of the early and post–Diaghilev/Ballets Russe period with the help of artists who danced in these productions. Performances, held from September through April, are given at Edison Theatre, Mallinckrodt Center, Washington University Campus, and other stages around town.

Prices: Usually about $15.

OTHER THEATERS & CONCERT FACILITIES

EDISON THEATRE, Mallinckrodt Center, Washington University, University City, MO. Tel. 935-6543.

Edison Theatre presents high-caliber performing artists in plays, dances, and concerts from throughout the country. It prides itself on presenting events that would not otherwise be brought to St. Louis, including contemporary and avant-garde theater productions and performances of the St. Louis Ballet.

Prices: Usually $18 adults, $12 senior citizens, $10 students.

FOX THEATRE, 527 N. Grand Blvd. Tel. 534-1678 or 534-1111 for tickets.

When the Fabulous Fox opened in 1929, it was considered one of the three most lavishly beautiful movie houses in the country. Completely restored in 1982 to its former neo-Byzantine glory, it has 4,500 seats, a 106-foot-high ceiling with a 2,000-pound chandelier made from 2,264 pieces of jeweled glass, and a giant four-manual Wurlitzer organ, one of five of its type ever built. The Fox features Broadway and off-Broadway productions as well as concerts by rock, pop, country and jazz performers. From September through May, it serves as the home of the Muny's Broadway musicals.

Tours: Tues, Thurs, and Sat by appointment at 10:30am; cost is $2.50 adults, $1.50 children under 12.

Prices: Usually between $5 and $35.

THE MUNY, Forest Park. Tel. 361-1900 or 534-1111 for information.

The Muny is a huge 12,000-seat open-air amphitheater in beautiful Forest Park. From June through August it stages Broadway musicals as well as rock and pop concerts. From September through May, The Muny presents a Broadway Series at the Fox Theatre.

Prices: Generally between $5 and $30.

RIVERPORT AMPHITHEATRE, 14141 Riverport Dr., Maryland Heights, MO. Tel. 298-9944.

Opened in 1991, this huge amphitheater has 7,000 reserved seats, with room for an additional 13,000 concertgoers on a specially designed grassy hill that allows unobstructed views of the 5,000-square-foot stage. Its state-of-the-art sound system incorporates custom-built speakers, strategically placed throughout the complex, that send clear and clean music to every fan in the audience. In addition, four video screens allow all concertgoers to experience a front-row view of such top-name entertainers as Rod Stewart, Paul Simon, Sting, Don Henly, and Bonnie Raitt. It's located near the I-70 and I-270 interchange, off Earth City Expressway.

Prices: Usually $10–$30.

DINNER THEATERS

BISSELL MANSION RESTAURANT, 4426 Randall Place. Tel. 533-9830.

Who's done it will keep you guessing as you participate in this Mystery Dinner Theater. Upon your arrival at the Bissell Mansion, built in the 1820s, you'll receive an identity, with murderers and suspects chosen randomly from the audience. The mystery unfolds as you partake a five-course dinner, including wine and your choice of three entrées. The shows change with the seasons, including, naturally, a Halloween show. Bissell Mansion is located off I-70 at the Grand Avenue exit, about 3½ miles from the Gateway Arch. Reservations are required. Incidentally, Bissell Mansion is also open for lunch and dinner throughout the week, when you can dine without having to wonder who did it. Open Friday through Saturday from 7 to 10:30pm and Sunday from 5 to 8:30pm.

Prices: Fri $27.95, Sat $30.95, Sun $25.95.

NATCHEZ RIVER REVUE, _Lt. Robert E. Lee,_ 100 S. Leonor K. Sullivan Blvd. Tel. 241-1282.

In the tradition of the old riverboats, a music revue is featured aboard the _Lt. Robert E. Lee,_ moored on the Mississippi River in the shadow of the Gateway Arch. The professional cast serves double time as the serving staff. Summer shows are given Tuesday through Sunday, and winter shows are given Thursday through Saturday; call for exact show times.

Prices: Show and dinner $18.95 adults, $9.95 children.

---

2. THE CLUB & MUSIC SCENE

Live music every night of the week? No problem. Laclede's Landing and Soulard lead the way in terms of quantity and quality—and what's more, many performances are free or charge only a nominal fee. Several establishments offer dance floors in addition to live music.

LIVE MUSIC

DOWNTOWN

AJ'S, in the Adam's Mark Hotel, 4th and Chestnut. Tel. 241-7400.

AJ's is so obviously popular and successful that to ignore it would be folly. Packed with both St. Louisans and out-of-towners, it boasts a dance floor with live entertainment nightly from 8:30pm featuring Top 40 tunes. There's a complimentary food buffet served Monday through Friday from 4:30 to 8pm, as well as daily promotionals. Thursday, for example, is ladies' night with reduced-price drinks for females. Thursday is also when in-house phones are placed throughout the club, each marked with a balloon sporting a number. Simply single out the person you want to talk to and call him or her up. There are also backgammon tables and bathrooms equipped with such high-class amenities as hairspray, makeup, and mouthwash. What will they think of next? Open Monday through Friday from 4:30pm to 3am and Saturday from 7pm to 3am.

Admission: Free.

JUST JAZZ, in the Hotel Majestic, 1019 Pine St. Tel. 436-2355.

This sophisticated jazz locale, with large windows and tall

ceilings, occupies the original lobby of the Hotel Majestic, built in 1913 in the Renaissance Revival style. It features two sets of live jazz every night, at 9 and 11pm, for which there is never a cover charge; there is, however, a two-drink minimum. Just Jazz offers a full-service menu that includes everything from sandwiches and salads to seafood.

Admission: Free.

KENNEDY'S 2ND STREET CO., 612 N. 2nd St. Tel. 421-3655.

One of the few establishments in Laclede's Landing open throughout the day, this locale offers live music nightly from 10:30pm to 2:30am. Possessing a distinct warehouse atmosphere with its tall ceiling, brick walls, and wood floors, it features original alternative and progressive music—from punk to heavy metal, funk, blues, jazz, and Motown. As one employee said, Top 40 hits are avoided here like the plague. There's a happy hour daily from 4:30 to 9:30pm with reduced-price drinks. The menu lists burgers, steaks, and sandwiches.

Admission: Free Mon and before 9pm; otherwise usually $2–$5.

LUCIUS BOOMER, 707 Clamorgan Alley. Tel. 621-8155.

Opened in 1978 and now one of the oldtimers in Laclede's Landing, this club has never flagged in popularity, due in large part to the tourists who flood the Landing. Boomer's specialty are its exotically named drinks, most of which are priced from $3.50 to $8: The Boomer Blaster sure does the job, mixing Malibu, vodka, schnapps, and cranberry and pineapple juices. Open daily from 8pm to 3am, it features a band that plays nightly from 9:30pm to 2:30am, sticking to Top 40 and recognizable tunes. There's an outdoor patio, too.

Admission: Free.

MISSISSIPPI NIGHTS, 914 N. 1st St. Tel. 421-3853.

This establishment in Laclede's Landing may well be the best place in the city to hear live music, as everyone from Jimmy Cliff and Tracy Chapman to the Talking Heads have performed here. Only 1,000 people can squeeze through its doors, and the music can get so loud that ear plugs are available at the front door. There's a dance floor, and when the big names aren't playing the music is usually rock and alternative rock. The doors open on Monday to Thursday at 7:30pm and on Friday and Saturday at 8pm, with live music starting at 8:30 or 9pm.

Admission: Usually $3–$5; $7–$20 for big names.

MUDDY WATERS, 724 N. 1st St. Tel. 421-5335.

Dichotomy, the house band here, has been raising a ruckus in Laclede's Landing for 15 years. Playing old rock-and-roll and country music, the band members are notorious for their between-song comments, which can only be classified as vulgar comedy, with most of the fun poked at the audience. Lord help any woman who gets up to go to the bathroom. The audience seems to eat it up, and this place is packed on most nights. There's an outdoor patio, and the house specialty is charbroiled catfish. It's open Monday through Saturday from 11am to 3am and Sunday from noon to midnight; the band and crowd ridicule begin at 9:30pm.

Admission: Free.

SUNDECKER'S, 900 N. 1st St. Tel. 241-5915.
   This place in Laclede's Landing is your typical college-crowd bar, with the added advantage of an outside deck with a view of Ead's Bridge. Open daily from 11am to 3am, it offers live music on Wednesday through Sunday at 9:30pm, with the emphasis on popular music from the 1950s to the present.
   Admission: $1 Fri–Sat, free the rest of the week.

SOULARD DISTRICT

HILARY'S, 1017 Russell Blvd. Tel. 421-3126.
   This is a great place to spend an evening listening to blues, jazz, or Motown; drinking; and dining on blackened redfish, filet mignon, or chicken chardonnay. It's a tiny place, but that doesn't stop people from pouring through its doors. Highly recommended, Hilary's has live music nightly from 9pm to 1am, with an additional set on Saturday from 4 to 7pm.
   Admission: Free Sun–Thurs; $2 Fri–Sat.

JOHN D. McGURK'S, 1200 Russell Blvd. Tel. 776-8309.
   A simple establishment with brick archways, a wooden floor, and an outdoor patio, this pub features live Irish music, either bands brought over from the old country or a local band that plays Irish tunes. Sometimes a Scottish group slips through. A lively place, it offers a variety of beers on tap and a menu featuring Irish stew, burgers, and smoked ham. It's open Monday through Friday from 11am to 1:30am, Saturday from noon to 1:30am, and Sunday from 2pm to midnight. There's live music on Sunday to Thursday beginning at 8:30pm and Friday and Saturday at 9pm.
   Admission: Free.

MIKE & MIN'S, 10th & Geyer. Tel. 421-1655.
   Formerly a dry-goods store dating from 1850 but the site of a tavern for almost 60 years, this establishment specializes in 30 different brands of imported beers, along with a full-service bar. Its bands, which perform on Thursday to Saturday from 9pm to 1am, play the blues. There's a happy hour on Monday through Friday from 4 to 7pm, plus extensive lunch and dinner menus. Mike & Min's is open Sunday through Wednesday from 11am to 11pm and Thursday through Saturday from 11am to 1:30am.
   Admission: Free Sun–Thurs, $2 Fri–Sat.

UNIVERSITY CITY

CICERO'S RESTAURANT AND BASEMENT BAR, 6510 Delmar Blvd., University City, MO. Tel. 862-0009.
   An informal place with a bar/restaurant serving Italian pizza and pastas on the ground floor and a live-music hall in the basement, Cicero's is a venue for jazz, folk, funk, and rock performed by both local and national acts. The ground-floor bar/restaurant is open daily from 11am to 12:30am. The basement music hall opens at 7:30pm, with live music from 9pm.
   Admission: $3–$5.

COMEDY CLUBS

CATCH A RISING STAR, in Union Station, 18th and Market. Tel. 231-6900.

Part of a national chain, this club in Union Station offers comedy six nights a week, with shows on Monday through Saturday at 8pm and a late show on Friday and Saturday at 10pm. In addition to nationally known headliners, it spotlights new and upcoming talent. There's a two-drink minimum per person, with drinks priced between $2.75 and $4.50.

Admission: $5 Mon, $8 Tues–Thurs, $10 Fri–Sat.

FUNNY BONE COMEDY CLUB, 940 West Port Plaza, Maryland Heights, MO. Tel. 469-6692.

Located in the West Port Plaza shopping-and-dining complex just off I-270, the Funny Bone offers live comedy seven nights a week. On Monday it's The Best of St. Louis featuring local comedians, while on Tuesday it's open mike. If you come before the show for dinner, you're guaranteed a reserved seat, but be sure to make a reservation beforehand. Entrées include seafood, pasta, chicken, and steak dishes. No one under 18 is admitted. Shows are on Monday through Thursday at 8:30pm, Friday at 8:30 and 10:45pm, Saturday at 7:45 and 10pm and midnight, and Sunday at 8pm.

Admission $5 Mon, $3 Tues, $7 Wed–Thurs and Sun, $9 Fri, $10 Sat.

3. THE BAR SCENE

BLUEBERRY HILL, 6504 Delmar Blvd., University City, MO. Tel. 727-0880.

If you're a rock-and-roll fan, chances are that you've already heard of Blueberry Hill. It's a St. Louis institution, an attraction in its own right, and a treasure trove of memorabilia as diverse as a Howdy Doody collection and record jackets nailed to the walls. This bar contains more memorabilia on Chuck Berry than any other place in the world, including his ES-350 Gibson, which he used to compose "Roll Over Beethoven." Other collections on display include Pee-wee Herman dolls, lunchboxes, the Smurfs, papier-mâché animals, and more. There are seven dart boards, and its CD juke box has been rated the best in the country, with at any one time a selection of 2,000 songs that are indexed by title, artist, and year. Live music is featured on Friday and Saturday nights from 9pm downstairs in the Elvis Room, where the cover charge ranges from $3 to $5. Blueberry Hill is open Monday through Saturday from 11am to 1:30am and Sunday from 11am to midnight.

DRESSEL'S, 419 N. Euclid Ave. Tel. 361-1060.

Located in the Central West End, this is one of my favorite pubs in St. Louis, a true Welsh pub that knows its beer and its pub grub. Dressel's walls are filled with portraits of writers and musicians, all done on commission by local artists or donated by friends and patrons of the bar. Beethoven, William Faulkner, Mozart, Count Basie, and Emily Dickinson are just some of those who stare down at you as you put away Welsh vegetarian pie or ploughman's lunch, washing it down with Welsh ale. Upstairs is The Pub Above, with a bar created from antique moldings; it features a jazz quartet on Wednesday and classical music on Saturday. Dressel's is open Monday through Friday from 11:30am to 2pm and again from 5pm to 1am, Saturday from noon to 1am, and Sunday from noon to midnight. The Pub Above is open only Wednesday through Sunday from 5:30pm to 1am.

HOULIHAN'S, in Union Station, 18th & Market. Tel. 436-0844.

Houlihan's, which had its beginnings in Kansas City and has since spread like prairie fire throughout the country, is a popular place for both drinking and dining. It features a happy hour on Monday to Friday from 4 to 7pm with drink specials and half-price appetizers as well as an extensive menu that ranges from quiche and fajitas to Cajun shrimp, fresh fish, sandwiches, and baby-back ribs.

There's another Houlihan's in the St. Louis Galleria shopping mall, at Clayton Road and Brentwood Boulevard (tel. 863-9116).

LYNN DICKEY'S SPORTS CAFE, in Union Station, 18th and Market. Tel. 436-1314.

This is the place to go if you enjoy watching sports, since that's what's featured on this establishment's 18 TVs and 2 big screens. Popular with the preppie/yuppie crowd, it has a happy hour on Monday through Friday from 4:30 to 7pm, with drink specials. On weekends it offers a DJ with a dance floor. Hours are daily from 11am to 2:30am; on Friday and Saturday there's a $2 cover charge after 9pm.

O'CONNELL'S PUB, 4652 Shaw, at Kingshighway Blvd. Tel. 773-6600.

Located on the edge of the Italian Hill district is this Irish pub, named after a street in Dublin. Opened in 1962, O'Connell's is famous for its burgers and also for its brew. This popular place is located in a hundred-year-old building with wooden floors and a pressed-tin ceiling. Open Monday through Saturday from 11:15am to 1:30am.

---

4. MOVIES

THE CENTER OF CONTEMPORARY ARTS [COCA], 524 Trinity Ave., University City, MO. Tel. 863-1004.

This center, devoted to the visual and performing arts, presents a year-round film series featuring international cinema.

Tickets: $4.

IMPRESSIONS

Meet me in St. Louis, Louis,
Meet me at the fair.
Don't tell me the lights are shining,
Any place but there.
We will dance the Hoochee Koochee,
I will be your tootsie wootsie,
If you will meet me in St. Louis, Louis,
Meet me at the fair.
—F. A. MILLS (1904)

ST. LOUIS ART MUSEUM, Forest Park. Tel. 721-0067.
Films are shown on Tuesday at 5:30 and 8pm and Friday at 1:30 and 7:30pm year-round at this great museum, usually on a certain cinematic theme—from French classics to film legends.
Tickets: $3 adults, $2 senior citizens and students.

TIVOLI PREMIER THEATRE, 6350 Delmar Blvd., University City, MO. Tel. 725-0220.
Alternative films, both domestic and international, are featured here, primarily those that are never shown at the regular movie houses.
Tickets: $5.50 adults, $3.50 children and senior citizens.

CHAPTER 11

EASY EXCURSIONS FROM ST. LOUIS

1. HANNIBAL, MO
2. SPRINGFIELD, IL

The two destinations in this chapter make easy half-day, day, or overnight trips.

1. HANNIBAL, MO

I wonder whether Mark Twain would recognize Hannibal today. As it is, Twain put Hannibal on the international map, and today it receives annually about a quarter of a million visitors who come to pay tribute to one of America's greatest authors and humorists. Twain's name is bestowed upon everything, from a campground and a motel to restaurants and sights. No doubt Twain would have given free reign to his thoughts about that, but even during his lifetime the town had changed. While on one of his visits, he noted with his usual dry wit, "Everything was changed, but when I reached Third or Fourth street the tears burst forth, for I recognized the mud."

Yet despite the fact that the town capitalizes heavily on Mark Twain's name, Hannibal remains remarkably and refreshingly small town. True, it does have souvenir shops and all the trappings that go with them, but Hannibal is not nearly the tourist trap it could be—it's simply not sophisticated enough for that. It remains friendly, charming, and unassuming, still that "white town drowsing in the sun." It's a great family destination.

ORIENTATION   Hannibal, located about 120 miles from St. Louis, is easily reached via Highway 61. The **Visitors and Convention Bureau** is located at 320 Broadway in the heart of Hannibal (tel. 314/221-2477)—open Monday through Friday from 8am to noon and from 1 to 5pm. In addition, there's an **Information Booth** set up during the warmer months at 402 N. Main Street (tel. 314/221-8300)—open daily Memorial Day to Labor Day from 9:30am to 5:30pm and on some weekends during April, May, September, and October.

Most of the town's major attractions are located on Main and Hill streets, just a stone's throw from the Mississippi River. The Bureau offers a free *Visitor's Guide* to Hannibal that contains a map.

THE *DELTA QUEEN* AND THE *MISSISSIPPI QUEEN*
Although you can drive to Hannibal from St. Louis in less than two hours, a much more relaxed and traditional way to travel there is by boat on the Mississippi River. The *Delta Queen* and the *Mississippi Queen* are the only two steamboats left in America that offer the unique opportunity to live aboard a luxury steamer, dine and sleep in

luxury, and watch the Mississippi valley roll by. The *Delta Queen,* built in 1926, is listed on the National Register of Historic Places and is also designated a National Historic Landmark. The *Mississippi Queen,* commissioned in 1976, is the largest steamboat the world has ever seen. Both boats make two round-trip journeys from St. Louis to Hannibal each summer, which includes three nights aboard ship and a day in Hannibal. Cabin prices as of 1992 ranged from $490 to $1,680. For information on sailing dates and current prices, call toll free 800/543-1949.

WHAT TO SEE

A town of approximately 18,000 people, Hannibal was founded in 1818 and is known worldwide as the boyhood home of Samuel Clemens, who lived here from 1839 to 1853 before going on to become a river pilot and a famous writer under the pen name of Mark Twain. Understandably, many of Hannibal's attractions relate to its most famous citizen.

MARK TWAIN BOYHOOD HOME AND MUSEUM, 208 Hill St. Tel. 314/221-9010.

Judge John Clemens moved his family to this small white-clapboard home in 1844, when Sam Clemens was four years old. Only two blocks from the Mississippi River, the home is featured in Twain's *The Adventures of Tom Sawyer* as the residence of Aunt Polly, Tom Sawyer, Sid, and Mary. It's a simple home that was recently restored to the way it looked back in the 1800s.

Adjoining the home is the Mark Twain Museum, which contains some photographs, one of Twain's legendary white coats, and first editions of Twain's books. There also are translations of *Tom Sawyer* in more than a dozen languages, including Japanese, Hungarian, Indian, and Afrikaans. Also included are some original paintings of Tom Sawyer by Norman Rockwell. Across the street are Judge John Clemens' law office and the home of Laura Hawkins, after whom Twain modeled his Becky Thatcher. And you can't miss that white-washed fence.

Admission: $4 adults, $2 children 6–12.

Open: Summer daily 8am–6pm; spring and autumn daily 8am–5pm; winter daily 10am–4pm. **Closed:** Thanksgiving, Christmas, and New Year's Day.

MARK TWAIN RIVERBOAT, Center Street Landing. Tel. 314/221-3222, or toll free 800/621-2322.

The Mississippi has always played an integral part in towns that sprang up beside it, and Hannibal is no exception. From May through October, you can join a one-hour cruise aboard the *Mark Twain,* built in 1964, and float past barges and the river valley while listening to a narrator describe legends, lore, and facts about the river. You'll learn, for example, that a barge can haul three times the amount a freight train can at 60% of the cost and that the Mississippi has an average depth of only 11 feet. In the evening are dinner cruises featuring baked chicken and barbecued beef, along with live music and dancing.

Admission: One-hour cruise $6.50 adults, $3.50 children; dinner cruise $20.95 adults, $14.95 children 3–12.

Open: Cruises in May daily 1:30pm and Fri–Sat 7pm; June, July, and Aug daily 11am and 1:30, 4, and 7pm; Sept–Oct daily 1:30 and 6:30pm, Sat 4pm.

MARK TWAIN CAVE, Missouri Route 79. Tel. 314/221-1656.

One mile south of Hannibal, this cave, discovered in 1819, was the one Sam Clemens played in as a young boy. Twain later used it in *Tom Sawyer* and *Huckleberry Finn* as the cave containing buried treasure, where Tom and Becky Thatcher were lost and where Injun Joe met his demise. In 1886 it became the first Missouri cave to be opened to the public, and six miles of passageways have been mapped. One-hour guided tours, departing every 15 minutes, cover less than a mile through the cave along smooth walkways carved ages ago by an underground stream. These tours are fun and informative and supply many anecdotes about Tom Sawyer and Huck Finn. Jesse James reportedly hid out here, too, and even wrote his name in the cave wall with a pencil.

Admission: $7 adults, $6 senior citizens 65 and older, $3.50 children 5–12.

Open: Apr–May and Sept–Oct 9am–6pm; June–Aug 8am–8pm; Nov–Mar 9am–4pm. The last tour departs one hour before closing. **Closed:** Thanksgiving and Christmas.

ROCKCLIFFE MANSION, 1000 Bird St. Tel. 314/221-4140.

Mark Twain gave a speech from this mansion's staircase during his last visit to Hannibal in 1902, and as many as 300 guests were able to hear it. This huge mansion was built by lumber magnate John Cruikshank around the turn of the century and served as his home until his death in 1924. The 30-room house was decorated, not in Victorian style but in art nouveau style, and it was equipped with all the modern conveniences of the day, including electric lights in all the closets that turned on automatically when the doors were opened. Everything is elaborately decorated, from the miniature copy of the Waldorf-Astoria's Turkish ballroom in New York to the dining-room wallpaper imported from Paris at $134 a roll. Forty-five-minute tours of the home are given throughout the day.

Admission: $4 adults, $1.50 children 6–11.

Open: Mar–Nov 9:30am–5pm (last tour); Dec–Feb 11:30am–3:30pm. **Closed:** Thanksgiving, Christmas, and New Year's Day.

WHERE TO STAY
MODERATE

FIFTH STREET MANSION, 213 S. 5th St., Hannibal, MO 63401. Tel. 314/221-0445, or toll free (reservations only) 800/874-5661. 7 rms (all with bath). A/C

$ Rates: (including breakfast, afternoon tea, and wine): $65–$90 double. Extra person $15. AE, DISC, MC, V.

This bed-and-breakfast, built in 1858 and listed on the National Register of Historic Places, is located in the heart of Hannibal. Built in Italianate style by a former Hannibal mayor, it has a huge Tiffany window on the first landing of the front staircase, 8 fireplaces, and a total of 21 rooms. Seven rooms are available for guests, each different from the others. On the top floor is a two-room suite that's perfect for families.

GARTH WOODSIDE MANSION, R. R. 1, Hannibal, MO 63401. Tel. 314/221-2789. 8 rms (all with bath). A/C
$ Rates (including breakfast): $58–$90 double. Extra person $15.

Situated on 39 rolling acres south of Hannibal, this bed-and-breakfast was built in 1871 as the summer residence of John and Helen Garth. Most of its Victorian furnishings are original to the mansion, including the gaslights and even the Victorian bed where Mark Twain is reputed to have slept while visiting the Garths. An elegant breakfast is served in the formal dining hall, and Victorian nightshirts are provided. In the summer, you'll want to sit on the wraparound veranda to enjoy the peaceful view; in winter you'll wish to warm yourself at the open fireplace. All in all, this is a perfect place for experiencing Mark Twain's Hannibal—but note that children under 12 are not accepted.

HOLIDAY INN, U.S. 61 at Market St., Hannibal, MO 63401. Tel. 314/221-6610, or toll free 800/325-0777. 238 rms, 3 suites. A/C TEL TV
$ Rates: $65 single; $70 double; $99 suite. Extra person $7. Children 19 and under stay free in parents' room. Weekday and special packages available. AE, CB, DC, DISC, MC, V.

Like Holidomes across the nation, this Holiday Inn is a favorite with families because it offers so much for kids to do. The rooms are similar to others in this chain and face either the Holidome or the outside. Besides offering a restaurant and a lounge with live music on Tuesday through Saturday evening, the Holiday Inn features laundry service and such facilities as an indoor pool, a sauna, a whirlpool, a game room, putting greens, outdoor tennis courts, a jogging track, a pool table, Ping-Pong tables, a convenience store, a gift shop, and a hair salon.

WHERE TO DINE

BUDGET

MARK TWAIN DINETTE AND FAMILY RESTAURANT, 3rd and Hill Sts. Tel. 221-5511.
Cuisine: AMERICAN. **Reservations:** Not necessary.
$ Prices: $3–$8. MC, V.
Open: Sun–Thurs 6am–10pm, Fri–Sat 6am–11pm.

Located a stone's throw from Mark Twain's Boyhood Home, this is the epitome of a small-town family restaurant, with informal and friendly service, artificial plants and flowers, and even a drive-in service out back. Locally owned and operated since 1942, it offers biscuits and gravy, pancakes, and eggs for breakfast; lunch and dinner include burgers, sandwiches, chili, grilled chicken, steak, pork chops, halibut, and catfish from the Mississippi River. There are a salad bar and a children's menu.

MISSOURI TERRITORY RESTAURANT & LOUNGE, 600 Broadway. Tel. 248-1440.
Cuisine: AMERICAN. **Reservations:** Recommended.
$ Prices: Lunch $4.25–$6; dinner $5.50–$18. AE, MC, V.
Open: Tues–Sat 11am–2pm and 5–9pm, Sun 11am–2pm and 5–8pm.

This restaurant occupies the first floor of what was once a federal courthouse, an impressive limestone building dating from 1888. Its luncheon specials include a variety of sandwiches, although diners are welcome to order from the dinner menu, which includes everything from more sandwiches to chicken, fish, seafood, prime rib, and steaks. There's a lounge downstairs.

DINNER THEATERS

MOLLY BROWN DINNER THEATER, 200 N. Main St. Tel. 221-8940.
   Cuisine: AMERICAN. **Reservations:** Required for evening show.
$ **Prices:** Lunch show $13.33 adults, $7.24 children including tax; evening show $17.50–$18.50 adults, $9.50–$10.50 children, plus tax. MC, V.
   Open: May–Oct lunch show noon–2:15pm, evening show 6:30–9:15pm. Call for show dates and reservations.
Mark Twain isn't Hannibal's only famous personality. The Unsinkable Molly Brown was born here in 1867, leaving at the age of 17 in search of a rich husband in Leadville, Colorado. This dinner theater features a musical revue honoring both citizens, with performances provided by professionals who also serve the food. Lunch includes an open-face barbecued beef sandwich, while dinner gives you a choice of roast sirloin, baked lemon-pepper catfish, and barbecue beef sandwich. Fun for the entire family.

MARK TWAIN OUTDOOR THEATRE, Route 3, New London. Tel. 221-2945.
   Cuisine: AMERICAN. **Reservations:** Recommended.
$ **Prices:** Show and dinner $15 adults, $8 children; show only $8 adults, $4 children.
   Open: Daily June–Oct buffet from 4pm; show starts at 8:30pm.
Located four miles south of Hannibal on Highway 61, this outdoor theater presents a two-hour show reflecting the life and times of Mark Twain, with scenes from *Tom Sawyer* and *Huckleberry Finn*. The stage is separated from the audience by a body of water, complete with a 50-foot replica of a Mississippi riverboat. Before the show, you can eat all you want at a buffet, after which it's just a short walk to the stage. You also can watch the show without eating dinner.

2. SPRINGFIELD, IL

In 1837 young Abraham Lincoln moved to Springfield, IL, where he practiced law and married Mary Todd, with whom he eventually had four sons. Almost a quarter of a century later he was elected 16th president of the United States and departed for his new office, never to return alive again.
   Springfield has never forgotten its favorite son, and Lincoln is buried here with his family. Today Springfield draws many visitors to its Lincoln Home, which presents lively tours that breathe life into the times of one of our most loved presidents. For children, the Lincoln Home is a tangible connection to Lincoln, making him much more real than the pages of a history book could. Not far from Springfield is New Salem, a reconstructed village where Lincoln lived,

worked, and studied law before moving to Springfield. If you're an architecture buff, you'll want to inspect the Dana-Thomas House, designed by Frank Lloyd Wright and recently completely restored.

ORIENTATION   The capital of Illinois with a population of about 105,000, Springfield is located at the intersection of I-55 and I-72, about 102 miles from St. Louis, 195 miles from Chicago, and 311 miles from Kansas City.

For information and brochures about Springfield, contact the **Springfield Convention and Visitors Bureau,** 109 N. 7th St. (tel. 217/789-2360, or toll free 800/545-7300)—open Monday through Friday from 8am to 5pm. More convenient, perhaps, is the Visitor Information booth at the **Lincoln Home Visitor Center,** 426 S. 7th St. (tel. 492-4150)—open daily from 8:30am to 5pm in winter and 8am to 8pm in summer—which is where visitors pick up tickets to tour the Lincoln Home.

WHAT TO SEE

LINCOLN HOME NATIONAL HISTORIC SITE VISITOR CENTER, 426 S. 7th St. Tel. 492-4150.

This should be the first stop, because you can pick up free tickets to tour the Lincoln Home, which are for a specific time and are issued on a first-come, first-served basis. The center contains an exhibit on Springfield during Lincoln's time and presents two 20-minute films throughout the day, *Mr. Lincoln's Springfield* and *At Home with Mr. Lincoln.* There's also a bookstore with volumes on Lincoln as well as a Visitor Information booth with brochures on sights in Springfield. Lincoln Home National Historic Site encompasses a four-block area administered by the National Park Service. In addition to the Lincoln Home, 12 neighboring homes dating from the 1800s have been preserved (many are now used as office space).

Admission: Free.

Open: Summer daily 8am–8pm; winter daily 8:30am–5pm. **Closed:** Thanksgiving, Christmas, New Year's Day.

LINCOLN HOME, 8th and Jackson Sts. Tel. 492-4150.

The only house Abraham Lincoln ever owned, this served as the Lincoln family home for 17 years, and it was here that three of Lincoln's four sons were born and one died. A modest wooden home built in 1839 and later enlarged by the Lincolns, who added the entire second floor, it has been restored as authentically as possible, right down to its wallpaper, carpets, and curtains. Furnished with original Lincoln belongings and reproductions of period pieces, the home reflects the taste of Mary Lincoln, who came from a prominent Kentucky banking family. The conducted tour presents a lively account of the life and times of Lincoln and his family.

Admission: Free. (Obtain tickets at the nearby Visitor Center, described above).

Open: Summer daily 8am–8pm; winter daily 8:30am–5pm. **Closed:** Thanksgiving, Christmas, New Year's Day.

LINCOLN TOMB STATE HISTORIC SITE, Oak Ridge Cemetery, entrance at 1500 N. Monument Ave. or N. Walnut St. Tel. 782-2717.

Lincoln was buried here in 1865, in a tomb that was built with public contributions. His wife, Mary, and three of their sons also are buried here. The site contains a number of Lincoln and Civil War sculptures, but most well known is the bust of Lincoln that guards the entrance to the tomb—generations of visitors have rubbed the nose in the belief that it will bring them luck, giving the nose a shining glow.

Admission: Free.

Open: Daily 9am–5pm. **Closed:** Martin Luther King, Jr.'s Birthday, President's Day, Veterans Day, Thanksgiving, Christmas, New Year's Day.

OLD STATE CAPITOL, Downtown Mall. Tel. 785-7961.

Only a five-minute walk from Lincoln's Home, this handsome building served as the state capitol from 1839 to 1876; it now houses the Illinois Supreme Court and a law library. Considered a perfect example of Greek Revival architecture, the capitol has been completely reconstructed, refurnished, and restored to how it looked during Lincoln's legislative years. Many of the objects now on display relate to famous people who used the building, including Stephen A. Douglas, Lincoln, and Ulysses S. Grant. On the ground floor is a handwritten copy of Lincoln's Gettysburg Address, the third of five surviving manuscripts. Tours of the building are conducted. Of special note are tours on Friday and Saturday (except in May), in which costumed interpreters portray historical characters of the times.

Admission: Free.

Open: Daily 9am–5pm (last tour 4:30pm). Costume tours Fri and Sat 10am–noon and 1–4pm (except May). **Closed:** Martin Luther King, Jr.'s Birthday, President's Day, Veterans Day, Thanksgiving, Christmas, and New Year's Day.

DANA-THOMAS HOUSE STATE HISTORIC SITE, 301 E. Lawrence Ave. Tel. 782-6776.

Designed by Frank Lloyd Wright and built in 1902, this is considered the best-preserved and most complete of Wright's early Prairie houses. It was constructed for Springfield socialite Susan Lawrence Dana, who entertained regularly, welcomed guests from all over the world, married three times, and ended up being declared incompetent by the courts and admitted to a local hospital a few years before she died. At any rate, what makes this house especially remarkable is that it contains more than 100 pieces of original Wright-designed furniture made specifically for the house, as well as 250 examples of art-glass doors and windows and about 200 original light fixtures.

Admission: Free. (Note: Admission may be charged in the future.)

Open: At press time, Thurs and Sat 1–4pm. Call beforehand, however, since hours can vary. **Closed:** Martin Luther King Jr.'s Birthday, President's Day, Veterans Day, Thanksgiving, Christmas, New Year's Day.

LINCOLN'S NEW SALEM STATE HISTORIC SITE, near Petersburg, IL. Tel. 632-7953.

Located about half an hour's drive northwest of Springfield on Illinois Route 97, New Salem is a reconstruction of a village that once existed here. Twenty-three log cabins have been authentically reproduced on the sites mentioned in interviews that were conducted in the 1880s of people who had lived here. Its heyday was in the 1830s, with a population of 125 recorded in 1832 (the same as Chicago at the time). Lincoln lived here from 1831 to 1837, working as a laborer, store clerk, merchant, county surveyor, postmaster, and captain of the local militia. This is also where he studied law on his own and was elected to the state legislature. In 1840 the town was abandoned.

The village contains a cooper shop (the only original building, more than 150 years old); a blacksmith's shop; a tavern; a carding mill; a saw and grist mill; stores; homes; and even gardens with corn, herbs, and other crops that were cultivated in the 1830s. From April through November, interpreters in period costume are on hand to describe the buildings and the various trades conducted there.

While here, you may wish to board the *Talisman River Boat,* a replica of an 1830s steamboat, for a one-hour trip on the Sangamon River (board near the grist mill). In addition, *The Great American People Show* is an outdoor dramatic portrayal of the life of Lincoln, including his struggle for the presidency and his years in office. For ticket reservations, call 217/632-7755.

Admission: Free to New Salem; *Talisman River Boat* $1.50 adults, $1 children 4–12; *The Great American People Show* $7.50 adults, $6 students and senior citizens; $21 family rate.

Open: New Salem summer daily 9am–5pm; winter daily 8am–4pm. **Closed:** Martin Luther King Jr.'s Birthday, Presidents Day, Veterans Day, Thanksgiving, Christmas, New Year's Day. *Talisman River Boat* May–Aug daily 9am–4pm; Sept–Oct weekends only 9am–4pm. *The Great American People Show* mid-June to mid-Aug Tues–Sun 8pm.

GEORGE COLIN FOLK ART, Route 97, Salisbury, IL. Tel. 217/626-1204.

As you travel on Route 97 between Springfield and New Salem, you'll pass an ordinary house made extraordinary by a profusion of colorful art in the yard. That's the home of George Colin, well known in these parts for his folk art, which takes whimsical shape mainly as benches, chairs, tables, and sculpture painted in bright colors. There are watermelon chairs, peacock tables, strawberry benches, Lincoln statues, and much more. In his studio/barn in the back, George also draws five chalk pictures a day, which he sells in his Chicago gallery. If George is busy, his wife, Winnie, will happily show people around.

Open: Whenever the Colins are at home.

WHERE TO STAY

EXPENSIVE

RAMADA RENAISSANCE HOTEL, 701 E. Adams St., Springfield, IL 62701. Tel. 217/544-8800, or toll free 800/228-9898. Fax 217/544-9607. 316 rms. A/C MINIBAR TV TEL

$ Rates: $94–$105 single; $111–$121 double; Executive Club floor $130 single, $145 double. Extra person $15. Children under 18 stay free in parents' room. Weekend and senior-citizen discounts available. AE, DC, MC, V.

This is Springfield's top hotel, a tall brick building located downtown. Each room is comfortably appointed, outfitted with either a king-size bed or two double beds as well as a minibar and cable TV with remote control and pay movies. If you feel like pampering yourself, stay at one of the Executive Club Level rooms on the top two floors, where the rooms are larger and have the added benefits of free sparkling water, terrycloth robes, hairdryers, telephones in the bathrooms, and free continental breakfast and afternoon hors d'oeuvres served in the private lounge.

Dining: Floreale, decorated with handblown chandeliers from Italy, is the hotel's signature restaurant, serving steaks and seafood. Lindsey's, more casual, serves breakfast, lunch, and dinner and is open on Sunday, when most downtown restaurants are closed. Globe Tavern is the hotel's bar, which serves lunch on weekdays.

Services: Babysitting, laundry/valet, room service until 2am, complimentary airport transportation.

Facilities: Indoor pool, whirlpool, health club, game room.

MODERATE

HOLIDAY INN EAST, 3100 S. Dirksen Parkway, Springfield, IL 62703. Tel. 217/529-7171, or toll free 800/ HOLIDAY. Fax 217/529-5063. 340 rms, 45 suites. A/C TV TEL

$ Rates: $65–$75 single; $74–$85 double. Extra person $8. Children under 18 stay free in parents' room. Corporate, family, and special packages available. AE, CB, DC, MC, V.

Located off I-55, about a 15-minute drive from Lincoln's Home, this is a great place for families. Its Holidome is about the size of a football field, with a lap pool, a snack bar, and a score of other diversions. The rooms were furnished by local decorators rather than by a designer from the Holiday Inn chain, giving them a more personal flavor in color schemes of light maroon and jungle green. As though its facilities weren't enough, the hotel will even rent you a VCR along with two videos for $5.

The Holiday Inn has a dining room, a coffee shop, a snack bar, and a lounge (with nightly entertainment). Its facilities include a gift shop (with souvenirs of Springfield), indoor and outdoor pools, an exercise room, a whirlpool and sauna, shuffleboard, a playground, a game arcade, a Ping-Pong table, pool tables, a putting green, an outdoor tennis court, and a coin-operated laundry.

BED & BREAKFAST

CORINNE'S BED & BREAKFAST, 1001 S. 6th St., Springfield, IL 62703. Tel. 217/527-1400. 5 rms (3 with bath). A/C (TEL and TV available)

$ Rates (including buffet breakfast): High season single or double $65 without bath, $75 with bath, $85 suite; low season $60, $65, and $75, respectively. MC, V.

Built in 1883 by a prominent grocer and banker, this Queen Anne home is in the center of town, about five blocks from Lincoln's Home. It has been beautifully decorated—with a cheerful and sunny breakfast room, a comfortable communal living room with a TV and fireplace, and guest rooms that show the feminine touch of its owners. Women traveling alone will especially appreciate the homey and friendly atmosphere here. Highly recommended.

WHERE TO DINE

You can't be in Springfield long before you hear about its famous Horseshoe, a local specialty since anyone can remember: Basically it's an open-face sandwich that originally featured ham and a cheese sauce and was served on a metal plate (the anvil) with french fries (representing the nails). Now there are many various kinds of Horseshoes, including turkey and hamburger; because the portions are massive, smaller Ponyshoes also are available.

If you're in downtown Springfield on a Sunday, when everything is closed, head for the Ramada Renaissance Hotel, where you'll find Lindsey's serving food daily from 6:30am to 11pm (see above).

INEXPENSIVE

CAPITOL TELETRACK, Chatham Square Center, 1766 Wabash Ave. Tel. 546-2111.
    Cuisine: AMERICAN. **Reservations:** Recommended.
$ **Prices:** Appetizers $4–$7.50; main courses $7.50–$16. AE, MC, V.
    Open: Tues–Sun noon–midnight.

If you like to wager on horses, you probably won't be able to stay away from this off-track wagering facility, with its 16 betting windows. Offering closed-circuit TV monitors that broadcast races from Fairmount Park and Chicago-area tracks, Capitol Teletrack is located on the west end of town in a shopping center. You must be at least 21 to enter, and no admission is charged. The Secretariat Dining Room is the facility's formal dining room, offering personal TV monitors and entrées ranging from prime rib and filet mignon to broiled swordfish, chicken, and spaghetti. If that's too formal, you can order sandwiches and snacks in the lounge area.

BUDGET

GEORGE WARBURTONS, South Shore Drive, Petersburg. Tel. 632-7878.
    Cuisine: AMERICAN. **Reservation:** Necessary on weekends.
$ **Prices:** Lunch $4–$8.50; dinner $4–$11. MC, V.
    Open: Sun and Tues–Thurs 11am–9pm, Fri–Sat 11am–10pm.

This is the best place to eat if you're visiting New Salem State Historic Site. To reach it, drive through the public parking lot and campground at New Salem and then take a right (or ask directions at New Salem). Open only since 1989, George Warburtons is a pleasant and casual family restaurant with an outdoor patio and a separate bar that's designed to resemble a library. It's owned by a man-and-wife team—she's a nutritionist, he's a pork producer. Naturally, pork is the specialty here, but there also are sandwiches (including the Horseshoe); for dinner there are also steaks, seafood, and chicken.

MALDANER'S, 222 S. 6th St. Tel. 522-4313.
    Cuisine: AMERICAN/CONTINENTAL. **Reservations:** Recommended for upstairs dining room.
$ **Prices:** Lunch $3.25–$6; dinner downstairs $4–$12; main courses upstairs $15–$22. AE, DC, MC, V.
    Open: Downstairs Mon–Fri 11am–9pm; upstairs Tues–Thurs 6–10pm, Fri–Sat 6–11pm.

Maldaner's has been a familiar name to the natives of Springfield ever since it first opened in 1884. Originally owned by a baker, confectioner, and caterer, it moved into its present building in 1896 and still boasts a pressed-tin ceiling and wainscot walls. The informal downstairs serves soups, salads, and sandwiches, including Horseshoes and Ponyshoes; its dinner menu changes often but includes an interesting variety of choices—from perhaps a vegetable stir-fry to blackened catfish; Thai chicken cakes; or fettucine with chicken, artichokes, and pesto. The more formal upstairs dining room, open only for dinner, also offers innovative selections, featuring perhaps grilled duck with apricot marmalade, sautéed veal with polenta and tomato ragoût, and beef Wellington.

NORB ANDY'S, 518 E. Capitol. Tel. 523-7777.
   Cuisine: AMERICAN. **Reservations:** Not necessary.
$ Prices: Lunch $3–$6; dinner $3–$12. AE, CB, DC, MC, V.
   Open: Mon–Thurs 11am–10pm, Fri–Sat 11am–11pm, Sun (no food served) 7–11pm.

Norb Andy's is a well-known tavern, popular in part because of its convenient location halfway between Lincoln's Home and the new state capitol. There's been a tavern here since the 1930s (operating as a speakeasy during Prohibition), and its specialty is the Horseshoe (nine different kinds). Norb Andy's also serves sandwiches and burgers for lunch and steaks and seafood for dinner. It doesn't serve food on Sunday, but it's open for live jazz, for which there's no cover charge. There's also jazz most Wednesday through Saturday evenings.

PART TWO

KANSAS CITY

CHAPTER 12

GETTING TO KNOW KANSAS CITY

Approximately 250 miles due west of St. Louis, Kansas City is a sprawling metropolis with approximately 1.5 million people living in the greater metropolitan area. Famous for its steaks, barbecue, jazz, and rich frontier history, Kansas City claims to have more boulevards than Paris and more fountains than any city outside Rome. As the starting point for the Santa Fe, Oregon, and California trails, the Kansas City area also claims that it, rather than St. Louis, served as the principal gateway to the West. But, alas, St. Louis registered the claim first.

1. ORIENTATION

Located mostly along the southern shore of the Missouri River, Kansas City straddles the boundary between the states of Missouri and Kansas, with the main part of the city—despite its name—on the Missouri side. The suburbs of Kansas City in Missouri include Independence, Liberty, Gladstone, Lee's Summit, Riverside, and North Kansas City. The suburbs in Kansas include Prairie Village, Shawnee, and Overland Park.

ARRIVING
BY PLANE

Kansas City International Airport (KCI; tel. 816/243-5237) is conveniently located about 25 minutes northwest of downtown, just off I-29, in Missouri. It's been rated one of the most congestion-free, user-friendly airports in the nation, due in part to its architectural configuration. Three C-shaped terminals allow drivers to drive virtually to their gate, with never more than a 75-foot walk from aircraft to curbside. An interterminal red bus makes continuous rounds to all three terminals.

GETTING INTO TOWN The easiest way to reach your hotel from the airport is by **taxi,** which averages about $27 for the trip downtown and takes about 25 minutes. Up to five people can ride for a single fare.

More economical is to take the **KCI Shuttle,** which delivers passengers to major hotels downtown and to Crown Center, Country

Amtrak Depot **6**
Bus Terminal **7**
City of Independence
Tourism Department **9**
Convention & Visitors Bureau
of Greater Kansas City **4**
Country Club Plaza **13**
Crown Center **8**
Downtown **5**
Garment District **3**
Independence, Missouri **10**
Kansas City
International Airport **1**
Kansas Visitor
Information Center **2**
Mission Hills **14**
Missouri Tourist
Information Center **12**
Overland Park **16**
Overland Park Convention
and Visitors Bureau **16**
Truman Sports Complex **12**
Westport **11**

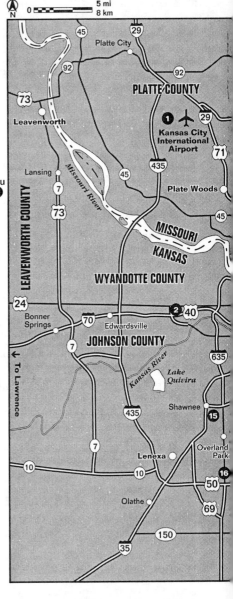

Club Plaza, and Johnson County (in Kansas). To reserve your seat, simply use a courtesy telephone in the airport arrival hall and dial 5000. After telling the operator the gate number you are calling from, you'll be picked up by a shuttle. One-way fares range from $10 to $15, depending on destination, and the hours of operation from the airport are about 6am to 11pm daily. Among the many hotels served by the KCI Shuttle are the Hilton Plaza Inn, Holiday Inn Crown Plaza, Westin Crown Center, Hyatt Regency Crown Center, Allis

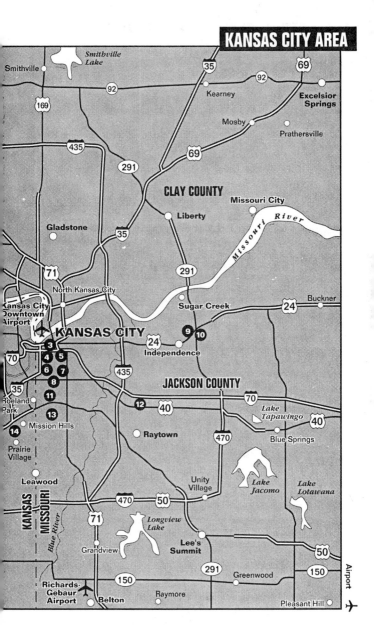

KANSAS CITY AREA

Smithville Lake

Smithville

Kearney

Excelsior Springs

Mosby

Prathersville

CLAY COUNTY

Missouri City

Liberty

Missouri River

Gladstone

North Kansas City

Buckner

Sugar Creek

Kansas City Downtown Airport

KANSAS CITY

9 **10**

Independence

JACKSON COUNTY

Roeland Park

Lake Tapawingo

Mission Hills

Raytown

Blue Springs

Prairie Village

Unity Village

Lake Jacomo

Lake Lotawana

Leawood

KANSAS
MISSOURI

Blue River

Longview Lake

Grandview

Lee's Summit

Richards-Gebaur Airport

Belton

Raymore

Greenwood

Pleasant Hill

Airport

Plaza, Ritz-Carlton, Embassy Suites, and Raphael. For more information call 816/471-2015, or toll free 800/243-6383.

The cheapest way to get from the airport to downtown is via the public **Metro Bus no. 29,** which departs from bus shelters on Bonn Circle (the circle drive that serves all three terminals). Buses depart only nine times per day on Monday through Friday, and the exact fare of 90¢ is required. For more information, call Metro Bus at 816/221-0660.

WHAT THINGS COST IN THE KANSAS CITY AREA	U.S. $
Taxi from airport to downtown Kansas City	$27.00
Bus from downtown to Country Club Plaza	.90
Local telephone call	.25
Double at Ritz-Carlton (expensive)	$150.00
Double at Embassy on the Park (moderate)	70.00
Double at downtown Travelodge (budget)	32.00
Lunch for one at Metropolis (moderate)	11.00
Lunch for one at Arthur Bryant's (budget)	6.00
Dinner for one, without wine, at The American Restaurant (expensive)	45.00
Dinner for one, without wine, at Bristol Bar and Grill (moderate)	25.00
Dinner for one, without wine, at Mario's (budget)	5.00
Pint of beer	2.00
Coca-Cola	1.00
Cup of coffee	.75
Roll of ASA 100 Kodacolor film, 36 exposures	5.50
Admission to Nelson-Atkins Museum of Art	4.00
Movie ticket	6.00
Ticket to Starlight Theatre	4.00–27.00

BY TRAIN

If you're traveling to Kansas City by train, most likely you'll arrive at the **Amtrak** depot at 2200 Main St. (tel. 816/421-3622, or toll free 800/872-7245). From there taxis are available to take to your final destination.

BY BUS

Kansas City is served by three intercity bus lines: **Greyhound/ Trailways, Jefferson,** and **TNM&O** (Texas, New Mexico, and Oklahoma). All use the same bus terminal, located at 12th Street and Troost (tel. 816/698-0080 or 221-2835).

BY CAR

If you're arriving in Kansas City by car, try to avoid rush hour, when I-70 and I-35 are particularly congested. Once in the city, you shouldn't have any problems driving or parking. Parking at most hotels and Country Club Plaza is free.

TOURIST INFORMATION

There are several visitor information centers ready to serve you in Kansas City. If you're driving into Kansas City from St. Louis on I-70, you can stop at the **Missouri Tourist Information Center** (tel. 816/861-8800), which overlooks Royals Stadium on the eastern end of town, off I-70 at the Blue Ridge Cutoff exit (Exit 9). In addition to information on Kansas City, it has information on other destinations in Missouri. Hours are daily from 8am to 5pm (closing an hour earlier on game days); closed on Sunday in December, January, and February.

Kansas City's main tourist office is the **Convention and Visitors Bureau of Greater Kansas City,** located downtown in the City Center Square Building, Suite 2550, 1100 Main St. (tel. 816/221-5242, or toll free 800/767-7700)—open Monday through Friday from 8:30am to 5pm. It distributes free brochures, maps, and other information.

Other tourist offices serving specific sections of greater Kansas City include the **City of Independence Tourism Department,** 111 East Maple, Independence, MO (tel. 816/836-8300); **Overland Park Convention and Visitors Bureau,** 10975 Benson Dr., Suite 360, Building 12, Overland Park, KS (tel. 913/491-0123); and **Kansas City, Kansas, Tourism,** 636 Minnesota Ave., KS (tel. 913/321-5800).

Incidentally, if you're driving west from Kansas City on I-70 to destinations in Kansas, you'll want to stop off at the **Kansas Visitor Information Center,** located about six miles into Kansas (Exit 415)—open daily in summer from 7am to 7pm and daily in winter from 9am to 5pm; closed Easter, Thanksgiving, Christmas, and New Year's Day.

For a weekly recording of festivals, concerts, activities, theatrical plays, sports events, and special events in the Kansas City metropolitan area, call the **Visitor Information Phone** at 816/691-3800. For information on where to hear jazz at Kansas City's various jazz clubs, call the **Jazz Hotline** at 816/931-2888.

CITY LAYOUT

Many newcomers are surprised to learn that the bulk of Kansas City, along with most of its attractions, is not in Kansas but in Missouri. Both the Missouri River and State Line Road serve as boundaries that divide the city, but the division is largely administrative only. For Kansas Citians, the entire metropolitan area is their city and playground, regardless of whether it's Johnson County in Kansas or Country Club Plaza in Missouri. Even a telephone call made throughout most of the city is a local call that does not require use of an area code, even if it's across the state line. A call placed from Independence, Missouri, to Overland Park, Kansas, for example, is a local call. The city covers 10 counties and includes more than 30 incorporated cities.

Downtown Kansas City is located in Missouri, approximately in the center of the greater metropolitan area. Although Kansas City's history is intertwined with the winding ribbon of the Missouri River, the city turned its back on the river more than a century ago when the railroads arrived. Today's downtown Kansas City is therefore about

KANSAS CITY AREA

Missouri

Kansas

Downtown

Barney Allis Plaza ⑦
Bartle Convention
  Center ⑥
Chamber of Commerce ②
City Center Square ④
City Hall ③
City Market ①
Convention & Visitors
  Bureau of Greater
  Kansas City ④
Crown Center ⑨
Greyhound/Trailways
  Terminal ⑤
Kemper Arena ⑧

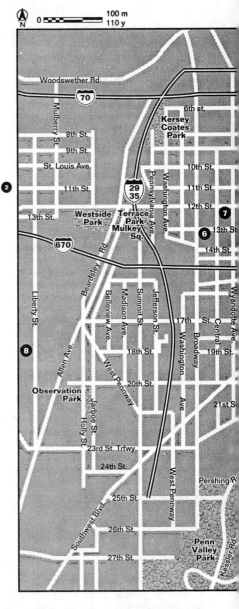

12 blocks south of the Missouri River, and it's here that you'll find its convention center, office buildings, shops, and a handful of hotels. In the past decade, the downtown has experienced a renaissance, because many of its historic buildings have been renovated and city planners are wooing people back from the suburbs into the inner city.

Most of Kansas City's major attractions, restaurants, and nightlife venues are located south of downtown. Crown Center, a huge

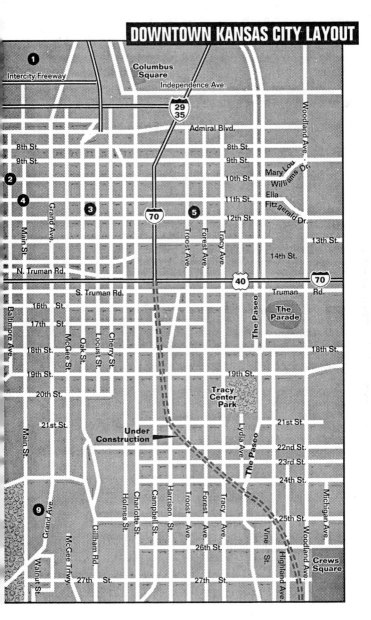

complex containing two luxury hotels, scores of shops, restaurants, entertainment facilities, and the Hallmark Visitors Center, is approximately 15 blocks due south. A 10-minute drive farther south are Westport, with its many bars and clubs; Country Club Plaza, the nation's oldest shopping center; and the renowned Nelson-Atkins Museum—all of which are in an area referred to by the locals as midtown. On the eastern edge of the greater Kansas City is Independence, Missouri, hometown of Harry S Truman and destination for a number of historic sites. On the other end of town, at its southwest corner, is Johnson County in Kansas, which contains Overland Park and Mission Hills, two of the city's most affluent neighborhoods.

MAIN ARTERIES & STREETS Although the majority of Kansas City's streets are arranged on a grid, many boulevards and avenues seem to wind without rhyme or reason. I grew up near Kansas City and usually end up where I want to be simply by heading in the right direction. Luckily, there are several landmark streets that are good standbys for orientation.

In every city I always have a favorite street, and in Kansas City it's Main Street. From the heart of downtown, it runs straight south, changing character as it passes through different parts of town. Main Street leads to several of the city's most popular destinations, including Crown Center, Westport, and Country Club Plaza. Bisecting Main Street (that is, streets that run east and west) are the numbered streets, beginning with 12th and 13th in the heart of downtown. Crown Center is near 24th and Main, Westport is just to the west of 40th and Main, and the Plaza is near 47th and Main.

The easiest way to get around is to take advantage of the various highways that cut through the city. I-70 is useful if you're traveling from downtown to Independence or the Royals stadium; I-35 travels straight through the city from its northeast corner to its southwest end; and I-435 forms a loop around the core of Kansas City.

FINDING AN ADDRESS As previously mentioned, much of Kansas City is composed of a grid, with numbered streets running east and west like the Missouri River. The lowest-numbered streets are closest to the Missouri in the north. Numbers increase as one moves south. The heart of downtown is between 9th and 14th streets; Crown Center is on 24th Street; Country Club Plaza spreads around 47th Street. Main Street serves as the dividing line for addresses designating east or west. Thus, 220 W. 43rd Street is located 43 blocks south of the Missouri River and two blocks west of Main Street.

Block numbers for north-south streets correspond to the numbered cross streets. For example, 7427 Main lies between 74th and 75th streets.

Incidentally, people in the Midwest tend to give directions using north, south, east, and west destinations. Even at home, they talk of the "east bedroom" or "the shelf against the west wall."

MAPS The Convention and Visitors Bureau of Greater Kansas City distributes a free map of the city, which includes both an outline to the entire city and a more detailed map of the downtown area. It's adequate for most purposes, but if you wish to explore the backroads of Kansas City, you might wish to purchase one of many city maps available. The H.M. Gousha *FastMap*™ of Kansas City is very helpful.

NEIGHBORHOODS IN BRIEF

There are so many neighborhoods and communities in the Kansas City area that I could write an entire guidebook on them alone. Following are descriptions of a few.

IMPRESSIONS

*Who in Europe, or in America for that matter, knows that
Kansas City is one of the loveliest cities on earth?*
—ANDRÉ MAUROIS (1946)

Downtown & the Garment District   One hundred years
ago, the Garment District was the hub of Kansas City's financial and
commercial center. It's named after the many garment industries
once located here, industries that in the mid-1940s ranked second
only to New York's in size and stature. The Garment District lies
immediately north of downtown's new commercial center, around
8th and Central. A cultural and financial desert just a decade ago, the
Garment District has been undergoing a renaissance, with many of its
older buildings being restored as offices, hotels, bars, restaurants, and
loft apartments.

River City Market   Located on the banks of the Missouri, the
River City Market area is being revitalized into a small but quaint
neighborhood of restored historic brick buildings, upscale loft
apartments, a bustling city market, and a museum featuring the
contents of a paddlewheel riverboat that sank in 1856. It's located
north of downtown, between I-70 and the Missouri River.

Crown Center   Crown Center is not really a neighborhood,
although it's big enough to encompass one; rather, it's a sprawling
complex containing two luxury hotels; an indoor shopping center;
restaurants; theaters; cinemas; and the corporate headquarters of
Hallmark Cards Inc., the greeting-card manufacturer. In fact, the
whole complex is owned by Hallmark Cards and is sort of a city
within a city. Cater-cornered from Crown Center is Union Station,
which unfortunately has not been renovated like the one in St. Louis
and has stood empty for years. It's the center of controversy over
what should be done with it and who should pay for the renovation.

Westport   Established in 1833 as a terminus for wagon trains
departing on the Santa Fe Trail, Westport predates Kansas City,
which has grown around it. It contains the two oldest buildings in the
city, both on the corner of Westport and Pennsylvania Avenue (one of
them is Kelly's, a well-known tavern). Today, Westport is one of the
hottest nightspots in Kansas City, with scores of bars and clubs
offering live music as well as shops and boutiques along tree-lined
boulevards. Its heart is Westport Road, Broadway, and Pennsylvania,
located to the west of Main between 39th and 44th streets. Country
Club Plaza is just a few blocks farther south.

Country Club Plaza   This was the nation's first shopping
center. Built in 1922 by J. C. Nichols, it was constructed in a Spanish
architectural style (Seville, Spain, is Kansas City's sister city)—with
red-roofed buildings; sparkling fountains; dozens of statues; and
fourteen blocks of shops, department stores, apartments, restaurants,
and bars. Horse-drawn carriages clatter down the streets, and at
Christmas the Plaza erupts into an extravaganza of 49 miles of
Christmas lights that outline the buildings, a tradition started in 1926.
The Plaza is located just west of Main, at 47th Street and Ward
Parkway.

NEARBY NEIGHBORHOODS

Independence   With approximately 112,000 residents, Independence is a separate city on the eastern edge of the metropolis, although where Kansas City starts and Independence begins is hard to say as you're driving along the highway. Founded more than 160 years ago and playing a vital role in the development of the Oregon, Californian, and Santa Fe trails, it was the hometown of Harry S Truman and today contains the Truman Home and the Truman Library and Museum. In addition, the Mormon Visitors Center, several historic mansions, and the new National Frontier Trails Center are here.

Overland Park   Located close by in Johnson County, KS, Overland Park is the region's fastest-growing community, with a population of about 112,000, most around 40 years old. It contains major shopping malls, Corporate Woods (a region of corporate buildings and headquarters), and a number of hotels and restaurants. Easy access to I-435 and I-35 make it a convenient place to stay.

2. GETTING AROUND

Because Kansas City is spread out, most people rely on their own automobiles. Public transportation is available, however. Of most interest to visitors is the Trolley.

BY PUBLIC TRANSPORTATION

BY TROLLEY   The easiest way to travel between downtown, Crown Center, Westport, and Country Club Plaza is by the **Trolley.** Painted bright red and green, these wheeled vehicles make a continuous circuit, with stops at the Town Pavilion and Barney Allis Plaza downtown, the Garment District, Crown Center, the Hyatt Regency Crown Center, Westport, the Nelson-Atkins Museum, and the Plaza. On Saturday from May through October, the Trolley also travels to the City Market near the riverfront.

   The fare is $3 per person (exact fare only), which allows you to get on and off the Trolley three times during the day at no additional cost. Children five and under are free; on Sunday and Monday, children under 12 can ride free when accompanied by an adult. Tickets are available from the driver or in advance at Crown Center Customer Service, the Town Pavilion Information Desk, or The Plaza Merchants Association near the corner of Wornall Road and 47th Street on the Plaza.

   Hours of operation during summer are Monday through Thursday from 10am to 10pm, Friday and Saturday from 10am to midnight, and Sunday from noon to 6pm. During March, April, May, and September through December, hours are Monday through Saturday from 10am to 10pm and Sunday from noon to 6pm. During January and February, the Trolley operates only on weekends, from 10am to 10pm on Saturday and from noon to 6pm on Sunday. For more information, call 221-3399.

BY BUS The **Metro** is Kansas City's public bus system, serving all counties except Johnson County, Kansas (which has its own bus system). There are 43 routes, most in a north-south direction, and buses are identified with both a number and a name. The base fare is 90¢ for regular buses and $1.10 for express buses (designated by one or two Xs following the route number). Children under 5 ride free; children 6 to 11 pay half fare. In any case, make sure you have exact change because the electronic fare boxes accept $1 bills and coins but do not give change. Free transfers are available upon request for a maximum of three trips on any bus going in any direction, valid for one hour during the day on Monday through Saturday and two hours for evening (after 7pm) and Sunday service. A transfer must be handed to the bus operator each time you board the bus. If your trip requires a transfer from a local bus to an express bus, you will need to pay an additional 10¢ or 20¢.

The primary problem, obviously, is finding the bus and the stop that you need. Bus no. 47 Roanoke is useful for travel between downtown (leaving from 10th and Main) and Country Club Plaza (Nichols Road and Jefferson). Bus no. 24 Independence makes runs from downtown (8th and Grand) and Independence. Bus no. 29 KCI Airport is useful for trips between downtown and the airport. To find out which bus you should take and where to board, call the Metro at 221-0660 on Monday through Friday from 6am to 6pm. In addition, there are racks with brochures of the various routes available at City Hall, 12th and Oak downtown, as well as at a number of other locations.

Johnson County maintains its own bus system, with service to downtown, Crown Center, Country Club Plaza, Oak Park Mall, and other locations. For more information, call the **Johnson County Transit** at 541-8450.

BY TAXI

All taxis in Kansas City are on a deregulated meter system, allowing each company to set its own rates. Thus, fares can vary widely. The cab's basic fare must be posted on the outside of the car, and when cabs are lined up, you are not required to take the first. You are not allowed to hail a cab from the street, but there are taxi stands on the street and at hotels. Up to five persons can ride for a shared single fare.

There are more than 30 taxicab companies listed in the Kansas City *Yellow Pages*. Both **Yellow Cab** (tel. 471-5000) and **American Cab Service** (tel. 421-5555) charge $1.30 for the first fifth of a mile, plus $1.10 for each extra mile. The fare from downtown to the airport runs about $27.

BY CAR

Kansas City is easy to navigate by car, especially if you stick to the main roads and highways, have a good map, and avoid rush-hour traffic. Unless otherwise posted, you can turn right on a red light, after stopping, in both Kansas and Missouri. Parking downtown is at a parking garage, on a pay parking lot, or at a meter. Crown Center also has a parking lot, with the first three hours free if you get validation from a merchant. There is no charge for parking at Country Club Plaza.

If you need to rent a car, **Avis** has an office both at the airport (tel.

243-5760) and in Johnson County at 9301 Metcalf (tel. 383-3374). **Budget** (tel. 262-9090) has five locations in Kansas City, including the airport and downtown. Other car-rental companies with locations at the airport include **Dollar** (tel. 243-5600), **Hertz** (tel. 243-5765), **National** (tel. 243-5770), and **Thrifty** (tel. 464-5670).

FAST KANSAS CITY

This section is designed to make your stay in Kansas City as problem-free as possible by answering questions you may have before and during your stay. Remember, too, that the concierge at your hotel is an invaluable source of information, as is the **Convention and Visitors Bureau of Greater Kansas City** (tel. 816/221-5242).

American Express American Express Travel Services is located at Country Club Place, 114 W. 47 St. (tel. 816/531-9114)—open Monday through Friday from 9am to 5pm.

Area Code The telephone area code for the Missouri side of Kansas City is **816;** on the Kansas side it's **913.** Note, however, that within all Kansas City, you can dial without using the area code, even if you're calling a number across the state line.

Airport **Kansas City International Airport** (KCI) is located about a 25-minute drive northwest of downtown. See "Orientation," above.

Auto Rentals See "Getting Around," above.

Babysitters Most of Kansas City's major hotels provide babysitting service or can contact a babysitter should the need arise.

Buses/Trolleys See "Getting Around," above.

Business Hours Office hours are generally Monday through Friday from 9am to 5pm, while most **banks** are open Monday through Friday from about 8am to 4 or 4:30pm. **Shops** are open longer, especially those in malls. Crown Center, for example, is open Monday through Wednesday and Saturday from 10am to 6pm, Thursday and Friday from 10am to 9pm, and Sunday from noon to 5pm. The Town Pavilion downtown is open Monday through Saturday from 10am to 6pm.

Car Rentals See "Auto Rentals," above.

Climate See "When to Go" in Chapter 2.

Dentists/Doctors Some of the expensive hotels offer the services of an in-house doctor or a doctor on call. Otherwise, check the *Yellow Pages* for a list of area doctors. An alternative is to call the **Metropolitan Medical Society of Greater Kansas City** (tel. 816/531-8432), which maintains a list of about 1,500 area physicians. If you need a dentist, contact the **Greater Kansas City Dental Society** (tel. 816/333-5454).

Drugstores There is no 24-hour drugstore in Kansas City. If you need medical attention in the middle of the night, your best bet is the **Trinity Lutheran Hospital,** 3030 Baltimore (tel. 816/751-3000), located three blocks south of Crown Center.

Emergencies As throughout most of the United States, the number to call in an emergency is **911** for police, fire, and ambulance. Also see "Dentists/Doctors" and "Hospitals" in this section.

Eyeglasses If you lose your eyeglasses and need a quick replacement, **Lenscrafters** offers custom-crafted eyeglasses in approximately one hour, with approximately 3,000 brands to choose from. Convenient locations include Bannister Mall, 5600 Bannister Rd., Kansas City (tel. 816/763-4930), and Oak Park Mall, 95th and Quivera, Overland Park (tel. 913/492-7713).

Gay & Lesbian Hotline   If you need to talk to someone while in Kansas City, **Gaytalk** is available evenings at 816/931-4470.

Hairdressers/Barbers   If your hotel does not have a barber shop or beauty salon, the concierge may be able to direct you to one to suit your style. Otherwise, refer to the *Yellow Pages.*

Holidays/Events   For a list of U.S. national holidays, see "Fast Facts: The Foreign Traveler" in Chapter 3. For information on the Kansas City area's special annual events, see "When to Go" in Chapter 2.

Hospitals   If you need to go to a hospital in an emergency, the ambulance will deliver you to the one best suited for your situation. There are more than 25 hospitals in the Kansas City area. Some of the more centrally located include **Trinity Lutheran Hospital,** 3030 Baltimore (tel. 816/751-2345 or 753-4600), which specializes in cardiology, diabetes, lung disease, and oncology; the **University of Kansas Medical Center,** 39th and Rainbow (tel. 913/588-5000), which has a burn center, a neonatal intensive care unit, and a cancer treatment center; and **Children's Mercy Hospital,** 24th St. at Gillham (tel. 816/234-3000), which has a poison center, a level-1 trauma center, and specialty pediatric services.

Information   Locations of Kansas City **tourist offices** are given in "Orientation," above.

Laundry/Dry Cleaning   All the expensive and most of the moderate hotels offer laundry and/or dry-cleaning service. Some of the budget accommodations offer coin-operated laundry machines.

Liquor Laws   The legal drinking age in both Kansas and Missouri is 21. In Kansas City, MO, bars in the "convention trade zones" may serve liquor daily until 3am. On Sunday, however, liquor is available in only restaurants and hotels. The remainder of Kansas City on the Missouri side follows these same guidelines, except that bars close at 1:30am. On the Kansas side, liquor by the drink is served in licensed restaurants and clubs daily from 9am to 2am.

Lost Property   There is no central lost-property office. If you lose something, call the nearest police station to report the loss.

Luggage Storage   If you need to store luggage in Kansas City and the hotel you are staying in cannot do so, your best bet is one of the lockers at the **Greyhound Bus Station,** 12th Street and Troost (tel. 816/221-2835). There's a 30-day limit, and the cost of a locker is $1 for the first day and $3 for each succeeding day.

Mail   The main **post office** of Kansas City is located at 315 Pershing (tel. 816/374-9180), near Crown Center in Midtown. It's open Monday through Friday from 8am to 6:30pm and Saturday from 8am to 12:30pm. Vending machines selling stamps are accessible 24 hours.

Maps   The Convention and Visitors Bureau of Greater Kansas City distributes a free map of the downtown area and city vicinity.

Newspapers/Magazines   Most hotels sell newspapers, including the *Kansas City Star.*

Photographic Needs   If you need film or camera equipment, ask your hotel concierge where the nearest photo shop is.

Police   The emergency number for police throughout most of the United States is **911.**

Religious Services   The Saturday edition of the *Kansas City Star* carries a religious section, with listings of places of worship according to denomination, their location, the times of services, and the pastor.

Restrooms   The best places to search for a public restroom are hotels and restaurants.

Safety   Whenever you're traveling in an unfamiliar city or country, stay alert. Be aware of your immediate surroundings. Wear a money belt and keep a close eye on your possessions. Never carry large amounts of cash and leave your expensive jewelry at home. Be particularly careful with cameras, purses, and wallets—all favorite targets of thieves and pickpockets.

Shoe Repair   You can have your shoes repaired while you wait at **Shoe Pro** in Crown Center, 2450 Grand Ave. (tel. 816/842-0870), in midtown. It's open Monday through Wednesday and Saturday from 10am to 6pm, Thursday and Friday from 10am to 9pm, and Sunday from noon to 5pm.

Taxes   The sales tax for Kansas City, MO, is 6.475%, which includes both state and local taxes and which is added to the price of all goods and food. The tax on hotels in most of Kansas City, MO, is 11.975%; for those near the airport, it's 11.725%. On the Kansas side, a tax of 5.75%, which includes both state and local taxes, is added to the price of all goods and food. If you're staying in a hotel on the Kansas side, a hotel tax of 9.75% will be added to the price of your room.

Taxis   See "Getting Around," above.

Telephone   A local call costs 25¢. Be sure to ask at your hotel whether a surcharge is added to calls made from your room.

Television/Radio   Kansas City's major network stations are NBC on channel 4, CBS on channel 5, and ABC on channel 9. Tune to channel 19 for PBS.

As for radio stations, tune to KCUR for National Public Radio (FM 89.3); KKFI for ethnic music and programs of interest to minorities, women, and other groups (FM 90.1); KFKF for country music (FM 94); KXTR for classical music (FM 96.5); and KCFX for classic rock and roll (FM 101.1).

Time Zone   Kansas City follows Central Standard Time. If it's noon in Kansas City, it's 1pm in New York and 10am in Los Angeles.

Tipping   As elsewhere in the United States, serving people should be tipped 15% to 20%, and bartenders should get at least 10%. Bellhops should receive 50¢ to $1 for each piece of luggage, cab drivers expect a tip of 15% of the fare, and chambermaids should be left $1 per night of stay.

Transit Information   For information on Kansas City's bus system, the **Metro,** dial 816/221-0660.

Weather   Weather information and the forecast can be obtained by dialing 816/531-4444 or 471-4840.

CHAPTER 13

KANSAS CITY AREA ACCOMMODATIONS

Kansas City and its environs offer a wide choice in accommodations—from historic hotels to bed-and-breakfasts, from glittering high-rises to nationwide chains. The hotels recommended in this chapter are divided according to location, but no matter where you choose to stay, you're never very far from the city's many attractions.

The rates quoted below are the standard rack rates, but keep in mind that you can often receive a discounted rate but only if you ask. Many hotels offer weekend rates that are as much as 50% off the regular weekday rate, with no extra charge for two or three extra persons in a room. There are also corporate rates available to business travelers; special packages are available at different times of the year, ranging from pre-Christmas packages to summer specials that include tickets to the theater or attractions. I'm convinced that most people end up paying less than the rack rate, so be sure to request the lowest special rate when making your reservation. Keep in mind that in addition to the rates given, a hotel tax will be added to your bill. For most of Kansas City, Missouri, it's 11.975%; for hotels near KCI Airport it's 11.725%. On the Kansas side, the tax averages about 9.75%.

When choosing a hotel, keep in mind that some offer in their rates a continental breakfast that consists of rolls, coffee, and perhaps juice and fruit. A few even offer complimentary cocktails during evening happy hours. Most hotels in Kansas City offer free parking.

The hotels are divided according to location and then further subdivided according to price. (Unless otherwise noted, all provide private baths.) The **expensive** hotels charge more than $120 per night for two persons; the **moderate** hotels offer rooms for two for $60 to $120; and the **budget** rooms are those that cost less than $60 for two. Generally speaking, the expensive hotels are those found in such choice locations as downtown, Crown Center, and Country Club Plaza. If you're on a budget, try one of the hotels in Kansas City, Kansas, or in other outlying areas. You might also consider staying in a campground.

1. DOWNTOWN

All these hotels are located in the heart of the city, near Kansas City's convention center and just off I-70 and I-35.

EXPENSIVE

ALLIS PLAZA HOTEL, 200 W. 12 St., Kansas City, MO 64105. Tel. 816/421-6800, or toll free 800/548-4782. Fax 816/421-6800. 550 rms, 23 suites. A/C MINIBAR TV TEL

$ Rates: $110–$120 single; $130–$140 double; $150 Corporate Club executive floor single or double; from $190 suite. Extra person $15. Children under 18 stay free in parents' room. Weekend and corporate rates and summer discounts available. AE, CB, DC, DISC, MC, V. **Parking:** Free.

Located across from Barney Allis Plaza and Bartle Hall convention center, this is *the* favorite hotel of the convention trade. A modern and rather unspectacular 22-story high-rise, the Allis Plaza makes up for its plain outward appearance with a lavishly appointed and spacious lobby, complete with a plant-filled atrium and an artificial waterfall dominating one entire wall. Facilities include everything you'd expect from a first-rate hotel: from a health club on the 22nd floor to a concierge desk that will help obtain tickets for everything from a Royals game to the theater.

Rooms are large, and each comes with a stocked refrigerator, two telephones, a TV with radio and full cable, and a bathroom equipped with a clothesline and a scale. Full-length bay windows provide a great view of the city—request a room facing Barney Allis Plaza. If you feel like pampering yourself, the Corporate Club executive level, located on the 20th and 21st floors, offers complimentary breakfast, happy-hour cocktails and hors d'oeuvres, and its own lounge with a concierge.

Dining/Entertainment: The hotel's restaurant serves steaks and a variety of meals in a relaxed setting. Afterward, you can enjoy a drink and listen to music at the 12th Street Bar.

Services: Room service until midnight, same-day laundry.

Facilities: Indoor pool, sauna, health club ($10 extra), outdoor tennis courts, gift shop, newsstand, florist shop.

MODERATE

EMBASSY ON THE PARK (formerly Days Hotel), 1215 Wyandotte, Kansas City, MO 64105. Tel. 816/471-1333. 176 rms, 13 suites. A/C TV TEL

$ Rates (including buffet or continental breakfast): $70 single or double; from $85 suite. Extra person $5. Children under 10 stay free in parents' room. Weekend, corporate, and special rates available. AE, CB, DC, DISC, MC, V. **Parking:** $2.

This is a small older hotel with character, located across from Barney Allis Plaza square. It was built in 1926 and still has such charming features as an old-fashioned letter drop beside the elevator that delivers letters to the ground floor and a small lobby with its original fixtures. What's more, Embassy on the Park offers lots of complimentary extras, from buffet break-

FROMMER'S SMART TRAVELER: HOTELS

VALUE-CONSCIOUS TRAVELERS SHOULD TAKE ADVANTAGE OF THE FOLLOWING:

1. Weekend discounts of up to 50% available at most expensive and moderately priced hotels in the Kansas City area.
2. Corporate rates usually offered to the business traveler may also be available to vacationers who present business cards.
3. Winter discounts available at some inexpensive hotels.
4. Less expensive hotels that often are located outside the downtown area.
5. Breakfasts included in the price of your hotel room.
6. Campgrounds and youth hostels at rock-bottom prices.

QUESTIONS TO ASK IF YOU'RE ON A BUDGET

1. Does the room rate include breakfast? Is breakfast served buffet-style, allowing you to eat all you want?
2. Is there a charge for parking? (Parking is usually free at hotels in Kansas City.)
3. Is there a surcharge for phone calls made from your room? (Some hotels offer free phone calls.)
4. Are discounts available? (Weekend rates can sometimes be less than those offered during the week.)

fasts on weekdays (continental on weekends) to evening cocktails. Rooms are comfortable, and those with the best view are on the top floor overlooking the square. The Embassy also offers a complimentary cocktail hour on Monday through Saturday from 5:30 to 6:30pm, free local phone calls, laundry facilities, and the free use of a nearby health club. If you like historic, European-style hotels, you'll like this place (though the lobby could do without the fake plants and flowers). Highly recommended.

HISTORIC SUITES, 612 Central, Kansas City, MO 64105. Tel. 816/842-6544, or toll free 800/733-0612. Fax 816/842-6544. 101 suites. A/C TV TEL

$ Rates (including buffet breakfast): $135 studio; $109 one-bedroom suite; $135 queen; $165 two-bedroom suite. Rollaway bed $10. Weekend and corporate rates and honeymoon package available; discounts for longer stays. AE, CB, DC, DISC, MC, V. **Parking:** Free.

I wish I could move in here permanently. Not only are all the suites huge, with tall ceilings and lots of windows, but also they're beautifully appointed—with separate living, dining, and sleeping areas. What's more, every suite has a fully stocked kitchen, with everything from a microwave oven, a dishwasher, a toaster, and a coffee machine down to a carrot peeler. The hotel's welcome pack includes complimentary coffee, tea, sugar, cream, and popcorn for the first night of your stay. And, as though that weren't

KANSAS CITY AREA

Allis Plaza Hotel **5**
Embassy on the Park **6**
Historic Suites **2**
Hotel Savoy **3**
Hyatt Regency
  Crown Center **7**
Radisson Suite Hotel
  Kansas City **4**
Travelodge **1**
Westin Crown Center **8**

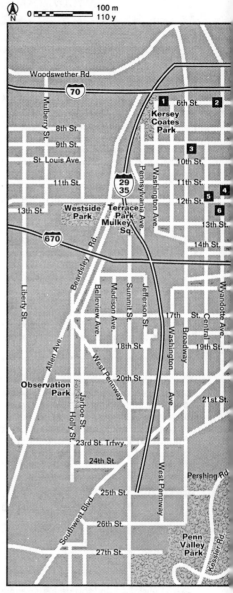

enough, the staff will do your grocery shopping for free (you pay for the goods, of course), the maid will clean all your dishes in the morning, and they provide free transportation to downtown businesses as well as same-day laundry and dry-cleaning services. Complimentary appetizers, wine, and beer are offered on Monday through Thursday from 5 to 7pm. And the facilities include an outdoor pool, a whirlpool and sauna, and a laundry. My kind of place.

Suites, ranging from studios that are much larger than regular hotel rooms to two-bedroom suites, are located in two restored brick buildings in the Garment District, both dating from the 1890s and listed on the National Historic Register. Most of the guests here are business travelers, some of whom stay for months. It's easy to see why.

HOTEL SAVOY, **9th and Central, Kansas City, MO 64105.** **Tel. 816/842-3575.** Fax 816/221-3131. 30 rms and suites. A/C TV TEL

$ Rates (including breakfast): $85 single or double; $97–$130 suite. AE, CB, DC, DISC, MC, V. **Parking:** Free.

Hooray, the Savoy lives! After years of neglect as a seedy and flea-bitten flophouse, the Savoy is now undergoing an ambitious and complete renovation, with the date of completion slated for 1993. That will bring to 80 the total number of rooms and suites, which offer modern conveniences without sacrificing historic quaintness. After all, this hotel, built in 1888, has the distinction of being the longest continuously run hotel west of the Mississippi with the same name. Both Teddy Roosevelt and Harry Truman ate at its renowned Famous Savoy Grill and Restaurant, and Houdini suffered the embarrassment of getting locked in a telephone booth from which he couldn't escape. Rooms have tall ceilings; some have brass, four-poster, or canopy beds; and bathroom fixtures include claw-foot tubs and old-fashioned sinks. The most expensive accommodations, called Deluxe Victorian Suites, each feature a fireplace, a wet bar, french doors separating the living room from the bedroom, and one-and-a-half baths. All rooms have coffee machines and free Kona coffee, and you receive complimentary Bailey's Irish Cream and free morning newspapers.

Breakfast is a luxurious affair with crisp white tablecloths, a maître d' decked out in black tuxedo and bow tie, and choices ranging from smoked salmon with caviar to veal chop.

RADISSON SUITE HOTEL KANSAS CITY, 12th at Baltimore, Kansas City, MO 64105. Tel. 816/221-7000, toll free 800/333-3333. Fax 816/221-7000. 214 rms and suites. A/C MINIBAR TV TEL

$ Rates (including breakfast): $99–$109 single or double; suite $119 single, $129 double. Extra person $10. Children under 18 stay free in parents' room. Weekend, senior-citizen, and corporate rates available. AE, CB, DC, DISC, MC, V. **Parking:** Free (valet $5).

This is another historic downtown hotel, built in 1930 and exalting in the art deco style. Recently renovated, the Radisson still has its original woodwork, marble, lighting, and fixtures—including an 11-foot-tall gilded statue called "Mother of the Stars," who stands on tiptoe on the crest of a wave overlooking the lobby. The hotel, a registered National Historic Landmark, stands on the site where Harry S Truman once had a gentleman's haberdashery. Geared toward corporate travelers, rooms offer remote-control TVs with in-house pay movies, alarm clocks with radios, bathrobes, king- or queen-size beds, separate vanity areas with makeup mirrors, large working desks, and two telephones each. Complimentary breakfasts are cooked to order.

The Radisson's restaurant serves steaks and prime rib, and the hotel also has a sports bar and a café, plus a business center and a 24-hour health club. Offered to guests are complimentary cocktails daily from 4:30 to 6:30pm, room service until 10pm, free morning newspapers, free coffee delivered to rooms, and same-day laundry service.

BUDGET

TRAVELODGE, (formerly Howard Johnson), 610 Washington, Kansas City, MO 64105. Tel. 816/421-1800. 180 rms, 5 suites. A/C TV TEL

ⓕ FROMMER'S COOL FOR KIDS: HOTELS

The Ritz-Carlton *(p. 175)* This ritzy hotel offers a special activity program for children 5 to 12 on Saturdays from 10am to 2pm. The program costs $20 per child and includes lunch, games, storytelling, adventure walks, and arts and crafts. Reservations are required.

Westin Crown Center *(p. 174)* Kids love the Westin's new Cush-N-Cubes playground, complete with eight activity cubes including a 16-foot tube slide, a web-crawl tube, a multilevel climber, a ball pit, and a punching-bag pit. The Westin also boasts a heated outdoor pool and a shuffleboard court.

$ Rates: $25 single; $32 double; from $50 suite. Extra person $8. Children under 18 stay free in parents' room. Corporate rates available. AE, CB, DC, DISC, MC, V. **Parking:** Free.

The advantage to staying in this hotel is that it's located right on I-70 (the Broadway exit), making it easy to find if you're arriving late at night. An older hotel, it offers a seventh-floor lounge with jazz on weekends and pleasant and clean rooms. Rooms facing north have large sliding-glass doors that open onto balconies overlooking I-70 and the river beyond, but they tend to be noisy with traffic. Ask for a room on a higher floor. Rooms facing south have a view of the Quality Hill residential area and do not have balconies. There are no-smoking rooms available. The Travelodge has a restaurant and two lounges, plus an outdoor pool, a game room, a laundry, and a gift shop. Services include room service until 10pm and one-day laundry and dry cleaning.

---

2. CROWN CENTER

Crown Center is a city within a city, complete with two hotels, restaurants, shops, and nightlife entertainment.

EXPENSIVE

HYATT REGENCY CROWN CENTER, 2345 McGee St., Kansas City, MO 64108. Tel. 816/421-1234, or toll free 800/233-1234. Fax 816/435-4190. Telex 434022. 689 rms, 42 suites. A/C MINIBAR TV TEL

$ Rates: $130 single; $160 double; $25 extra for Regency Club executive floor; from $215 suite. Extra person $15. Children under 18 stay free in parents' room. Weekend rates available. AE, CB, DC, DISC, MC, V. **Parking:** $8.50.

Linked to Crown Center via an enclosed skywalk, the Hyatt Regency is known for its excellent service and personal touches. Soaring 42 stories, the hotel has a spacious and dramatic lobby, patterned after the 115-year-old Galleria in Milan, Italy, and featuring a five-story atrium with skylights, plants, and a bubbling fountain.

Rooms are generously large, with original artwork and fresh plants giving them a homey and comfortable atmosphere. The top two floors are reserved for the Regency Club, which features its own lounge, full-time concierge service, free continental breakfast, and free happy-hour appetizers, as well as such extra touches as terry-cloth robes, shoe-shine machines, hairdryers, and complimentary mineral water and candies.

Dining: The Peppercorn Duck Club is one of Kansas City's best restaurants, known for its steaks and seafood. Skies is a revolving restaurant high above the city; The Terrace is a casual, bright, and spacious restaurant open throughout the day.

Services: 24-hour room service, same-day laundry and dry cleaning.

Facilities: Outdoor pool, tennis courts, sauna, whirlpool, exercise room, gift shop.

WESTIN CROWN CENTER, One Pershing Rd., Kansas City, MO 64108. Tel. 816/474-4400, or toll free 800/228-3000. Fax 816/391-4490. 676 rms, 49 suites. A/C MINIBAR TV TEL

$ Rates: $150 single; $175 double; Executive Club floor $20 extra; from $330 suite. Extra person $30. Children under 18 stay free in parents' room. Weekend, corporate, and other rates available. AE, CB, DC, DISC, MC, V. **Parking:** $8.50.

Located right in Crown Center, the Westin Crown Center is one of Kansas City's premier hotels, and this will be evident as soon as you walk into the lobby. The hotel was built into the side of a limestone cliff, which was retained and utilized in the construction—it was turned into a dramatic five-story indoor waterfall and rock garden. Service is excellent, from the front desk to the room service to the restaurants. But what appeals to most guests is that they can walk out of the hotel and right into shops, theaters, restaurants, and the attractions of Crown Center.

All rooms are luxuriously appointed, complete with remote-control TVs, minibars, and glass-sliding doors that open onto small balconies. Guests can receive messages either by written note or by voice mail over the telephone. On the 17th floor is the Executive Club, where guests are treated to such extra services as complimentary continental breakfasts; free soft drinks and snacks throughout the day; complimentary evening cocktails; free morning newspapers; and hairdryers, makeup mirrors, and mini-TVs in the bathrooms.

Dining: Benton's is one of Kansas City's best steak houses, made even better by the fact that it offers a rooftop view of the city. Trader Vic's serves a variety of international dishes in a tropical setting; the Brasserie offers American and continental dishes in a relaxed, bistrolike atmosphere.

Services: 24-hour room service, valet and same-day laundry, limousine service.

Facilities: Year-round heated outdoor pool, two tennis courts, health club, sauna, steam room, jogging track, children's playground, putting green, games court, shuffleboard, live theater, business center.

3. COUNTRY CLUB PLAZA

Although the Plaza is considered a part of midtown, it's important enough to warrant its own heading. Because of the Plaza's choice location, hotels on or near it tend to be expensive.

EXPENSIVE

THE RITZ-CARLTON, 401 Ward Pkwy., Kansas City, MO 64112. Tel. 816/756-1500, or toll free 800/241-3333. Fax 816/756-1635. 352 rms, 21 suites. A/C MINIBAR TV TEL
$ **Rates:** $150–$190 single or double; $225 Club Executive floor; from $275 suite. Extra person $20. Children under 18 stay free in parents' room. Weekend and other packages available. AE, CB, DC, DISC, ER, MC, V. **Parking:** Free.

The Ritz-Carlton gets my vote as the ritziest hotel in town. It opened in 1990 in what was formerly the Alameda Plaza, which is where Ronald Reagan stayed during the 1976 Republican convention. Located across the street from Country Club Plaza and offering great views, it follows the Ritz tradition with 18th- and 19th-century antiques and artwork throughout, elaborate floral arrangements, imported carpets, and crystal chandeliers. Its lobby is one of understated elegance, with a low ceiling, a marble floor, chandeliers, and mahogany walls. The service is as good as it gets anywhere, and the facilities and extra guest amenities leave nothing to be desired. This is the place to be if you wish to be pampered.

Rooms are traditionally furnished in antique reproductions, with such luxuries as imported Italian marble bathrooms, hairdryers, plush terry-cloth robes, room safes, bathroom scales, and three telephones each. The more expensive rooms have balconies. For unbridled indulgence, stay on the Ritz-Carlton Club floors (10 and 11), with private access, a concierge staff, and a private lounge. Guests here are treated to six food presentations a day, from a complimentary continental breakfast to afternoon tea with pastries and evening cocktails and hors d'oeuvres. Highly recommended.

Dining: The Grill is the hotel's signature restaurant, offering elegant dining with a view of the Plaza and American cuisine ranging from steaks to seafood. The Café offers more casual dining, including tables on a terrace with a view of the pool and Plaza, with a menu that serves light and hearty fare along with fitness cuisine. The Lounge serves an afternoon tea as well as cocktails throughout the afternoon and evening.

Services: 24-hour room service, same-day laundry, limousine service, complimentary morning newspaper, babysitting.

Facilities: Fitness exercise room, heated outdoor pool, sauna, car-rental agency, gift boutique and sundry shop.

SHERATON SUITES ON THE COUNTRY CLUB PLAZA (formerly the Marriott Plaza), 770 W. 47th St., Kansas City, MO 64112. Tel. 816/931-4400, or toll free 800/325-3535. Fax 816/561-7330. 259 suites. A/C MINIBAR TV TEL
$ **Rates:** $150 single; $175 double. Extra person $10. Children under 12 stay free in parents' room. Weekend and other packages available. AE, CB, DC, DISC, MC, V. **Parking:** Free.

This modern high-rise is the newest addition to the Country Club Plaza. It offers only suites, each consisting of a living room and a bedroom separated by french doors and including two remote-control TVs, two telephones, a large desk, a coffeemaker and coffee, a hairdryer, and an iron and ironing board. Most suites also have a sofa bed in the living room, and bedrooms boast either a king-size bed or two double beds. Since room rates are the same no matter where you stay, request a room on the 18th floor facing the Plaza for the best view.

Dining: The hotel's restaurant features beef and seafood specialties, as well as lighter fare served in a casual atmosphere. There's also a lobby bar.

Services: Room service until 11pm, same-day laundry, free newspaper and coffee.

Facilities: Indoor/outdoor pool, whirlpool, health club, sundry shop.

MODERATE

HILTON PLAZA INN, 1 E. 45th St., Kansas City, MO 64111. Tel. 816/753-7400, or toll free 800/525-6321. Fax 816/753-4777. 230 rms, 10 suites. A/C MINIBAR TV TEL
$ Rates: $99–$110 single; $109–$115 double; from $175 suite. Extra person $10. Children under 18 stay free in parents' room. Weekend and corporate rates available. AE, CB, DC, DISC, ER, MC, V. **Parking:** Free (valet).

Located on the corner of Main and 45th streets, about a five-minute walk from the Plaza, this is one of the more economical hotels in the vicinity. The Hilton Plaza is built around a heated outdoor pool, and across the street is a popular mile track with workout stations along the way.

Each room is equipped with a minibar; a remote-control TV with pay movies; a clothesline in the bathroom; and such amenities as a sewing kit, mouthwash, and shoe polish. Some rooms facing the outside have a view of the Plaza, while some of those facing the inner courtyard have sliding doors that open onto the pool.

Dining/Entertainment: Main Street Grill specializes in seafood and Kansas City steaks. M.J.'s Piano Lounge offers live piano music six nights a week.

Services: Courtesy shuttle to Westport and Plaza, valet laundry, babysitting, free coffee mornings in the lobby, room service until 11pm.

Facilities: Heated outdoor pool, cardiovascular workout center, beauty shop, barber shop, gift shop.

HOLIDAY INN CROWN PLAZA, (formerly Marriott Plaza Hotel), 4445 Main St., Kansas City, MO 64111. Tel. 816/531-3000, or toll free 800/HOLIDAY. Fax 816/531-3007. 278 rms, 18 suites. A/C TV TEL
$ Rates: $109 single; $119 double; $129 Concierge Executive floor; from $350 suite. Extra person free. Weekend, corporate, and other discounts available. AE, CB, DC, DISC, ER, MC, V. **Parking:** Free.

Located right beside the Hilton Plaza Inn, the Holiday Inn is more luxuriously appointed than the Hilton, with only slightly higher prices. The small marble lobby is elegantly simple; the guest rooms each offer a remote-control cable TV, pay movies, and two telephones (with call waiting). There are five no-smoking floors, and the 19th Concierge floor includes a complimentary continental breakfast and evening hors d'oeuvres in its prices.

Dining: Curios Restaurant offers a wide variety of cuisines and presents a lunch buffet of different national cuisine daily, ranging from Asian to Italian. After dinner you can retire to the Plaza Bar, which has a dance floor.

Services: Room service until midnight, same-day laundry.

Facilities: Health club with complete Nautilus circuit, whirlpool, indoor pool, sunning deck, gift shop.

THE RAPHAEL, 325 Ward Pkwy, Kansas City, MO 64112. Tel. 816/756-3800, or toll free 800/821-5343. Fax 816/756-3800. 33 rms, 90 suites. A/C MINIBAR TV TEL

$ Rates (including continental breakfast): $90–$105 single; $111–$125 double; $115–$125 single suite, $135–$145 double suite. Extra person $20. Children under 18 stay free in parents' room. Weekend, corporate, and other rates available. AE, CB, DC, DISC, MC, V. **Parking:** Free.

Located across the street from the Plaza, the Raphael occupies a beautiful brick building that was built in 1927 to house apartments and was converted into a hotel in 1975. Fashioned after the small and elegant hotels of Europe, it is a delightful place to stay if you prefer intimacy rather than convention crowds.

Rooms are large, each equipped with either a queen- or king-size bed, a sofa bed, a TV with remote control, and a stocked minibar. Some rooms have a view of the Plaza at no extra charge; suites, on the other hand, are charged according to whether they have a view of the Plaza. The lobby was recently renovated—next on the agenda are the rooms, which, although adequate, could do with a bit of spiffing up.

Dining: The Raphael, a romantic restaurant just off the lobby, offers international cuisine and a cocktail bar.

Services: 24-hour room service, same-day laundry, complimentary continental breakfast delivered to room, free morning newspaper, babysitting.

BED-&-BREAKFAST

SOUTHMORELAND ON THE PLAZA, 116 E. 46th St., Kansas City, MO 64112. Tel. 816/531-7979. Fax 816/531-2407. 12 rms (all with bath). A/C TEL

$ Rates (including breakfast): $95–$125 single; $105–$135 double. Corporate rates and winter discounts available. AE, MC, V. **Parking:** Free.

This bed-and-breakfast comes as something of a surprise. Located in the center of Kansas City within walking distance of both the Plaza and the Nelson-Atkins Museum of Art, it nevertheless has a countryside New England flair, imparted perhaps by its formal gardens, antique furnishings, and cozy ambience. A three-story Colonial Revival mansion built in 1913, it features a cheery solarium with wicker furniture; a comfortable living room with a communal TV and VCR and a library of more than 100 classic films; and 12 unique guest rooms, each slightly different from the others and named after famous Kansas Citians, including Thomas Hart Benton, Satchel Paige (whose room comes with two box seats to a Royals game during baseball season), and George Caleb Bingham. Half the rooms have private decks; four have fireplaces; one is handicapped accessible. There are such personal touches as decanters of sherry, along with fresh flowers and fruit. Note, however, that smoking is prohibited in guest rooms and is restricted to the living room and public veranda. In addition, children under 13 are not allowed. Guests are allowed free use of the nearby Rockhill Tennis Club, which also offers swimming and a health club. Highly recommended.

4. WESTPORT & MIDTOWN

Westport is Kansas City's nightlife hot spot, with plenty of bars and restaurants.

EXPENSIVE

EMBASSY SUITES HOTEL, 220 W. 43rd St., Kansas City, MO 64111. Tel. 816/756-1720, or toll free 800/EMBASSY. Fax 816/756-3260. 266 suites. A/C TV TEL
$ Rates (including buffet breakfast): $139 single or double; $149 triple or quad. Extra person $10. Children under 12 stay free in parents' room. Weekend, corporate, and senior-citizen rates available. AE, CB, DC, DISC, MC, V. **Parking:** Free.

In keeping with the Spanish architecture of the nearby Plaza, this Embassy Suites features a dramatic inner courtyard that soars 12 stories above its stone floor, embellished with plants ringing each floor and topped with a skylight. A fountain bubbles in the middle of it. The hotel is located just off J. C. Nichols Parkway, less than two blocks from Westport and four blocks from the Plaza. Complimentary breakfasts here are buffet style, along with cooked-to-order dishes; the pool has two tiers connected by a waterfall.

As with all hotels in this chain, the rooms are two-room suites, each complete with a kitchenette stocked with a stove, refrigerator, coffeemaker, and coffee. Cooking utensils are available on request. There are two TVs, one in the living room and one in the bedroom, with pay movies. A good choice for longer stays, the Embassy is very popular with business travelers. All suites open onto walkways that ring the inner atrium as well as onto tiny balconies on the outside of the building (not for the acrophobic). No-smoking suites are available.

Dining/Entertainment: The Plaza Grill serves everything from sandwiches and pasta to steaks and chicken. There's also a lounge featuring live piano music on weekends and a dance floor.

Services: Complimentary two-hour evening cocktail service.

Facilities: Indoor pool, whirlpool, sauna, steam room, game room, pool tables, gift shop.

MODERATE

COMFORT INN, 801 Westport Rd., Kansas City, MO 64111. Tel. 816/931-1000. 109 rms. A/C TV TEL
$ Rates (including continental breakfast): $62–$70 single; $70–$80 double. Extra person $7. Children under 18 stay free in

parents' room. Weekend and corporate rates available. AE, CB, DC, DISC, ER, MC, V. **Parking:** Free.

This is a good choice in inexpensive lodging just a few minutes' walk from the nighttime action of Westport. Rooms are large and pleasant enough, with hints of the Southwest in their earth-tone pastels and artwork featuring Native Americans. A variety of rooms are available, including those with king-size beds or two double beds; no-smoking rooms and handicapped-accessible rooms also are available. Breakfast here consists of coffee, juice, and pastries. Also offered are complimentary snacks and sodas on Tuesday through Thursday from 4:30 to 6:30pm and valet laundry service.

THE QUARTERAGE HOTEL WESTPORT, 560 Westport Rd., Kansas City, MO 64111. Tel. 816/931-0001, or toll free 800/942-4233. 115 rms, 8 suites. A/C TV TEL

$ Rates (including continental breakfast): $75 single; $92 double; from $140 suite. Extra person $15. Children under 16 stay free in parents' room. Weekend and corporate rates available. AE, DC, DISC, MC, V. **Parking:** Free.

You can't get closer to Westport than this handsome brick hotel. Comfortable, spotless, and relatively new, it's tastefully decorated throughout and offers the basics plus a few extras. Each room features a remote-control cable TV, full-length mirrors, a clock-radio, two phones, and a desk. The Quarterage's facilities include an exercise room, a sauna, and a whirlpool, and it offers complimentary cocktails on Monday through Saturday from 5 to 7pm, free local phone calls, and laundry service.

BUDGET

TRAVEL INN, 3240 Broadway, Kansas City, MO 64111. Tel. 816/531-9250, or toll free 800/255-3050. 52 rms. A/C TV TEL

$ Rates: $43 single; $49 double. Extra person $5. Children under 18 stay free in parents' room. AE, CB, DC, DISC, MC, V. **Parking:** Free.

Centrally located only a five-minute drive from downtown or the Plaza, this is an older three-story hotel that is slowly receiving a much needed facelift, which should be completed by the time you read this. Rooms come with the basics; free coffee is available in the lobby. Although there's no restaurant in the hotel, there's a Pancake House Restaurant next door.

BED-&-BREAKFASTS

Both bed-and-breakfasts listed here are on the edge of Hyde Park in midtown, about a seven-minute ride from both the Plaza and the Crown Center.

DOANLEIGH WALLAGH, 217 E. 37th St., Kansas City, MO 64111. Tel. 816/753-2667. 5 rms (all with bath). TV TEL

$ Rates (including breakfast): $80–$110 double. Extra adult or child $10. AE, MC, V. Monthly rates available. **Parking:** Free.

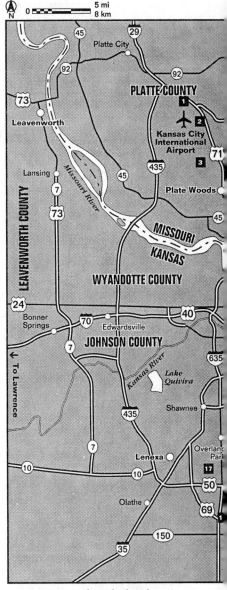

⭐ This is a turn-of-the-century mansion furnished with antiques and decorative objects culled from travels and local treasures, including furniture and silver from the old Muehlbach Hotel, which served as a landmark in downtown Kansas City for many years. The Doanleigh is owned by friendly Carolyn and Edward Litchfield, who bring their personal touches and flair to their home. Carolyn, a former home-economics teacher, places fresh cookies in guest rooms every day; breakfasts include such dishes as French toast with honey glaze, Russian pancakes, omelets, and eggs Benedict. Rooms, all with cable TV offering four movie channels, come in a variety of styles and prices. The Hyde Park Master Suite, for example, is the most expensive, complete with a four-poster queen bed and a working fireplace. The Westport Room has a porch. Communal facilities include a living room with big-screen TV, a VCR and videos, and a grand piano. Children are accepted only by prior arrangement.

MILFORD HOUSE, 3605 Gillham Rd., Kansas City, MO 64111. Tel. 816/753-1269. 4 rms (all with bath). A/C TV

$ Rates (including breakfast): $65 single; $75 double. AE, MC, V.
Parking: On the street.

Just across the park from the bed-and-breakfast above, this accommodation is a red-painted brick home, a combination of Queen Anne and Dutch colonial styles. Built in 1889 and opening as a bed-and-breakfast a century later, Milford House is owned by Ian and Pat Mills. Pat hails from Mississippi, while Ian was born and raised in the original Milford House in England. Guest rooms here are named after English royalty. Robes are provided for rooms with shared bathrooms, and in the living room is a piano (Margaret Truman's music teacher is rumored to have lived here). Note the three-story circular wooden staircase and the 70-square-foot stained-glass window in the living room, modeled after a Tiffany landscape.

5. OVERLAND PARK, KS

Both hotels below are located near the intersection of I-435 and Highway 169 (Metcalf Avenue), on the southern end of Kansas City in the suburb of Overland Park, KS. I-35 and the Corporate Woods development park are close by, and downtown Kansas City is 10 miles north.

MODERATE

HOLIDAY INN EXPRESS (formerly Best Western Overland Park Inn), 7200 W. 107th St., Overland Park, KS 66212. Tel. 913/648-7858, or toll free 800/HOLIDAY. Fax 913/648-1867. 80 rms. A/C TV TEL

$ Rates (including continental breakfast): $60–$65 single; $66–$71 double. Extra person $6. Children 18 and under stay free in parents' room. Weekend, corporate, senior-citizen, and other discounts available. AE, DC, MC, V. **Parking:** Free.

This is a streamlined version business-oriented hotel of the Holiday Inn, which is why many people stay here. Rooms are clean and comfortable, each offering a remote-control cable TV and a clock-radio; no-smoking rooms are available. Also offered are complimentary newspapers, free local phone calls, in-room coffee machines, and vending machines. The facilities include an outdoor pool and a laundry room.

COURTYARD BY MARRIOTT, 11301 Metcalf Ave., Overland Park, KS 66212. Tel. 913/339-9900, or toll free 800/321-2211. Fax 913/339-6091. 137 rms, 12 suites. A/C TV TEL

$ Rates: $79 single; $89 double; suite from $94 single, $104 double. Extra person free. Weekend rates and discounts for longer stays available. AE, CB, DC, DISC, MC, V. **Parking:** Free.

The Courtyard was designed with the business traveler in mind—from its large desks to such facilities as an exercise room for working off stress and a whirlpool for relaxation. Opened in 1989 on the edge of town, away from the mainstream of traffic, this hotel is built around an inner courtyard that contains an expanse of green and a terrace. Rooms each come with a remote-control cable TV with pay movies, a clock-radio, a sofa, a sink separated from the bathroom, and in-room coffee service. Some rooms face the inner courtyard and come with balconies but not higher rates. No-smoking rooms are available. The hotel contains a restaurant and a lounge, plus an indoor pool, a sunning terrace, a whirlpool, an exercise room, and a laundry.

6. NEAR THE TRUMAN SPORTS COMPLEX

Both hotels below are located on I-70 at the Blue Ridge Cutoff exit, approximately a 12-minute drive east of downtown Kansas City. The Truman Sports Complex is across the highway, making this area a convenient place to stay if you're here mainly to watch the baseball Royals or the football Chiefs. In addition, Worlds of Fun and attractions in Independence are close by.

EXPENSIVE

ADAM'S MARK, 9103 E. 39th, Kansas City, MO 64133. Tel. 816/737-0200, or toll free 800/444-ADAM. Fax 816/737-0200. 365 rms, 9 suites. A/C TV TEL

$ Rates: $95–$130 single; $120–$150 double; from $330 suite. Extra person $16. Children under 18 stay free in parents' room. Weekend, corporate, and other rates available. AE, CB, DC, DISC, MC, V. **Parking:** Free.

This hotel caters largely to group and convention travelers, many of whom want to take advantage of the Royals and Chiefs stadiums across the street. On game days, the hotel even offers a free shuttle bus to the Sports Complex. A sister hotel to the landmark Adam's Mark in downtown St. Louis, this has dependably good service and a wide range of facilities.

Rooms are pleasant and clean, with either queen-size or king-size beds or two double beds. Rooms on the 15th floor have higher ceilings and tend to be quieter than those closer to the highway. The best views are those of the stadiums or downtown Kansas City.

Dining/Entertainment: Remington's, the hotel's premier restaurant, serves steaks and seafood in the tradition of the American West. The Pantry is a casual dining room open for breakfast through dinner. The Players Lounge has a big-screen TV before which you can drink and watch sports; Quincy's is the hottest night spot around, offering live entertainment and dancing as well as happy-hour drinks and buffets.

Services: $1 shuttle to Truman Sports Complex, valet laundry, room service until 11pm.

Facilities: Indoor and outdoor pools, sauna, whirlpool, exercise room, tennis courts, gift shop.

MODERATE

DRURY INN, 3830 Blue Ridge Cutoff, Kansas City, MO 64133. Tel. 816/923-3000, or toll free 800/325-8300. Fax 816/923-3000. 133 rms. A/C TV TEL

$ Rates (including continental breakfast): $58–$63 single; $69–$74 double. Extra person $6. Children under 18 stay free in parents' room. Senior-citizen discount. AE, CB, DC, DISC, MC, V. **Parking:** Free.

S Drury Inn is a St. Louis–based hotel chain that offers clean and comfortable accommodations at remarkably low prices. Half the rooms here are no-smoking, and all offer remote-control cable TVs with pay movies. Located across the street from the Adam's Mark, the Drury Inn features an outdoor pool and free local phone calls and coffee. There's a Denny's restaurant next door.

7. KANSAS CITY, KS

Kansas City, KS, is less than a five-minute drive west of downtown Kansas City, MO. Thus, the two hotels listed here are good choices if you wish to stay close to downtown but don't want to pay downtown prices. To reach them, take I-70 west from downtown to the Minnesota Avenue exit.

BUDGET

CIVIC CENTRE HOTEL, 424 Minnesota Ave., Kansas City, KS 66101. Tel. 913/342-6919, or toll free 800/542-2983. Fax 913/342-6919. 201 rms. A/C TV TEL
$ Rates: $55 single, $60 double. Extra person $6. Children under 13 stay free in parents' room. Weekend and other packages available. AE, CB, DC, DISC, MC, V. **Parking:** Free.
Formerly a Holiday Inn, this eight-story hotel needs to be renovated but offers simple accommodations, plus a few added extras. Rooms are clean and comfortable, and the best views are those afforded by the higher floors with a southern exposure, from which you can see the river and the downtown skyline. The Civic Centre has a restaurant and a lounge, plus an outdoor pool.

GATEWAY GARDENS INN, 425 Minnesota Ave., Kansas City, KS 66101. Tel. 913/621-3085. 208 rms. A/C TV TEL
$ Rates: $33 single or double. Extra person $5. Children under 18 stay free in parents' room. Weekend discounts available. AE, DC, DISC, MC, V. **Parking:** Free.
Located across the street from the Civic Centre Hotel (above), Gateway Gardens Inn is an older and slightly seedy hotel with inexpensive rooms. If all you want is a place to lay down your head at night, this is a good choice. Rooms are simply decorated with just the basics of TVs, phones, and self-controlled air conditioning and heating. The next year should see a few rooms outfitted with new carpets, drapes, bedspreads, and a fresh coat of paint. When making a reservation, ask for a renovated room.

8. NEAR THE AIRPORT

The hotels below are northwest of downtown, near Kansas City International Airport. They are reachable via I-29.

EXPENSIVE

KANSAS CITY AIRPORT MARRIOTT, 775 Brasilia, Kan-

sas City, MO 64153. Tel. 816/464-2200, or toll free 800/228-9290. Fax 913/451-5914. 382 rms. A/C TV TEL

$ **Rates:** $145 single or double; Concierge Executive floor $155 single or double. Extra person $10. Children under 18 stay free in parents' room. Weekend and corporate rates and extended-stay discounts available. AE, CB, DC, DISC, ER, MC, V. **Parking:** Free.

Its location beside an artificial lake right next to the airport assures this hotel one of the highest occupancy rates in town. The Airport Marriott is the hotel closest to the airport, and it offers such conveniences as a free shuttle bus to the terminals and a park-and-fly policy that allows hotel guests to keep their cars in the hotel parking lot for up to two weeks free.

Rooms, decorated on an Asian theme, each offer remote-control cable TV with pay movies; the TV also doubles as a screen for calling up hotel bills and messages. Large windows feature double panes to shut out the noise of overhead planes, and the best view is that of the lake.

Dining: The King's Wharf serves American food throughout the day, with tables overlooking the lake. Cocktails are served in the Windjammer Lounge.

Services: Free shuttle to airport, free newspaper, same-day laundry, room service until 11pm.

Facilities: Indoor pool, exercise room, sauna, whirlpool, gift shop.

MODERATE

AIRPORT HILTON PLAZA INN, I-29 and N. W. 112th St., Kansas City, MO 64195. Tel. 816/891-8900, or toll free 800/525-6322. Fax 816/891-8030. 348 rms. A/C TV TEL

$ **Rates:** $99–$109 single; $109–$129 double. Extra person $10. Children under 18 stay free in parents' room. Weekend and corporate rates available. AE, CB, DC, DISC, ER, MC, V. **Parking:** Free.

Located off I-29 (Exit 12), about a five-minute drive from the airport, this 11-story hotel has recently undergone a much-needed restoration. Request a south-facing room, from which you have a view of downtown far in the distance. There are four no-smoking floors; handicap-accessible rooms; room windows can be opened; and the hotel attracts business, group, and convention clientele. Besides two restaurants and two lounges, the Airport Hilton offers indoor and outdoor pools, a whirlpool and sauna, tennis courts, an exercise room, a business center, a laundry room, a basketball court, and a gift shop. Services provided here include a free 24-hour shuttle to the airport, free coffee from midnight to 6am, same-day dry cleaning, and room service until 11pm.

BUDGET

MOTEL 6, 8230 N.W. Prairie View Rd., Kansas City, 64152. Tel. 816/741-6400. 86 rms. A/C TV TEL

$ **Rates:** $29.95 single; $35.95 double. Extra person $6. Children under 18 stay free in parent's room. AE, CB, DC, DISC, MC, V. **Parking:** Free.

Known for inexpensive lodging, Motel 6 is a nationwide chain that offers the basics of a room and a few added extras. This one has an outdoor pool and soda-vending machines. Rooms, equipped with showers instead of tubs, have TVs with free in-house movies; local telephone calls are free. Guests can park near their rooms, and there are both no-smoking and handicapped-accessible rooms. Pets are allowed. Ask for a room as far away from I-29 as you can get, to cut down on traffic noise. Motel 6 is located off I-29 at the Barry Road exit (Exit 8), approximately four miles south of the airport.

9. CAMPING

KOA KAMPGROUNDS, P.O. Box 191, Oak Grove, MO 64075. Tel. 816/625-7515. 77 trailer sites, 23 tent sites.

$ Rates: $14–$19 for two people. Extra person $2; children under 5 free. MC, V. **Season:** Mar–Oct.

This KOA is located 16 miles east of Kansas City, just off I-70 at the Oak Grove exit (Exit 28). Facilities include a store, showers, a laundry, a snack bar, ice and firewood, mini-golf, video games, a pool, and a playground.

TRAILSIDE CAMPERS' INN, Grain Valley, MO 64029. Tel. 816/229-CAMP. 83 trailer sites, 20 tent sites.

$ Rates: $10–$16 for two people. Extra person $1.50; children 5 and under free. MC, V. **Season:** Year round.

This eight-acre campground is located 20 minutes east of downtown Kansas City, off I-70 at the Grain Valley exit (Exit 24). Facilities here include showers, a pool, a hot tub, a laundry room, a store, a playground, and a game room.

CHAPTER 14

KANSAS CITY AREA DINING

Kansas City is justifiably famous for its steaks and barbecue. This is the place to come if you're hungering for a 25-ounce steak or wish to dine at a different barbecue restaurant every night for two months solid. Kansas Citians love to argue about which barbecue restaurant is the best, each convinced that his or her favorite is it. But the fact that the city supports more than 60 barbecue restaurants is testimony to the fact that "best" often signifies just a difference in tastes. There are probably more different types of barbecue sauces in Kansas City than anywhere else in the world—ranging from the gritty, cayenne-flavored sauce of Arthur Bryant's to the hot and tangy sauce of Gates & Sons.

Kansas City barbecue is always slow-smoked over wood, usually hickory, and it includes barbecued pork, ribs, brisket, ham, sausage, and chicken. Once the food of Kansas City's poor black population with a tradition that stretches back to the 1920s, barbecue is still served in simple and no-nonsense establishments, with the most popular dish consisting of brisket piled high on white bread and slathered with thick sauce, accompanied by a mountain of fries. This is roll-up-your-sleeves cuisine, and if by chance you become addicted, most restaurants sell bottles of their sauce that you can take home.

But Kansas City is more than beef and barbecue. Italian, French, Greek, Asian, Mexican, Cajun, and other ethnic restaurants have found an enthusiastic welcome in Kansas City, as have restaurants dishing out hearty portions of American food, both traditional and nouvelle.

The restaurants below have been divided according to location and then further subdivided by price. **Expensive** restaurants are those where dinners probably will cost you more than $25 per person, excluding wine, drinks, and tip. **Moderate** restaurants range from $15 to $25 for a meal, while **inexpensive** restaurants offer meals that cost from $7 to $15. At **budget** restaurants, you can dine for less than $7. Keep in mind, however, that many restaurants offer a cheaper menu and daily specials during lunch hours. Thus, you can splurge for lunch at a restaurant that may be way out of your price range for dinner.

Remember that a 6.475% tax will be added on to restaurant bills in Kansas City, MO; on the Kansas side the tax averages about 5.75%. Tips should run about 15%, rising to 20% at the better restaurants or for special service.

1. DOWNTOWN

Restaurants listed here range from those located in the heart of downtown to those near the City Market, the old stockyards, and other locations within a few minutes' drive to the south and east of downtown.

EXPENSIVE

SAVOY GRILL, 9th and Central. Tel. 816/842-3890.
   Cuisine: AMERICAN. **Reservations:** Recommended.
$ **Prices:** Lunch $5–$16; dinner main courses $12.50–$26; fixed-price dinners $27–$38. AE, CB, DC, DISC, MC, V.
   Open: Mon–Thurs 11am–11pm, Fri–Sat 11am–midnight, Sun 4–10pm.

The Savoy Grill opened in 1903 and has been a Kansas City landmark ever since. It's a restaurant in the old tradition—with turn-of-the-century stained-glass windows; high-backed booths; wainscoting; wall murals with scenes of the Santa Fe Trail; white tablecloths; and gallant, efficient service. There's no other place in town that better conveys what Kansas City was like during its cowtown heyday, when West was best and the nearby stockyards were at their zenith.

The food is unabashedly straightforward and traditional American cuisine, featuring seafood and steaks. There are about two dozen selections of fish and seafood, including a mixed crab plate, lobster, broiled salmon, gulf shrimp, channel catfish, and frog legs. Other main courses include baked lobster pie, chateaubriand, veal marsala, and T-bone steak. Lunch ranges from sandwiches to heartier entrées, such as broiled sole, red snapper, crabmeat crêpes, prime rib, and braised lamb with artichokes and lemon.

MODERATE

BLVD CAFE, 703 Southwest Blvd. Tel. 816/842-6984.
   Cuisine: SPANISH/MIDDLE EASTERN/MEDITERRANEAN. **Reservations:** Recommended for dinner.
$ **Prices:** Lunch $5.50–$7.50; dinner appetizers $3–$7, main courses $12–$14, MC, V.
   Open: Lunch Tues–Fri 11am–2pm; dinner Tues–Thurs 5–10pm, Fri–Sat 5–11pm; Sun brunch 10am–2pm.

The Blvd Café is a favorite haunt of some friends of mine who happen to be going to chef's school and are therefore interested in virtually every restaurant in the city. They like the

Blvd because of its unique blend of Spanish, Mediterranean, and Middle Eastern cuisines and because it's hip, cool, and laid-back. Orange-sponged walls, large windows framed in electric-blue sills, tiled tables, and plants give it a breezy atmosphere that's reminiscent of an oasis in the middle of a desert. Tuesday evenings feature live Brazilian jazz, while at Sunday brunch a live jazz duo performs. The dinner menu offers an intriguing array of hot and cold appetizers, including hummus (chickpea-tahini dip with lemon, garlic, and olive oil), magmoor (ragout of eggplant, tomato, and chickpeas with yogurt and mint), avocado shrimp, Egyptian chicken (kabob marinated in saffron and yogurt and cooked with pepper, onion, and tomato), and shrimp in cilantro sauce. In fact, the appetizer list of tapas and mezze are so long that many diners order a string of them and nothing else. Friday and Saturday evenings offer the national dish of Spain, paella, featuring clams, mussels, shrimp, chicken, chorizo sausage, and vegetables on a bed of saffron rice. If you come for lunch, you'll find a menu offering everything from feta-and-olive omelet to Moroccan phyllo turnover stuffed with spicy chicken chunks, almonds, and herbs. A culinary festival!

FOUNTAIN CITY DINING ROOM, 931 Broadway. Tel. 816/ 474-1468.

Cuisine: AMERICAN. **Reservations:** Recommended for lunch.

$ Prices: Lunch $5.25–$10; dinner $10–$20. AE, MC, V.

Open: Lunch Mon–Fri 11am–2pm; dinner Tues–Thurs 5–9:30pm, Fri–Sat 5–10pm.

Opened as a saloon in 1911 by James E. Fitzpatrick and operating as such until Prohibition closed its doors, Fountain City still retains many of its original architectural features—including its tile floor, molded-tin ceiling, plaster molding, and copper facade. A colorful mural adorning one wall pays tribute to famous people who once lived in Kansas City—Count Basie, Thomas Hart Benton, George Caleb Bingham, Walt Disney, Ernest Hemingway, Charlie Parker, Frederic Remington, and others. The lunch menu includes sandwiches, pasta bolognese, frittata, grilled chicken breast, and salads; dinner includes pheasant breast, salmon, steak, chicken, veal saltimbocca, filet of sole, and rack of lamb roasted in a pistachio crust and laced with sauvignon sauce.

GAROZZO'S, 526 Harrison. Tel. 816/221-2455.

Cuisine: ITALIAN. **Reservations:** Recommended on weekends.

$ Prices: Lunch $4.30–$9.60; dinner pasta main courses $7.50–$15, meat courses $9.25–$22. AE, DISC, MC, V.

Open: Mon–Thurs 11am–10pm, Fri 11am–11pm, Sat 4–11pm.

"Fine Italian Cuisine at Family Prices" is the motto of this newcomer to the Italian food scene in Kansas City. Located north of I-70 and east of the City Market, Garozzo's is a casual establishment in the heart of the city's old Italian district, which now includes new waves of Asian immigrants. Specialties include a lightly breaded veal sautéed in butter and lemon, with fresh mushrooms, capers, and black olives; and beef medallions breaded and charbroiled, then topped with melted cheese and served in a sauce of white wine, butter, lemon, and fresh mushrooms. More than a dozen pastas dishes are available, including such popular choices as fettucci-

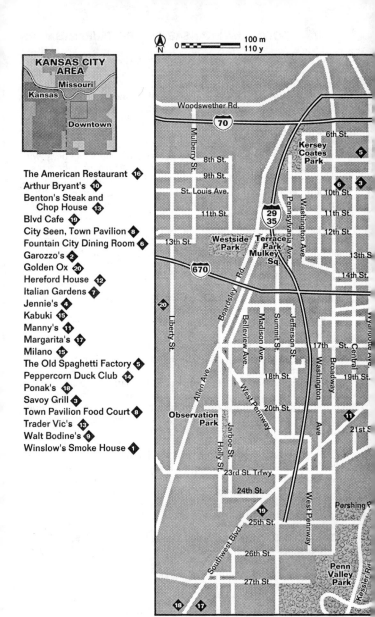

ne served in a spicy tomato sauce with shrimp, calamari, clams, and fresh mussels; ziti in cream sauce with fresh broccoli and mushrooms; and rigatoni with tomato sauce, cream sauce, peas, mushrooms, and prosciutto.

HEREFORD HOUSE, 20th and Main. Tel. 816/842-1080.
  Cuisine: STEAKS. **Reservations:** Recommended for lunch.
$ Prices: Lunch $4.95–$15; dinner main courses $9–$27. AE, CB, DC, DISC, MC, V.

DOWNTOWN KANSAS CITY DINING

Intercity Freeway

Columbus Square

Independence Ave.

Admiral Blvd.

Woodland Ave.

8th St.
9th St.
10th St.
11th St.
12th St.
13th St.
14th St.

Mary Lou Williams Dr.
Ella Fitzgerald Dr.

Grand Ave.
Main St.

N. Truman Rd.
S. Truman Rd.

Troost Ave.
Forest Ave.
Tracy Ave.

Truman Rd.

The Paseo

The Parade

16th St.
17th St.
18th St.
19th St.
20th St.
21st St.

Baltimore Ave.
McGee St.
Oak St.
Locust St.
Cherry St.

19th St.

Tracy Center Park

Under Construction

Lydia Ave.

The Paseo

21st St.
22nd St.
23rd St.
24th St.
25th St.
26th St.
27th St.

Main St.

Grand Ave.
McGee Trfwy.
Gilliam Rd.
Holmes St.
Charlotte St.
Campbell St.
Harrison St.
Troost Ave.
Forest Ave.
Tracy Ave.
Vine St.
Highland Ave.
Woodland Ave.
Michigan Ave.

Walnut St.

Crews Square

Airport

Open: Mon–Thurs 11am–10pm, Fri 11am–10:30pm, Sat 4–10:30pm, Sun 4–9pm.

This Kansas City steak house, decorated with pictures of the old West and the days of the cattle drives, has been serving cuts of prime beef since 1957. A happy hour featuring specials on drinks and appetizers is offered Monday through Friday from 3 to 6pm. Lunch includes everything from more than half a dozen varieties of burgers to chicken, seafood, sandwiches, and steaks. Dinner is heavy on steaks, lobster, fish, and shrimp, with the specialty of the house a 12-ounce filet mignon. All dinners include salad, baked potato or french fries, and bread.

INEXPENSIVE

CITY SEEN, Town Pavilion, 1111 Main. Tel. 816/472-8833.
   Cuisine: AMERICAN/INTERNATIONAL. **Reservations:** Not required.
$ **Prices:** $5.75–$15. AE, MC, V.
   Open: Mon–Thurs 11am–6pm, Fri–Sat 11am–10pm.
One of the few restaurants in the heart of downtown, this is the only one in Town Pavilion shopping center that remains open past 6pm (Friday and Saturday only). Its food is fun and creative, including international recipes with a liberal use of spices and seasonings. You might wish to start with oysters served with ginger-saffron glaze; Vietnamese spring rolls; or chicken breast strips rolled in bread crumbs and shredded coconut, fried, and served with honey-mustard sauce. The list of sandwiches includes such tempting combinations as charbroiled chicken breast with Cajun seasoning, cheese, and barbecue sauce; and Ozark ham served with Jarlsberg cheese and tomato chutney on focaccia. Main courses include sautéed chicken breast,

---

 FROMMER'S SMART TRAVELER: RESTAURANTS

VALUE-CONSCIOUS DINERS SHOULD TAKE ADVANTAGE OF THE FOLLOWING:

1. Lunch menus offering main courses at cheaper prices than those on dinner menus; save money by eating a big meal at noon.
2. Daily specials offered by many restaurants, which are not on the regular menus and may offer a main course and side dish at a good price.
3. Fixed-price meals, each of which includes an appetizer or soup, a main course, and a dessert, at prices much cheaper than ordering à la carte.
4. Inexpensive entrées, such as chicken or pasta, offered by some of the more expensive restaurants, where even budget travelers can dine in style by choosing carefully.
5. Kansas City's steaks and barbecue, hearty portions at inexpensive prices.
6. Food offered by many pubs, bars, and taverns, usually hearty portions at bargain prices (see Chapter 18).

QUESTIONS TO ASK IF YOU'RE ON A BUDGET

1. Does the main course come with a side dish such as a vegetable or potato? (If so, it may be all you want to order, unless you have a voracious appetite.)
2. Is there a special of the day or a fixed-price meal not listed on the regular menu?

calamari steak, veal, pasta, and steak—all also available by the half order for diners with smaller appetites.

GOLDEN OX, 1600 Genessee. Tel. 816/842-2866.

Cuisine: STEAKS. **Reservations:** Recommended.

$ Prices: Lunch $3.30–$8 sandwiches, $5.50–$18 steaks; dinner main courses $7–$17. AE, CB, DC, DISC, M, V.

Open: Mon–Fri 11:30am–10pm, Sat 4:30–10:30pm, Sun 4–9pm.

The Golden Ox opened in 1950, primarily to satisfy the hearty appetites of ranchers bringing their livestock to the stockyards next door. Now the stockyards are gone, but the Golden Ox continues to draw crowds, with beef aged and cut on the premises. Prime rib and steaks broiled over a hickory charcoal flame are the specialties—all served with a choice of baked potato or french fries, garlic toast, and salad. The dining hall has maintained its 1950s look, with wood paneling and shining busts of golden ox heads everywhere. To reach the restaurant from downtown, take 12th Street west or I-35 south to the Kemper-Genessee exit.

ITALIAN GARDENS, 1110 Baltimore. Tel. 816/221-9311.

Cuisine: ITALIAN. **Reservations:** Not required.

$ Prices: Lunch $4.70–$12, fixed-priced lunch $4.90; dinner pasta courses $7–$12.50, pizza $6–$14, meat courses $9–$16. AE, CB, DC, MC, V. **Parking:** Valet (free, after 5pm).

Open: Mon–Thurs 11am–10pm, Fri–Sat 11am–11pm.

This popular restaurant has been in continual operation since 1925. An informal family restaurant with red-and-white-checked tablecloths and a children's menu, Italian Gardens specializes in homemade pizza, lasagne, ravioli, chicken, and veal dishes and features daily lunch specials. Don't pass up the cheesecake. Adjoining the restaurant is the Ciao Lounge.

JENNIE'S, 511 Cherry St. Tel. 816/421-3366.

Cuisine: ITALIAN. **Reservations:** Not required.

$ Prices: Lunch $4.50–$7; dinner pasta courses $8–$9, meat courses $9.50–$16. AE, DC, MC, V.

Open: Mon–Thurs 11am–9pm, Fri 11am–10pm, Sat noon–10pm, Sun noon–8pm.

This is another long-standing Italian restaurant, open since 1938 and now managed by Jennie's grandson, Thomas Barelli. Specializing in Sicilian food, it caters to two distinct crowds—bringing in downtown white-collar workers during lunch and serving as a blue-collar family establishment for dinner. Adjoining the restaurant is a bar, a watering hole for people who live and work in the area. Most of the food is made from scratch, and Jennie's was probably the first establishment in town to serve pizza. It excels in red sauces, with lasagne and cheese ravioli its most popular dishes. Dinner main courses include veal, steak, chicken parmigiana, and eggplant parmigiana. Jennie's is located in the old Italian district, north of I-70 and east of the City Market.

BUDGET

ARTHUR BRYANT'S, 1727 Brooklyn. Tel. 816/231-1123.

Cuisine: BARBECUE.

$ Prices: $5–$7. No credit cards.

Open: Mon–Thurs 10am–9:30pm, Fri–Sat 10am–10pm, Sun 11am–8pm.

This, the granddaddy of barbecue restaurants in Kansas City, was once rated by writer Calvin Trillin as the "single, best restaurant in the world." Former presidents Harry Truman and Jimmy Carter made a point of dining here on visits to Kansas City, as did Emperor Haile Selassie of Ethiopia back in 1937.

But you'd never guess at Arthur Bryant's fame by looking at the place, a simple two-story brick building located a few minute's drive east of downtown in what is a predominately black neighborhood. Hungry customers from throughout the city are willing to stand in line for the privilege of ordering from the counter of this no-frills establishment. This is the place to indulge yourself without reservation. Sandwiches are the specialty, piled sky high with beef, pork, ham, sausage, or chicken, best ordered with side dishes of french fries or baked beans. There are also ribs. Arthur died in 1982, and even though his successors have cleaned up the place a bit (customers used to be able to skid across the floor on a layer of grease and french fries), little has changed—many Kansas Citians consider this the best barbecue place in town. Arthur Bryant's sauce, gritty and made with a secret recipe that includes cayenne, paprika, vinegar, and celery, is for sale at the restaurant. Highly recommended.

MANNY'S, 207 Southwest Blvd. Tel. 816/474-7696.
   Cuisine: MEXICAN.
$ Prices: $3–$11. AE, MC, V.
   Open: Mon–Thurs 11am–10pm, Fri–Sat 11am–11pm.
This is a large, popular Mexican restaurant, located between downtown and Crown Center, where Southwest Boulevard, 20th Street, and Central Street all converge. Manny's strives for authenticity in its homemade tamales, as well as in its preparation of tacos, chile rellenos, enchiladas, fajitas, and burritos. Burgers and a children's plate also are available; a house specialty is its margaritas, available by the pitcher or the glass.

MARGARITA'S, 2829 Southwest Blvd. Tel. 816/931-4849.
   Cuisine: MEXICAN.
$ Prices: A la carte items $2–$8; fixed-price meals $6–$8. AE, DISC, MC, V.
   Open: Mon–Thurs 11am–10pm, Fri–Sat 11am–11:30pm, Sun noon–10pm.
"Always a party scene" is how one employee described this popular restaurant, one of the many Mexican establishments that stretch along Southwest Boulevard beside the railroad tracks, about a five-minute drive southwest of downtown. Margarita's is so crowded that customers expect to belly up to the bar while waiting for a table, drinking some of the 40 gallons of margaritas that are mixed and sold each day. The food, prepared by Mexican cooks, includes a dozen selections of complete meals along with some à la carte items. The most popular platter is the Margarita's Special, which features a flour tortilla stuffed with pork, beef, beans, cheese, and onions and topped with chili con queso and served with rice. Happy hour is daily from 3 to 6pm.

PONAK'S, 2856 Southwest Blvd. Tel. 816/753-0775.
   Cuisine: MEXICAN.

$ Prices: A la carte items $1.50–$5; fixed-price meals $5–$7.50. AE, MC, V.

Open: Mon–Thurs 11am–10:30pm, Fri–Sat 11am–11:30pm. Sun noon–9pm.

When this restaurant opened in 1978 in the Hispanic part of town, none of the cooks spoke English. Today the original recipes are faithfully followed in the open kitchen, but now all the cooks speak English. All the meat is cut and ground on the premises, and the chile rellenos and tamales are homemade. Ponak's is the place to dine if you want menundo (a soup made with tripe and hominy in a clear broth—considered a good cure for a hangover) or chicken mole. Another popular item is the guacamole platter, which features one burrito, one tostada, one enchilada with avocado dip, Spanish rice, and beans. More than 50 different brands of beer are available, including nine draft beers.

THE OLD SPAGHETTI FACTORY, 304 W. 8th St. Tel. 816/842-1801.

Cuisine: ITALIAN.

$ Prices: Lunch $3.25–$5.50; dinner $4.50–$8. MC, V.

Open: Summer lunch Mon–Thurs 11:30am–2pm; dinner Mon–Thurs 5–10pm, Fri–Sat 5–11pm, Sun 4–10pm. Winter lunch Mon–Fri 11:30am–2pm; dinner Mon–Thurs 5–9:30pm, Fri 5–11pm, Sat 4:30–11pm, Sun 4–9:30pm.

This chain of spaghetti restaurants has a branch here in Kansas City, serving inexpensive pasta dishes in a comfortable and historic setting. Similar in decor and concept to the Factory restaurant in St. Louis, it occupies part of a former hotel, boasting tall ceilings with embellished pillars, stained-glass windows, a polished wood floor, antique lamps, and a trolley car in the middle of the dining room. The menu is limited and straightforward, offering pasta dinners ranging from spaghetti with meat sauce to lasagne, spinach tortellini with Alfredo sauce, and ravioli. Dinners come with a salad, French bread, a drink, and ice cream—all for less than $8. A bargain.

TOWN PAVILION FOOD COURT, 3rd floor, 1111 Main St. Tel. 816/472-9600.

Cuisine: INTERNATIONAL.

$ Prices: $1.50–$6.50. No credit cards.

Open: Mon–Sat 10am–6pm.

Town Pavilion is a downtown mall with more than 40 shops and restaurants. On the third floor is its food court, a bright and cheerful place with skylights and a pleasant dining area separate from the various food counters, giving it a restaurant atmosphere. Burgers; hot dogs; barbecue; pizza; tacos; salads; sandwiches; and Chinese, Mexican, and Greek specialties are available.

WINSLOW'S SMOKEHOUSE, 20 E. 5th St. Tel. 816/471-RIBS.

Cuisine: BARBECUE.

$ Prices: $3.50–$13. AE, DISC, MC, V.

Open: Summer daily 10am–9pm; winter Mon–Sat 10am–6pm.

This family-owned and -operated restaurant, serving barbecue at the City Market for more than 20 years, is famous for its ribs and spicy smoked chicken wings. It uses certified black Angus beef, slow-cooked over green hickory, and its sauce is made with fresh produce along with blackstrap molasses. Also on the menu of this informal eatery are sandwiches and smoked sausage. Winslow's is a good place for lunch if you're visiting City Market, located north of I-70.

2. CROWN CENTER

For choices other than those listed below, be sure to check "Specialty Dining" at the end of this chapter for hotel restaurants and restaurants with a view, including Benton's Steak and Chop House and the Peppercorn Duck Club.

EXPENSIVE

THE AMERICAN RESTAURANT, Crown Center, 200 E. 25th St. Tel. 816/426-1133.
   Cuisine: AMERICAN. **Reservations:** Recommended on weekends.
$ Prices: Appetizers $7.50–$16; main courses $28–$35. AE, MC, V.
   Open: Mon–Thurs 6–10pm, Fri–Sat 6–11pm. **Parking:** Free (valet).

 Gourmet American cuisine best describes the food served by this great restaurant, one of the best in Kansas City. Its dining room (with only 21 tables) is an unexpected delight, featuring a dramatic 25-foot-high ceiling and floor-to-ceiling windows that are shuttered against the daylight but opened after nightfall to reveal a view of the city. A pianist appears nightly.

The menu capitalizes on regional specialties that include such

---

🅕 FROMMER'S COOL FOR KIDS: RESTAURANTS

Italian Gardens *(p. 193)* This family-style restaurant, serving a variety of pasta and pizza dishes for decades, also offers a children's menu.

Stephenson's Apple Farm *(p. 208)* This has been a popular family destination for decades, for both its home cooking and its rustic antique setting.

Tasso's *(p. 207)* Children love the drama at Tasso's, a Greek restaurant that features a live band and the lively personality of Tasso himself.

Winstead's *(p. 201)* Show your child what a 1940s diner was all about. Hamburgers are served wrapped in tissue, sodas are made the old-fashioned way, and there's a jukebox with tunes of the 1950s and early 1960s.

ingredients as buffalo, cracked Kansas wheat, and morels. The menu changes often but may include such main courses as roasted salmon with lemon grass and ginger, pan-roasted pheasant breast with morels, and grilled T-bone steak with onions and tomato-horseradish salsa. There are also evening specials, and the wine list is extensive. Jackets are required for men, but ties are optional.

MODERATE

KABUKI, Crown Center, 2450 Grand Ave. Tel. 816/472-1717.

    Cuisine: JAPANESE. **Reservations:** Recommended for lunch and weekend dinners.

$ Prices: Lunch $7–$9; dinner main courses $11–$21. AE, DC, MC, V.

    Open: Lunch Mon–Fri 11:30am–2pm, Sat noon–2pm; dinner Mon–Thurs 5:30–10pm, Fri–Sat 5:30–11pm, Sun 5–10pm.

This place gets my vote as the best Japanese restaurant in town. Decorated in traditional style with paper screens and bamboo, it has a Japanese staff and offers a wide variety of Japanese cuisine—including tempura (deep-fried meats and vegetables), teriyaki, tonkatsu (breaded pork cutlets), sukiyaki (thinly sliced beef cooked in broth with vegetables), and sushi. There are no knife-brandishing teppanyaki chefs in sight.

MILANO, Crown Center, 2450 Grand Ave. Tel. 816/471-2003.

    Cuisine: ITALIAN. **Reservations:** Recommended.

$ Prices: Lunch main courses $6.25–$12; dinner pizza and pasta $6.50–$12, meat courses $11–$17. AE, MC, V.

    Open: Mon–Thurs 11:30am–2:30pm and 5–9pm, Fri–Sat 11:30am–2:30pm and 5–10pm, Sun 11:30am–8pm.

This has to be one of the most pleasant dining rooms in Kansas City. Light and airy, with so many skylights and plants that eating here is like dining in a greenhouse, Milano serves Northern Italian cuisine. Pasta dishes include bow-tie pasta with four cheeses and a shrimp linguine; pizza choices range from artichoke and oven-dried tomato to Italian sausage. Main courses include shellfish risotto, sautéed veal, and broiled salmon medallions.

3. COUNTRY CLUB PLAZA

For information on the Grill at The Ritz-Carlton, check "Specialty Dining" at the end of this chapter.

EXPENSIVE

FEDORA CAFE AND BAR, 210 W. 47th St. Tel. 816/561-6565.

    Cuisine: CONTINENTAL. **Reservations:** Recommended for dinner.

$ Prices: Lunch $6.50–$10; dinner pizza and pasta courses $9–$11, meat courses $13–$22. AE, CB, DC, DISC, MC, V.
Open: Lunch Mon–Sat 11:30am–2:30pm; dinner Sun–Thurs 4:30–10pm, Fri–Sat 4:30–11pm; Sun brunch 10:30am–3pm.

This is a favorite choice for many Kansas Citians when they are celebrating special occasions, from birthdays to anniversaries; it is a place to see and be seen. The clientele is always smartly dressed, and the restaurant, boasting an open kitchen, has a decor that gives it a turn-of-the-century art nouveau elegance. The innovative menu, which changes once a year, offers both familiar and exotic choices. Past dishes, for example, have included Thai noodles stir-fried with shrimp and vegetables; pizza topped with barbecued chicken, red onions, Kansas City barbecue sauce, and cilantro; veal sweetbreads with morels, ham, cognac, and heavy cream; and a quesadilla with grilled quail and barbecued shrimp. Lunch offers lighter fare, including salads, pasta, pizza, and sandwiches.

LA MEDITERRANEE, 4742 Pennsylvania. Tel. 816/561-2916.
Cuisine: FRENCH. **Reservations:** Recommended.
$ Prices: Lunch $6–$10; dinner main courses $14–$25. AE, MC, V.
Open: Lunch Mon–Fri 11:15am–1:45pm; dinner Mon–Sat 6–9:45pm.

French restaurants have never hit it big in Kansas City, but this intimate and elegant one has been serving what's probably the best French food in the city for more than 20 years, which means that it must be doing something right. Dining is in three cozy rooms that make the place seem more like a private home than a restaurant. Many dishes are prepared tableside.

French owner/chef Gilbert Jahier offers an extensive menu with selections of fish, seafood, veal, steak, duck, and lamb, as well as wild game in season (wild boar, pheasant, or partridge). Main courses in the past have included frog legs in menthe sauce; sweetbreads in a lobster, shrimp, and cognac sauce; Kansas City steak with sauce béarnaise, crabmeat, and asparagus; beef Wellington; and chateaubriand with goose liver in truffle-and-mushroom sauce. Lunch is lighter, including salads, omelets, fish, pasta, and daily specials.

VENUE, 4532 Main. Tel. 816/561-3311.
Cuisine: AMERICAN. **Reservations:** Recommended.
$ Prices: Lunch $6–$9; dinner main courses $17–$21; fixed-price dinners $35. AE, CB, DC, DISC, MC, V.
Open: Lunch Mon–Fri 11:30am–2:30pm; dinner Mon–Thurs 5:30–10pm, Fri–Sat 5:30–11pm; Sun brunch 10am–2:30pm.

This bright new star in Kansas City's culinary scene features American cuisine prepared in a contemporary style. Its setting is modern yet unpretentious, with a plain wooden floor, brightly painted walls, white tablecloths, a changing exhibit featuring local artists, and attentive service. If you enjoy well-prepared food but shun the stuffiness that seems to accompany many of the better restaurants, this is the place for you. There's a separate bar where you can enjoy a drink before or after dinner, plus live music every Friday from 11am to 3pm.

Its menu is fun and creative—with past appetizers including such interesting combinations as artichoke lasagne and wild mushroom stuffed cabbage and main courses ranging from seafood fettucine and spicy roast fish on a lentil pancake to beef sirloin with shiitake mushrooms, shallots, and garlic. Especially recommended are the two fixed-price dinners.

MODERATE

BRISTOL BAR AND GRILL, 4740 Jefferson. Tel. 816/756-0606.
    Cuisine: SEAFOOD. **Reservations:** Recommended, especially on weekends.
$ **Prices:** Lunch $6.50–$12; dinner main coures $12.95–$21.95; Sun brunch $9.95. AE, CB, DC, DISC, MC, V.
    Open: Lunch Mon–Fri 11:30am–2:30pm, Sat 11:30am–3pm; dinner Mon–Thurs 5:30–10:30pm, Fri–Sat 5–11:30pm, Sun 5–9:30pm; Sun brunch 10am–2pm.

Bristol Bar and Grill, first opened on the Plaza in 1980, has proved so successful that it has opened at several locations across the country. Its slightly masculine decor is reminiscent of that in venerable seafood restaurants in England, with a molded-tin ceiling, brass railings, stained-glass lamps, newspapers hanging from a rack, and a marble-top bar with a brass foot rail. Its specialty is seafood—including oysters, swordfish, lobster, Alaskan king crab legs, jumbo shrimp, sea scallops, and daily specials that usually include a dozen or so fresh fish. Particularly recommended is the shellfish cioppino, which contains fresh fish, sea scallops, Maine mussels, shrimp, clams, and stone crab claw, served in red-wine tomato-herb sauce. Steaks also are available. All main courses include a soda biscuit (deliciously flaky) and a choice of potatoes or pasta.

FIGLIO, 209 W. 46th St. Tel. 816/561-0505.
    Cuisine: ITALIAN. **Reservations:** Recommended.
$ **Prices:** Lunch $6.75–$8.50; dinner pasta and pizza $7.50–$9, meat courses $12.25–$17.50. AE, CB, DC, DISC, MC, V.
    Open: Lunch Mon–Fri 11:30am–2:30pm. Sat 11:30am–3:30pm; dinner Mon–Thurs 5–10pm, Fri–Sat 5–11pm, Sun 4–10pm.

Figlio, one of Kansas City's newer Italian restaurants, offers great food at modest prices. Simply decorated with hardwood floors, pink walls, modern lighting, palm trees, and an open kitchen, it specializes in Northern Italian food. Especially recommended are the homemade pasta and the gourmet pizza that's cooked in a wood-burning oven. Try the Spaghettini Napoletana (thin spaghetti with roma tomatoes, garlic, olive oil, and fresh basil); three-cheese ravioli; or Stromboli Figlio, which is a rolled pizza stuffed with prosciutto, mushrooms, and romano and mozzarella cheeses. For a main course, you might consider tender beef marinated in fresh herbs and Bardolino wine, grilled with vegetables over hardwood coals and served on linguine. Finish your meal with homemade chocolate mousse wrapped in sponge cake that's been soaked in espresso and Amaretto.

INEXPENSIVE

ANNIE'S SANTA FE, 100 Ward Parkway. Tel. 816/753-1621.
    Cuisine: MEXICAN. **Reservations:** Recommended.

$ Prices: $6.50–$10. AE, CB, DC, DISC, MC, V.
   Open: Mon–Thurs 11am–11pm, Fri–Sat 11am–midnight. Sun
   10am–10pm.
Serving an American version of Mexican food, this has long been a
favorite restaurant on the Plaza. Fajitas are its most popular dish, but
platters offer everything from Mexican pizza or tamales to
chimichangas, enchiladas, empanadas, and tacos. The flautas are
wonderful. An especially good deal is the lunch buffet offered on
Monday through Friday for $5.50.
   Other branches are at 5600 E. Bannister Rd. (tel. 816/966-1400)
at Bannister Mall and 11855 W. 95th St. (tel. 913/492-6121) in
Overland Park.

HOULIHAN'S OLD PLACE, 4743 Pennsylvania. Tel. 816/ 561-3141.

   Cuisine: AMERICAN. **Reservations:** Not required.
$ Prices: $6.50–$14. AE, CB, DC, DISC, MC, V.
   Open: Sun–Thurs 11am–11pm, Fri–Sat 11am–midnight.
This was the very first Houlihan's, open for almost two decades and
now part of a chain with more than 50 locations nationwide. It's a
fun and informal place, popular with a professional working crowd
and families (there's a children's menu). The menu is extensive—
including burgers; sandwiches; quiches; salads; and an eclectic mix of
main courses that range from fajitas and Cajun shrimp to barbecued
ribs, teriyaki steak, chicken stir-fry, and blackened chicken quesadilla.
Happy hour is on Monday through Friday from 4 to 8pm, with
discounts on drinks and appetizers.

ROZELLE COURT, in the Nelson-Atkins Museum of Art, 4525 Oak. Tel. 816/751-1279.

   Cuisine: CONTINENTAL. **Reservations:** Not required.
$ Prices: Salads $2.50–$4.50; main courses $6. MC, V.
   Open: Tues–Thurs 10am–3pm, Fri 10am–4pm and 5–8pm, Sat
   10am–3:30pm, Sun 1–3:30pm.
This is one of the most unusual and beautiful places to dine in
Kansas City, a light and airy Venetian courtyard with a stone
floor, a fountain, pillars, and a super-high ceiling topped with a
skylight. The food, served cafeteria style, includes a changing
selection of salads; sandwiches; soup; and main courses that may
include lasagne, game hen, crabcakes, catfish, and veal stew. Since
Rozelle Court is located in the Nelson-Atkins Museum of Art, east
of the Plaza, you have to pay the $4 museum admission in order to eat
here. Highly recommended, it even features live jazz on Friday
evenings.

BUDGET

GATES & SONS BAR-B-Q, 47th & Paseo. Tel. 816/921-0409.

   Cuisine: BARBECUE.
$ Prices: $4.45–$11.99. No credit cards.
   Open: Mon–Sat 10am–2am, Sun 10am–midnight.
Gates & Sons' trademark is the manner in which employees
greet customers, yelling "May I help you?" as soon as someone
walks through the door. In business since 1945, it ranks

alongside Arthur Bryant's as one of the best barbecue restaurants in Kansas City; it gets my vote as having the best sauce in town, particularly its hot and spicy version (available for sale in bottles). The menu includes sandwiches, ribs, sausage, chicken, and mutton. This branch, easily recognizable with its red roof, is located a few minutes' drive east of the Plaza, past Troost.

Other locations include 12th and Brooklyn (tel. 816/483-3880) and 10440 E. 40 Highway (tel. 816/353-5880) in Independence.

WINSTEAD'S, 101 Brush Creek. Tel. 816/753-2244.
Cuisine: BURGERS.
$ Prices: $1.50–$3. No credit cards.
Open: Sun–Fri 6:30am–midnight, Sat 6:30am–1am.

Winstead's is a nostalgic trip back to the days of the diner, when waitresses wore pinafores and hamburgers were served in tissue. Its jukebox features music of the 1950s and early 1960s. A Kansas City tradition since 1940, Winstead's is the place to go for hamburgers or grilled-cheese sandwiches or to satisfy cravings for ice-cream sodas, milk shakes (my children say these are the best they've ever had), root-beer floats, cheesecakes, and sundaes. It's located about a five-minute walk east of the Plaza on 47th Street.

Other locations include 8817 W. 63rd (tel. 816/384-2224), 8333 W. 95th (tel. 816/383-3330), and 1428 Noland Rd. (tel. 816/252-9363) in Independence.

4. WESTPORT & MIDTOWN

Most of the following restaurants are located either in the heart of Westport (Pennsylvania Street and Westport Road) or north of Westport on West 39th Street, near the University of Kansas Medical Center.

EXPENSIVE

CAFE ALLEGRO, 1815 W. 39th St. Tel. 816/561-3663.
Cuisine: CONTINENTAL. **Reservations:** Recommended.
$ Prices: Lunch $7.50–$11; dinner main courses $19–$26. AE, CB, DC, MC, V.
Open: Lunch Mon–Fri 11:30am–2pm; dinner Mon–Sat 6–10pm.

A well-heeled older crowd patronizes this cheerful restaurant, which manages to be casual, civilized, and artsy at the same time. Café Allegro features exposed-brick walls, cane chairs, flower arrangements, white tablecloths, and original artwork. The service is attentive, and the food, with French, Italian, and Asian influences, is artfully arranged and presented.

This restaurant has one of the most extensive wine lists in Kansas City, mainly American but also page after page of French vintages. Approximately 40 wines are available by the glass at any one time, but you may wish to opt for one of its 400 choices in bottles. Highly recommended food choices are the rack of lamb, marinated and charcoal-grilled over a wood fire and served with a crust of mustard and pine nuts; the duck breast with caramelized sweet garlic; the veal tenderloin with garlic-parmesan mashed potatoes; and the peppered filet with bleu cheese.

MODERATE

CALIFORNOS, 4124 Pennsylvania. Tel. 816/531-7878.
   Cuisine: AMERICAN. **Reservations:** Recommended on week-ends.
$ **Prices:** Appetizers $4.50–$6; main courses $6–$20. AE, CB, DC, MC, V.
   Open: Lunch Mon–Sat 11am–3pm; dinner Mon–Thurs 5–10pm, Fri–Sat 5–11pm, Sun 5–9pm; Sun brunch 11am–2pm.
California-inspired cuisine is featured in this bright bistrolike restaurant in the heart of Westport. Decorated in hot pink with white tablecloths and black chairs, Californos offers both indoor and outdoor seating and live piano music every evening. For an appetizer, you might consider an artichoke-chile cheese spread or shrimp tostada. Main dishes include grilled tuna, crab strudel, king salmon, swordfish with pesto butter, and grilled chicken with homemade salsa. Steaks, lamb chops, and lobster round out the menu. There are also a selection of entrée salads along with sandwiches, pizza, and pasta.

METROPOLIS, 303 Westport Rd. Tel. 816/753-1550.
   Cuisine: INTERNATIONAL. **Reservations:** Recommended for dinner.
$ **Prices:** Lunch $6.50–$11; dinner pizza $9.95–$10.95; main courses $11–$18. AE, DC, MC, V.
   Open: Lunch Mon–Fri 11:30am–2:30pm; dinner Tues–Thurs 5:30–10pm, Fri–Sat 5:30pm–11pm.
This is an ultramodern, chic restaurant, one small room sleekly decorated in black and teal, with black tables, a black carpet, and neon-colored placemats. Even the service staff are dressed in black. One of the two owners is always on hand to greet customers. The dishes, artfully presented, are an imaginative blend of regional American cuisine with international ingredients, including Italian and Asian. For the first course, you might select Vietnamese-style eggrolls or beef carpaccio. There are several choices of pizza and pasta; main courses include salmon stuffed with chorizo sausage and topped with caviar-and-cheese sauce; tandoori sea bass; curried chicken; and grilled steak. For dessert, try the white-chocolate flan or the cheesecake.

INEXPENSIVE

ATHENA ON BROADWAY, 3535 Broadway. Tel. 816/756-3227.
   Cuisine: GREEK. **Reservations:** Not required.
$ **Prices:** Lunch $6.50–$9; dinner main courses $10–$16. AE, MC, V.
   Open: Lunch Mon–Fri 11:30am–2pm; dinner Mon–Thurs 6–10:30pm, Fri–Sat 6–11pm.
You can't tell upon entering that this is a Greek restaurant—no blaring bouzouki music, no belly dancing, and no pictures of the

Acropolis. Rather, there are paintings and artwork that are for sale, with fresh flowers on the tables. Athena is a casual and subdued establishment that offers great Greek food, including moussaka, souvlaki, homemade Greek sausage, grilled octopus, and baklava. There are also daily specials that range from fresh fish to grilled rack of lamb; lunch features sandwiches and lighter dishes.

FOOD FOR THOUGHT, 1808 W. 39th. Tel. 816/756-5304.
Cuisine: INTERNATIONAL. **Reservations:** Recommended for lunch.

$ **Prices:** Lunch $4.50–$6.50; dinner appetizers $1.50–$2.50, main courses $7–$12. No credit cards.

Open: Lunch Mon–Fri 11:30am–2pm; dinner Wed–Sat 6–9:30pm.

This restaurant is so alternative that the first time I came here it didn't even have a telephone. Now it has different owners and a new menu, but it still looks like a relative's living room with an odd assortment of mismatched tables and chairs, area rugs, plants, and original artwork—cozy and casual. It's especially recommended for its long list of international appetizers (more than three dozen), which run the gamut from Thai chile-and-mushroom won ton, chicken wings with peanut-coconut sauce, and Tuscany white beans with sage to pâté with truffles and hummus with hazelnuts, sesame seeds, and coriander. You can even make a meal of them. Main courses include Moroccan chicken with couscous, enchilada with potatoes and black beans, and lentil-and-eggplant moussaka. There are plenty of choices for vegetarians.

JIMMY AND MARY'S, 3400 Main. Tel. 816/753-9397.
Cuisine: ITALIAN/STEAKS. **Reservations:** Not required.

$ **Prices:** Sandwiches $3.80–$7; pasta courses $5.25–$10; meat courses $8.25–$15. AE, CB, DC, DISC, MC, V.

Open: Wed–Thurs 5–11pm, Fri–Sat 5pm–1am, Sun 4–10pm.

Sizzling steaks served on hot platters have been a specialty at this family-owned and -operated restaurant ever since it opened in 1944; other specialties are lasagne, spaghetti, ravioli, and sautéed chicken liver with onions. Additional dishes include chicken broiled with garlic butter, veal parmigiana, chicken cacciatore, lobster tail, catfish, and sandwiches. There's also a children's menu. Telly Savalas, Bill Cosby, and Neil Diamond have walked through the doors to Jimmy and Mary's, which is delightfully unpretentious, right down to its fake flowers.

KIKI'S BON TON, 1515 Westport Rd. Tel. 816/931-9417.
Cuisine: CREOLE/CAJUN. **Reservations:** Recommended for Wed and Sat.

$ **Prices:** Lunch $5.50–$8, dinner $5.50–$11. AE, DC, MC, V.

Open: Mon–Thurs 11am–10pm, Fri 11am–11pm, Sat 11am–midnight.

This is a fun and funky kind of place, with stucco alligators crawling on the walls and lobsters stenciled below a pressed-tin ceiling. The walls are painted a deep bayou green; there are palm trees; and charts on the walls show various species of fish, mushrooms, and sea life. Above the bar is a collection of accordions, along with a neon sign that proclaims "Laissez les Bonton Roulez," which is exactly what happens every Wednesday at 9:30pm and Saturday at 10:30pm, when the Bon Ton Soul Accordion Band plays (reservations a must). The menu includes gumbo, soup, alligator sausage, crayfish pie, Creole crabcakes, red beans and rice, jambalaya, and po-boy sandwiches. There's an extensive collection of hot sauces available—if you bring in a variety not already available, you'll get a free drink in trade.

BUDGET

MARIO'S, 204 Westport Rd. Tel. 816/531-7187 or 531-9898.
Cuisine: ITALIAN.
$ **Prices:** Sandwiches and grinders $3.30–$3.90, main courses $3.30–$5. MC, V.
Open: Mon–Sat 10:30am–7:30pm.

One of the best deals in Westport, Mario's is a simple and inexpensive establishment selling grinders, sandwiches, and main courses ranging from spaghetti and lasagne to steak parmigiana. Food, served in styrofoam containers, is available either for carry-out or for dining at one of the tables covered with red-and-white-checked tablecloths. There's additional seating up on the second floor.

TORRE'S PIZZERIA, 4112 Pennsylvania. Tel. 816/931-0146.
Cuisine: ITALIAN.
$ **Prices:** $2.40–$11. AE, DISC, MC, V.
Open: Mon–Thurs 11am–10pm, Fri–Sat 11am–1:30am, Sun 4–10pm.

The specialty here is pizza, available by the slice ($1.50), in four different sizes, and as a stuffed pie. There are also sandwiches and a salad bar. Torre's is located in the heart of Westport, in a building dating from 1856.

WESTPORT FLEA MARKET BAR AND GRILL, 817 West-port Rd. Tel. 816/931-1986.
Cuisine: BURGERS/HOT DOGS.
$ **Prices:** $3.50–$5. No credit cards.
Open: Mon–Sat 9am–midnight, Sun 11am–1:30am.

As its name implies, this very casual bar and grill is located in the middle of an indoor flea market (the market itself is open only on Saturday and Sunday). It's best known for its gigantic hamburgers, made with 10 ounces of ground chuck. Also on the menu are hot dogs, Polish dogs with sauerkraut, Italian sausage, chicken-breast sandwiches, soups, and salads. There are happy-hour appetizer and drink specials on Monday through Friday from 3 to 7pm, when 16-ounce draws of beer go for $1. Sunday features live rock-and-roll music.

5. OVERLAND PARK, KS

Nearby Overland Park, KS, is located southwest of downtown Kansas City, MO.

INEXPENSIVE

BANGKOK PAVILION, Windmill Square Shopping Center, 7249 97th St., Overland Park. Tel. 913/341-3005.
Cuisine: THAI. **Reservations:** Not required.
$ Prices: Fixed-price lunches $4.25–$5.75; dinner main courses $6.50–$12. AE, MC, V.
Open: Lunch Mon–Sat 11:30am–2:30pm; dinner Mon–Thurs 5:30–10pm, Fri–Sat 5:30pm–10:30pm, Sun 5:30–9pm.

Authentic Thai food is served in this pleasant and unpretentious restaurant located southwest of Kansas City, just north of I-435 on the corner of Metcalf Avenue and 97th Street. My favorite way to start a Thai meal is with Tome Khah Gai—chicken soup with galanga, lemon grass, and coconut milk—and an appetizer of grilled beef with mint leaves and lemon. Main courses include a wide selection of chicken, seafood, pork, beef, noodles, rice, and vegetarian dishes, including the national dish, Phad Thai noodles. Fixed-price lunches are a bargain, including soup, an appetizer, fried rice, and a choice of entrées ranging from cashew chicken or beef and broccoli in oyster sauce to spicy shrimp.

K. C. MASTERPIECE BARBECUE AND GRILL, 110th and Metcalf Ave., Overland Park. Tel. 913/345-1199.
Cuisine: BARBECUE. **Reservations:** Not required.
$ Prices: Lunch $5.25–$10; dinner $6.50–$15. AE, CB, DC, DISC, MC, V.
Open: Mon–Thurs 11am–10pm, Fri–Sat 11am–11pm, Sun 11am–9:30pm.

There are some who believe that any respectable barbecue joint must carry with it a layer of grease and a homey air of neglect. K. C. Masterpiece, located just south of I-435, defies all that. Neither greasy nor falling apart, it's in suburbia, is spotless, and is a phenomenal success, with bottles of its sauces now marketed throughout the region. K. C. Masterpiece uses hickory for slow cooking and grilling meats and fish. It's best known for its baby-back ribs, which are so tender that the meat practically falls off the bone, and its hickory-smoked filet of pork. Other items on the menu include beef brisket, smoked chicken, skewered shrimp, and sandwiches.

6. SOUTH KANSAS CITY & MARTIN CITY

South Kansas City refers to the southern part of Kansas City, MO, close to I-435. Most of the following restaurants are either on or near Wornall Road, north of I-435, or in Martin City, which is about as far south in the metropolitan area as you can get. Although the restaurants are a bit out of the way, they warrant a trip.

EXPENSIVE

JASPER'S, 405 W. 75th St. Tel. 816/363-3003.
Cuisine: ITALIAN. **Reservations:** Recommended, especially on weekends.

$ Prices: Appetizers $7.50–$9.50; main courses $17.50–$30. AE, CB, DC, DISC, MC, V.
Open: Mon–Thurs 6–10pm, Fri–Sat 6–11pm.

⭐ It's easy to see why many consider this Kansas City's best restaurant. Jasper's, in operation for almost 40 years, was the first restaurant in the city to receive a four-star *Mobil Travel Guide* Award, which it has won consistently for more than a decade. It also has an AAA Four Diamond Award. The atmosphere is elegant without being too stuffy, and the service is excellent. It's a favorite destination for Kansas Citians celebrating special occasions.

Jasper's cuisine is Northern Italian, but it also offers steaks, fish, and veal. Pasta dishes include homemade ravioli stuffed with lobster and served in a pink lobster sauce, and linguine with lobster, crab, scallops, and shrimp in a tomato sauce. For a main course, you might choose baby veal stuffed with prosciutto and cheese in piquant sauce; prime tenderloin of beef with crabmeat, white asparagus, and Barolo wine sauce; or shrimp sautéed with mushrooms, garlic, tomato, and white wine. Jackets are required for men. In a separate bar area you can enjoy an after- or before-dinner drink.

INEXPENSIVE

JESS & JIM'S STEAK HOUSE, 517 E. 135th St., Martin City. Tel. 816/942-9909.
Cuisine: STEAKS. **Reservations:** Not required.
$ Prices: Lunch $3.50–$6; dinner main courses $8.50–$25. AE, DC, DISC, MC, V.
Open: Mon–Sat 11am–11pm, Sun noon–9pm.

⭐ A 25-ounce boneless steak is Jess & Jim's claim to fame, bringing in hungry carnivores by the droves. Even if your appetite dictates one of the smaller cuts of beef (eight types and sizes are available), you'll still want to gawk at that huge chunk of meat in the glass-enclosed display case in the front room. This is a no-nonsense eating establishment that has been in operation since 1938, the kind of place where no one takes notice of the nondescript decor and fake plants. Rather, people come here for steaks served sizzling hot, although lobster tail, catfish, shrimp, rainbow trout, frog's legs, pork chops, and chicken also are available. Main courses come with a salad, choice of potato, and bread. Lunch offers digestible sizes of beef, a wide range of sandwiches, and daily specials.

PRINCESS GARDEN, 8906 Wornall Rd. Tel. 816/444-3709.
Cuisine: CHINESE. **Reservations:** Not required.
$ Prices: Lunch $4.20–$5.30; fixed-price lunches $4; dinner main courses $6.75–$22; fixed-price dinners $10–$14. AE, DISC, MC, V.
Open: Lunch Mon–Sat 11:30am–2pm; dinner Mon–Thurs 5–10pm, Fri–Sat 5–11pm, Sun noon–10pm.

This pleasant restaurant, decorated with Chinese lanterns, a dragon-motif ceiling, and subdued lighting, serves authentic Mandarin and Szechuan cuisine prepared and served by a Chinese staff. Of the more than 100 items listed on the dinner menu, standouts include the Hunan beef in hot garlic sauce, Peking duck, and Mandarin noodles. The fixed-price lunches and dinners are real bargains.

There's another branch at 8505 College Blvd. (tel. 913/339-9898) in Overland Park.

SMOKE STACK, Holmes Rd. and 135th St., Martin City. Tel. 816/942-9141.

Cuisine: BARBECUE. **Reservations:** Not accepted.

$ Prices: Lunch $4.50–$8; dinner $6.50–$13. AE, MC, V.

Open: Mon–Thurs 11am–10pm, Fri 11am–10:30pm, Sat 11:30am–10:30pm, Sun 11:30am–10pm.

This place is always packed, even though it's on the edge of nowhere. A family-owned business since 1957, it is a cozy and casual restaurant, with a low wooden ceiling, wooden tables, and plants. Smoke Stack serves ribs and barbecued beef, pork, sausage, turkey, and chicken as well as Cajun chicken breast, hickory-grilled beef kabob, steaks, fresh seafood, grilled pork chops, lamb ribs, and sandwiches. All dinner main courses come with french fries, cole-slaw, and toasted French bread; there's a wide selection of beers, including about 30 different kinds of imports.

STROUDS, 1015 E. 85th St. Tel. 816/333-2132.

Cuisine: CHICKEN. **Reservations:** Not required.

$ Prices: Sandwiches from $3.50; main courses $8.70–$15. AE, DISC, MC, V.

Open: Mon–Thurs 4–10pm, Fri 11am–11pm, Sat 2–11pm, Sun 11am–10pm.

This is a Kansas City tradition, specializing in pan-fried chicken prepared the old-fashioned way ever since its opening in 1933. Strouds is a plain and almost painfully modest establishment, a wooden building with a wooden floor and red-and-white-checked tablecloths. Yet the food is so famous that it's been written up in a number of publications through the years, including *People, Esquire, The New York Times,* and *USA Today.* Strouds also offers steak, pork chops, shrimp, catfish, and sandwiches. All main courses come with a salad or soup, choice of potato, green beans, gravy, and homemade cinnamon rolls. It's located just east of Holmes Road.

TASSO'S, 211 W. 75th St. Tel. 816/363-4776.

Cuisine: GREEK. **Reservations:** Recommended on weekends.

$ Prices: Lunch $4.95–$5.95; dinner main courses $9.50–$14; sandwiches $3.50–$5. AE, MC, V.

Open: Lunch Tues–Fri 11am–2:30pm, Sat noon–5pm; dinner Tues–Thurs 5:30pm–midnight, Fri–Sat 5:30pm–1am.

Fun is the catchword here, and owner Tasso is always on hand to make sure that even the most surly succumb to the merriment. The decor gives you something to smile about—fake grapes galore, kitsch everywhere, walls painted a Mykonos white and blue, and obligatory pictures on the wall (thankfully, Tasso's wife says, she didn't let him decorate their home). There's also a Greek band and belly dancing nightly, and, as though that weren't enough, Tasso has been known to dance impromptu on the tables and to break dishes in hot-blooded Greek fashion, just to add drama to the occasion. The liveliest evenings are Friday and Saturday. The menu includes all the Greek favorites, from moussaka and souvlaki to pastitsio (macaroni and beef in béchamel sauce), spring lamb, gyros, and kabobs. There are a daily fresh fish and vegetarian specials, as well as combination plates that let you sample a variety of dishes. An adjoining grocery store sells Greek specialties. It's located off Wornall Road.

7. EAST KANSAS CITY & INDEPENDENCE

In addition to the restaurants listed below, Gates & Sons' Bar-B-Que has a branch at 10440 E. 40 Highway (tel. 816/353-5880) and Winstead's serves its burgers at 1428 Noland Rd. (tel. 816/252-9363), both in Independence. For details, see Section 3 above. The city of Independence borders Kansas City on the east.

MODERATE

STEPHENSON'S APPLE FARM RESTAURANT, Hwy. 40 at Lee's Summit Rd. Tel. 816/373-5400.
Cuisine: BARBECUE. **Reservations:** Recommended.

$ Prices: Lunch $6–$12; dinner main courses $14–$23. AE, DISC, MC, V.

Open: Mon–Fri 11:30am–10pm, Sat 11:30am–11pm, Sun 10am–9pm; Sun brunch 10am–2pm.

What started out in 1946 as a modest restaurant begun by twin brothers on the edge of their family's fruit orchard has blossomed into one of the Kansas City area's best-known restaurants, popular with families and groups. The farm still produces apples, peaches, berries, and sweet cider, but the modest original restaurant has now grown into a huge barnlike structure, filled with antiques. There are a variety of dining rooms, each one different from the others but all decorated in slightly corny country style. The mock apple-orchard room, for example, features a plastic apple tree in the center and wrought-iron patio chairs. But what the heck, this is Americana kitsch at its best, and the food is great. Stephenson's specializes in hickory-smoked chicken, brisket, loin pork chop, whitefish, pork ribs, and jumbo shrimp—all slow-cooked over hickory. The enormous dinner main courses each come with baked potato with cheese sauce, green rice casserole, hot bread and apple butter, relish, salad, and hot apple fritter. Alcoholic specialties include apple and peach daiquiris and fruit wine. Stephenson's is located about a 15-minute drive east of downtown, off I-70 (turn south on Lee's Summit Road).

THE RHEINLAND RESTAURANT, 208 N. Main, Independence. Tel. 816/461-5383.
Cuisine: GERMAN. **Reservations:** Recommended on weekends.

$ Prices: Lunch $5.50–$6.50; dinner $9.50–$13. AE, DISC, MC, V.

Open: Tues–Sat 7am–9pm, Sun 11am–3pm.

For a bit of authentic German food in the heart of the Midwest, go to this casual family restaurant. It is owned and operated by Heinz and Rosie Heinzelmann, who immigrated from Germany in 1986 and opened this restaurant in 1991. The menu, using ingredients imported from Germany, includes such perennial favorites as smoked pork chops, several variations of Schnitzel (lightly breaded pork or veal cutlet), and Rouladen (rolled beef filled with pickles, onions, mustard, and spices). There are also daily specials. All dinner main courses are served with a salad, roll, and side dishes that range from spaetzle (Swabian noodles) to red cabbage or french fries. The lunch menu features sandwiches, including a Reuben, open-faced varieties, and Wurst (sausage). Conveniently located between the Truman Ticket and Information Center and Independence Square, the restaurant features live music on Saturday nights.

INEXPENSIVE

THE COURTHOUSE EXCHANGE, 113 W. Lexington, Independence. Tel. 816/252-0344.
   Cuisine: AMERICAN. **Reservations:** Recommended on weekends.
$ Prices: $3–$16. MC, V.
   Open: Mon–Sat 11am–9pm.
Located across from the courthouse on Independence Square, in the heart of town, this is a convenient place to eat if you're visiting the many sites in the vicinity. The Courthouse Exchange is an informal basement establishment, with exposed rafters, wooden booths, and a separate bar area that offers happy-hour specials weekdays from 5 to 7pm. The menu includes steaks, pork chops, fried chicken, shrimp, deep-fried catfish, grilled chicken breast, and more than 20 different kinds of sandwiches. There's a salad bar.

BUDGET

CLINTON'S, 100 W. Maple, Independence. Tel. 816/833-2625.
   Cuisine: BURGERS.
$ Prices: $1.40–$2.50. AE.
   Open: Mon–Thurs 11am–8pm. Fri–Sat 11am–10pm, Sun noon–6pm.
Harry S Truman got his first job here at Clinton Drugstore, opening the store every morning at 6:30, cleaning, and working the fountain. After he worked there for a year, his employer asked him to dust the entire stock of bottles—and Harry decided to look for a job somewhere else. Today Clinton's is a nostalgic reminder of the soda fountains of yore, complete with a marble counter at which you can sip on sodas, malts, and shakes and eat burgers, hot dogs, or sandwiches. It's located on Independence Square across from the courthouse, a stone's throw from the Truman Visitor's Center.

8. SPECIALTY DINING

HOTEL DINING

DOWNTOWN

Expensive

WALT BODINE'S, in the Radisson Suite Hotel Kansas City, 12th at Baltimore. Tel. 816/221-7000.
   Cuisine: STEAK. **Reservations:** Not required.

$ Prices: Lunch $5.50–$20; dinner main courses $15–$25. AE, CB, DC, DISC, MC, V.
Open: Lunch Mon–Fri 11:30am–2pm; dinner Sun–Thurs 5–10pm, Fri–Sat 5–11pm.

Named after a longtime Kansas City broadcaster, food critic, and local personality, Walt Bodine's is located in a historic downtown hotel, complete with original 1930s lamps and woodwork and an open kitchen. The limited menu, featuring steaks, includes prime rib, Kansas City strip steak, and filet mignon. There are also a fresh fish of the day, lobster tail, and chicken. Lunch focuses on lighter fare, including a variety of salads, sandwiches, and beef.

CROWN CENTER
Expensive

PEPPERCORN DUCK CLUB, in the Hyatt Regency Crown Center, 2345 McGee St. Tel. 816/421-1234.
Cuisine: CONTINENTAL. **Reservations:** Imperative on weekends.
$ Prices: Lunch $10–$16; dinner main courses $24–$30. AE, CB, DC, DISC, MC, V.
Open: Lunch Mon–Fri 11:30am–2pm; dinner Sun–Thurs 5:30–10pm, Fri–Sat 5:30–10:30pm; Sun brunch 10am–2pm.

The Peppercorn Duck Club is considered one of the top restaurants in the city, famous for its spit-roasted duck cooked in a rotisserie built especially for the restaurant. In the middle of the restaurant is Market Island, a buffet featuring a fantastic array of domestic and imported cheeses, terrines, pâtés and galantines, and innovative salads; and the Ultra Chocolatta Bar with its fresh pastries and chocolates prepared by the house pastry chef. Diners can choose the Market Island as a main course for both lunch and dinner, eating to their heart's content. Other lunch selections include fresh seafood, crabcakes, barbecued shrimp, spit-roasted duck, and steak; dinner offers a wider choice of seafood, beef, veal, lamb, and game entrées—including salmon, lobster, steak, rack of lamb, braised pheasant breast, and duck. Coats and ties are required for men.

TRADER VIC'S, in the Westin Crown Center, One Pershing Rd. Tel. 816/391-4444.
Cuisine: INTERNATIONAL. **Reservations:** Not required.
$ Prices: Lunch $7.50–$15; dinner main courses $16–$28. AE, CB, DC, DISC, MC, V.
Open: Lunch Mon–Fri 11:30am–2:30pm; dinner Sun–Thurs 5–10pm, Fri–Sat 5–11pm.

Apart from the wonderful selection of international dishes, the thing I like most about Trader Vic's is that dining here is like taking a minivacation. Decorated as though it were a thatched-roof cottage on a beach in the South Seas, Trader Vic's is an escape into the world of exotic tropical cocktails (more than 50 on the menu) and a cuisine that takes its inspiration from China, the South Seas, and Southeast Asia.

You might wish to begin your meal with a Mai Tai, a rum concoction invented by Trader Vic in the 1940s, or such favorites as the Suffering Bastard, the Navy Grog, or the Black Widow. Appetizers not to miss include the crab rangoon; the crisped prawn with lemon grass; the sliced barbecue pork; and the grilled bamboo

IMPRESSIONS

*Not all the best restaurants in the world are in Kansas City,
just the top four or five.*
—CALVIN TRILLIN, IN *THE NEW YORKER*

---

skewers of swordfish, scallops, prawns, and chicken. Your next choice
should be the Bongo Bongo, a soup of puréed oyster and spinach
bisque. Main courses include a variety of meats grilled in the
restaurant's special Chinese smoker oven, including ginger chicken,
Indonesian lamb roast, sirloin steak, salmon, and Chinese roasted
pork. Other intriguing dishes are marinated duck served with chutney
and bok choy, shiitake chicken, Thai-spiced sea scallops, and almond
duck. There also are a variety of curry dishes, as well as seasonal
dishes that may include Hawaiian paella, swordfish with lime sauce,
and medallions of veal.

DINING WITH A VIEW

CROWN CENTER

Expensive

**BENTON'S STEAK AND CHOP HOUSE, in the Westin
Crown Center, One Pershing Rd. Tel. 816/474-4400.**
Cuisine: STEAK. **Reservations:** Recommended.
$ Prices: Dinner $20–$35. AE, CB, DC, DISC, MC, V.
Open: Dinner only Mon–Sat 5:30–10pm; Sun brunch 10am–
2:30pm.

Benton's, named after Kansas City artist Thomas Hart Benton,
features his original artwork, including one oil painting and
some lithographs. Located on the 20th floor of the Westin
Crown Center, it affords a view of the city in a nonfussy setting of
simple blond wood, brass fixtures, large windows, and plants.
Benton's specializes in Kansas City steaks and chops as well as fresh
seafood, all charbroiled and brought sizzling from the grill. All main
courses, ranging from steak and filet mignon to prime rib, chicken,
veal chops, and salmon steak, come with a bucket of shrimp, breads,
a salad, a vegetable of the day, and a choice of potato or rice pilaf.
Jackets are recommended, but not necessary, for men. There's an
adjoining lounge, where you may come solely for a drink.

Moderate

**SKIES, in the Hyatt Regency Crown Center, 2345 McGee
St. Tel. 816/421-1234.**
Cuisine: AMERICAN. **Reservations:** Recommended on week-
ends.
$ Prices: Appetizers $4.50–$8; main courses $14–$28. AE, CB,
DC, DISC, MC, V.
Open: Dinner only Sun–Thurs 5:30–9:30pm, Fri–Sat 5:30–
10:30pm.

You can't dine nearer to heaven than this 42nd-floor restaurant,
which is also the only revolving restaurant in town. Skies gives a
fantastic view over the entire city—and it is also a great place from
which to watch those Midwest sunsets or even thunderstorms come

rolling in. The limited menu opens with such appetizers as a corn-and-crab chowder, oysters, and lobster ravioli; main courses include roasted lamb medallions, king crab legs served with prime rib, mesquite-broiled veal chops, lobster tails, fresh fish, and black Angus beef. On the same floor is Skies Lounge, open from 4pm.

COUNTRY CLUB PLAZA
Expensive

THE GRILL, in The Ritz-Carlton, 401 Ward Parkway. Tel. 816/756-1500.
   Cuisine: AMERICAN. **Reservations:** Recommended, especially on weekends.
$ Prices: Appetizers $7.50–$10; main courses $22–$33. AE, CB, DC, DISC, MC, V.
   Open: Dinner only Tues–Sat 5:30–10pm; Sun brunch 10:30am–2pm.

This restaurant, located on the 12th floor of The Ritz-Carlton, has long been a favorite with Kansas Citians, especially the well-heeled older generation who come to celebrate anniversaries, birthdays, and other special occasions. The Grill is fitted with authentic English and French antiques, bronze sculptures, a crystal chandelier, and a working fireplace. It offers great views of the Plaza, which is especially impressive from Thanksgiving to New Year's Day, when the entire Plaza is outlined in festive lights. There's live piano music, and on the same floor is also a bar with live entertainment and a view of the Plaza.

The menu, which focuses on seafood and steaks, highlights regional specialties prepared in unusual ways. You may wish to start your meal with the Kansas City corn chowder, steak-and-potato soup, or perhaps oysters on the half shell. Seafood selections may include a 2½-pound Maine lobster, Ozark trout, or grilled tuna steak. From the grill there are Kansas City strip steak, beef tenderloin, an extra-thick cut of veal chop, and a 24-ounce porterhouse steak. Other specialties on the changing menu have included pan-fried capon breast with grilled eggplant, mozzarella, and marinara sauce; roast prime rib of beef with Yorkshire pudding and horseradish sauce; and baked, deep-dish spinach tortellini with three cheeses and prosciutto.

LIGHT, CASUAL & FAST FOOD
BUDGET

BARNEY'S CAFE, Barney Allis Plaza, 12th and Wyandotte. Tel. 816/871-3798.
   Cuisine: BURGERS/SNACKS.
$ Prices: $1–$4. No credit cards.
   Open: Mon–Fri 11am–3pm.
This is a café located on an open-air square in the heart of downtown Kansas City, with both indoor and outdoor seating. It serves hamburgers, hot dogs, nachos, salads, ice cream, sodas, and beer, as well as a daily lunch special.

LAMAR'S DONUTS, 240 E. Linwood. Tel. 816/931-5166.
   Cuisine: DOUGHNUTS.
$ Prices: 20¢–60¢. No credit cards.

Open: Mon–Sat 6am–6pm, Sun 6:30am–4pm.

Lamar's, located in a converted service station not far from 31st and Main streets, hasn't changed much since it opened in 1933. There are some Kansas Citians so hooked on these doughnuts that they cannot let a week go by without dropping in; when the place opens up there's usually a line already waiting at the door. As many as 500 people will pass through before 10am, loading up on the 30-some variety of doughnuts. Lamar's is famous for its cinnamon twist, but other varieties are German chocolate, French, apple spice, blueberry, chocolate glazed, and double chocolate. At day's end, whatever is left is donated to the Salvation Army, soup kitchens, nursing homes, and halfway houses.

SUNDAY BRUNCH

All hotels in the expensive and moderate ranges have restaurants that serve breakfast; many of them also offer Sunday brunch. The **Peppercorn Duck Club,** located in the Hyatt Regency Crown Center, offers Sunday brunch from 10am to 2pm, featuring a huge spread with an omelet station, prime rib, cured ham, two types of duck, three types of egg dishes, fish, fresh lunch meats, fruit, pastries, desserts, and even champagne. The all-inclusive price is $18.95 for adults and $13.95 for children.

Also at Crown Center is **Benton's Steak and Chop House,** where diners are awarded the extra treat of a panoramic view of the city. Its Sunday brunch, available from 10am to 2:30pm, features a bountiful spread of assorted fresh fruits, pastries, croissants, breads, spinach and romaine salads, cheeses, omelets, bacon, sausage, biscuits and gravy, roast beef, assorted cold meats, pasta dishes, country-style fried potatoes, fresh salmon, oysters, and fresh seafood. It costs $15.95 for adults and $8.95 for children.

On the Plaza, the favored spot for Sunday brunch is **The Grill** at The Ritz-Carlton, served from 10:30am to 2pm. If you're lucky enough to get a window seat, you'll dine with a view of the Plaza. Costing $24.50 for adults and $9.50 for children, brunch features an appetizer table with salads, cold cuts, cheeses, smoked fish, fruits and berries, pâtés, pastries, muffins, croissants, and fruit bread. There's a different roast offered each week; the main buffet table runs the gamut from breakfast eggs and meats to lunch entrées. Of course, there's also a dessert table.

More recommendations for Sunday brunch on the Plaza include **Fedora Café and Bar,** 210 W. 47th St. (tel. 816/561-6565), which from 10:30am to 2:30pm offers a selection of breakfast entrées ranging in price from $6.95 to $12.95, including trips to a buffet laden with fruit and pastries; and **Bristol Bar and Grill,** 4740 Jefferson (tel. 816/756-0606), which charges $10.95 per person for its brunch from 10am to 2pm.

Within a three-minute walk from the Plaza is the smartly decorated **Venue,** 4532 Main St. (tel. 816/561-3311), which offers a simple menu ranging from bagels with lox and cream cheese and pecan buttermilk pancakes to scrambled eggs with fettucine and cottage cheese. Main courses here, ranging from $5.50 to $8, are served Sunday from 10am to 2:30pm.

One of my personal favorites for Sunday brunch is the Classic Cup, which has two convenient locations. The **Classic Cup Sidewalk Café,** 301 W. 47th St. (tel. 816/753-1840), located on the

Plaza, offers outdoor sidewalk seating. One of the few places on the Plaza that is open for breakfast throughout the week, it also offers a Sunday brunch from 10am to 3pm with main courses ranging from $5.95 to $8.95. There's another **Classic Cup** in Westport at 4130 Pennsylvania (tel. 816/756-0771), a great place to start the day. Its main courses, which change weekly but may range from buttermilk pancakes and chicken enchiladas to omelets and other egg dishes, cost $6.95 to $8.95 and are served with a fruit dish. Hours here are 11am to 2pm.

And, finally, there's the lively Sunday brunch at **Blvd Café,** 703 Southwest Blvd. (tel. 816/842-6984), with live jazz music. It features an international range of main courses, including a feta-and-olive omelet; Moroccan phyllo turnover; vegetarian quiche; Mexican-style eggs; and freshly baked scones, muffins, and assorted cakes and pastries. All entrées are priced at $6.95 and are served from 10am to 2pm.

LATE-NIGHT/24-HOUR
BUDGET

LUCILLE'S, 1604 Westport Rd. Tel. 816/561-5111.
　Cuisine: AMERICAN.
$ **Prices:** $4.50–$10. AE, CB, DC, DISC, MC, V.
　Open: Mon–Thurs 6:30am–midnight, Fri–Sun 24 hrs.

Lucille's in midtown is a reproduction of a 1950s diner; with its polished-chrome facade and Formica tabletops, Lucille's looks more 1950s than anything ever did back then. It's decorated with a delightful assortment of nostalgic kitsch—including Sputnik-inspired lamps, gaudy table lamps, tableside juke boxes, and other feasts for the eyes. Water is served in Mason jars. Unfortunately, the food doesn't live up to the decor, but who cares at 2am? Part of the fun in dining here is in seeing what other poor souls are wandering the streets at such an ungodly hour. Breakfasts range from omelets to Mexican-inspired dishes; lunch and dinner include burgers, sandwiches, and platters of fried chicken, catfish, or lasagne that include side dishes.

NICHOLS LUNCH, 39th and S. W. Trafficway. Tel. 816/561-5200.
　Cuisine: AMERICAN.
$ **Prices:** Sandwiches $2.50–$5; fixed-price dinners $4.50–$7.50. No credit cards.
　Open: Tues–Sun 24 hrs. **Closed:** Mon.

Nichols, near Westport, has been the place to go for late-night dining in midtown ever since it opened back in 1921. It features old-fashioned home cooking, with more than 100 items on the menu and changing dinner specials for less than $5 that range from catfish and cod to pork chops, fried chicken, meatloaf, and macaroni and cheese. Breakfast is always available.

PICNIC FARE & WHERE TO EAT IT

The best place to buy picnic ingredients is Country Club Plaza because it offers a variety of specialty stores clustered together. Both Volker Park and Brush Creek Park are located immediately east of the Plaza, so they are ideal places for picnicking. The largest park in town is Swope Park, located at Meyer and Gregory boulevards; it offers picnic shelters (tel. 363-7800 for reservations), hiking trails, and rolling hills.

THE BETTER CHEDDAR, 604 W. 48th St. Tel. 816/561-8204.

Open: Mon–Sat 9am–9pm, Sun 11am–6pm.

If you buy bread at La Bonne Bouchée (below), come here to buy things to put on the bread. This shop sells imported cheeses, sausage, chutney, mustard, jams, caviar, imported gourmet items, wine, and gift baskets.

THE GOURMET GROCER, 614 W. 48th St. Tel. 816/561-5888.

Open: Mon–Sat 7am–9pm, Sun 9am–5pm.

OK, so you want to go on a picnic but want someone else to prepare the food? The Gourmet Grocer sells the ultimate in picnic food: gourmet items to go (there's even a drive-through window). Items include salads, sandwiches, soups, a dozen or more vegetarian dishes, quiches, potato dishes, and entrées. Salads range from pasta primavera to couscous and curried rice; entrées include beef Wellington, lasagne, and seafood Florentine. There also are complete box lunches, each of which includes a sandwich, a salad, a dessert, utensils, and a napkin—beginning at $6.

LA BONNE BOUCHEE, 618 Ward Pkwy. Tel. 816/931-5230.

Open: Mon–Fri 7am–6pm, Sat 8am–5pm, Sun 8am–2pm.

This is the place to go for freshly baked breads, rolls, croissants, boules, baguettes, cookies, tarts, cakes, and desserts. As its name implies, it features French breads and pastries, baked each day in an imported French oven.

MUEHLBACH'S WEST, 4807 Jefferson. Tel. 816/756-1115.

Open: Mon–Sat 8am–8pm, Sun 10am–6pm.

Grocers since 1874, Muehlbach's serves as a full-line grocery store for people living around the Plaza, carrying everything from fruits, vegetables, and meats to health food, liquor, and canned goods. Buy all your essentials here.

CHAPTER 15

WHAT TO SEE & DO IN THE KANSAS CITY AREA

Kansas City and environs do not have as many major museums and renowned attractions as St. Louis. In fact, the three biggest draws—Royals baseball games, the Worlds of Fun theme park, and Woodlands racetrack—are not types of attractions unique to the Kansas City area. However, Kansas City does offer a wide variety of things to do and see—the fine Nelson-Atkins Museum of Art, with its Henry Moore Sculpture Garden; historic forts; Country Club Plaza; cruises on the Missouri River; and some unusual museums.

SUGGESTED ITINERARIES

The sights are spread throughout Kansas City's metropolitan area, including Independence and Leavenworth, making it necessary to plan your itinerary geographically.

IF YOU HAVE ONE DAY

If you have only one day in Kansas City, I suggest you start downtown and slowly work your way south, using Main Street as your guide to both Crown Center and Country Club Plaza. It's best to have your own car to see Kansas City in a day, but even without an automobile you can see most of the sights listed in this day's outing by boarding the Trolley downtown at Barney Allis Plaza on 12th Street and taking it to Crown Center, the Nelson-Atkins Museum, and the Plaza.

If you're sightseeing on Saturday, you should begin your day by rising early and heading for the City Market, located near the Missouri River, just north of downtown at 5th and Walnut streets.

First erected in 1888 and recently restored, the market is at its busiest on Saturday but is still worth a visit during the week. Surrounding the market is an old district of brick warehouses, which are gradually being renovated as loft apartments and offices.

From the market, head south across I-70 to the old Garment District, located in downtown Kansas City, around 8th and Central. Once the hub of Kansas City's financial and commercial district, it contains many fine old buildings. (See Chapter 16 for more information.)

Next head south on Main to Pershing, where you'll see the now-defunct Union Station to your right (empty for years and still the object of debate about its future) and Crown Center to your left. A city within a city, Crown Center occupies 85 acres of land and contains two hotels; offices; indoor shops and restaurants; and the Hallmark Visitors Center, where you can learn about the history of Hallmark cards and how they're made. If you're hungry for a snack or lunch, refer to Chapter 14 for restaurants in Crown Center, the Hyatt Regency, and Westin Crown Center.

From Crown Center head to the Nelson-Atkins Museum of Art, one of the most comprehensive art museums in the country. If you visit only one museum in the Kansas City area, this should be it. In addition to its outstanding Oriental collection and outdoor Henry Moore Sculpture Garden, it has a delightful restaurant.

Finally, complete your quick tour of Kansas City at America's oldest shopping center, Country Club Plaza, renowned for its Spanish architecture, statues, fountains, shops, and restaurants. Refer to Chapters 14 and 18 for recommendations on restaurants and bars.

IF YOU HAVE TWO DAYS

Day 1   Follow the itinerary outlined above.

Day 2   Devote your energies to pursuing your own special interest, whether it's more shopping at Crown Center or the Plaza, a Royals baseball game, or a trip to Fort Osage or Fort Leavenworth. One of the Kansas City area's newer, but immensely popular, attractions is the Woodlands racetrack, featuring horses in summer and grey-hounds the rest of the year. If you have children, head for the Worlds of Fun theme park; the Green Mill Candy Factory, with its samples of peanut brittle; or the Kaleidoscope, a creative art exhibit sponsored by Hallmark Cards Inc., in Crown Center. Missouri Town 1855 is a reconstructed 1800s Missouri town, with original homes and shops brought from other locations and reconstructed here. For evening entertainment, head for Westport, located in midtown, just north of Country Club Plaza.

IF YOU HAVE THREE DAYS

Days 1–2   Follow the itinerary outlined above.

Day 3   Head for Independence, MO, a 15-minute drive from downtown Kansas City (take I-70 east to Noland Road, then head north, watching for the many signs). This was the hometown of Harry S Truman, 33rd president of the United States. Your first stop should be the Truman Home Ticket and Information Center, Truman Road and Main Street, to pick up your ticket to tour the Truman Home. You'll learn more about Truman, his life in Independence, and his

? DID YOU KNOW . . . ?

- More than one-third of the U.S. population resides within 600 miles of Kansas City.
- Kansas City has more miles of boulevards than Paris and more fountains than any city except Rome.
- Kansas City leads the country in underground storage space and the publishing of greeting cards.
- The Kansas City area served as the starting point for the Santa Fe, California, and Oregon trails.
- Kansas means "People of the South Wind" in the language of the Kansas Indians.
- At one time it was against the law to serve ice cream on cherry pie in Kansas.

days in office at the Harry S Truman Library and Museum. Other sights worth seeing in Independence include the National Frontier Trails Center, dedicated to those who traveled the Santa Fe, Oregon, and California trails; the Mormon Visitors Center, with exhibits relating Mormon history, settlement in Independence, and relocation to Salt Lake City; and Vaile Mansion and the Bingham-Waggoner Estate, two restored mansions open to the public. For evening entertainment, consider a cruise on the *America* or *Missouri River Queen,* which offer such diversions as blues, gospel, and other live music on trips along the Missouri River. Alternatives include an outdoor concert or musical at the beautiful Starlight Theatre in Swope Park or a late-night jam session of jazz at the Mutual Musician's Foundation.

IF YOU HAVE FIVE DAYS OR MORE

Day 1 Spend the day in downtown Kansas City, beginning with a trip to the city market, with its colorful displays of fruits and vegetables. Here also is the newly opened *Arabia* Steamboat Museum, with its fascinating displays of cargo recovered from a steamboat that sank in the Missouri River in 1856. Next, head for City Hall to begin a walking tour of Kansas City's most famous buildings (see Chapter 16). Top off the day with a meal at the historic Savoy Grill.

Day 2 In the morning, head for Crown Center, with its many shops, restaurants, and attractions. Next on your itinerary should be the Nelson-Atkins Museum of Art, one of the country's finest art museums. From there it's just a short drive to Country Club Plaza, America's oldest shopping center (for a walking tour, see Chapter 16).

Day 3 Head for Independence, MO, following the itinerary outlined above under "If You Have Three Days."

Days 4–5 Devote your energies to pursuing your own interest, whether it's visiting more museums, shopping, or attending a Royals baseball game. See Day 2 under "If You Have Two Days" for more suggestions on what to do. Better yet, read the rest of this chapter.

1. THE TOP ATTRACTIONS

In addition to the attractions listed here, other top Kansas City area draws are the Worlds of Fun theme park (see the "Cool for Kids" section below), and also Royals baseball games and the Woodlands racetrack (see "Sports & Recreation" at the end of this chapter).

NELSON-ATKINS MUSEUM OF ART, 4525 Oak St., Kansas City, MO. Tel. 816/561-4000.

Located about a 15-minute walk east of Country Club Plaza in midtown, the Nelson-Atkins Museum of Art boasts one of the most comprehensive art collections in the country. Founded in 1933 by William Rockhill Nelson, the flamboyant owner of the *Kansas City Star,* it is a massive building constructed primarily in Greek classic style. Its galleries represent all civilizations, from Sumeria in 3,000 B.C. to paintings and sculpture in modern times— including Oriental, European, Classical, African, pre-Columbian, American, and modern art.

Particularly outstanding is the museum's collection of Oriental art, including Japanese art and screens and Chinese porcelain, furniture, and sculpture. Among the works to look out for are the seated guanyin, Chinese deity of mercy and compassion, dating from about the 11th century, and pottery figures produced during the Tang dynasty (A.D. 618–906) and used in important Temple burials. Both are located on the second floor in the Chinese Temple room.

In the museum's European collections are works representing all important schools and periods, including early Italian Renaissance and Venetian works; French paintings, furniture, and decorative arts; and Dutch, Flemish, Spanish, and English paintings. Many artists are represented: Degas, Monet, Pissarro, van Gogh, Gauguin, Paul Klee, Max Beckmann, Emil Nolde, Rembrandt, and others. American artists also are well represented, with works by native son Thomas Hart Benton, Georgia O'Keeffe, Andrew Wyeth, George Caleb Bingham, John Singer Sargent, Raphaelle Peale, and Willem de Kooning.

On the museum's south lawn is the Henry Moore Sculpture Garden, with 12 sculptures spread on 17 acres. It is the largest collection of monumental bronze sculptures by Moore outside England. The museum also contains a fine book and gift store and a delightful restaurant called Rozelle Court, which resembles a Venetian courtyard.

Admission: Free to Henry Moore Sculpture Garden; Nelson-Atkins Museum of Art $4 adults, $1 students and children; children 5 and under free. All permanent collections free Sat.

Open: Tues–Sat 10am–5pm, Sun 1–5pm. **Closed:** July 4, Thanksgiving, Christmas, New Year's Day.

COUNTRY CLUB PLAZA, 47th St. and Ward Pkwy., Kansas City, MO. Tel. 816/753-0100.

Country Club Plaza in midtown, usually referred to simply as the Plaza, opened in the early 1920s as America's first shopping center. Built in Spanish architectural style with red-tiled roofs, it's a delightful area for strolling, shopping, and dining. The wide boulevards are lined with trees, and the ornate buildings are topped with towers; throughout the Plaza are more than $1 million worth of fountains and bronze sculptures. A peculiarity of the Plaza is that there are no stoplights or stop signs, in keeping with the belief of Plaza founder J. C. Nichols that all visitors to the Plaza would behave so courteously that no such measures would be necessary. Maybe that was true back then, but experience has taught

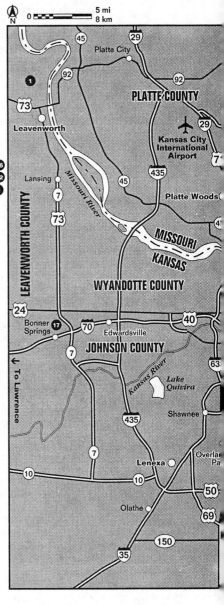

me to look both ways before venturing from the curb. Another characteristic of the Plaza is that parking is absolutely free. Highlights include the Christmas lighting ceremony, which takes place every year on Thanksgiving evening, and the Plaza Art Fair in September. For more information on the Plaza, refer to Chapter 17 on shopping.

Admission: Free.

Open: Most shops Mon–Sat 10am–6pm, Sun noon–5pm. Many open Thurs until 9pm.

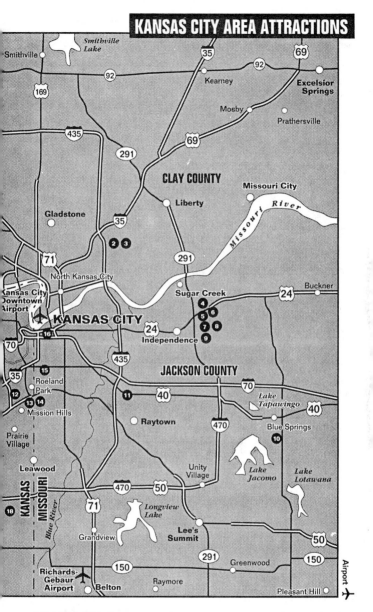

KANSAS CITY AREA ATTRACTIONS

CROWN CENTER, 2450 Grand Ave., Kansas City, MO. Tel. 816/274-8444.

Located between the Plaza and downtown, Crown Center is a huge living-and-working environment occupying 85 acres. Of interest to visitors are its three levels of shops, boutiques, and restaurants, as well as its outdoor ice-skating rink (open winter only), the American Heartland Theatre, and the Coterie Children's Theatre. Kaleidoscope is a free creative art workshop that allows children 5 to 12 to participate and create their own works of art (see "Cool for Kids" later in this chapter for more information).

The entire Crown Center complex is under the management of Hallmark Cards, Inc., the world's largest greeting-card company, which publishes cards in some 20 languages. Be sure to see the Hallmark Visitors Center, with its displays chronicling more than 75 years of Hallmark history. Free to the public, the Visitors Center's twelve exhibits include sections devoted to the Hallmark Hall of Fame TV series, the production of Hallmark's many products, their distribution around the world, and a film about craftspeople at work. During summer there are free outdoor concerts every Friday at 8pm on Crown Center Square.

Admission: Free to Crown Center and Hallmark Visitors Center.

Open: Shops Mon–Wed and Sat 10am–6pm, Thurs and Fri 10am–9pm, Sun noon–5pm. Hallmark Visitors Center Mon–Fri 9am–5pm, Sat 9:30am–4:30pm. **Closed:** Thanksgiving, Christmas, New Year's Day.

HARRY S TRUMAN HOME, 219 N. Delaware St., Independence, MO. Tel. 816/254-7199 or 254-9929.

Americans still flock to Independence to pay tribute to Harry S Truman, 33rd president of the Unites States, with a visit to the Truman Home. (Note: Because Truman's middle name was just the letter S, not a name beginning with that letter, the *S* is usually not followed by a period.) Built in 1867 by Bess Truman's grandfather, this 14-room Victorian housed four generations of her family. Modest for a president's home, it's still furnished exactly as it was when Harry and Bess Truman retired here in 1953 after Truman's two terms in the White House, with the Truman's 1972 Chrysler still in the garage and Harry's hat and coat still hanging in the foyer. After Bess Truman died in 1982 at age 97, the home became a National Historic Site under the administration of the National Park Service. According to Bess Truman's will, only the ground floor is open to the public as long as the couple's only daughter, Margaret Truman Daniel, is still alive.

Note: Tours, which depart every 15 minutes and last slightly less than half an hour, must be booked through the Harry S Truman Ticket and Information Center, 223 N. Main St. Tickets are distributed on a first-come, first-served basis, with no advance reservations. Be sure to come here first upon your arrival in Independence. The Center offers a 12-minute slide show on Truman, from his courtship of Bess to his grave. You can reach the Truman Home by car via I-70 (Noland Road exit) or U.S. 24.

Admission: $1 adults; children 16 and younger and seniors 62 and older free.

Open: Harry S Truman Ticket and Information Center daily 8:30am–5pm. Tours in summer daily 9am–4:45pm (last tour); in winter (Labor Day to Memorial Day) daily Tues–Sun 9am–4:45pm. **Closed:** Thanksgiving, Christmas, New Year's Day.

HARRY S TRUMAN LIBRARY AND MUSEUM, Hwy. 42 and Delaware St., Independence, MO. Tel. 816/833-1400.

The Harry S Truman Library contains more than 14 million pages of manuscripts, books, and other historical materials relating to the former president. Of the most interest to the more than 150,000 visitors per year, however, is the adjoining museum that focuses on Truman's life and career. Serving as vice president only 82 days before being sworn in as president upon Franklin Roosevelt's death on April 12, 1945, Truman was in office during the end of World War II, went on to win a surprise victory over opponent Thomas Dewey in the 1948 presidential election, and served as president during the Korean War. All these events are faithfully chronicled in the museum's excellent displays.

Also in the museum is an exact reproduction of the Oval Office as it appeared in the 1950s, complete with a voice recording of Truman describing the items in his office. On display are many gifts that were given to the Trumans from all over the world, including a silver tea set sent by the Dalai Lama of Tibet in 1945, a carpet from Iran with 29 million hand-tied knots, and a dining set from the Philippines. In the lobby of the museum is a large mural by Thomas Hart Benton entitled *Independence and the Opening of the West.* Both Harry and Bess Truman are buried in the courtyard of the library.

Admission: $2 adults; children 15 and under free.

Open: Daily 9am–5pm. **Closed:** Thanksgiving, Christmas, New Year's Day.

2. MORE ATTRACTIONS

MUSEUMS

AGRICULTURAL HALL OF FAME AND MUSEUM OF FARM-ING, 630 N. 126th St., Bonner Springs, KS. Tel. 913/721-1075.

Kansas is a fitting place for this memorial to the American farmer, set amid rolling hills 15 miles west of Kansas City, just off I-70. It boasts the country's largest and most varied exhibit of agricultural artifacts, as well as items relating to everyday life on the American farm. Altogether there are more than 5,000 items on display—every one donated by individuals. Included are rustic toys, kitchenware, antique washing machines, a collection of old telephones (which had a profound influence on isolated farm life), a collection of barbed wire, a blacksmith's shop, a one-room schoolhouse, and a harness-maker's shop.

The museum's agricultural machinery collection (10 times larger than the Smithsonian's) contains thousands of engines, vehicles, machines, tools, and tillers—including a replica of the 1831 McCormick reaper, a 1903 Dart farm truck, a horse-drawn plow used by Harry S Truman as a young man, an original sodbuster plow, a 1781 Native American plow, tractors of the 1916–29 era, and threshing machines. The Hall of Fame honors individuals who helped in the advancement of agriculture, from Squanto to Eli Whitney and George Washington Carver.

Admission: $4 adults, $3 seniors, $2 children 6–16.

Open: Mon–Sat 9am–5pm, Sun 1–5pm (must enter by 4pm). **Closed:** Dec–Mar.

ARABIA **STEAMBOAT MUSEUM, 400 Grand Ave., Kansas City, MO. Tel. 816/471-4030.**

In 1856, the steamboat *Arabia* sank in the Missouri River, taking with it more than 200 tons of cargo. After some 130 years and countless floods, the boat lay buried 45 feet beneath a farm field, half a mile from the Missouri River. In 1988, five families of the Kansas City area began uncovering the ship and its contents. Although the ship itself proved too fragile for removal, its cargo was in mint condition, preserved by the dark, cold, damp mud. In 1991, the *Arabia* Steamboat Museum opened on the edge of the city market, not far from the Missouri. It contains the largest collection of pre–Civil War steamboat cargo in the world, a time capsule of frontier life in 1856.

After viewing a 12-minute film about the ship's excavation, visitors can wander through the museum, with exhibits re-creating the look and feel of 1856 steamboat life, including a 171-foot full-scale replica of the *Arabia*'s steamboat deck with a 28-foot working paddlewheel. Recovered goods and artifacts, all bound for trade in the West, offer a fascinating look at frontier life. These include an amazing 4,000 leather boots and shoes; more than 1,000 pieces of china; 65 bolts of fabric; 10,000 buttons; tools and hardware ranging from square nails to doorknobs; jewelry; perfume; blankets; cigars; hairbrushes; pencils; spittoons; and even glass bottles containing pickles, ketchup, and pie fillings.

Admission: $5.50 adults, $5 seniors, $3.25 children 4–12.

Open: Tues–Sat 10am–6pm, Sun noon–5pm. **Closed:** Easter, Thanksgiving, Christmas, New Year's Day.

CITY MARKET, 5th and Main, Kansas City, MO. Tel. 816/421-0053.

Kansas City's main produce market, in operation since the 1840s, is located just north of downtown, between I-70 and the Missouri River. Its handsome art deco buildings were recently renovated, and a new addition is the *Arabia* Steamboat Museum (see above). Saturday is the busiest day, when fruit, vegetables, T-shirts, nuts, baked goods, ice cream, live chickens, and plants and flowers are for sale. There are also vendors selling everything from barbecue and Chinese food to chili dogs.

Admission: Free.

Open: Mon–Fri 8am–3pm, Sat 6am–5pm.

LIBERTY MEMORIAL AND MUSEUM, Penn Valley Park, 100 W. 26th St., Kansas City, MO. Tel. 816/221-1918.

Located downtown on the crest of a hill near Crown Center and Union Station, this is the only military museum and archives in the United States devoted to World War I. Its towering Torch of Liberty, a familiar Kansas City landmark, rises 300 feet and contains an elevator and an observation platform affording a panoramic view of the downtown skyline. The small museum, located to the west of the tower, starts with an explanation of the causes of World War I and continues with displays relating to America's role in the Great War. Also displayed are military clothing, items the doughboy carried in his pack, gas masks, medals and decorations, posters urging enlistment, and other memorabilia. There's even a full-scale replica of a trench and underground.

Admission: Free to museum; Torch of Liberty tower $1 adults, 25¢ children 6–11.

Open: Wed–Sun 9:30am–4:30pm. **Closed:** Thanksgiving, Christmas, New Year's Day.

NATIONAL FRONTIER TRAILS CENTER, 318 W. Pacific Ave., Independence, MO. Tel. 816/254-0059.

⬥ Opened in 1990, this museum commemorates Independence's historic role as the only location that served as the starting point for the three major westward trails—the Santa Fe, California, and Oregon. Housed in a former flour mill near a spring

---

⬥ **FROMMER'S FAVORITE KANSAS CITY EXPERIENCES**

Lunch at Arthur Bryant's Once rated by *New Yorker* writer Calvin Trillin as the "single, best restaurant in the world," Arthur Bryant's is the city's best-known barbecue restaurant and has served presidents and kings. It's a roll-your-sleeves-up kind of place, the place to indulge yourself without reservation. Worth the wait in line as people from around the city come for that famous meat piled high on white bread and doused with Bryant's legendary sauce.

A Stroll through Country Club Plaza Country Club Plaza is the nation's oldest shopping center, a 14-block area with tree-lined streets, horse-drawn carriages, Spanish architecture, and more than $1 million worth of fountains and statues. Come for a meal, shopping, browsing, and strolling. Great also for people-watching.

City Market on Saturday For more than 100 years, the City Market has been selling fruit, vegetables, flowers, live chickens, eggs, and other produce to Kansas Citians. Recently renovated, the City Market is still going strong, with Saturday bringing in huge crowds that also shop for T-shirts, kitchen appliances, and other goods. A new attraction is the *Arabia* Steamboat Museum. Great fun.

A Royals Baseball Game The Royals bring in more visitors to Kansas City than any other attraction—and for good reason. Watching baseball is a great summertime activity, and the Royals stadium is one of the best.

An Evening at Starlight On a warm summer evening, there's no better place for an outdoor concert or musical than the Starlight Theatre. Set amid the lush greenery of Swope Park, this amphitheater features brick architecture that faintly resembles a castle, vine-covered trellises, and sometimes a full moon hovering above the stage. Very romantic.

Late-Night Jam at the Mutual Musicians Foundation This place doesn't open until after midnight, when jazz musicians who have finished their regular gigs come here to jam the rest of the night away. Don't plan on going to bed before dawn.

where pioneers filled their water barrels, the museum gives visitors, through letters and diary entries, a vivid description of what life was like for those who made the arduous trek westward. A young girl writes of her family's emotional parting with families and friends as they begin their voyage westward, never to return; another girl writes of her sister's death on the trail. There are passages describing the beauty of the prairies, encounters with Native Americans, death, dust, and tribulations of the five months it took to travel the 2,000-mile Oregon Trail. A 14-minute movie describes the paths and purposes of the three trails. You can reach here by car via I-70 (Noland Road exit).

Admission: $2 adults, $1.50 seniors, 50¢ children 10–15.

Open: Mon–Fri 9am–4:30pm, Sat–Sun 12:30–4:30pm. **Closed:** Veteran's Day, Thanksgiving, Christmas, New Year's Day.

TOY AND MINIATURE MUSEUM, 5235 Oak St., Kansas City, MO. Tel. 816/333-2055.

This restored 1911 mansion in midtown contains a fantastic collection of antique toys and fine, exact-to-scale miniatures, including houses, rooms, and furniture. Even if you've never given much thought to the world of toys and miniatures, you'll be captured by the spell woven by the museum's beautiful displays: You can peek inside doll houses so realistic that in a photograph they would be indistinguishable from the real thing or marvel at a violin that has been opened up to reveal a violin-maker's shop inside, complete with tiny playable violins strung with human hair. There also are antique lead figures, dolls, puppets, marionettes, and toy kitchens that prepared girls for their future.

Admission: $3 adults, $2.50 seniors, $2.50 students over 12, $1.50 children 5–12.

Open: Wed–Sat 10am–4pm, Sun 1–4pm. **Closed:** Major hols and first two weeks of Sept.

HISTORIC SITES

FORT LEAVENWORTH AND THE FRONTIER ARMY MUSEUM, U.S. 73, near Leavenworth, KS. Tel. 913/684-3191 or 684-4051.

Located about 35 miles northwest of Kansas City, MO, and reached by taking I-70 west and then U.S. 73 north, Fort Leavenworth was established in 1827 to protect those traversing the Santa Fe Trail and later pioneers traveling the California and Oregon trails. The first fort established west of the Mississippi River, it, in contrast to many other forts in the area, is still in service. Serving as an education center for the U.S. Army, Fort Leavenworth is home for some 1,500 enlisted men, 2,500 officers, and approximately 11,000 students. The fort occupies a bluff overlooking the Missouri River and contains beautiful brick and Victorian wood homes. Custer, Eisenhower, and Patton all passed through Fort Leavenworth.

Your first stop should be the Frontier Army Museum on Reynold's Avenue. In addition to its displays portraying Fort Leavenworth's role in the opening of the West, including exhibits of uniforms, sabers, and other artifacts, it boasts one of the largest and best collections of carriages and wagons in the United States. This collection contains a Conestoga wagon, a carriage used by Abraham Lincoln, a sleigh that once belonged to General Custer, surries, stagecoaches, sleighs, and buggies. At the museum, be sure to pick up a brochure outlining a self-guided tour through Leavenworth, which takes visitors past the U.S. Disciplinary Barracks (with approximately 1,400 inmates); the National Cemetery; and the Rookery, built in 1832 and Kansas's oldest house.

Admission: Free.

Open: Fort open 24 hrs; museum Mon–Fri 9am–4pm, Sat 10am–4pm, Sun and hols noon–4pm. **Closed:** Easter, Thanksgiving, Christmas, New Year's Day.

FORT OSAGE, Sibley, MO. Tel. 816/881-4431 or 249-5737.

Fort Osage was erected in 1808 as the first U.S. outpost following the Louisiana Purchase, on a site chosen by William Clark (of Lewis and Clark fame). Abandoned in 1827 after the frontier pushed westward, Fort Osage has been reconstructed on its original site, complete with stockades, hewn log barracks, five blockhouses, officers' quarters, and other buildings. Living history interpretations are featured by staff and volunteers dressed in period costumes and portraying the work and life of fort residents, from soldiers to traders. To reach Fort Osage, 14 miles northeast of Independence, take U.S. 24 from downtown Kansas City to Buckner, MO, where you should turn north onto Sibley Street and travel 3 miles to Sibley Orchards. The fort is one mile north of Sibley.

Admission: $3 adults, $2 seniors and children 5–13.

Open: Mid-Apr to mid-Nov Wed–Sun 9am–5pm; mid-Nov to mid-Apr Sat–Sun 9am–5pm. **Closed:** Thanksgiving, Christmas, New Year's Day.

MISSOURI TOWN 1855, Lake Jacomo, Blue Springs, MO. Tel. 816/881-4431.

Missouri Town 1855 is a collection of original mid-19th-century structures brought to their present site from throughout western Missouri and arranged to resemble a typical Midwestern farming community. Occupying approximately six city blocks, the town contains more than 30 structures, including houses with barns and outbuildings, a schoolhouse, a church, a tavern, a lawyer's office, a livery stable, and slave quarters. These structures represent a variety of architectural styles prevalent from the 1820s through the 1850s— Greek Revival, Georgian, New England–style, and so on. Staff members, dressed in 1850s attire, provide insight into the lives and work of people of the times. To reach Missouri Town 1855, take I-70 east to I-470 south, then exit at Colbern Road, turning east (left) on Colbern to Cyclone School Road, where you should turn north (left) and follow it for two miles.

Admission: $3 adults, $2 seniors and children 5–13.

Open: Mid-Apr to mid-Nov Wed–Sun 9am–5pm; mid-Nov to mid-Apr Sat–Sun 9am–5pm. **Closed:** Thanksgiving, Christmas, New Year's Day.

THOMAS HART BENTON HOME, 3616 Belleview, Kansas City, MO. Tel. 816/931-5722.

This two-and-a-half-story stone house in midtown Kansas City, built around the turn of the century on a tree-lined residential street, was the home and studio of Kansas City's most famous contemporary artist from 1939 until his death in 1975. The house, which contains many of Benton's personal belongings, displays a handful of originals, some reproductions, and some prints and lithographs. Benton's studio in a former carriage house holds many of his tools and equipment.

Admission: $2 adults, $1.25 children 6–12.

Open: Summer Mon–Sat 10am–4pm, Sun noon–5pm; winter Mon–Sat 10am–4pm, Sun 11am–4pm. **Closed:** Easter, Thanksgiving, Christmas, New Year's Day.

JOHN WORNALL HOUSE, 146 W. 61st Terrace, Kansas City, MO. Tel. 816/444-1858.

This pre–Civil War brick home, built in 1858 in Greek Revival style, was once located on 500 acres of farmland but is now surrounded by the city. Used as a hospital for the wounded of both the Confederate and the Union armies during the Battle of Westport in 1864, it belonged to John Wornall, a well-to-do farmer. Tours of the home, offered throughout the day, impart interesting bits of information about life in the 1800s—such as the fact that women required their own style of chairs, due to the fact that they wore hooped skirts and didn't lean back and the fact that wives arose every morning two hours early just to start the coals for breakfast and then had to contend with flies, mice, and long skirts that could easily catch fire.

Admission: $2.50 adults, $1.50 seniors, 50¢ children under 12.

Open: Tues–Sat 10am–4pm, Sun 1–4pm. **Closed:** All major hols.

BINGHAM-WAGGONER ESTATE, 313 W. Pacific Ave., Independence, MO. Tel. 816/461-3491.

Built in 1855, occupied by Missouri artist George Caleb Bingham from 1864 to 1870, and then serving as the home of the Waggoner family for nearly a century until 1976, this grand building sits on a 20-acre estate. It features a porch that wraps around the entire house, 26 rooms furnished almost entirely with belongings of the Waggoner family, 8 coal-burning fireplaces, marble washbasins throughout, mahogany imported from Africa, a walk-in ice box, and an intercom system from the kitchen to the second floor. Tours, lasting 45 minutes, are offered throughout the day. There's a large gift shop in the former carriage house.

Admission: $2.50 adults, $2 seniors 62 and older, 50¢ children 3–11.

Open: Mon–Sat 10am–4pm, Sun 1–4pm. **Closed:** Nov 1 to day after Thanksgiving and Jan–Mar.

VAILE MANSION, 1500 N. Liberty, Independence, MO. Tel. 816/833-0040.

This 31-room mansion, built in 1881 at a whopping cost of $150,000, is a fine example of Second Empire Victorian architecture; it once boasted a lake, arbors, fountains, and a greenhouse on its grounds. The house has had a checkered past—Sophia Vaile killed herself here with an overdose of morphine in 1883, a year after she and her husband, Harvey, moved in; following Harvey Vaile's death in 1894, the home was used successively as an inn, a private mental institute and sanatorium, and then a nursing home. The Vaile Mansion contains furnishings of the period, as well as nine marble fireplaces and some beautifully handpainted ceilings. Tours last approximately 40 minutes.

Admission: $2.50 adults, $2 seniors, 50¢ children 12 and under.
Open: Mon–Sat 10am–4pm, Sun 1–4pm. **Closed:** Nov–Mar.

1859 JAIL AND MARSHAL'S HOME, 217 N. Main St., Independence, MO. Tel. 816/252-1892.

Located next to the Truman Home Ticket and Information Center, this 12-cell jail held prisoners from 1859 to 1933 and also served as the marshal's living quarters. Famous prisoners included Frank James, brother of Jesse, and William Quantrill, a Confederate guerilla. In the courtyard is an 1870 schoolhouse, relocated here in 1960.

Admission: $2.50 adults, $1.75 seniors 62 and older, 50¢ children 12 and under.

Open: Summer Mon–Sat 10am–5pm, Sun 1–4pm; winter Tues–Sat 10am–5pm, Sun 1–4pm. **Closed:** Jan, Thanksgiving, Christmas.

SIGHTSEEING MISCELLANY

NCAA VISITORS CENTER, 6201 College Blvd., Overland Park, KS. Tel. 913/339-0000.

This facility, opened in 1990, salutes intercollegiate athletics with photographs and videos highlighting all 21 sports and 76 championships administered by the National Collegiate Athletic Association (NCAA). The displays begin in the lobby, with a 96-foot mural outlining the history of the NCAA and depicting various aspects of college sports: The displays continue with photographic and multimedia presentations chronicling some of the great moments and significant achievements in NCAA history, from basketball and baseball to lacrosse, volleyball, gymnastics, golf, wrestling, skiing, soccer, and track and field. It's located in Overland Park just south of I-435, between Roe and Metcalf avenues, on the southern border of Kansas City.

KANSAS CITY BOARD OF TRADE, Third floor, 4800 Main, Kansas City, MO. Tel. 816/753-7500.

Founded in 1856, the midtown Kansas City Board of Trade is the world's predominant marketplace for wheat and grain sorghum, as well as a trading place for soybeans, corn, and oats. A visitor's gallery on the third floor allows guests to observe futures trading in the pit, with explanations describing what's going on.

Admission: Free.
Open: Mon–Fri 8:30am–3:15pm. **Closed:** Major hols.

MORMON VISITOR'S CENTER, 937 W. Walnut Ave., Independence, MO. Tel. 816/836-3466.

Members of the Church of Jesus Christ of Latter-day Saints (Mormons) immigrated to Independence in 1831, along with their leader and church president, Joseph Smith. He hoped to build the city of Zion, a community based on righteous living and unselfish cooperation. Persecution, however, drove the Mormons onward to Utah by the end of the decade, but before they left Smith designated land in Independence as site for a temple. This visitor's center describes the history of the Mormons and the concepts of their faith through displays, a slide show, and free 20-minute guided tours.

Admission: Free.

Open: Daily 9am–9pm.

RLDS AUDITORIUM, 1001 W. Walnut Ave., Independence, MO. Tel. 816/833-1000.

Built in the 1920s next to the Mormon Visitor's Center above, this huge auditorium serves as world headquarters of the Reorganized Church of Jesus Christ of Latter-day Saints. Occupying a section of the temple lot designated by Joseph Smith, it contains the 110-rank Aeolian Skinner organ, one of the largest church organs in the country with 6,500 pipes. Twenty-minute tours of the auditorium are given throughout the day; try to schedule a visit during an organ recital.

Admission: Free.

Open: Tours Mon–Sat 9am–noon and 1–5pm, Sun and hols 1–5pm. Organ recitals: Summer daily 3pm; winter Sun 3pm. **Closed:** Thanksgiving, Christmas, New Year's Day.

---

3. COOL FOR KIDS

WORLDS OF FUN, I-435, Exit 54, Kansas City, MO. Tel. 816/454-4545.

This 230-acre family entertainment park is one of Kansas City's top attractions, drawing more than 1.3 million visitors per year. It's based on Jules Verne's *Around the World in Eighty Days* and is divided into five areas—the Orient, Scandinavia, Europa, Africa, and Americana—throughout which are more than 140 rides, stages featuring live entertainment and shows, arcades, food outlets, and other attractions. Its leading rides are the Timber Wolf, a 4,230-foot wooden roller coaster that includes a 95-foot drop, and the Orient Express, a steel-track roller coaster with two interlocking loops. Other popular rides include the Fury of the Nile, Viking Voyager, Monsoon, and Python Plunge—all water rides. Families with small children should head for Pandemonium, with more than a dozen rides and attractions, including a carousel, playground, and small Ferris wheel. Worlds of Fun is located in the northeastern part of Kansas City, north of the Missouri River off I-435.

Admission (includes all rides and attractions): $21.95 adults, $14.95 seniors 60 and over and children 4–11. Combination ticket to Worlds of Fun and Oceans of Fun: $26.95 adults and children.

Open: Apr, May, Sept, and Oct Sat–Sun from 10am; June, July, and Aug daily from 10:30am. Telephone for closing times, which vary widely. **Closed:** Labor Day weekend; Nov–Mar.

OCEANS OF FUN, I-435, Exit 54, Kansas City, MO. Tel. 816/454-4545.

Located beside Worlds of Fun, this is the Midwest's largest tropically themed water park, featuring 60 acres of water slides, lakes, and pools. It offers more than 35 water-related attractions, including a million-gallon wave pool designed for body surfing and rafting, and Caribbean Cooler, 800 feet of gently rushing water in a tropical setting through which you can swim or float. Be sure to bring your swimsuit.

Admission: $14.95 adults, $11.95 seniors 60 or over and

children 4–11. Combination ticket with Worlds of Fun, $26.95 adults and children.

Open: Memorial Day weekend to Labor Day weekend, daily from 10am. Telephone for closing times, which vary.

KALEIDOSCOPE, Crown Center, 25th and McGee, Kansas City, MO. Tel. 816/274-8300 for information or 274-8301 for reservations.

Sponsored by Hallmark Cards, Inc., Kaleidoscope is a creative art workshop that encourages children to touch, participate in, and create their own works of art. Only children ages 5 to 12 are allowed to join the 1½-hour sessions, which begin with a journey through the Discovery Room and end in the Art Studio, where children are allowed to create their own art. Parents are not allowed to enter Kaleidoscope but can watch the activities through one-way mirrors.

Admission: Free, with tickets issued 30 minutes before each session on a first-come, first-serve basis.

Open: Summer (mid-June to late Aug) Mon–Fri 10:30am and 12:30, 1:30, 2:30pm; Sat 10am, noon, and 1:30, and 3pm. Winter Mon–Fri 9 or 9:30am, 10:30am, 1pm; Sat 9:30, 11, 1:30am, and 3pm. Since winter is reserved mainly for school groups, telephone beforehand to confirm the schedule and make a reservation.

THE COTERIE CHILDREN'S THEATRE, Crown Center, 25th St. and Grand Ave., Kansas City, MO. Tel. 816/474-6552.

This professional theater company stages seven productions per year—primarily for children and their families—from classics of children's literature to original material. Past shows have included George Orwell's *Animal Farm;* a musical adaptation of Hans Christian Andersen's *The Ugly Duckling;* and *Pooh,* adapted from the stories of A. A. Milne.

Admission: $5 children and adults.

Performances: Tues–Fri 10am, sometimes also 12:30 or 1pm; Sat and Sun usually 2pm or 7pm. **Closed:** Jan and between performances.

THE MARTIN CITY MELODRAMA & VAUDEVILLE CO., 13440 Holmes Rd., Kansas City, MO. Tel. 816/942-7576.

Martin City is fun entertainment for the whole family, with melodramas that invite audience participation through booing, hissing, and cheering. Local professionals perform six different shows a year in a rustic barnlike atmosphere, and refreshments range from popcorn, cookies, and hot dogs to hot cider and sarsaparilla (no alcohol is served). It's a good place to bring your teenagers.

Admission: $8.50 adults; $7.50 seniors, students, and children.

Performances: Thurs–Sun 7:30pm, Sun matinee 3:30pm. **Closed:** Between performances (call for schedule and reservations).

GREEN MILL CANDY FACTORY, 2020 Washington, Kansas City, MO. Tel. 816/421-7600, or toll free 800/369-2462.

This downtown Kansas City candy factory, in operation since 1914, produces peanut brittle, peanut clusters, and cream candies. It offers four tours daily, which last about 45 minutes and include a film presentation on the manufacture of chocolate and a look at the production of peanut brittle and chocolate. Each tour participant receives free confections fresh off the assembly belt, plus a box of peanut brittle. There's also a factory outlet here should you feel tempted.

Admission: $1.50 per person.

Tours: Mon–Fri 9am–2pm (call for reservations).

---

4. ORGANIZED TOURS

BOAT CRUISES One of the most relaxing ways to enjoy the Kansas City skyline is on a cruise along the Missouri River, on either the *Missouri River Queen* or the *America*. Both boats are moored in Kansas City, Kansas, off I-70 at the Fairfield Industrial District exit. They travel from the Kansas River onto the Missouri River, with views of the skyline and rural countryside.

The **Missouri River Queen** is a replica of a 19th-century paddlewheeler, an ornate triple-decked boat. In operation from March through October, it offers a variety of cruise options—including a one-hour sightseeing cruise that departs daily at 2pm through the summer and on Saturday and Sunday at 2pm during March, April, May, September, and October; it costs $6 for adults, $5.40 for seniors 60 and older, and $3 for children 12 and under. There's also a 2½-hour dinner cruise with a buffet of prime rib and live entertainment, offered on Friday and Saturday only during March and April and on Tuesday through Sunday evening from May through October; it costs $26.95 per person on Saturday evening; the rest of the week it's $24.95 for adults, $22.95 for seniors, and $12.50 for children. Other options include a two-hour Moonlight Entertainment Cruise offered on Friday and Saturday at 9pm; a popular two-hour Country Western Entertainment Cruise offered every Monday at 7:30pm from May through October; and a two-hour Sunday brunch at 11:30am from April through October.

The **America,** a modern luxury liner, offers a wide variety of options throughout the year, including a two-hour lunch cruise that departs daily at noon June through October and costs $16.95 for adults, $15.25 for seniors, and $8.50 for children 3 to 12. A 2½-hour dinner cruise, departing every night except Monday, offers dinner with live entertainment; the cost is $31.95 per person on Friday and Saturday night; the rest of the week it's $29.95 for adults, $27 for seniors, and $15 for children. On Friday and Saturday there's a two-hour Moonlight Cruise departing at 10pm, and on Monday at 7:30pm there's a two-hour Gospel Cruise, featuring live gospel entertainment and a buffet with fried chicken.

For more information on these cruises, prices, and reservations, call 913/281-5300 in Kansas City, or toll free 800/373-0027.

BUS TOURS With the help of this guide, you should be able to see all of Kansas City's major sights on your own. However, for orientation purposes you may wish to join a tour upon your arrival and then return later to explore at leisure. The **Gray Line** offers a two-hour Kansas City tour, which departs daily at 10am and costs $10 per person. This tour takes in the sights of downtown, Westport, Country Club Plaza, and other areas. The **Truman Country Tour,**

which lasts three hours beginning at 1pm and costs $15 per person, tours Independence's main attractions, including the Truman Library. For more information, call Gray Line at 913/268-5252.

5. SPORTS & RECREATION

SPECTATOR SPORTS

BASEBALL The Kansas City Royals, 1985 World Champions, provide the best in American League baseball action from April to October, with more than 80 home games each year. The **Harry S Truman Sports Complex,** on I-70 at the eastern edge of the city, is the site of both Royals Stadium and the Kansas City Chiefs' Arrowhead Stadium for football. Ticket prices range from $5 for general admission (sold 1½ hours prior to each game at Gates C and D). to $13 for box seats. For ticket information, call 816/921-8000. You can also charge tickets to your credit card by calling 921-4400 in Kansas City, or toll free outside Kansas City at 800/422-1969. You can order tickets by mail at Kansas City Royals, Ticket Office, P.O. Box 419969, Kansas City, MO 64141-6969.

FOOTBALL The Kansas City Chiefs, winners of the 1970 Super Bowl, play at **Arrowhead Stadium** in the Truman Sports Complex from August to December, with approximately 10 home games each season. Ticket prices range from $20 to $25. The Arrowhead ticket office (tel. 816/924-9400) is open Monday through Friday from 8:30am to 5pm; you can charge tickets to your credit card by calling 931-3330. Outside Kansas City, call toll free at 800/676-5488.

HORSE & GREYHOUND RACING Although open only since 1989, the Woodlands is already among the top three attractions in Kansas City, with both horse- and dog-racing courses. The Woodlands is located in Kansas City, KS, on I-435 two miles north of its intersection with I-70. For information on both horse and greyhound racing, call 913/299-3636 or 299-9797.

The horse-racing season is from mid-August through September and features both Thoroughbred and quarter horses on a one-mile track. Races are held Wednesday through Sunday at 1pm or 3pm, with prices ranging from $2 for general admission to $5 for the club house. Parking is $2. Patrons are invited to view the action from the infield of the track, where they can spread a blanket and have a picnic.

Greyhound racing, held from November to mid-August on a quarter-mile track, takes place at 1:30pm on Wednesday, Friday, Saturday, and Sunday and at 7:30pm on Monday, Wednesday, Thursday, Friday, and Saturday. Prices here range from $1 for general admission to $3 for the club house, plus $1 for parking.

ICE HOCKEY The Kansas City Blades, of the minor-league International Hockey League, skate from October through April at Kemper Arena, near downtown in the former stockyards district. Kemper's circular, pillarless structure provides unobstructed views from all 16,300 seats, and fans are never farther than 200 feet from the action. Tickets, available at Kemper Arena's Blades ticket office on Monday to Friday from 8:30am to 5pm, range from $7.50 to $12 for adults and $5 to $8 for children and seniors. Tickets are also available at Ticketmaster outlets. For more information, call 816/842-1063.

RECREATION

Swope Park, with 1,769 acres of greenery and facilities, is one of the largest city parks in the nation. Located in Kansas City, MO, at Gregory and Meyer boulevards, it offers a number of recreational facilities, including two 18-hole public golf courses, a swimming pool, two fishing lakes, boating areas, bicycle paths, two tennis courts, picnic tables, and shelters. The **Blue River Golf Course** (tel. 816/523-5830) charges green fees of $10 on weekdays and $11 on weekends and holidays; the **Swope Memorial Golf Course** (tel. 816/523-9081) charges $11 on weekdays and $13 on weekends and holidays. The **Swope Park Pool** on Lewis Road and Riverside Drive, open every day except Monday, charges a $1.50 admission.

Other recreational diversions are almost limitless. For more information on recreation in Kansas City, contact Kansas City's tourist office or consult the *Yellow Pages*.

CHAPTER 16

STROLLING AROUND KANSAS CITY

1. DOWNTOWN
2. COUNTRY CLUB PLAZA

Because sights and attractions are spread throughout the city, Kansas City doesn't lend itself to many sightseeing strolls. Two exceptions are the downtown area and Country Club Plaza, both notable for their architectural styles.

WALKING TOUR 1 — Downtown

Start: City Hall, 12th and Oak.
Finish: Town Pavilion, 11th and Main.
Time: Allow approximately two hours, not including stops.
Best Times: Weekdays, when buildings and restaurants are open.
Worst Times: Saturday and Sunday, when some buildings and most shops are closed.

FROM CITY HALL, 12TH & OAK, TO THE SAVOY, 9TH & CENTRAL This stroll introduces you to some of Kansas City's most significant architectural treasures, from grand brick buildings dating from the 1880s to the city's wealth of art deco treasures. Start your stroll at:

1. **City Hall,** completed in 1937, a 30-story building on the corner of 12th and Oak. It's built in typical art deco style, with a cluster of stepbacks near the top of the building, emphasized by light-colored verticals and darkened window spandrels. On the top floor is an observation deck that you can reach by taking the elevator to the 28th floor and then the stairs to the 30th. Open free to the public on Monday through Friday from 8am to 5pm, it affords a clear view of the city.

   From City Hall, walk west two blocks on 11th Street and make a right onto Grand Avenue. At the corner of Grand and 11th is the:

2. **Professional Building,** one of half a dozen major office buildings under construction in downtown Kansas City when the Great Depression hit. Across the street, at 1101 Grand, is the:

3. **Bryant Building,** one of the city's best examples of art deco with a beaux arts tower. Take a peak at its ornate lobby.

   Continue walking north on Grand to the:

4. **Federal Reserve Bank,** 925 Grand Ave., one of 12 Federal Reserve banks in the country. Built in 1921 and renovated in the mid-1980s, this beautiful neoclassical building contains a Visitor's Center on its mezzanine, with displays that explain the

function of the Federal Reserve System and the history of money and banking. It's open free to the public Monday through Friday from 8am to 5pm. After touring the Visitor's Center, be sure to stop by the Information Counter in the lobby and ask for a free souvenir—a bag of shredded paper currency. Just off the lobby is another place of interest, the Roger Guffey Gallery, open free to the public on Monday through Friday from 8am to 5pm. It stages changing exhibitions that have ranged from Hollywood poster art to photographs by Gordon Parks and paintings by Thomas Hart Benton.

Just a stone's throw from the Federal Reserve Bank is one of my favorite buildings in the city, the:

5. **Scarritt Building,** located on the northwest corner of 9th and Grand. Constructed in 1906, it was one of the city's first modern skyscrapers and shows strong influences from the Chicago style of architecture, particularly in its terra-cotta embellishments and its vertical thrust. Walk through the lobby, head downstairs through the corridor, and you'll find yourself in the wonderful:

6. **Scarritt Arcade** (located behind the Scarritt Building), with its four-story atrium and skylight. Beautifully constructed, it's a sight to behold.

Exit Scarritt Arcade onto 9th Street and head west, where immediately on your right will be the:

7. **New York Life Building,** 20 W. 9th St., an impressive and massive brownstone. At the time of its completion in the late 1880s, it was the largest and most distinguished building in the city and is still considered by many to be the most significant historic building downtown. Currently undergoing renovations that will transform its interior into luxury apartments, it is guarded by an imposing Augustus Saint-Gaudens bronze eagle perched above its entryway. Nearby is another building of the same period, the:

8. **New England Building,** 112 W. 9th St., designed by a Boston firm and noted for its projecting corner window and the seals of the five New England states carved below its first set of windows. Just a minute's walk farther west on 9th Street is the:

9. **Savoy Hotel and Grill,** 9th and Central. It was built at the turn of the century, with a restaurant that claims to be the city's oldest continuous restaurant and still highly recommended for its atmosphere, steaks, and seafood. Note the stylistic lead windows, a rare example of art nouveau in the United States. The Savoy building, a sorely rundown flophouse just a few years ago, is now being restored and offers rooms with turn-of-the-century charm.

REFUELING STOPS You can't go wrong dining at the **Savoy Grill,** 9th and Central, one of Kansas City's most famous historic restaurants. Almost as old is **Fountain City Dining Room,** 931 Broadway, which opened in 1911 and serves moderately priced American food. It still boasts a molded-tin ceiling, plaster molding, and a bright copper facade.

FROM THE SAVOY AT 9TH & CENTRAL TO BARNEY ALLIS PLAZA, 12TH & WYANDOTTE From the Savoy, walk one block south on Central, turn right onto 10th, and walk one more

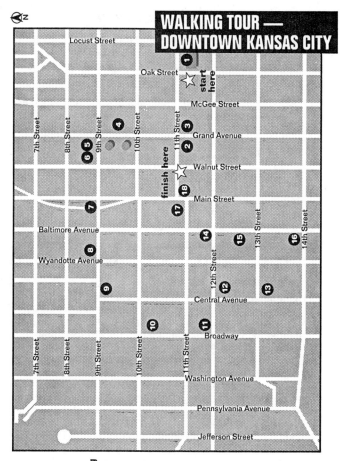

WALKING TOUR —
DOWNTOWN KANSAS CITY

Locust Street

Oak Street

start here

McGee Street

7th Street
8th Street
9th Street
10th Street
11th Street

Grand Avenue

Walnut Street

finish here

Main Street

Baltimore Avenue

Wyandotte Avenue

12th Street
13th Street
14th Street

Central Avenue

7th Street
8th Street
9th Street
10th Street
11th Street

Broadway

Washington Avenue

Pennsylvania Avenue

Jefferson Street

① City Hall
② Professional Building
③ Bryant Building
④ Federal Reserve Bank
⑤ Scarritt Building
⑥ Scarritt Arcade
⑦ New York Life Building
⑧ New England Building
⑨ Savoy Hotel and Grill
⑩ Coates House
⑪ Folly Theater
⑫ Barney Allis Plaza
⑬ Municipal Auditorium
⑭ Radisson Suite Hotel
⑮ Midland Theater
⑯ Kansas City Power and Light Building
⑰ City Center Square
⑱ Town Pavilion

block to the corner of 10th and Broadway. Here you'll see the
beautifully restored:

10. Coates House, completed in 1891 and once the most lavishly
appointed hotel in the city. (Presidents Grover Cleveland and
Benjamin Harrison stayed here.) Empty for years, now housing
apartments, it is the crowning restoration achievement of surrounding Quality Hill. Once one of the wealthiest residential
districts after the Civil War, Quality Hill suffered almost a
century of decline and neglect before vigorous redevelopment

began in the 1980s, changing more than 45 historic structures into residences and mixed-use commercial space.

From Coates House, walk two blocks south on Broadway, turning left onto 12th Street. At the end of the block on your left, at 300 W. 12th St., is the:

11. Folly Theater, built in 1900 and now Kansas City's only turn-of-the-century theater still in existence. Used for burlesque revues before shutting down in 1973, it has been lovingly restored and now features all types of entertainment, including concerts and theater.

Just cater-cornered from the Folly is:

12. Barney Allis Plaza, a large open square bounded by Kansas City's convention center. That monumental structure on the southern edge of the plaza is the:

13. Municipal Auditorium, completed in 1934 in art deco style and a venue for concerts, theater, and exhibitions.

REFUELING STOPS If the weather's fine, a great place for a snack is **Barney's Café,** located on Barney Allis Plaza and offering open-air seating where you can sip a beer and munch on nachos. Much more uptown is **Hitter's,** located on the corner of 12th and Baltimore, an ultramodern sports bar with TV screens and happy-hour specials from 4:30 to 7pm on Monday to Friday. If you're ravenous, head for **Italian Gardens,** 1110 Baltimore, in operation since 1925 and specializing in home-made pizza, lasagne, and daily specials at low prices.

FROM BARNEY ALLIS PLAZA TO TOWN PAVILION, 11TH & MAIN From Barney Allis Plaza, head east on 12th Street, where on the corner of 12th and Baltimore you'll find the:

14. Radisson Suite Hotel. Built in 1930 and exalting in the art deco style, it boasts a great statue in the lobby above the entryway, an 11-foot-tall gilded statue called "Mother of the Stars," standing on tiptoe on the crest of a wave.

Take a right onto Baltimore and to your right will soon be the:

15. Midland Theater, 1221 Baltimore, built in the 1920s as the grandest movie theater the city had ever seen. Ornate and opulent in Renaissance Revival style, it serves as a center for the performing arts.

Less than two blocks farther south, at 14th and Baltimore, is my most favorite building (I do have several favorites), the:

16. Kansas City Power and Light Building, probably the best example of art deco in town. Completed in 1931, it soars to a height of about 480 feet and for many years was the tallest building in Missouri. Its upper six stories feature a lighting system that changes colors at night, which always fascinated me as a child.

Backtrack north on Baltimore to 11th Street, where you should take a right and walk one block east to Main. Here, at 1100 Main, is:

17. City Center Square, where on the 25th floor you'll find offices of the Convention and Visitors Bureau of Greater Kansas

City. Stop here for brochures and information on the city if you haven't already done so.

Across the street, at 1111 Main, is:

18. Town Pavilion, a new building that nevertheless incorporates art deco concepts to make it compatible with the older buildings around it. It houses a number of shops and food outlets as well as a museum with changing exhibits.

FINAL REFUELING STOPS On the third floor of Town Pavilion is a **food court,** a bright and cheerful dining hall with various counters serving everything from barbecue and burgers to tacos and Chinese food. For more formal dining, **City Seen,** located on the ground floor of Town Pavilion, offers international cuisine, steaks, and sandwiches. For some famous Kansas City jazz, backtrack northwest to **The Phoenix,** 302 W. 8th St., where live jazz is offered on Monday to Saturday from 5pm to 1am. Boasting the motto "Never a Cover," it occupies the former old Phoenix Hotel, with brick walls and ceiling fans, and is a fine place to end the day.

WALKING TOUR 2 — Country Club Plaza

Start: J. C. Nichols Memorial Fountain, 47th Street and J. C. Nichols Parkway.
Finish: Swansons, 47th and Wyandotte.
Time: Allow approximately one hour, not including stops.
Best Times: Monday through Saturday, when all stores are open.
Worst Times: Sunday morning, when shops are closed.

Located just five miles south of downtown, Country Club Plaza was developed in 1922 and is the oldest shopping center in the country. This 14-block area is modeled after Seville, Spain (Kansas City's sister city), with pastel-colored buildings topped by tiled roofs and ornate towers. Most people come here to shop in its more than 150 stores and boutiques or to eat at one of its two dozen restaurants, with nothing more than a quick glance at the 30-some statues and fountains (many imported from Europe) that grace the Plaza's tree-lined streets. This walking tour will direct you to the Plaza's highlights.

FROM J. C. NICHOLS MEMORIAL FOUNTAIN AT 47TH AND J. C. NICHOLS PARKWAY TO SEVILLE SQUARE, PENNSYLVANIA & NICHOLS ROAD On the corner of 47th Street and J. C. Nichols Parkway is:

1. Mill Creek Park, dominated by a massive fountain of thrashing horses and heroic horsemen. Dedicated to the developer of the Plaza, this fountain was sculpted in Paris in 1910 by Henri Greber. From the fountain, walk west on 47th Street, crossing J. C. Nichols Parkway. To your left is:

2. Giralda Tower, a close reproduction of Giralda Tower in

Seville, except that this one is only two-thirds the original's size. Of the 14 towers on the Plaza, this is the tallest, and it sounds carillon bells throughout the day.

Continue walking west on 47th Street to Central, where on the corner to your left you'll see:

3. **Function Junction,** a favorite Kansas City outlet for practical and functional items for kitchen and home. Behind it is a small shop:

4. **Asiatica,** a women's clothing store that shows Asian designer influence. One block farther west is:

5. **Sharper Image,** 333 W. 47th St., a store for extravagant gadgets.

At the intersection of 47th and Broadway is another statue of note:

6. **Sleeping Child,** sculpted in 1963 by the Romanelli Studios in Florence and made of Carrara marble. Also at this intersection is:

7. **Dillard's,** a dependable and popular department store.

Head south on Broadway, where immediately on your right you'll see:

8. **The Nature Company,** part of a fast-growing chain of stores specializing in high-quality gifts and gadgets that usually have a connection with the outdoors or nature, including bird feeders, gardening books, T-shirts, and educational toys. Continue heading south on Broadway to Nichols Road, where you should take a right. This is the heart of the Plaza, with its tree-lined streets and horse-drawn carriages available for hire. At the corner of Nichols Road and Pennsylvania is:

9. **Saks Fifth Avenue,** one of the Plaza's most upmarket stores, as well as:

10. **Seville Square,** with many indoor shops. Across the street are a number of small boutiques, including Crabtree and Evelyn, Gucci, and The Gap. And next to Seville Square is McDonald's, in front of which is a statue of a boy eating—you guessed it—a hamburger.

REFUELING STOPS If you're looking for a fun place for a drink, in the basement of Seville Square is the **Longbranch Saloon,** known for its food specials, drinks, and "Kansas City's Meanest Waitresses." Nearby, at 4743 Pennsylvania, is the original **Houlihan's Old Place,** which opened almost two decades ago and now has branches across the country. Cater-cornered from Houlihan's is **Parkway 600 Grill,** a place to be seen for Kansas City's upwardly mobile. More important, it offers outdoor seating and is one of the few places serving alcohol in the morning. For serious dining, head for the **Bristol Bar and Grill,** 4740 Jefferson, great for seafood, or **La Mediterranée,** a posh restaurant serving Kansas City's best French cuisine.

FROM SEVILLE SQUARE, PENNSYLVANIA & NICHOLS, TO SWANSONS, 47TH & WYANDOTTE Backtrack one block east on Nichols Road, where on Broadway you'll find the:

11. **Mermaid Pool,** the Plaza's oldest work of art. Made of Carrara marble and dating from about 1680, it features

mermaids guarding a pool inlaid with ceramic tile. Throw in some coins—they go to Children's Mercy Hospital.

Back on Nichols, continue heading east one block, where on the corner of Nichols and Central you'll see:

12. Boy and Frog, one of the more bizarre statues on the Plaza. Take a look at it and decide for yourself what's going on. It was purchased in 1928 and is an original by Raffaello Romanelli of Florence, whose father, Pasquale, founded the Romanelli Studios in 1860. Cater-cornered from the statue is:

13. Halls, another department store. Across Wyandotte Street is:

14. Swanson's, a chic apparel store.

FINAL REFUELING STOPS   Quench your thirst at a local watering hole, **Fred P. Ott's,** 4770 J. C. Nichols Pkwy., which has a small patio. Next door is **Annie's Santa Fe,** great for margaritas and Mexican food. **Fedora Café and Bar,** 210 W. 47th St., offers upscale dining with an innovative menu. **Figlio,** 209 W. 46th St., serves great Italian food at modest prices in a modern setting.

CHAPTER 17

KANSAS CITY AREA SHOPPING

1. SHOPPING CENTERS

2. ANTIQUES & ART

In the days of wagon caravans heading west along the Santa Fe, California, and Oregon trails, Independence and Westport served as important trading and outfitting centers. Those days have long gone, and the Kansas City area has never regained a reputation as a shopper's paradise. Nevertheless, it offers a unique shopping experience—Country Club Plaza, the nation's oldest shopping center. In addition, one can spend hours exploring area malls and antiques shops.

---

1. SHOPPING CENTERS

KANSAS CITY

CITY MARKET, sandwiched between the Missouri River and I-70 at 5th and Main, just north of downtown, has been the scene of a colorful and brisk Saturday business ever since covered stalls were first erected in 1888. Although a few vendors are on hand Monday through Friday from about 8am to 3pm to sell produce and flowers, the busiest day of the week is Saturday, when a great multitude of vendors, shoppers, and browsers converge on the scene to make it one of the liveliest places in the city.

One of the great things about the recently renovated City Market is that it is just that—a city market that draws a wide mix of people, blue-collar and white-collar workers, young and old, and various ethnic backgrounds. Second- and third-generation families sell fruit, vegetables, flowers, plants, live chickens, and eggs, while entrepreneurial newcomers hawk T-shirts, kitchen appliances, and odds and ends (nothing used is allowed to be sold at the market). Fast food is available, from hot dogs to barbecue, as well as soft drinks. The Saturday market begins at about 6am and continues to about 4 or 5pm. On Saturday, the Trolley includes City Market on its circuit.

COUNTRY CLUB PLAZA, located five miles south of downtown, is the nation's oldest shopping center, dating from 1922. It's a 14-block, 55-acre shopping district modeled after Seville, Spain, complete with pastel-colored buildings topped with red-tiled roofs and towers, tree-lined boulevards, horse-drawn carriages, and notable fountains (more than 40) and statues (more than 50). To reach the Plaza from downtown, take Main Street south to 47th Street, where you should turn right.

The main draws of Country Club Plaza are its shops, department stores, and boutiques, which number more than 150 and offer a wide variety of goods and services. Department stores include Dillard's on the corner of 47th Street and Broadway; Saks Fifth Avenue on the corner of Pennsylvania and Nichols Road; and Halls at Nichols Road and Central. Seville Square, at Nichols Road and Pennsylvania, is a shopping center with approximately 40 boutiques.

Clothing stores on the Plaza include Asiatica with its Asian-influenced designs for women, AnnTaylor, Banana Republic, Benetton, Brooks Brothers, The Gap, Jaeger International, Laura Ashley, N. Valentino, Outrigger, Overland Outfitters, Plaza Pendleton, Polo/Ralph Lauren, Swanson's, and Woolf Brothers.

Shops and boutiques offering specialty items include Gucci, for accessories; Bennett Schneider, a bookstore; Crabtree and Evelyn, for soap, sachets, and other products; Sharper Image, for gadgets, accessories, and playthings; Function Junction, for household items and kitchenware; The Nature Company, for gifts and unique educational toys that relate to the outdoors and nature; and Tivol, Inc., a family-owned jewelry store.

Parking throughout the Plaza is free, and most shops are **open** Mon through Sat from 10am to 6pm and Thurs to 9pm. Sun hours are noon or 12:30pm to 5 or 5:30pm. If you have questions regarding the Plaza or its retail outlets, stop by the **Plaza Association,** 4625 Wornall Rd. (tel. 816/753-0100), located just north of the 47th Street and Central intersection.

CROWN CENTER, located between downtown and the Plaza, at 2450 Grand Ave., is a $500-million complex financed by Hallmark Cards Inc. Virtually a city-within-a-city, the 85-acre development includes Hallmark's international headquarters, the Hallmark Visitors Center, two luxury hotels, apartments and condominiums, offices, theaters, cinemas, an outdoor ice-skating rink, and retail outlets.

Most interesting to shoppers, of course, is Crown Center's trilevel retail complex with more than 50 boutiques, shops, and stores. These include The Custom Shop Shirtmakers, for custom and ready-to-wear shirts; Victoria's Secret, for fine lingerie; The Best of Kansas City, for souvenirs and edibles of the city; Cat's Meow, packed with gifts for felines and their friends; Everyday's A Holiday, with decorations for Christmas and other holidays; Function Junction, Kansas City's most popular store for household items and kitchenware; Second Star to the Right, for Disney collectibles; and Hallmark Live!, a showcase of Hallmark greeting cards and related products. Halls Crown Center is a large department store with quality merchandise.

Crown Center offers a variety of customer services, including gift wrapping, mail wrapping, and UPS shipping. There's also a Ticketmaster outlet, and tickets for the Trolley are sold here. For information on Crown Center and a brochure listing all its shops and food outlets, stop by the Crown Center Information Booth, located on Level 2. As for parking, Crown Center allows three hours of free parking with validation from any Crown Center shop, no purchase necessary. An additional three hours of parking is awarded with the purchase of $25 in goods or food. On the weekend, parking is free, without validation. Crown Center is **open** Mon to Wed and Sat from 10am to 6pm, Thurs and Fri from 10am to 9pm, and Sun from noon to 5pm.

TOWN PAVILION, one of Kansas City's newest shopping centers, is located right in the heart of downtown at 1111 Main St. It's built in sleek art deco style to match the city's surrounding architecture. Its anchor is the Jones Store Company, and there are more than three dozen retail stores and food outlets. Shops include Hurst's Diamond Shop, which has been selling jewelry for more than 80 years; Demaree Stationery, opened since 1895 and selling fine writing instruments, leather briefcases, and office supplies; McClendon's Hats, Kansas City's oldest millinery; and St. Moritz Chocolatier.

A One Hour Photo shop will develop film in one hour; at the Pavilion Personal Services you can have your shoes repaired or your laundry done or altered, mail a letter or package by express delivery, or have a key duplicated. Parking is free the first three hours with validation on Monday through Friday; on Saturday it's free. For more information, drop by the Information Desk located next to the north escalator on Level 1. Town Pavilion is **open** Mon to Sat from 10am to 6pm.

BANNISTER MALL is located in South Kansas City just east of I-435 (take the 87th Street or Bannister Road exit) at 5000 Bannister Rd. It is a huge mall with approximately 180 retail shops and outlets. Dillard's, Jones, J. C. Penney's, and Sears serve as anchor department stores, with many other shops selling clothing, shoes, accessories, formal and bridal wear, toys, home furnishings, jewelry, gifts, records, and more. An information booth is located in the center of the second floor, near Dillard's. Bannister Mall is **open** Mon to Sat from 10am to 9pm and Sun from noon to 6pm.

OVERLAND PARK, KS

OAK PARK MALL is located just off I-35 at 95th and Quivera streets in Overland Park, KS, which is southwest of Kansas City, MO. the two-level Oak Park Mall has 160 stores, shops, and food outlets. Major stores include J. C. Penney's, Montgomery Wards, and Dillard's. Its information booth is located in the center of the Lower Level, near Dillard's. Among its many food outlets and restaurants, particularly recommended is Paradise Diner, an upscale diner with a sleek white interior and a fun menu serving sandwiches and innovative dishes. Oak Park Mall is **open** Mon to Sat from 10am to 9pm and Sun from noon to 5:30pm.

2. ANTIQUES & ART

ANTIQUES

At 45th and State Line is the heart of antiques heaven in Kansas City, a three-block area with more than 20 independent dealers. Located in midtown just six blocks west of Country Club Plaza, it is the best place in town to browse for high-quality antiques, many imported from Europe. Victorian birdcages, furniture, silver, glass, carousel figures, stained-glass windows, jewelry, decorative objects, light fixtures, Depression glass, miniatures, old books, and collectibles are for sale. **The Antique Mall,** 4510 State Line Rd., is the largest shop, with 40 dealers under one roof. Most shops are **open** Tues to Sat from 10am to 5pm; a few are open Mon with the same hours.

CHEEP ANTIQUES, 201 Main St., Kansas City, MO Tel. 816/471-0092.

This huge, warehouselike store is one block north of City Market, near the Missouri River. I always enjoy coming here after visiting City Market on a Saturday. Cheep Antiques specializes in antique furniture, mostly wardrobes, kitchen tables, headboards, and buffets, spread on two floors of an old building. Lots to look at. Great prices. The store is **open** on Sat and Sun from 9am to 5pm.

WESTPORT FLEA MARKET, 817 Westport Rd., Kansas City, MO. Tel. 816/931-1986.

Just west of the nightlife action of Westport in midtown, this is the city's oldest and largest indoor flea market. In operation for about 20 years, it houses dozens of dealers selling furniture, clothing, jewelry, and collectibles. A lot of the items are plain junk, but it's fun to walk through. Prices are low, and I've picked up some real bargains here. The hamburgers at the Bar and Grill in the center of the market, by the way, are the biggest I've ever seen. The flea market is **open** on Sat and Sun from 10am to 5pm.

ART

CENTRAL PARK GALLERY, 1644 Wyandotte, Kansas City, MO. Tel. 816/471-7711.

This is a beautiful gallery, both in space and in content. Located in downtown Kansas City, it occupies what was formerly Wester School, built in 1885 and listed on the National Register of Historic Places. The gallery's grounds boast a garden, an aviary, and a fountain stocked with Japanese carp. The gallery itself is so large, with 15,000 square feet of space, that it seems more like a museum than a retail gallery. Opened in 1989, it is the largest gallery in the Midwest, with two floors offering a mix of 1,500 paintings, sketches, watercolors, sculptures, and ceramics by approximately 50 regional and nationally acclaimed artists. Every item is marked with the price, and many are identified with biographies of the artists as well. Featured artists include Wong Shue, Watanabe, Eyvind Earle, Lu Hong, Yamin Young, Andreas Nottebohm, Marco Sassone, Michel-Henry, and Jim Buckels. The gallery is **open** Tues through Fri from 9am to 5pm and Sat from 10am to 4pm.

KANSAS CITY'S ARTISTS COALITION, 201 Wyandotte, Kansas City, MO. Tel. 816/421-5222.

Founded in 1976, the Kansas City Artists Coalition is a nonprofit organization designed to promote the area's visual-arts awareness through exhibitions, publications, and public talks. Local and regional artists display their works here in changing exhibits; the first Friday of every month is the opening reception. Housed in a restored warehouse, the gallery is located in the River Market area, north of downtown and just a stone's throw from the Missouri River. It's **open** Wed through Sat from 11am to 4pm; additional hours on the first Fri of each month are 7 to 9pm.

CHAPTER 18

KANSAS CITY AREA NIGHTS

1. THE PERFORMING ARTS
2. THE CLUB & MUSIC SCENE
3. THE BAR SCENE
4. MOVIES

Kansas City and its environs offer a wide variety of nightlife diversions, with something for everyone. You can sip a cocktail in a subdued and sophisticated lounge while watching the city lights twinkle in the distance, dance to the latest in aggressive rock, listen to some of the finest jazz in the country, eat at a dinner theater, or watch a musical being performed under the stars. And that's only the beginning.

Of course, Kansas City is most famous for its jazz, which it owes largely to such former local greats as Charlie Parker and Count Basie. The Kansas City Jazz Commission, the only group of its kind in the country, is dedicated to preserving and promoting the distinctive Kansas City style of jazz, which makes use of saxophones and background riffs. To find out what's going on in the weekly jazz scene in clubs across the city, call the Jazz Hotline, maintained by the Jazz Commission, at 816/931-2888.

To find out about upcoming productions in the theater, concerts, and other nightlife entertainment, pick up a copy of *The Fun Calendar,* a quarterly entertainment calendar published and distributed by the **Convention and Visitors Bureau of Greater Kansas City,** located downtown on the 25th floor of City Center Square, 1100 Main St. (tel. 816/221-5242). The bureau also maintains a 24-hour **Visitor Information Phone** (tel. 816/691-3800), with recordings of this week's events.

In addition, *The Kansas City Star* features comprehensive listings of current and upcoming activities in its Friday and Sunday editions. Finally, available at various bars and restaurants throughout the city are free copies of *Pitch, The New Times,* and *The Note,* Kansas City's nightlife scene in depth.

Capital Automated Ticket Services (CATS), is the largest ticket service in the metropolitan area, located at record shops and the Jones Stores. You can charge tickets for major events by calling Ticketmaster at 816/931-3330.

1. THE PERFORMING ARTS

MAJOR PERFORMING-ARTS COMPANIES

OPERA

LYRIC OPERA OF KANSAS CITY, 11th and Central. Tel. 816/471-7344.

Two operas are presented each spring, followed by three in the fall. Under the artistic direction of Russell Patterson, all productions are sung in English and performed in this stately former Masonic Temple and movie theater, located downtown.

Prices: $6–$35.

SYMPHONY ORCHESTRA

THE KANSAS CITY SYMPHONY, Lyric Opera, 11th and Central. Tel. 816/471-0400.

The Kansas City Symphony, under music director and conductor William McGlaughlin, presents a variety of programs at the Lyric Opera hall. The Main Series features both classical and contemporary symphonies with guest soloists. The Family Series and the Discovery Series are based on themes, while Nightlights teams the orchestra with major jazz and pop artists.

Prices: Main Series $13–$29; Family Series $11; Discovery Series $13; Nightlights $17–$30.

THEATER

AMERICAN HEARTLAND THEATRE, Crown Center, 2450 Grand Ave. Tel. 816/842-9999.

This small 440-seat theater offers professional Broadway plays, musicals, mysteries, and dramas in an intimate setting. It's located on Level 3 of Crown Center, with the second, more intimate Stage Two located in the Westin Crown Center Hotel.

Prices: $13.50–$19.50.

MISSOURI REPERTORY THEATRE, Spencer Theatre, 4949 Cherry. Tel. 816/276-2700.

Celebrating more than a quarter of a century of live performances, this is Kansas City's best professional theater company. Located downtown, it presents approximately seven shows per year, with productions ranging from the great classics to premieres. *A Christmas Carol* is presented annually.

Prices: $17–$25.

QUALITY HILL PLAYHOUSE, 303 W. 10th at Central. Tel. 816/421-7500.

Located near Quality Hill and the Garment District downtown, this 150-seat new theater presents contemporary plays, comedies, and musicals.

Prices: $8–$14.

UNICORN THEATRE, 3820 Main. Tel. 816/531-7529.

This 200-seat midtown theater offers off-Broadway–style productions, with an emphasis on contemporary, avant-garde, and original scripts. It is one of only two companies in the country accessible for performers in wheelchairs.

Prices: $9–$14.

DANCE

STATE BALLET OF MISSOURI, Midland Center, 1228 Main. Tel. 816/471-8600.

This resident ballet company, starting its second decade under the artistic direction of Todd Bolender (who was a principal dancer with George Balanchine's New York City Ballet), presents a wide variety of dance, from classics to contemporary. Performances are downtown at the historic Midland Center for the Performing Arts in October, around Christmas (when *The Nutcracker* is an annual favorite), and in February and May.

Prices: $5–$30.

MAJOR CONCERT HALLS, THEATERS & AUDITORIUMS

FOLLY THEATER, 300 W. 12th St. Tel. 816/474-4444 for tickets or 842-5500 for information.

This is Kansas City's only surviving turn-of-the-century playhouse, which served as a venue for burlesque, films, vaudeville, boxing, wrestling, and even strip tease before its renovation and reopening in 1981. On the National Register of Historic Places, the downtown Folly now serves as a stage for a wide variety of events and concerts, including its own 12th Street Jazz Series, the Children's Sampler Series, and dance.

Prices: Vary according to performance. Jazz Series $16–$24; Children's Sampler Series $7.

MIDLAND CENTER FOR THE PERFORMING ARTS, 1228 Main St. Tel. 816/471-8600.

The Midland opened downtown in 1927 as one of the region's most lavishly decorated movie palaces. It is still very ornate, with a three-story-high lobby, walnut wainscoting with gold overleaf, a 12-foot-wide marble staircase, chandeliers, and custom-cut Tiffany glass. Retaining many of its original furnishings and art objects, it seats 2,800 in its five-story-high auditorium, where Broadway hits, musicals, comedies, Las Vegas headliners, and other performances are held. It is also home of the State Ballet of Missouri.

Prices: Vary according to the performance, with $15–$40 charged for most Broadway shows.

MUSIC HALL, Municipal Auditorium, 13th and Central. Tel. 421-8000.

Located downtown in Municipal Auditorium, this beautiful art deco theater was constructed in the early 1930s and is now a versatile facility, offering presentations ranging from dance, symphonies, and concerts to Broadway musicals.

Prices: Vary according to performance.

SANDSTONE, 130th and State Ave., Bonner Springs, KS. Tel. 913/721-3300.

This natural amphitheater, off I-70 west of Kansas City in Bonner Springs, Kansas, is where many visiting top artists perform. There are 3,000 permanent seats, but most people opt to bring blankets to spread out on the terraced lawns, where there is room for approximately 15,000.

Prices: Vary according to performance.

STARLIGHT THEATRE, Swope Park, Meyer Blvd. and Swope Pkwy. Tel. 816/363-STAR, or toll free 800/776-1730.

You couldn't ask for a more delightful setting for musicals or outdoor concerts than this 7,862-seat amphitheater set in lush Swope Park. Since its opening in the early 1950s, the Starlight has served as a venue for Broadway musicals and top-name concerts, with 4 musicals and approximately 15 concerts performed each season (mid-May to October). Musicals have ranged from *West Side Story* and *Oklahoma!* to *Grease* and *Annie,* while performers have included Bette Midler, Tina Turner, and Elton John.

Prices: Musicals $6–$27.

DINNER THEATER

THE NEW THEATRE RESTAURANT, 9229 Foster, Overland Park, KS. Tel. 913/649-SHOW.

This new dinner theater, a 600-seat renovation of the former Overland Park Convention Center, is the only professional nonchildren's theater in Kansas. It features comedies and musicals year round, and its buffet spread includes main dishes ranging from beef and poultry to seafood and pork.

Prices: Tues–Thurs and Sun $21.95, Fri $24.95, Sat $26.95.

2. THE CLUB & MUSIC SCENE

LIVE MUSIC

Most of the Kansas City area's live music features jazz or blues, though rock and alternative music are also offered.

DOWNTOWN

THE PHOENIX, 302 W. Central. Tel. 816/472-0001.

This jazz piano bar located in the old Garment District occupies the former Phoenix Hotel, built a century ago. Featuring brick walls and ceiling fans, it's popular with downtown businesspeople. The pianist, who plays Kansas City–style swing be-bop, is usually joined by local jazz artists, with live music beginning at 5pm on Monday to Saturday. The Phoenix is open Monday to Saturday from 11am to 1am, with happy hour's reduced-price drinks offered from 4 to 6pm.

Admission: Free.

THE TUBA, 333 Southwest Blvd. Tel. 816/471-6510.

This small informal establishment, located on the corner of Southwest Boulevard and Broadway, offers live music on Monday through Saturday from 9pm to 1am. This is one of the best places in town to hear rhythm and blues, though jazz is also featured. Happy hour here is on Monday to Friday from 3 to 7pm.

Admission: Usually $3; more for nationally known musicians.

VINE DISTRICT

In the 1930s, Kansas City jazz flourished, with more than 60 clubs in the Vine jazz district alone. At that time, most clubs were centered around 12th and Vine. The action today has shifted a few blocks farther south to 18th and Vine, with these two locales featuring black musicians playing largely to black audiences, although all ages and races are welcome.

BIRDLAND, 19th and Vine. Tel. 816/842-8463.

This is an old-fashioned establishment, complete with vintage 1950s furnishings and fixtures, including wrought-iron railings, red vinyl chairs, Formica tabletops, and glowing red lamps. The clientele ranges from young couples to the middle-aged, and there's a small dance floor. This place, mellow and laid-back, is a lot of fun. A band plays only on weekends, from 8pm on Friday and from 9pm on Saturday. The bar is open on Monday to Saturday from 4pm to 1:30am.

Admission: Free.

MUTUAL MUSICIANS FOUNDATION, 1823 Highland St. Tel. 816/471-5212 or 421-9297.

The Mutual Musicians Foundation is a nonprofit social club for professional musicians and jazz buffs and was chartered in 1917 as an all-black Musicians Association. In the 1930s its membership included some of the greatest musicians in jazz history—Bennie Moten, Count Basie, Andy Kirk, Harlan Leonard, Lester Young, Jay McShann, and Charlie Parker. It has been at the same location off Vine since 1930, in a modest two-story building; it now offers after-hour jam sessions on Friday and Saturday nights, from sometime after midnight until dawn. This is where area musicians congregate after their regular gigs to jam all night long, with participants ranging from local celebrities to older men who once played with Count Basie and similar bands. There's also a Saturday practice session, from about 11:30am to 1:30pm.

Admission: Donation of $3 is appreciated.

COUNTRY CLUB PLAZA

THE BAR, in The Ritz-Carlton, Wornall Rd. at Ward Pkwy. Tel. 816/756-1500.

This snazzy bar, located on the 12th floor of The Ritz-Carlton hotel, features live jazz on Wednesday through Saturday from 8:30pm to 12:30am. The Russ Long Trio, the house band, performs with guest artists.

Admission: Free.

CITY LIGHT JAZZ CLUB, 4749 Pennsylvania Ave. Tel. 816/753-0000.

Located in the basement beneath the Plaza III Steakhouse, this sophisticated jazz club is cozy and intimate and tends to draw in an older crowd, many of whom come for dinner as well. The house band, the City Light Jazz Ensemble, ranks as one of the best in the city, playing mostly contemporary jazz but also accomplished at swing, be-bop, and rhythm and blues. Led by pianist Joe Cartwright, the ensemble, with occasional guest musicians, plays every night except Monday.

Admission: Tues–Thurs $2, Fri–Sat $4, Sun $3; $6–$8 for special events.

WESTPORT & MIDTOWN

BLAYNEY'S, 415 Westport Rd. Tel. 816/561-3747.

This is an unrefined, basement establishment, popular with a college crowd ever since its 1973 opening. The live music starts at 10pm and features blues, rhythm and blues, and old-style rock-and-roll from the late 1960s and early 1970s. There's a small dance floor, plus two pool tables. The doors open at 8pm on Monday to Saturday.

Admission: Mon–Thurs $1, Fri–Sat $2.

THE GRAND EMPORIUM, 3832 Main St. Tel. 816/531-1504.

This place is nothing fancy—in fact, it's kind of a dive—but it consistently brings in some of the best music in Kansas City and is certainly the best place in town to listen to blues, as well as alternative rock and reggae. It's also a good place for barbecue, prepared by Grace, who is known for her sauce, ribs, ham, beef, and red beans and rice. The building itself dates from the 1920s and through the years has served as a plumbing shop, candy factory, grocery store, pool hall, speakeasy, brothel, and saloon. It's a small place, long and narrow, with a tiny stage, an even tinier dance floor, and walls plastered with promotional posters of various bands. If you're looking for Kansas City's most popular music house and dance hall, this is it, open Monday to Saturday from 10am to 3am.

Admission: $4–$8 for most bands, sometimes higher for national acts.

THE HURRICANE, 4048 Broadway. Tel. 816/753-0884.

Located off Westport Road in the heart of the nightlife district, the Hurricane is a showcase for regional alternative acts, including bands that perform original material, whether it's blues, zydeco, or rock. There are a dance floor and an outdoor stage in the summer, making it the only place in Westport where you can listen to music outside. Live music starts at 10pm on Monday through Thursday and at 5pm on Friday and Saturday, but the bar itself is open Monday to Saturday from 3pm to 3am. Happy hour, with reduced-price drinks, is from 4 to 7pm on Monday to Thursday.

Admission: $1–$3.

JIMMY'S JIGGER, 1823 W. 39th St. Tel. 816/753-2444.

This casual establishment opened the day after Prohibition ended. Its location near the University of Kansas Medical Center brings in an older crowd, including doctors, nurses, and medical students, who come not only for a drink but also for the food. Jimmy's Jigger has gained a deserved reputation for good barbecue, prepared with its own sauce in its own smoker, including ribs and various sandwiches. There's live music every Friday and Saturday from 9pm and every Sunday from 5pm, featuring mostly jazz but also bluegrass, rock-and-roll, and zydeco. Hours are Monday to Saturday from 8am to 1:30am and Sunday from 11am to midnight.

Admission: $2–$3.

THE LEVEE, 16 W. 43rd St. Tel. 816/561-2821.

What a great place to while away a sunny afternoon, sitting on the Levee's outside patio or deck and sipping a beer. It's so pleasant that you'll be easily persuaded to stay through the evening to hear the band. Jazz and blues are the featured music. Bands play in the main room on the ground floor, but you can still hear the music on the second floor and even outside. Live music begins at 8:30pm on Monday to Thursday, 9pm on Friday, and 3pm on Saturday. The bar is open Monday to Saturday from 11am to 1:30am. With its exposed-brick walls, ceiling fans, and wooden floor, the Levee manages to be casual and stylish at the same time, attracting people of all ages. Salads and burgers are available. The Levee is located between Westport and the Plaza.

Admission: Fri–Sat $1, Mon–Thurs free.

THE POINT, 917 W. 44th St. Tel. 816/531-9800.

Ida McBeth, a local jazz and blues singer who has gained a faithful following of devoted fans, packs them in when she performs at the Point every other Thursday. Friday and Saturday nights feature blues, jazz, and rock performers, with live music beginning at 9pm. There are two floors, each with its own bar, and the main floor can get so crowded that there's hardly room to move, much less dance on the small dance floor. There are also pool tables and video games. Deli-type food, including soup and sandwiches, is available. This establishment, open Monday to Saturday from 11:30am to 1:30am, is located a couple of blocks southwest of Westport.

Admission: Thurs (for Ida McBeth) $4, Fri and Sat free.

THE SHADOW, 510 Westport. Tel. 816/561-2222.

This large music hall, located in the heart of Westport, features alternative and rock music. Its black walls are splattered with brilliant fluorescent paint. There's a dance floor in the middle of the hall, lower than the circle of tables around it, kind of like a pit arena. The Shadow is open on Tuesday to Thursday from 8pm to 3am and on Friday and Saturday from 5pm to 3am. The bands, which play Tuesday, Thursday, Friday, and Saturday nights, hit the stage at 10:30pm. On Wednesdays it's disco, with a local DJ.

Admission: Tues and Thurs–Sat $2–$5.

DANCING

In addition to the places listed below, a number of establishments described above offer both live music and dancing. These include Birdland, the Grand Emporium, the Hurricane, the Point, and the Shadow.

WESTPORT & MIDTOWN

GUITARS AND CADILLACS, 3954 Central Ave. Tel. 816/756-2221.

Claiming to have the largest dance floor in Kansas City, Guitars and Cadillacs is worlds apart from the other establishments in Kansas City—this is where you'll find cowboy boots, cowboy hats, and even some real cowboys. Co-owned by country-music star T. G. Sheppard, Guitars and Cadillacs is the place to go for country music. There's a live band on Mondays, but otherwise there's a DJ, along with such promotionals as swimsuit contests (you won't find many feminists here), free dance lessons, and Friday happy hour that features reduced-price drinks and a buffet. On Saturdays, KFKF, the local country-music radio station, broadcasts live from here. It's open Monday to Friday from 5pm to 3am and Saturday from 7pm to 3am.

Admission: Mon, Tues, and Thurs $1; Wed $2 (ladies free); Fri–Sat $2; occasional concerts $5–$10.

LYNN DICKEY'S, 535 Westport Rd. Tel. 816/756-1010.

A popular sports café during the day, with 17 TV screens showing mainly sports, Lynn Dickey's transforms into a wild and crazy disco on Wednesday through Saturday nights. The clientele, either college-age or college-educated, ranges from the preppie to the yuppie. There are a happy-hour buffet and special drink prices on Monday to Friday from 4:30 to 7pm. It's open daily from 11am to 3am.

Admission (after 9pm): Thurs $3, Fri–Sat $2.

3. THE BAR SCENE

Many establishments listed in the preceding section are open throughout the day and are also good places for a drink.

DOWNTOWN

HITTER'S, in the Radisson Suite Hotel Kansas City, 12th St. at Baltimore. Tel. 816/472-8900.

This ultramodern bar broadcasts the latest in sports on its 11 TV screens, which can be found even in the bathroom to assure that fans won't miss a minute of the action. One of the few bars in the downtown area, it offers a limited menu of sandwiches, salads, and burgers. Open every day from 11am, it closes at midnight on Monday through Thursday, at 1am on Friday and Saturday, and at 10pm on Sunday. Happy hour is on Monday to Friday from 4:30 to 7pm.

CROWN CENTER

SKIES, in the Hyatt Regency Crown Center, 2345 McGee St. Tel. 816/421-1234.

Skies is Kansas City's only revolving restaurant, with a separate lounge where you can come simply for a drink. Located high above the city on the 42nd floor, it offers a fantastic panoramic view in a sophisticated cocktail-lounge setting. The best time to come is during happy hour from 4 to 7pm, when drinks and appetizers are half price. Otherwise, hours here are Monday to Thursday from 4pm to midnight, Friday and Saturday from 4pm to 1am, and Sunday from 4pm to 11:30pm.

COUNTRY CLUB PLAZA

FRED P. OTTS, 4770 J. C. Nichols Pkwy. Tel. 816/753-2878.

This simple bar has the extra advantage of a small outdoor patio. In addition, happy hour on Monday to Friday from 4 to 7pm offers discounted prices for drinks and food. The menu lists typical bar fare, including hamburgers, sandwiches, chili, and potato skins. The bar is open Monday to Saturday from 11am to 3am and Sunday from noon to 3am.

HOULIHAN'S OLD PLACE, 4743 Pennsylvania. Tel. 816/561-3141.

Just about everyone has a good time at Houlihan's, including families, the college crowd, and working professionals. Opened two decades ago, this is the original in a chain that has since spread throughout the country. Happy-hour specials with discounts on food and drinks are offered on Monday to Friday from 4 to 8pm. The food menu is extensive, with a wide assortment of soups, salads, burgers, sandwiches, and main courses. Houlihan's is open Sunday to Thursday from 11am to 11pm and Friday and Saturday from 11am to midnight.

LONGBRANCH SALOON, Seville Square, Pennsylvania and Nichols Rd. Tel. 816/931-2755.

Pay no attention to this establishment's claim that it has the city's "meanest waitresses" or that there's a 10-drink minimum. Instead, enjoy the convivial atmosphere over a beer or cocktail ("No Foo Foo Drinks," the menu says, "—This is a Saloon not a Drink Boutique") and take advantage of the daily food specials or such regular menu items as hamburgers, steaks, and sandwiches. The saloon is open Monday to Saturday from 11am to 3am and Sunday from 11am to midnight.

PARKWAY 600 GRILL, 600 Ward Pkwy. Tel. 816/931-6600.

This is *the* place to come in summer for an after-work drink on the Plaza, primarily because of its outdoor patio. In fact, so many people want to drink here that you'll probably have to wait for a table (be sure to get your name on the waiting list) unless you get here early. Because this is one of the few places on the Plaza serving alcohol in the morning, you can get here very early indeed. It's open Monday to Friday from 7am to 11pm, Saturday from 11am to 11pm, and Sunday from 9am to 11pm.

WESTPORT & MIDTOWN

FUZZY'S SPORTS BAR AND GRILL, 4113 Pennsylvania. Tel. 816/561-9191.

Yes, this is yet another sports bar, except that this one claims to be the oldest one in Kansas City. Decorated with trophies, pennants, photographs, and other sports memorabilia, Fuzzy's features five TV screens and is its rowdiest during big sports events. According to the management, everyone from business workers and young people to "sports nuts" make up its clientele. Happy hour is on Monday to Friday from 4 to 7pm. Otherwise, it's open daily from 11am to 3am.

HARPO'S, 4109 Pennsylvania. Tel. 816/753-3434.

This is a beautiful building, one of the first to be renovated back in the 1970s when Westport awakened as a nightlife district. After several reincarnations, it is now a bar with a two-story atrium topped by a skylight. Out back is a tree-shaded brick patio, a great place for an afternoon drink. Hours are Monday to Saturday from 10:30am to 3am.

KELLY'S, Pennsylvania Ave. and Westport Rd. Tel. 816/753-9193.

Kelly's has the distinction of occupying the oldest building in Kansas City, built in 1837 when Westport served as an outfitting post for wagon trains heading for Santa Fe. In the 1850s, a grandson of Daniel Boone set up shop here. Today Kelly's still has that unrefined, rustic atmosphere—a tavern in the true sense of the word. It is very popular with a young and enthusiastic drinking crowd. If you want beer for breakfast, this is the place to go. It's open Monday to Saturday from 6am to 3am.

4. MOVIES

GRANADA THEATRE, 1015 Minnesota Ave., Kansas City, KS. Tel. 913/621-2232 or 621-7177.

Built in the 1920s in the style of a Spanish courtyard, this movie theater features silent movies, which are even accompanied by a theater pipe organ, just like they were in the olden days. There are approximately 75 films in the Granada's archives, with another 2,000 available from a private collection. Silent movies are shown approximately twice a month; also shown are classic films. Call for exact dates.

Tickets: $5–$7 adults; $4–$5 seniors, students, and children.

TIVOLI, 425 Westport Rd., Kansas City, MO. Tel. 816/756-1030.

This movie theater, located in the heart of Westport, shows alternative and international films that never make it to the regular box offices.

Tickets: $5.50.

INDEX

GENERAL INFORMATION

ST. LOUIS AREA

KANSAS CITY AREA

SIGHTS & ATTRACTIONS

ST. LOUIS AREA

KANSAS CITY AREA

Note: An asterisk (*) after an attraction name indicates an Author's Favorite.

ACCOMMODATIONS

ST. LOUIS AREA

KANSAS CITY AREA

Key to Abbreviations B = Budget; E = Expensive; M = Moderate; VE = Very expensive; B&B = Bed & Breakfast; CG = Campground; YH = Youth Hostel; * = Author's Favorite; $ = Super-Special Value

RESTAURANTS

ST. LOUIS AREA

AFTERNOON TEA
Adam's Mark, downtown (*I*), 96–7
Ritz-Carlton, downtown (*I*), 97

AMERICAN
Busch's Grove, Ladue (*M*), 89
Caleco's, downtown (*I*), 74–5
Cardwell's, Clayton (*E$*), 87–8
De Menil Mansion Restaurant, Soulard (*B*), 92
Faust's, downtown (*E*), 93–4
Grappa, Central West End (*M*), 83
Key West, Union Station (*B*), 78–9
Lt. Robert E. Lee, downtown (*M*), 72–4
Miss Hullings, downtown (*B$*), 76
Norton's Cafe, Soulard (*B*), 92
Park Avenue Cafe, Soulard (*M*), 91
Patty Long Cafe, Soulard (*M*), 91–2
Redel's, Forest Park (*I$*), 84–5
The Restaurant, Clayton (*E*), 95
Sunshine Inn, Central West End (*B**), 86
Top of the Riverfront, dining with a view (*M*), 95–6

BAR FOOD
Blueberry Hill, University City (*B**), 86–7
Culpeppers, Central West End (*B*), 85
Riddles Penultimate Cafe and Wine Bar, University City (*I*), 86

BRUNCH, SUNDAY
Balaban's, Central West End (*I*), 96
Museum Café, Forest Park (*I*), 96
Schneithorst's, Clayton (*I*), 96
Sunshine Inn, Central West End (*I*), 96
Top of the Riverfront (*I*), 96

CHINESE
Silk Road, Central West End (*B$*), 86
Yen Ching, Richmond Heights (*B*), 91

CONTINENTAL
Al Baker's, Clayton (*E*), 87

Balaban's, Central West End (*M**), 82–3
Chez Louis, Clayton (*E*), 94–5
Museum Cafe, Forest Park (*I*), 84
Park Avenue Cafe, Soulard (*M*), 91
Patty Long Cafe, Soulard (*M*), 91–2
The Restaurant, Clayton (*E*), 95

FAST FOOD
Food Court, Union Station (*B*), 78
A Taste of St. Louis, downtown (*B*), 77

FRENCH
Balaban's, Central West End (*M**), 82–3
Cafe de France, downtown (*E*), 70
Chez Louis, Clayton (*E*), 94–5
Fio's La Fourchette, Richmond Heights (*E**), 88
L'Auberge Bretonne, Clayton (*E*), 88–9

FROZEN CUSTARD
Ted Drewes, Chippewa (*B**), 96

GERMAN
Bevo Mill, South St. Louis (*I*), 92–3
Schneithorst's Hofamberg Inn, Ladue (*I*), 90

HAMBURGERS
McDonald's, Gateway Arch (*B*), 96
O'Connell's Pub, Hill District (*B$*), 81–2

INTERNATIONAL
Duff's, Central West End (*I*), 84

ITALIAN
Al Baker's, Clayton (*E*), 87
Amighetti Bakery, Hill District (*B$*), 81
Cafe Napoli, Clayton (*I$**), 89–90
Caleco's, downtown (*I*), 74–5
Charlie Gitto's, downtown (*B*), 76
Cunetto House of Pasta, Hill District (*I$**), 80–1
Dominic's, Hill District (*E**), 79
Gian-Peppe's, Hill District (*M**), 80

Gian-Tony's, Hill District (*M$*), 80
Giovanni's, Hill District (*E**), 79–80
Girarrosto, Clayton (*I*), 90
Kemoll's, downtown (*E*), 70–1
Lou Boccardi's, Hill District (*I$*), 81
Premio, downtown (*M*), 74
Rigazzi's, Hill District (*B$**), 82
Tony's, downtown (*E**), 71–2
Zia's, Hill District (*I*), 81

MEXICAN
Burrito Brothers, University City (*B$*), 87
La Sala, downtown (*I*), 75–6

PASTA
The Old Spaghetti Factory, downtown (*B$*), 76–7
The Pasta House Company, Central West End (*B$*), 85

SANDWICHES
Lettuce Leaf, downtown (*B*), 76
O'Connell's Pub, Hill District (*B$*), 81–2
Riddles Penultimate Cafe and Wine Bar, University City (*I*), 86
Saint Louis Bread Company, Central West End (*B*), 85

SEAFOOD
Boston's, Union Station (*M*), 77
Key West, Union Station (*B*), 78–9
Nantucket Cove, Forest Park (*M*), 83–4

SEAFOOD/STEAK
Al's Steak House, downtown (*E*), 70
Dierdorf & Hart's, Union Station (*M*), 77–8
Station Grille, Union Station (*E*), 94

STEAK
Ruth's Chris Steak House, downtown (*M*), 74

VEGETARIAN
Sunshine Inn, Central West End (*B**), 86

KANSAS CITY AREA

Please Send Me the Books Checked Below

FROMMER'S COMPREHENSIVE GUIDES
(Guides listing facilities from budget to deluxe, with emphasis on the medium-priced)

	Retail Price	Code		Retail Price	Code
☐ Acapulco/Ixtapa/Taxco 1993–94	$15.00	C120	☐ Jamaica/Barbados 1993–94	$15.00	C105
☐ Alaska 1990–91	$15.00	C001	☐ Japan 1992–93	$19.00	C020
☐ Arizona 1993–94	$18.00	C101	☐ Morocco 1992–93	$18.00	C021
☐ Australia 1992–93	$18.00	C002	☐ Nepal 1992–93	$18.00	C038
☐ Austria 1993–94	$19.00	C119	☐ New England 1993	$17.00	C114
☐ Austria/Hungary 1991–92	$15.00	C003	☐ New Mexico 1993–94	$15.00	C117
			☐ New York State 1992–93	$19.00	C025
☐ Belgium/Holland/ Luxembourg 1993–94	$18.00	C106	☐ Northwest 1991–92	$17.00	C026
☐ Bermuda/Bahamas 1992–93	$17.00	C005	☐ Portugal 1992–93	$16.00	C027
			☐ Puerto Rico 1993–94	$15.00	C103
☐ Brazil, 3rd Edition	$20.00	C111	☐ Puerto Vallarta/ Manzanillo/ Guadalajara 1992–93	$14.00	C028
☐ California 1993	$18.00	C112			
☐ Canada 1992–93	$18.00	C009			
☐ Caribbean 1993	$18.00	C102	☐ Scandinavia 1993–94	$19.00	C118
☐ Carolinas/Georgia 1992–93	$17.00	C034	☐ Scotland 1992–93	$16.00	C040
			☐ Skiing Europe 1989–90	$15.00	C030
☐ Colorado 1993–94	$16.00	C100			
☐ Cruises 1993–94	$19.00	C107	☐ South Pacific 1992–93	$20.00	C031
☐ DE/MD/PA & NJ Shore 1992–93	$19.00	C012	☐ Spain 1993–94	$19.00	C115
			☐ Switzerland/ Liechtenstein 1992–93	$19.00	C032
☐ Egypt 1990–91	$15.00	C013			
☐ England 1993	$18.00	C109	☐ Thailand 1992–93	$20.00	C033
☐ Florida 1993	$18.00	C104	☐ U.S.A. 1993–94	$19.00	C116
☐ France 1992–93	$20.00	C017	☐ Virgin Islands 1992–93	$13.00	C036
☐ Germany 1993	$19.00	C108	☐ Virginia 1992–93	$14.00	C037
☐ Italy 1993	$19.00	C113	☐ Yucatán 1993–94	$18.00	C110

FROMMER'S $-A-DAY GUIDES
(Guides to low-cost tourist accommodations and facilities)

	Retail Price	Code		Retail Price	Code
☐ Australia on $45 1993–94	$18.00	D102	☐ Israel on $45 1993–94	$18.00	D101
			☐ Mexico on $50 1993	$19.00	D105
☐ Costa Rica/ Guatemala/Belize on $35 1993–94	$17.00	D108	☐ New York on $70 1992–93	$16.00	D016
			☐ New Zealand on $45 1993–94	$18.00	D103
☐ Eastern Europe on $25 1991–92	$17.00	D005			
			☐ Scotland/Wales on $50 1992–93	$18.00	D019
☐ England on $60 1993	$18.00	D107			
☐ Europe on $45 1993	$19.00	D106	☐ South America on $40 1993–94	$19.00	D109
☐ Greece on $45 1993–94	$19.00	D100	☐ Turkey on $40 1992–93	$22.00	D023
☐ Hawaii on $75 1993	$19.00	D104			
☐ India on $40 1992–93	$20.00	D010	☐ Washington, D.C. on $40 1992–93	$17.00	D024
☐ Ireland on $40 1992–93	$17.00	D011			

FROMMER'S CITY $-A-DAY GUIDES
(Pocket-size guides with an emphasis on low-cost tourist accommodations and facilities)

	Retail Price	Code		Retail Price	Code
☐ Berlin on $40 1992–93	$12.00	D002	☐ Madrid on $50 1992–93	$13.00	D014
☐ Copenhagen on $50 1992–93	$12.00	D003	☐ Paris on $45 1992–93	$12.00	D018
☐ London on $45 1992–93	$12.00	D013	☐ Stockholm on $50 1992–93	$13.00	D022

FROMMER'S TOURING GUIDES
(Color-illustrated guides that include walking tours,
cultural and historic sights, and practical information)

	Retail Price	Code		Retail Price	Code
☐ Amsterdam	$11.00	T001	☐ New York	$11.00	T008
☐ Barcelona	$14.00	T015	☐ Rome	$11.00	T010
☐ Brazil	$11.00	T003	☐ Scotland	$10.00	T011
☐ Florence	$ 9.00	T005	☐ Sicily	$15.00	T017
☐ Hong Kong/Singapore/ Macau	$11.00	T006	☐ Thailand	$13.00	T012
			☐ Tokyo	$15.00	T016
☐ Kenya	$14.00	T018	☐ Venice	$ 9.00	T014
☐ London	$13.00	T007			

FROMMER'S FAMILY GUIDES

	Retail Price	Code		Retail Price	Code
☐ California with Kids	$17.00	F001	☐ San Francisco with Kids	$17.00	F004
☐ Los Angeles with Kids	$17.00	F002			
☐ New York City with Kids	$18.00	F003	☐ Washington, D.C. with Kids	$17.00	F005

FROMMER'S CITY GUIDES
(Pocket-size guides to sightseeing and tourist accommodations
and facilities in all price ranges)

	Retail Price	Code		Retail Price	Code
☐ Amsterdam 1993–94	$13.00	S110	☐ Minneapolis/St. Paul, 3rd Edition	$13.00	S119
☐ Athens, 9th Edition	$13.00	S114			
☐ Atlanta 1993–94	$13.00	S112	☐ Montréal/Québec City 1993–94	$13.00	S125
☐ Atlantic City/Cape May 1991–92	$ 9.00	S004	☐ New Orleans 1993–94	$13.00	S103
☐ Bangkok 1992–93	$13.00	S005	☐ New York 1993	$13.00	S120
☐ Barcelona/Majorca/ Minorca/Ibiza 1993–94	$13.00	S115	☐ Orlando 1993	$13.00	S101
			☐ Paris 1993–94	$13.00	S109
☐ Berlin 1993–94	$13.00	S116	☐ Philadelphia 1993–94	$13.00	S113
☐ Boston 1993–94	$13.00	S117	☐ Rio 1991–92	$ 9.00	S029
☐ Cancún/Cozumel/ Yucatán 1991–92	$ 9.00	S010	☐ Rome 1993–94	$13.00	S111
			☐ Salt Lake City 1991– 92	$ 9.00	S031
☐ Chicago 1993–94	$13.00	S122			
☐ Denver/Boulder/ Colorado Springs 1990–91	$ 8.00	S012	☐ San Diego 1993–94	$13.00	S107
			☐ San Francisco 1993	$13.00	S104
			☐ Santa Fe/Taos/ Albuquerque 1993–94	$13.00	S108
☐ Dublin 1993–94	$13.00	S128			
☐ Hawaii 1992	$12.00	S014	☐ Seattle/Portland 1992– 93	$12.00	S035
☐ Hong Kong 1992–93	$12.00	S015			
☐ Honolulu/Oahu 1993	$13.00	S106	☐ St. Louis/Kansas City 1993–94	$13.00	S127
☐ Las Vegas 1993–94	$13.00	S121			
☐ Lisbon/Madrid/Costa del Sol 1991–92	$ 9.00	S017	☐ Sydney 1993–94	$13.00	S129
			☐ Tampa/St. Petersburg 1993–94	$13.00	S105
☐ London 1993	$13.00	S100			
☐ Los Angeles 1993–94	$13.00	S123	☐ Tokyo 1992–93	$13.00	S039
☐ Madrid/Costa del Sol 1993–94	$13.00	S124	☐ Toronto 1993–94	$13.00	S126
			☐ Vancouver/Victoria 1990–91	$ 8.00	S041
☐ Mexico City/Acapulco 1991–92	$ 9.00	S020	☐ Washington, D.C. 1993	$13.00	S102
☐ Miami 1993–94	$13.00	S118			

Other Titles Available at Membership Prices

SPECIAL EDITIONS

	Retail Price	Code		Retail Price	Code
☐ Bed & Breakfast North America	$15.00	P002	☐ Where to Stay U.S.A.	$14.00	P015
☐ Caribbean Hideaways	$16.00	P005			
☐ Marilyn Wood's Wonderful Weekends (within a 250-mile radius of NYC)	$12.00	P017			

GAULT MILLAU'S "BEST OF" GUIDES
(The only guides that distinguish the truly superlative from the merely overrated)

	Retail Price	Code		Retail Price	Code
☐ Chicago	$16.00	G002	☐ New England	$16.00	G010
☐ Florida	$17.00	G003	☐ New Orleans	$17.00	G011
☐ France	$17.00	G004	☐ New York	$17.00	G012
☐ Germany	$18.00	G018	☐ Paris	$17.00	G013
☐ Hawaii	$17.00	G006	☐ San Francisco	$17.00	G014
☐ Hong Kong	$17.00	G007	☐ Thailand	$18.00	G019
☐ London	$17.00	G009	☐ Toronto	$17.00	G020
☐ Los Angeles	$17.00	G005	☐ Washington, D.C.	$17.00	G017

THE REAL GUIDES
(Opinionated, politically aware guides for youthful budget-minded travelers)

	Retail Price	Code		Retail Price	Code
☐ Able to Travel	$20.00	R112	☐ Kenya	$12.95	R015
☐ Amsterdam	$13.00	R100	☐ Mexico	$11.95	R016
☐ Barcelona	$13.00	R101	☐ Morocco	$14.00	R017
☐ Belgium/Holland/ Luxembourg	$16.00	R031	☐ Nepal	$14.00	R018
			☐ New York	$13.00	R019
☐ Berlin	$11.95	R002	☐ Paris	$13.00	R020
☐ Brazil	$13.95	R003	☐ Peru	$12.95	R021
☐ California & the West Coast	$17.00	R121	☐ Poland	$13.95	R022
			☐ Portugal	$15.00	R023
☐ Canada	$15.00	R103	☐ Prague	$15.00	R113
☐ Czechoslovakia	$14.00	R005	☐ San Francisco & the Bay Area	$11.95	R024
☐ Egypt	$19.00	R105			
☐ Europe	$18.00	R122	☐ Scandinavia	$14.95	R025
☐ Florida	$14.00	R006	☐ Spain	$16.00	R026
☐ France	$18.00	R106	☐ Thailand	$17.00	R119
☐ Germany	$18.00	R107	☐ Tunisia	$17.00	R115
☐ Greece	$18.00	R108	☐ Turkey	$13.95	R027
☐ Guatemala/Belize	$14.00	R010	☐ U.S.A.	$18.00	R117
☐ Hong Kong/Macau	$11.95	R011	☐ Venice	$11.95	R028
☐ Hungary	$14.00	R118	☐ Women Travel	$12.95	R029
☐ Ireland	$17.00	R120	☐ Yugoslavia	$12.95	R030
☐ Italy	$13.95	R014			